The Transpersonal Relationship
in Psychotherapy

The Hidden Curriculum of Spirituality

The Transpersonal Relationship in Psychotherapy

The Hidden Curriculum of Spirituality

PETRŪSKA CLARKSON

Friend, we're travelling together.
Throw off your tiredness. Let me show you
one tiny spot of the beauty that cannot be spoken.
I'm like an ant that's gotten into the granary,
ludicrously happy, and trying to lug out
a grain that's way too big. (1991: 110)

(From Rumi, first dictated
1207–1273 in Koyna, Turkey

W
WHURR PUBLISHERS
LONDON AND PHILADELPHIA

© 2002 Whurr Publishers

First published 2002 by
Whurr Publishers Ltd
19b Compton Terrace, London N1 2UN, England
325 Chestnut Street, Philadelphia PA19106, USA

Reprinted 2002

British Library Cataloguing in Publication Data

A catalogue record for this book is available from the
British Library.

ISBN 1 86156 249 7

Printed and bound in the UK by Athenaeum Press Limited,
Gateshead, Tyne & Wear.

Contents

Dedicated to my dogs, who have taught me more about living and dying in God than any book:

Remote from universal nature, and living by complicated artifice, man in civilization surveys the creature through the glass of his knowledge and sees thereby a feather magnified and the whole image in distortion. We patronize them for their incompleteness, for their tragic fate of having taken form so far below ourselves. And therein we err, and greatly err. For the animal shall not be measured by man. In a world older and more complete than ours they move more finished and complete, gifted with extensions of senses we have lost or never attained, living by voices we shall never hear. They are not brethren, they are not underlings; they are other nations, caught with ourselves in the net of life and time, fellow prisoners of the splendour and travail of the earth.

(Beston 1928: 155–56)

Preface

There are guides who can show you the way.
Use them. But they will not satisfy your longing.

Keep wanting that connection,
with all your pulsing energy.

The throbbing vein
will take you farther
than any thinking,

Muhammed said, 'Don't theorize
about Essence!' All speculations
are just more layers of covering.
Human beings love coverings!

They think the designs on the curtains
are what's being concealed.

Observe the wonders as they occur around you.
Don't claim them. Feel the artistry
moving through, and be silent.'

. . . The saying, Whatever God wills, will happen,
does not end, 'Therefore be passive.'

Rather it means, Forget yourself,
and get ready to help . . .

The way you distinguish a true commentary
from a false is this:
Whichever explication
makes you feel fiery and hopeful, humble
and *active*, that's the true one.

If it makes you lazy, it's not right.

(Rumi 1991: 95–96)

This book is written with the sap of three disciplines – philosophy, psychology and physical science: the study of **thinking,** the study of the **psyche** and the study of **nature**. It comes from a lifelong engagement with the meaning of life, death and transformation for me and for others, which has included a dedication to the mystic traditions in several religions. In my experience and from my studies, their commonalities far outweigh their differences (which are usually those of their formal ideological embodiment in language) in the same way that 'schoolism' is today preventing us from rendering our best and most creative service to those who seek our help.

Through my researches I have come to understand that the transpersonal (however defined) is always with us. It permeates the work of creativity, healing, growth and decay wherever this occurs – particularly in all the healing relationships we call psychotherapy. The spiritual is the hidden curriculum. (When I write psychotherapy, I include psychoanalysis, counselling, counselling and clinical psychology and any other form of healing through **attending the psyche**.) Whether acknowledged or not, it is the invisible relationship within which we live and die and do our work.

The word I, as a white European, prefer using to refer to this is *physis* (or *phusis*). It means being **and** nothingness. It is an ancient Greek word used by the pre-Socratic Heraclitus in the occidental tradition some 2 | 500 years ago. It has many, many synonyms which makes it easy for most other cultures to identify its equivalent in their own languages. (And let us not forget that it was the Africans who taught the Egyptians and the ancient Greeks.) Marimba Ani (1994) calls the universal life force NTU. God is only one of its meanings. In English, *physis* is the root word of 'physicist' and 'physician':

> *Physis* was associated with the ultimate *a priori*, the first of everything about the human world and thus (for those with the sensitivity for it) the most obvious fact of all. Yet it is generally overlooked, not primarily because of some human defect but above all because it [physis] 'prefers to hide' (Heraclitus Frag. 53) in the sense of being 'ultimately unfathomable'.
>
> (Sheenan 1993: 82)

The workers from the chaos and complexity sciences have shown us the creative order evolving from chaos and how life is always re-creating itself. The word they use for this is *auto-poiesis* (e.g. Mingers 1995) It is another name for 'physis' arcing across 2 | 500 years of human endeavour in the Western world.

Quantum physics has shown us that the world **is** relationship and we will explore this idea throughout this book. The discipline of philosophy serves us to 'think and act well'. The seven-level model described here can help us think and act better in the realms of soul-healing.

The mediaeval alchemists, in search of the philosopher's stone, the grail, the goal of self-realization named the phases of the work of transforming dirt or faeces into real or symbolic gold according to the different colours manifested by the raw material in the process of transformation. These colour-stages were identified as (a) the blackening *(nigredo)*; (b) the whitening *(albedo)*; (c) the yellowing *(citrinitas)*; and (d) the reddening *(rubedo)*: 'This division has survived the entire history of alchemy' (Roob 1997: 30).

So, the four names of these stages in the alchemical work (although there have been many sub-divisions) refer to the changes in colour which the primal material goes through during the alchemical work of creating the philosopher's stone. I liken these to the stages of the soul's journey of transformation from (a) 'the loss of meaning and agonies of the spirit' (the dark night or *nigredo*), through (b) 'getting better' *(albedo)*, to (c) facing the even darker 'greater night of the soul' *(citrinitas)*, towards (d) transformation, renewal and rebirth which follow on from the *rubedo* stage.

The 'philosopher's stone' has numerous synonyms, but generally it symbolically indicates the goal, the grail, enlightenment. I also adhere to this symbolic alchemical sequence in the extended case study and it forms the underlying metaphorical spine of the whole book. (For further reading on this theme see Jung 1968; Von Franz 1980; Fabricius 1994; Klossowski de Rola 1973)

The inspirational poets say everything more sublimely. I could have followed Rumi's advice, but like he himself said:

> I know I ought to be silent,
> but the excitement of this keeps opening
> my mouth as a sneeze or a yawn does.
>
> (Rumi 1991: 70)

I am grateful to my teachers, but they are not responsible for what I have made of their teachings. I am grateful to my other teachers – clients and students who have learned with me – but there is not a single real person in this book. Just everybody.

How to form an effective working alliance relationship with this book

When I use the word 'client', please fill in according to your particular circumstances: patient, patients, client, clients, keyworking case, group participant. When I use the word 'psychotherapist' or 'psychotherapy', please fill in according to your particular circumstances: psychoanalyst, analytic psychologist, clinical psychologist, therapeutic counselling psychologist, counsellor, keyworker, social worker, doctor, psychiatrist or whatever.

As usual I follow Muhlhausler and Harré's 1991 recommendation to use the vernacular device of the gender-neutral third person singular usage of *they*, *their*, and *them* where appropriate. I sometimes insert female pronouns in square brackets where the original authors write as if their words only apply to males. All non-English words are at their first usage italicized and thus standardized also throughout quotations. I use **bold** to emphasize particularly important summary points and crucial highlights for ease of skimming or finding significant markers in the work.

Overall, don't expect one answer. Realities are multi-layered. Even where I sound convinced, what I think, feel and believe may already have changed by the time this is printed. Our world moves on. I write as part of an ongoing conversation and research into the world – to stimulate, to ignite the imagination, to remind of things already known or perhaps forgotten, perhaps sometimes to conceive of possibilities not yet dreamed of . . .

A young rabbinical student attended three talks by a very famous visiting rabbi. When his friends asked him about them he said: 'The first one was very good, because I understood everything. The second sermon was however even better. I did not understand it, but the rabbi did. The third lecture was the very best of the three. It was very profound and deep – even the rabbi did not understand it.'

Those three kinds of lectures are here presented in one book. Where you don't understand or don't like something, you can just skip it. You may come back to it (or not) at any future time when the questions you are experiencing are more relevant to the theme I was exploring in that section. But before looking at later chapters, please attempt to read through Chapter 1, about the seven levels of experience or epistemological domains related to the transpersonal relationship in psychotherapy. It is important to warn the reader that:

> Every attempt to follow the train of thought will therefore meet with obstacles. That is good. Questioning thereby becomes more genuine. Every question that does justice to its issue is already a bridge to the answer. Essential answers are always only the last step in questioning . . . The essential response is only the beginning of a responsibility. In such responsibility, questioning awakens in a more originary manner. For this reason too the genuine question is not super-seded by the answer that is found.
>
> (Heidegger 1998: 232)

The Seven-level Model will make more and more sense in time as you relate to it and even more when you use it for problems of living and healing. I have sometimes taken the liberty of emphasizing the word 'level' when it occurs in the quotations of other authors throughout the book to show how some appreciation of the coexistence of a multiplicity of **levels** or domains in human experience (not just coexistent dualisms) is to be found throughout our literature.

Even after some thirty years of intensively teaching and healing with the seven-level model, I certainly don't fully understand it yet. But every time I refer to it, I learn something – even if it is only the next question. (On the other hand, no matter what your education or experience, you may just simply easily and happily 'get it'.)

The philosophers, logicians and doctors of law were drawn up at Court to examine Nasrudin. This was a serious case, because he had admitted going from village to village saying: 'The so-called wise men are ignorant, irresolute and confused.' He was charged with undermining the security of the State.

> 'You may speak first,' said the King.
> 'Have paper and pens brought,' said the Mulla.
> Paper and pens were brought.
> 'Give some to each of the first seven savants.'
> They were distributed.
> 'Have them separately write an answer to this question: "What is bread?"'
> This was done.
> The papers were handed to the King, who read them out.
> The first said: 'Bread is a food.'
> The second: 'It is flour and water.'
> The third: 'A gift of God.'
> The fourth: 'Baked dough.'
> The fifth: 'Changeable, according to how you mean "bread".'
> The sixth: 'A nutritious substance.'
> The seventh: 'Nobody really knows.'

'When they decide what bread is,' said Nasrudin, 'it will be possible for them to decide other things. For example, whether I am right or wrong. Can you entrust matters of assessment and judgement to people like this? Is it or is it not strange that they cannot agree about something which they eat each day, yet are unanimous that I am a heretic?' (Shah 1985: 27.)

Chapter 2 concerns an overview of the **transpersonal relationship** in all psychotherapies, while Chapter 3 is specifically concerned with can be called **transpersonal psychotherapy**. I think the transpersonal, like the other four dimensions of the therapeutic relationship, is an intrinsic part of the embedded relational matrix present in all forms of healing – whether acknowledged or not.

Chapters 4 to 9 follow a structured sequence resembling an order (usually overlapping and interpenetrating) which sometimes emerges in the healing journey – that of the alchemical search for the philosopher's stone (*lapis*). This mythical stone is conceived of as the goal of the work, the grail, the fountain of enlightenment – the objective of undertaking the healing or learning journey. The names given to each of the stages in the alchemical work are supposed to reflect the different colours the material takes on through the various stages of becoming the philosopher's stone.

Each chapter contains a section with some relevant theoretical material as well as a section containing some practical guidance on using the material in clinical practice. Modify, disagree or ignore anything that you don't find useful.

There is also a case study of a middle-aged man's depression organized to fit in and elucidate each one of the phases in the alchemical (or psychotherapeutic) work. You could read the case study through first as a whole (pages $$–$$) to give an encapsulated overview of all the book's major themes.

The primal material – that which forms the basis for commencing the work – is discussed in Chapter 4, while the Nigredo phase of the healing journey – 'the lesser dark night of the soul' – is explored in Chapter 5. Chapters 6 and 7 are concerned with the Albedo phase – whitening or getting better – and the Citrinitas phase – 'the greater dark night' – of the healing journey. The final, Rubedo phase of the healing journey – reddening or rebirth – is dealt with in Chapter 8.

Chapter 9 is about the end, and about beginning again (the philosopher's stone is never finally achieved); Chapter 10 looks at training, supervision and continuing professional development that is inclusive of the transpersonal relational dimension – whatever psycho-language you prefer.

Appendix 1, 'The psychotherapy of the dead', is intended as a humorous piece – possibly helping to puncture some of the 'preciousness' around the transpersonal which alienates so many people's yearnings. Perhaps it may also help us to laugh at ourselves.

I include Appendix 2, 'Jesus Christ and the relational five-dimensions', by popular demand. It is concerned with Christian themes. For people to whom this story has little or no meaning, it can be fruitfully ignored. However, it could equally well be adapted to any of the many faiths and mystical traditions with which I have some familiarity.

Appendix 3 is a gift from someone who has 'come through'. It is a privilege to publish it.

Appendix 4 is a very brief summary of Systemic Integrative Relational Psychotherapy.

Appendix 5 is a transcript of a supervision session using the scientist-practitioner paradigm.

Any book is a co-creation of all of those – living and dead – with whom the named writer has ever been in relationship. (Nonetheless the labourer is worthy of his or her reward because it is the author who put in the hours or years of perspiration.)

There even are those like Derrida (1992) who think that it is not the author, but the reader who, in an important sense, 'writes' the book. In a certain sense this is accurate. This book is meant to stimulate your being a psychotherapist or supervisor more fully by inviting you into thinking and feeling in conversation with me and the relatively small number (of many) valuable guides I have brought together here. **You** are indeed already creating this text.

What is meant by this is that it is the resonances of your body; your subjective feelings; your word associations and personal images; the filters of your culture, values and beliefs; your habits of thought, logic and previous 'knowledge'; your theories and myths; and your capacity to tolerate ambiguity and the 'not knowing' which is constructing the true meaning of the words arranged on these printed pages.

To paraphrase Rumi: 'We have written so much. Remember what we haven't said' (1991: 122).

Finally, don't expect Aristotelian non-contradiction. The transpersonal relationship for me is all about the coexistence of opposites in cyclic manifestation, paradox, simultaneously distressingly and delightfully mysterious labyrinths. Above all, it is about **inarticulateness**. I offer this work in that Spirit.

Acknowledgements

Every effort has been made to obtain permission to reproduce copyright material throughout this book. If any proper acknowledgement has not yet been made, the copyright holder should contact the author.

Chapter 1
What is the transpersonal?

. . . Awe is the salve
that will heal our eyes.

And keen, constant listening.
Stay out in the open like a date palm
lifting its arms. Don't bore mouseholes
in the ground, arguing inside some
doctrinal labyrinth.

(Rumi, 1207–73; 1990: 76)

Be fiery, cold one, so heat can come.
Endure rough surfaces that smooth you.
The subject of all this is not *two camels*.
There's only one lost camel,
but language has difficulty saying that.

Muhammed said: 'Whoever knows God, stammers.'
Speaking is like an astrolabe pointing at the sky.
How much, really, can such a device know?

Especially of that Other Sky,
to which this one is a piece of straw?
That Other Sun, in which this is a fleck of dust?

(Extract from 'The Lost Camel',
Rumi: 1988: 30–31)

The human search for meaning

Humankind has been engaged in the search for meaning since the beginning of time. Creation myths from all cultures, oral histories and biblical
stories contain the kernels of this human desire to make meaning of the
'thrownness' (Heidegger's *Geworfenheit*) of our existence. According to

1

Brock's notes on Heidegger: 'The underlying thought would appear to be that in being-there (*Dasein*) we are "thrown there" and left derelict, like a thing cast up by the waves on the seashore' (Brock 1949: 369). From the existentialists came the clearest articulation last century of the devastating consequences of meaninglessness – alienation, moral despair, nihilism and suicide (Sartre 1938; Genet 1963; Camus 1948).

For me as a psychologist and psychotherapist, however, the foundational work from this oeuvre is Frankl's *Man's Search for Meaning* (1973). In this testament to the human spirit, born from the Nazi concentration camps, Frankl calls the ultimate human striving the 'will to meaning' (102): 'He who has a *why* to live can bear with almost any *how*' (vii). What precisely this 'why' is doesn't seem to matter – it can be individually different or shared with millions of others. But the 'force of the why' in human history cannot be denied.

'Where do we come from? Where are we going? What is the meaning of this life? That is what every heart is shouting, what every head is asking as it beats on chaos' (Kazantzakis 1960: 128). For the sake of the 'whys' – the meanings we make of our lives – wars are fought. Sometimes with the same God's priests on either side praying for victory and seeking solace in defeat. In the name of a loving Christ, millions of South Americans have died from torture, hunger or simply being worked to death in the mines. Apartheid was created because white South Africans believed that 'their' Biblical God wanted them to do it. Furthermore:

> The destruction of the [American] Indians was written into the first chapter of the successful colonization in America. The pure ideals of Christianity were easily molded into a racist ideology that matched the economic and social needs of expanding settlers.
>
> (Jacobs et al. 1971: 156)

For the sake of the 'why', brother will turn on and kill brother, mothers and fathers will abuse their children, people will risk their families and their lives or die for a cause in which they believe. We can think of IRA hunger strikers in prisons, Christian martyrs in the Colosseum of Rome, a South African girl (called Rageltjie) who dies from exposure in a snowstorm covering her baby brother's body with her own – giving up her life to save his.

Human beings will die (and do die) from loss of meaning more violently than from hunger, illness or deprivation. Is it possible that the shocking rise in young male suicides in Britain in the last decade testifies to a crisis of meaning for them in this country? Certainly, even in a secular society, there seems to be a deep need for spiritual experience:

The proportion of British people involved in some form of organised religion dwindles as each year passes. [However] there are now more than 600,000 sites associated with religion . . . and spirituality on the world wide web. Every mainstream denomination has its place in cyberspace, as have hundreds of churches, synagogues and mosques. It is possible to make a confession on-line . . . which is erased as soon as they have left the site. Jewish visitors can go to the Window on the Wall section, type in a message and the site promises to print it out and place it in the wall. Hindus, evangelical Christians and many other varieties of faith are catered for. For example Muslims can avail themselves of the five times a day on-line *azan* or call to prayer, for those using internet mobile phones.

(Daily Mail, 30 May 2000: 53)

There is so much that we cannot solve in life – loss, our bodies, time, other people, illness, bereavement, life's catastrophes. Of course when people come to counselling, psychotherapy or psychoanalysis they are seeking relief from pain, or further development. Often this occurs through changing the meanings we used to attach to our lives for new ones – creating a new narrative.

But, however much we can, and do, help, psychotherapy is not an inoculation against the vicissitudes of existence: 'Without suffering and death human life cannot be complete' (Frankl 1973: 67). Pain hurts. But the reasons we make up for why we are in pain can lead to bearing it with more courage – or to despair. In this sense all religions (and all psychotherapies) are attempts to answer the question: 'How to live in the face of death?'

Freud's (1907) confident splitting apart of religion from 'science', typical of his time, has been undermined from many angles: Michael Polanyi (1958) has shown how the notion of scientific truth rests upon subjective and emotion-laden choices; philosophers of language have shown how the world we perceive is inescapably structured by the language we inhabit. Theologians such as Raimon Panikkar (1989) have come to speak of the different religions as essentially different structures of language (Black 2000).

However, modern psychoanalysts such as Field (1996) are beginning to question the nineteenth century scientific paradigm inherited from Freud and even beginning to 'suppose' something like physis – a natural healing tendency. Arden for example writes:

I have become increasingly convinced that the so-called scientific attitude in psychoanalysis is a serious limitation . . . I want to suggest that the transference relationship with the analyst as a good parent engenders a healing process which exists in its own right. If we think about mental processes as analogous to physical processes, we can suppose there is a natural healing tendency in the mind that corresponds to the healing of physical wounds. The separation of mind and body is no longer tenable.

(Arden 1993: 151)

The poet Kazantzakis puts it this way:

> We have seen the highest circle of spiralling powers. We have named this circle God. We might have given it any other name we wished: Abyss, Mystery, Absolute Darkness, Absolute Light, Matter, Spirit, Ultimate Hope, Ultimate Despair, Silence.
>
> But we have named it God because only this name, for primordial reasons, can stir our hearts profoundly. And this deeply felt emotion is indispensable if we are to touch, body with body, the dread essence beyond logic.
>
> (1960: 101)

Transpersonal psychology

In 1969, Sutich (with Maslow, a founder of the *Journal of Transpersonal Psychology*) wrote that transpersonal psychology was concerned with the

> *empirical*, scientific study of, and responsible implementation of the findings relevant to, becoming, individual and species-wide meta-needs, ultimate values, unitive consciousness, peak experiences, B-values, ecstasy, ultimate meaning, transcendence of self, spirit, oneness, cosmic awareness, individual and species wide synergy, maximal interpersonal encounter, sacralization of everyday life, transcendental phenomena, cosmic self-humour and playfulness, maximal sensory awareness, responsiveness and expression; and related concepts, experiences and activities.
>
> (Sutich 1969: 15)

According to another definition (Clarkson 1995a: 18), the transpersonal relationship refers to the spiritual or inexplicable dimensions of relationship in all forms of psychotherapy and counselling. This category of relationship can be seen to range across

- a simple miscellaneous conceptual basket into which we place all those aspects of the healing relationship which do not fit into any other relational category;
- those imagos of therapy which are concerned with notions of chaos and complexity as well as quantum physics where modernist norms of causality and duality become redundant; and
- those aspects of mystical or transcendent relationships which correspond to the esoteric, mystical or archetypal universes of discourse. These may or may not include notions such as religion, spirituality and the traditional healing practices of most of the world's cultures. (I have discussed this extensively in *The Therapeutic Relationship*, Clarkson 1995a). However, for our purposes here, a summary is necessary.

In 1995, I published a definition of psychotherapy as the '**intentional** use of relationship' (Clarkson 1995a: 5). Of course any relationship, including the therapeutic one, is a co-creation of the people involved. However, the therapist is doing it to alleviate suffering and facilitate development. The therapist is ethically responsible for their avoided or enacted intentions in this co-created relationship. The client is responsible for their life.

I have been teaching much of this material since the late 1970s. After overcoming my 'writer's block' I have since published my findings that there are **five** primary relationship modes which are the **embedded relational matrix** present in any relationship. These five modes (aspects, dimensions or facets) are present in all relationships from supervision to parent–child relationships to casual sexual encounters – and particularly in psychotherapy and psychological counselling (Clarkson 1990, 1995a and 1996b). The five relational dimensions are:

– the working alliance
– the transference/countertransference (or biased) relationship
– the developmentally needed or reparative relationship
– the dialogic or person-to-person relationship
– the transpersonal relationship

The **working alliance** is the aspect of the client–psychotherapist relationship that enables the client and therapist to work together even when the patient or client experiences strong desires to the contrary.

The **transferential/countertransferential (biased)** facet of the relationship is the experience of wishes and fears transferred on to or into the therapeutic partnership which distorts the working alliance.

The **reparative/developmentally needed** facet of the relationship is the intentional provision by the psychotherapist of a corrective, reparative, or replenishing relationship or action where previous relationships were deficient, abusive or overprotective.

The **person-to-person facet** of the relationship is the real relationship or dialogic subject-to-subject relationship – as opposed to object relationship.

The **transpersonal** facet of the relationship is thus the timeless facet of the psychotherapeutic relationship, which is impossible to describe, but refers to the spiritual dimension or post-positivist scientific aspects of the healing relationship. (It is important to remember these are not stages but states in psychoanalysis, often subtly 'overlapping', in and between which a client creates his or her unique experiences.)

In the first instance, therefore, the transpersonal relationship refers to all kinds of transactions, relationships, phenomena and concepts which do not fit into one of the other four categories of therapeutic relationship. Although one can see the five as separate therapeutic relationships for the purposes of analysis, research or teaching, it would be more precise to describe them phenomenologically as aspects, modes or facets of one intrinsically whole and indivisible relationship – not an integrative framework, but an integrated whole. In this way I liken it again to the phenomenological discovery of the five modes best conceptualized as the **fractal of relationship**:

> The word 'fractal' was coined by [the chaoticist] Mandelbrot (1974) to describe the phenomenon of a repeating pattern – elements of the whole are repeated in every fragment, and spiral off each other towards creative evolution. 'Above all, fractal meant self-similar. Self-similarity is symmetry across scale. It implies recursion, pattern inside of pattern.'
>
> (Gleick 1989: 103).

The five relational dimensions can also be considered as a fractal, self-similar across scale, for relationships across all scales – larger or smaller wholes of any system which are each also wholes in and of themselves. (The research supporting it is available in Clarkson 1996b.) We can speak of having five kinds of relationship with ourselves (e.g. see Mountjoy, in press).

We can also consider any couple as having their mutual relationship across these five dimensions (see Appendix in Clarkson 1995a: 338–48). Its use as a framework for the practice of and training in Integrative Psychotherapy and Counselling Psychology (or Integrative Systemic Relational Psychotherapy) as well as for Diploma training and supervising of supervisors has been well documented (e.g. see Clarkson 1992a; Appendix 4 of this book; and the PHYSIS website: www.physis.co.uk).

This 'fractal' of relationship has been successfully used in organizational consultancy (Clarkson 1995b) and organizational culture change (Clarkson and Nicolopoulou, in press) as well as in psychological research (Clarkson 2000a: Chapter 14). It applies to casual relationships, business, friendships, sales and sports teams as well as to governments. We could even consider the relationship of all human beings with the planet earth herself as having all five of these dimensions – and it doesn't take much to see how our distorted relationship with the earth could benefit from a better working relationship at the very least!

So, at a micro scale we could focus on the five dimensions of a person's relationship with themselves; at a meso scale we could focus on the five dimensions of family relationships; at a macro scale we could focus on the five dimensions as they present themselves in the culture of an organization, a nation or the world. In between there are of course many, many other scales and gradations.

Fiumara (1995) writes that when constrained to an objective factual literalism (as in many academic journals, which use exclusively an 'objective' language stripped of metaphoric life) language becomes divorced from the body, from liveliness, and then language functions 'only as a deadening filter' which may be

> only apparently free of conflicts, but which ultimately leads to nullifying vital relations. Speakers become tied into a sort of benumbed state which is perhaps the most widespread and most concealed of all forms of degradation. Paradoxically, the more our life can be described as 'intimate', 'profound', 'subjective', the more its development is dependent upon the quality of the interpersonal relationships which affect the crucial distinction between mirroring and relating.
>
> (Fiumara 1995: 130)

Chaos and complexity science is, along with quantum physics, a postmodern scientific area with fascinating implications for psychologists and psychotherapists, since it concerns itself with what does not submit to objective, linear, simplistic, causal, rationalistic formulations alone:

> The first Chaos theorists . . . had an eye for pattern, especially pattern that appeared on different scales at the same time. They had a taste for randomness and complexity, for jagged edges and sudden leaps. Believers in chaos speculate about determinism and free will, about evolution, about the nature of conscious intelligence. They feel that they are turning back a trend in science toward reductionism, the analysis of systems in terms of their constituent parts . . . they believe that they are looking for the whole.
>
> (Gleick 1989: 5)

This, again, is true of our life and belief systems, which can also be seen as fractals. Psychotherapists know that you can go on repeating certain patterns of belief to infinity too, for example habitual self-deception, or letting addictive habits become the very meaning of life: 'When we try to pick out anything by itself, we find it hitched to everything else in the Universe . . . The whole wilderness is unity and interrelation is alive and familiar' (Muir, in Wolfe 1951: 123).

It is not that chaos is without order – it is that it **is** order, with its own creative nature and in a new dimension. Bohm (1980) has addressed this wholemaking tendency in his thought-provoking book *Wholeness and the Implicate Order*. I also find illumination in the Holism theory of Smuts (1987, first published in 1926), the South African philosopher-warrior who was developing similar ideas well before Bohm or the Chaos Theorists.

Sometimes I say
The Sun within the Sun inside the Sun,
and claim to be describing God.
I'm talking in my sleep.
(Rumi 1990: 7)

It is possible to distinguish for the sake of clarity three categories of referring to the transpersonal relationship mode or the transpersonal domain in psychotherapy and counselling.

That which is currently unknown or not yet understood constitutes the first category, and to this can be consigned whatever is inexplicable, wordless, ineffable. Thus the fact that the therapist dreams of the client in distress calling him, and this subsequently corresponds to an actual event, can be safely consigned to coincidence. Meeting someone at a conference who has had similar experiences is probably no more likely than chance. Finding a scarab beetle knocking at the window when someone is talking about their psychological 'carapace' is simply accidental – except that one's client or patient may wish to attach significance and meaning to such 'untoward events'. (Jung's scarab example is discussed in Chapter 3.) One could of course dismiss these kinds of things as 'unscientific fantasies', symptoms of psychosis in need of specialized psychiatric treatment – or simply hocus-pocus. This is one category of referring to what I mean by the transpersonal relationship.

Secondly, the category of transpersonal relationship refers to images, metaphors, notions and ideas from the worlds of quantum physics or chaos and complexity science. What is meant here is simply the fact that these comparatively new sciences present us with capacities and categories to deal with ambiguity, uncertainty, paradox, contradiction, simultaneity, permanent uncertainty and the quantum leaps (or more accurately 'quantum drops') which tend to categorize individual human change as well as the scientific revolutions which Kuhn (1970) described. As Koestler puts it:

> The cycle which results makes the evolution of ideas appear as a succession of repeated differentiations, specializations and re-integrations on a higher **level** – a progression from primordial unity through variety to more complex patterns of unity in variety.
>
> (Koestler 1972: 290)

Thirdly, however defined, some implicit or explicit recognition of the possibility, if not the existence, of an explicitly transpersonal relationship between **healer** and **healed** as it unfolds within the psychotherapeutic *vas* (container) is gradually beginning to gain more acceptance (Clarkson 1990). Then the spiritual, mystical, transcendent or numinous can be brought out openly into the conversation. This is particularly relevant as we recognize that there can be no multicultural psychotherapy without some kind of respectful relationship with the religious and spiritual practices in which many, if not most, cultures are steeped.

There is not a great deal of documentation about the transpersonal relationship in psychotherapy and counselling except for Cortright (1997) and Rowan's contribution to surveying and expanding the field (1993). Thorne's (1998) volume – *Person-centred Counselling and Christian Spirituality – the Secular and the Holy* – is a fine and rare contribution from a Christian perspective.

The classic text by Braud and Anderson (1998) contains one of the best summaries of research methods generally that I have come across so far. Boorstein's excellent and comprehensive edited volume (1996) represents a wide variety of approaches and techniques with some illustrative case studies. Valle's volume *Phenomenological Inquiry in Psychology – Existential and Transpersonal Dimensions* (1998), which has contributions from many leading transpersonal psychologists, is also highly recommended.

In her inspiring book on the psychological experience of ritual, *Susceptible to the Sacred*, the Jungian Bani Shorter writes that:

> while serious psychologists and psychotherapists have themselves abstained from interference with religion, by and large religion has disregarded psychology, accepting it only in so far as it has been found relevant to pastoral care. Fortunately, the imagery of psyche itself makes no such distinctions.
>
> (Shorter 1996: 32)

Peck (1978) uses the concept of 'grace', like Buber (1937: 1987 edition) before him, as the ultimate factor which operates in the healing encounter and which may make the difference between whether a patient gets better or not. Berne, the founder of transactional analysis, was also aware of it when he quoted: '"Je le pensay, et Dieu le guarit" . . . we treat them, but it is God who cures them' (Agnew, in Berne 1966: 63).

Use of the transpersonal in psychotherapy and counselling discourses: explicit acknowledgements and specific examples

According to Black (2000) there has even been a shift in psychoanalysis from the 'orthodoxy of atheism' to acknowledging that there are forms of 'mature' religion (as opposed to 'primitive' religion):

> By 'primitive' religion [Symington 1994] means a form of magical thinking, aimed at personal protection and survival; 'mature' religion is rational, thoughtful and able to debate important themes such as truth, love, evil and goodness.
>
> (Black 2000: 14).

Black sees, for example, the Semitic (Judaeo-Christian) and the Indian religions as two of the 'great families of highly developed religion' (2000: 16). However, later in this article he comments on how the Kleinian analyst Jaques (1988) continues, a little surprisingly in view of his general attitude of disparagement of religion, to speak with great feeling of the possible serenity and confidence of old age, using the sublime imagery of Dante's Paradiso: 'my desire and my will, like a wheel that spins with even motion, were revolved by the Love that moves the sun and other stars' (2000: 23).

In the history of psychoanalysis I have always been interested in Groddeck's concept of the *It* (1988: 10–15). He was particularly successful with healing organic diseases through his self-confessedly 'wild analysis'.

It therefore comes as no surprise that he came to the conclusion that 'the distinction between body and mind is only verbal and not essential, that body and mind are one unit, that they contain an It, a force which lives us while we believe we are living' (Groddeck 1988: 9). He also commented on how the It creates illness to save a person from perhaps more serious dangers. He does not differentiate between illness and health because he sees illness or neurosis as a sign of life. For Groddeck, 'illness is not an evil in itself but always a meaningful process' (1988: 10).

Groddeck's notion of the *It* is exactly the same as what I understand by 'physis':

> There is no such thing as an I, it is a lie, a misrepresentation to say: I think, I live. It ought to be: it thinks, it lives. It, i.e. the great mystery of the world. There is no I . . . It is the most important thing about people . . . [but] only a fool would try to understand it. There is nothing there to understand . . . All definitions are thus made null and void, they have nothing but a momentary meaning, are only justified in so far as they are useful.
>
> (Groddeck 1988: 11)

Freud, who valued Groddeck's work highly, wrote to him (18 June 1925) that he did not 'recognise my civilised, bourgeois, demystified Id in your It. Yet you know that mine is derived from yours' (in Groddeck 1988: 14). Groddeck elaborates:

> The It, moreover, manifests itself as independent and as mutually dependent in the life as a whole as in the parts of a living human being's existence, or, in other words, there is apparently a similar relation between the whole human being and the cell or even smaller entities, the tissues, the individual organ or part of the body as was expressed by the terms macrocosmos and microcosmos in former times to describe the universe and its parts . . .
>
> (Groddeck 1988: 15–16)

Within the Jungian tradition, Jung himself, with Pauli (Jung and Pauli 1955), and more recently Field recognize 'the life force that the therapy tries to mobilise' (Field 1996: 31). Hauke's exemplary book, *Jung and the Postmodern* (2000), also shows an increasing acknowledgement of the influence of the qualities which at present transcend the limits of our understanding within analytical psychology thinking. ('There are more things in heaven and earth, Horatio, than are dreamt of in your philosophy' – *Hamlet*: 1.5.166.)

> The psychotherapist and the client find themselves in a relationship built on mutual unconsciousness. The psychotherapist is led to a direct confrontation of the unreconciled part of himself. The activated unconsciousness of both the client and the therapist causes both to become involved in a transformation of the 'third'. Hence, the relationship itself becomes transformed in the process.
>
> (Archambeau 1979: 162)

The transpersonal relationship is generally characterized by its timelessness. In Jungian thought it is conceived of as 'the relationship between the unconscious of the analyst and the unconscious of the patient not mediated by consciousness' (Guggenbühl-Craig 1971). 'Insofar as the [psychoanalytic interpretation] clarifies this psychoanalytic object, it will acquire dimensions in the sense of myth, of meaning and of theory' (Grinberg et al. 1975: 67).

The existentialist Van Deurzen-Smith even uses the notion of 'soul'. She writes that, in addition to the physical, social and personal dimension, there is also a spiritual dimension: 'On this dimension we connect through what we may think of as our soul to the absolute world of ideas and their concrete significance in our everyday existence' (1997: 101).

Rogers (1961), father of the person-centred psychotherapy tradition, frequently writes about the self-actualizing tendency. In later life he became almost a mystic by recognizing the constant influence of the transpersonal in all our lives – our participation in a larger universal formative tendency. He wanted to develop the creative potential – the natural tendency towards growth – within a person and within society. He writes about the 'mysterious laws' which we can intuit from physics, and the transcendent, even timeless, sense of life and the universe unfolding as a whole.

Perls (1969a) of Gestalt fame was seriously influenced by Zen Buddhism. He talked about the *élan vital* – the energy of life, the vitality of the life force which permeates all living beings and is for him the soul:

> Now normally the *élan vital*, the life force, energizes by sensing, by listening, by scouting, by describing the world – how is the world there. Now this life force

> apparently first mobilizes the center – *if* you have a center. And the center of the personality is what used to be called the soul: the emotions, the feelings, the spirit.
>
> (Perls 1969a: 63–64)

I don't think Ellis (1962) overtly espouses any religious doctrine, but he does write about the goal of Rational Emotive Therapy including a 'joy of being' (1962: 366). The existentialist philosopher Heidegger (1987) recognized that *being* means *physis* – an ancient Greek word for the life energy in everything and nothing. Ellis even writes that the Zen Buddhist notion of *satori* (enlightenment) would not be incompatible with some of the goals that 'a devotee of rational emotive living might seek for himself' (1962: 366). He also suggests as a cure for the pains of being human that people acquire a good philosophy of life which will enable us to live successfully and happily in spite of our intrinsic biological limitations as human beings.

The similarities between the experimental-cognitive models of unconscious information processing and Milton Erickson's conception of 'unconscious mind' have been pointed out by Liotti (1989: 36) and I shall return to this later. (Erickson is but one exemplar of a practitioner working with the notion of the 'intelligent unconscious' – an idea which is far richer and elaborate than the 'unconscious' of Freud.) The phenomenologist Merleau-Ponty writes:

> But quantum physics has doubtless taught us to introduce 'acausal' givens into our image of the physical world, behind which there is no reason in principle for affirming a causality of the classical type . . . In order to maintain definitively the originality of vital categories, it would be necessary to make every organism a whole which produces its parts, to find in it the simple act from which the partial phenomena derive their being, to return therefore to the notion of vital *élan*.
>
> (Merleau-Ponty 1983: 154–55)

Transcultural perspectives

In history, as well as in two thirds of the world, of course, there is hardly a culture which does not use traditional healing practices based on ancient appreciations of the power of shamans, medicine people and other kinds of prophet-healers to invoke the supreme powers of God (or whatever the life force may be called locally) to assist in healing, helping and harvesting. Sometimes it is called *NTU* as in some parts of North Africa (Ani 1994), or *kiruenugii* by the Japanese (Nippoda, personal communication) or *phusis* by the ancient Greeks. All such words and many more refer to the life force through which we/the universe live and breathe and have our being.

Fpr Ani, **anxiety** – such a theme for white male existentialists and psychoanalysts – is seen as emanating from the fact that **Spirit cannot be controlled**:

> The African world-view, and the world-views of other people who are not of European origin, all appear to have certain themes in common. The universe to which they relate is sacred in origin, is organic, and is a true 'cosmos'. Human beings are part of the cosmos, and, as such, relate intimately with other cosmic beings. Knowledge of the universe comes through relationship with it and through perception of spirit in matter. The universe is one; spheres are joined because of a single unifying force that pervades all being. Meaningful reality issues from the force. These world-views are 'reasonable' but not rationalistic: complex yet lived. They tend to be expressed through a logic of metaphor and complex symbolism.
>
> (Ani 1994: 30)

Ani goes on to show how the African-centred view of the universe is alive with energy – 'the whole life-flow of creation' (1994: 102). In contrast to the European cultural determination to subdue (and torture) Nature, Africans – and others, for example North American Indians – experience that all the various forms of life are interdependent and form a rich tapestry enlivened by difference, diversity and **mystery** – which is the strength of creation. Ani suggests that the European world-view is at variance with the world-view of the majority cultures of the world because Europeans view themselves in a superior evolutionary position – 'more developed' than first world cultures.

Some people may find this view flawed or irrelevant. I think it is important to take account of what 'we' (the authors of most psychoanalytic and psychotherapy texts, for example) look like to people from other cultures. In particular, it is rare to find such a scholarly and clear exposition of the African-centred vertex. Why is it so important? One reason is because we live in a multicultural world and people from many cultures may seek or want to offer psychotherapy (e.g. see Bird 1999).

Another reason is that the findings from quantum physics and complexity science are 'almost identical to our description of the African world view' (Ani 1994: 100).

Yet a review of the major formally prescribed texts in psychotherapy and counselling psychology in the UK (Clarkson 1999) showed that (a) race and culture are **not** on the curriculum or in the indexes; (b) the three traditional approaches favoured in UK psychotherapeutic psychotherapy neglect or exclude non-Eurocentric approaches; (c) there is almost no mention at all of transpersonal, spiritual or post-positivistic sciences in any of the texts.

Maslow once said:

> If there is any primary rule of science, it is . . . acceptance of the obligation to
> acknowledge and describe all of reality . . . It must accept within its jurisdiction
> even that which it cannot understand, explain . . . that which cannot be measured
> . . . It includes all **levels** or stages of knowledge, including . . . subjective experi-
> ence'.
>
> (Leytham 1995: 80)

My colleague Bill Wahl told me that when he was teaching psychology on
an American Indian 'reservation', the curriculum required him to teach
Freud and he did. One day he was giving a lift to one of his Sioux students
when he noticed the student clearly wanted to say something to him.

'Yes, Running Water, what is it?'

'Well, you see Bill I don't really want to tell you. I think it will embarrass
you.'

'Go on,' said Bill, 'tell me what's in your heart.'

'Well, you know what you were telling us today about how you people
want to kill their fathers and want to have sexual intercourse with their
mothers?'

'Yes,' said Bill.

'Well,' said Running Water, 'I don't know how to break this to you but,
since you're my friend, I feel you should know . . . we're not like that.'

People from the two-thirds world cultures are, with some exceptions,
generally deeply spiritual or religious. For people from these traditions,
the life force, ancestors, the entanglement of individuals and community,
of body and mind, of nature and spirit are not ideas, they are living realities. Eurocentric psychologies or psychotherapies as they are generally
practised have little or no place for such realities. Like it was for the
ancient Greeks, a split between nature and spirit is inconceivable. In
Rumi's words again: 'No image can describe what of our fathers and
mothers, our grandfathers and grandmothers remains . . . Language does
not touch the One who lives in each of us' (1991: 15).

Too often a harsh interpretative reductionism is applied to explain the
transpersonal away, for example in terms of 'internalized object
relations', or religious worship is defined as coming from the 'psychotic
part of the personality'. For the African-Jamaican community in this
country, for example, Christianity in various forms is part of people's
daily lives in a way which is almost impossible for other people to
imagine. Yet our Eurocentric psychotherapies too often make 'God-talk
beyond the pale'.

This is of course a natural microcosm of what has been called our Eurocentric cultural imperialism. The *Hutchinson Encyclopaedia of Living Faiths* (1988 reprint) includes Dialectical Materialism (Marxism) as a living faith, but there is no mention of any African-centred faith or any of the spiritual traditions of the first world. The following quotation is representative:

> Thus for the Jain the soul, which is identified with the life (*jiva*) is finite and has variable though definite size and weight. Moreover, **primitive animistic ideas** must have originally inspired the Jain's attribution of life to entities and objects not thought to be living by other [more developed?] Indian sects. Not only are, human beings, demons, animals and insects believed to be inhabited by souls, but also plants of all species, earth and stones and everything derived from the earth, rivers, ponds, seas and raindrops, flames and all fires, and gases and winds of every kind. Thus the whole universe is full of life . . . 'A bird, I have been seized by hawks or trapped in nets, or held fast by bird-lime, and have been killed an infinite number of times.' . . . 'a tree, with axes and adzes by the carpenters an infinite number of times, I have been felled, stripped of my bark, cut up, and sawn into planks.'
>
> (257, my emphasis)

The physicist David Peat writes in *Blackfoot Physics* that 'Native people not only have knowledge of what comes by direct experience, but [also] access to the knowledge of the birds, insects, animals, rocks and trees' (1996: 250); he adds that 'there is no division between science and spirituality for every act and every plant and animal is sacred' (1996: 262). But Plato, according to Ani,

> . . . sought to construct a world made up totally of conceptual reality. In this world there was little room for sense perceptions. They occupied a very inferior position. He wanted the citizen to become more and more acculturated to this conceptual reality. Doing so meant that the citizen's senses were trusted less and less, until European culture ended up at one end of the spectrum of which Africa might be at the other. Europeans are not trained to use their sense nor to be 'perceptive' (insofar as that is taken by them to mean 'non-intellectual') whereas Africans relate to the universe using sense perceptions as highly developed tools – media, if you will – that are a valued part of the human intellectual apparatus.
>
> (1994: 43, and also further)

It was the great white Western male Descartes who hoped 'that those who understood all that has been said in this [his] treatise will, in future, see nothing whose cause they cannot easily understand, nor anything that gives them any reason to marvel' (Descartes 1969: 349). (Well, so much for marvelling then.)

About the Enlightenment project (that science and reason would explain all) Mary Midgley writes:

> The literature of early modern science is a mine of highly-coloured passages that describe Nature, by no means as a neutral object, but as a seductive but troublesome female, to be unrelentingly pursued, sought out, fought against, chased into her inmost sanctuaries, prevented from escaping, persistently courted, wooed, harried, vexed, tormented, unveiled, unrobed [like Draupadi in the Mahabharat] and 'put to question' (i.e. interrogated under torture), forced to confess 'all that lay in her most intimate recesses', her 'beautiful bosom' must be laid bare, she must be held down and finally 'penetrated', 'pierced' and 'vanquished' (words which constantly recur) . . . they would subdue 'Nature with all her children, to bind her to your service and make her your slave'.
>
> (1992: 77)

Midgley also quotes Sedgewick as describing the true scientific method as putting 'nature to the torture in order to wring new secrets from her' (1992: 78); 'Matter, fully debunked, was from now on to be recognized as what the New Philosophy declared it to be – mere inert, passive, mindless stuff, devoid of spontaneity, of all interesting properties such as sympathy and antipathy, and above all destitute of any creative power' (1992: 76). Here, as elsewhere, *physis* (spirit) and *nomos* (the law) are seen to be one.

Chanter, an Irigaray scholar, poses this question:

> The [Platonic-initiated] clash between *physis* and *nomos*, the personal and the political, individual and universal, family and state, divine and human, between the old gods and the new, youth and age, inner and outer, implicit and explicit, unconscious and conscious, night and day, pleasure and discipline, and finally between female and male is brought to a head in a confrontation between nature and culture. How far is man's struggle against nature also his struggle against woman?
>
> (Chanter 1995: 120)

How 'primitive' and 'undeveloped' to think that we humans have a soul-full relationship with all of life – especially the 'inferior', 'lower' or 'inanimate' forms of it! How quaint to think that some people from 'the third world' believe that people interpenetrate and that they are not 'other'. Just like some Western babies (see e.g. Costall et al. 1997; Draghi-Lorenz et al. in press), some faiths have not even developed to the point where they believe that the mind and body are separate and that the natural world is there to be 'mastered' – or tortured till all her secrets are forced out of her.

Marimba Ani (1994) speaks for these ignored faiths when she laments:

We used their definitions of ourselves
to disconnect our consciousness
Lines drawn in denial of deeply textured souls
Okra/Ka/Se
Life/Force/Energy
Nyama . . .
We have allowed the earth to be defiled.
The wake of two thousand seasons
Of Spiritless matter.

(Ani 1994: xx)

Is it any wonder that so many people with an African heritage do not return after one session of formal time-boundaried and touchless psychotherapy based on individualistic linear models, when we so patently fail to deal with what is most important in their lives. In fact we even lack a vocabulary which is not at best archetypal (Adams 1997; see also Bird 1999; MIND Report 2000; and Cleminson, in press). Hogan writes:

For more than a quarter century the mental health professions have brought to bear a panoply of weapons in waging a fierce battle to control the field of psychotherapy. However, their efforts, made in the name of protecting the public from harm, have probably caused more harm than good. What we should have at this date in history is plentiful services delivered to all populations at a reasonable cost and with minimal risk. Instead, what we have are fewer services at higher costs and with many populations totally unserved. And it is not at all clear that the public has been protected.

(Hogan 1999: 1)

I think that unless we take a transpersonal dimension into every moment of our psychotherapeutic psychology work (or at least all **five** facets of all our relationships) there is no place for God (or Physis/Umendu, the life force). If there isn't place for **God** in our psychotherapeutic psychology, there isn't place for the **African** experience in it either.

Describing the transpersonal

The nature of the transpersonal dimension is thus quite difficult to describe, because it is both rare in the European literature and not easily accessible to the kind of descriptions that can easily be used in discussing the other forms of psychotherapeutic relationships:

The *numinosum* is either a quality belonging to a visible object or the influence of an invisible presence that causes a peculiar alteration of consciousness.

(Jung 1969d: 7)

The invisibility at the heart of things was traditionally named the *deus abscon-ditus*, the 'concealed god', that could be spoken of only in images, metaphors and paradoxical conundrums, gems of immense worth buried within giant mountains, sparks that contain the flammable force of wildfire.

(Hillman, in Moore 1996: 285)

We struggle to make this Spirit visible, to give it a face, to encase it in words, in allegories and thoughts and incantations, that it may not escape us.
　　But it cannot be contained in the twenty-six letters of an alphabet which we string out in rows; we know that all these words, these allegories, these thoughts, and these incantations are, once more, but a new mask with which to conceal the Abyss.
　　Yet only in this manner, by confining immensity, may we labor within the newly incised circle of humanity.

(Kazantzakis 1960: 101)

Poetry embarrasses some people. Plato would ban poets from his ideal republic. He says:

We cannot, therefore, allow poetry in our ideal state. The gravest charge against poetry still remains. It has a terrible power to corrupt even the best characters, with very few exceptions . . . poetry has the same effect on us when it represents sex and anger, and the other desires and feelings of pleasure and pain which accompany all out actions. It waters them when they ought to be left to wither.

(Plato 1987: 436–37)

It is also possible that there may be a certain amount of embarrassment in Western psychotherapists who have to admit that after all the years of training and personal analysis and supervision, ultimately we may still not know **precisely** what it is that we are doing or how and what difference it really makes.
　　This is the kind of statement that one can only be sure will be understood by experienced psychotherapists who have been faced repeatedly with incomprehensible and unpredictable outcomes – the person of whom you despaired suddenly, and sometimes apparently inexplicably, gets well, thrives and actualizes themselves beyond all expectation. At the other polarity, the client for whom the analyst had made an optimistic prognosis reaches plateaux from which in effect they never move, and the analysis is abandoned with a lingering sense of potential glimpsed but never reached.
　　The kinship relationship which is characterized by the creation of space as well as fruitful substance between the psychotherapeutic partners is analogous to that of the marital pair which may give birth to a third – the continuation of life itself. Indeed, in Jung's work (1966) the archetypal sexual relationship is used to represent the alchemical process of transfor-

mation. Of course, the conjunction was to be symbolic, not consummated in an unethical, incestuous way.

In an illuminating paper, Nuttall explores the ancient woodcuts of the Rosarium first applied by Jung through Fairbairn's theory of object relations, setting them alongside Clarkson's five-dimensional model of the therapeutic relationship. He concludes that the 'Rosarium contains all those elements that Clarkson has identified as invariably present in the optimum therapeutic process' (2000: 92).

The transpersonal relationship is paradoxically also characterized both by a kind of intimacy and by an 'emptying of the ego' at the same time. It is rather as if the ego (of even the personal unconscious of the psychotherapist) is 'emptied out' of the psychotherapeutic space, leaving room for something numinous (glowing) to be created in the 'between' of the relationship. This space can then become the '*temenos*' (sacred space) or 'the *vas bene clausum* [beneficial closed container] inside which transmutation takes place' (Adler 1979: 21). (Numinous means something like sacred.) This dimension in the psychotherapeutic relationship cannot be 'proved'. Buber concludes: 'Nothing remains to me in the end but an appeal to the testimony of your own mysteries . . .' (1987: 174).

Implied in the transpersonal relationship as I see it is a **letting go** of skills, a surrender of knowledge, the forgetting of experience, the yielding of preconceptions – even of the desire to remember, to heal or to be present. Grinberg et al. comment on Bion's observations:

> We can say that the reality we deal with as analysts, i.e. psychic reality, is infinite and has many facets . . . 'O' is 'the unknown, new and as yet not evolved. We assume it can develop to a point where our intuition can grasp it and make it coherent. The developments or evolutions of O are presented to the analyst's intuition and he must wait for such evolution to take place before he can formulate an interpretation . . . The process called *evolution* is the union, through a sudden intuition, of a mass of apparently disparate phenomena, thus giving them coherence and meaning. What is the adequate mental state for the intuitive grasp of the evolutions of O? Bion proposes the systematic avoidance of memory and desire . . . [He] extends 'memory' to all memory; he suggests that the analyst forget what he already knows about the patient and consider him a new patient in every session . . . He points out the importance of the capacity to tolerate the suffering and frustration associated to 'not knowing' and 'not understanding'. A lack of tolerance for this type of frustration can promptly lead the analyst to look for 'fact and reason' to relieve him of his uncertainty, even though it may enhance knowledge, opposes discovery and the insight that is closely linked to becoming 'O'. *The language of achievement* derives from the possibility of tolerating half-doubts, half mysteries and half truths. It is the language that is at the same time a prelude to action and a type of action in itself. It is the language the analyst must achieve, and this language is related to the

'capacity to forget, the ability to eschew desire and understanding when in contact with the patient during the unique and incommunicable experience of each psychoanalytic session' [Bion 1970: 51].

(Grinberg et al. 1975: 55)

It is essentially allowing the kind of 'passivity', yielding and receptiveness for which preparation is always inadequate. But paradoxically one has to be full in order to become empty. The story is told of a famous professor from an eminent Japanese university who went to visit an illustrious Zen master to learn the wisdom of life from him. When the Zen master, during the extremely formal tea ceremony, just poured and poured the tea into the professor's cup until it flowed all over the table and the floor, the professor was outraged. Why? The Zen master explained that the professor's tea cup was already full when he came. If he really wanted to have his cup filled, it would first need to be empty. He was demonstrating vividly the futility and waste of trying to receive where there is no emptiness.

We have to lose our souls to gain our souls. It cannot be **made** to happen. It can only be encouraged in the same way that the inspirational muse of creativity cannot be forced. The ground needs to be seized in the serendipitous moment of readiness. What **can** be prepared are the conditions conducive to its emergence.

Whereas Freud used the term 'unconscious' to apply to one person or something within that person, both Jung and Erickson conceive of unconscious processes as also **shared**. (It's important to note that I see consciousness along a continuum of awareness, not split into two or three sections.) According to Rank:

Dessoir, in his Aesthetics, gives this mysterious something [a genius in the artist or collective] the designation of the unconscious – a dubious psychological conception in any case – he has not elucidated any of its mysteriousness by so doing. For if one is not prepared to interpret the unconscious in the rationalistic sense of psycho-analysis as the repressed impulse, it remains but a pseudo-scientific metaphor for the inconceivable, the divine, just as the collectivity resolves itself according to Utiz into a social representation of the unconscious divinity.

(Rank 1989: xxvi)

TO PUT IT MORE PRECISELY, I SEE THE CREATOR-IMPULSE AS THE LIFE IMPULSE MADE TO SERVE THE INDIVIDUAL WILL. When psycho-analysis speaks of a sublimated sexual impulse in creative art, meaning thereby the impulse diverted from its purely biological function and directed towards higher ends, the question as to what diverted and what directed is just being dismissed with an allusion to repression. But repression is a negative factor, which might divert, but never direct . . . [it says nothing about the] 'VITAL IMPULSE' of which the neurotic suffers from an excessive check, the artist not . . .

(Rank 1989: 40)

This leads us to the profoundest source of the artistic impulse to create, which I can only satisfactorily explain to myself as the struggle of the individual against an inherent striving after totality, which forces him equally in the direction of a complete surrender to life and a complete giving of himself in production.

(Rank 1989: 60)

This corroborates Winnicott's statement that creativity 'is the retention throughout life of something that belongs properly to infant experience: the ability to create the world' (1986: 40).

But the regression in the case of aesthetic creation—in contrast to these other cases—is purposive and controlled.

(Koestler 1989: 253)

The fact that art and discovery draw on unconscious sources indicates that one aspect of all creative activity is a regression to ontogenetically or phylogenetically earlier **levels**, an escape from the restraints of the conscious mind, with the subsequent release of creative potentials—a process paralleled on lower **levels** by the liberation from restraint of genetic potentials or neural equi-potentiality in the regeneration of structures and functions.

(Koestler 1989: 462)

For Jung the collective unconscious is that primary substratum which has 'never been in consciousness and reflects archetypal processes' (Samuels et al. 1986). To quote Jung directly:

The personal unconscious rests upon a deeper layer, which does not derive from personal experience and is not a personal acquisition, but is inborn. The deeper layer I call the collective unconscious . . . this part of the unconscious is not individual but universal.

(Jung 1951: para. 3)

It might exist across our evolutionary history, across world cultures, across species – even perhaps across humans and animals and so-called 'inanimate matter'.

Field (1996) points out that Jung held that individual consciousnesses are 'like islands showing up in the ocean; at the **level** of the sea-bed we are joined . . . The fact of our connection is the primary reality and our separateness [as individuals] a secondary one' (1996: 42). Would our collective unconscious connection only be with other human beings to the exclusion of all else in the universe?

For Erickson and Kubie (in Haley 1967):

[Our] observation stresses from a new angle a fact that has often been emphasized by those who have studied unconscious processes but which remains nonetheless mysterious – namely, that underneath the diversified nature of the consciously organized aspects of the personality, the unconscious talks in a language which has remarkable uniformity; furthermore that that language has laws so constant that the unconscious of one individual is better equipped to understand the unconscious of another than the conscious aspect of the personality of either.

(Haley 1967: 545)

Shades of Lacan (1968)? A trainee reports:

When I first started learning it was like trying to learn a new language, say French, but when I saw a very experienced psychotherapist working it appeared to me that she was speaking an entirely different language such as Chinese. The more I have learnt the more I have come to realize that she does indeed speak French, she just speaks it very well. And sometimes she speaks Chinese.

(Clarkson 1995a: 20)

This comment arose from a context in which he has perceived the supervisor at times intuitively to know facts, feelings or intentions of patients without there being any prior evidence to lead to the conclusions. It is these intuitive illuminations which seem to flourish the more the psychotherapist dissolves the individual 'ego' from the psychotherapeutic container, allowing wisdom and insight and transformation to emerge as a process. The essence of it can be said to lie in the heart of the shared silence of being-together in a dimension which is impossible to articulate exactly, too delicate to analyse and yet too pervasively present in all healing practices to deny.

Another trainee in supervision brought as an ethical problem the fact that he had seen a particular client for several years, who was seriously disturbed and showed no sign of improvement. He had utilized all the major interpretations and intervention strategies for such cases to no avail. Indeed she even refused to form any working alliance in the shape of an agreed goal for her. It was exceedingly uncertain what benefit there could be for her, yet she continued coming because (we speculated) this was the only single human relationship which was alive for her in a physically and emotionally impoverished life.

The psychotherapist questioned, responsibly, whether she should be referred to another treatment facility. Yet he feared that she would experience this as an abandonment. In our supervision we explored the possibility that he should let go of expectations that she should be different from the way she was. The psychotherapist was even willing and able to let go of the healer archetype, allowing himself to become an empty vessel, a container wherein healing **space** could be manifest, or **beingness** could be validated, without any expectation even of the acceptance. This needs to be truly done in good faith and not based on the trickery of paradoxical interventions where expectations are removed **in order** for the patient to change. The atmosphere is more suspension of ego-consciousness – a trance-like meditation. The quality is conveyed by the **being-with** of creative psychotherapists such as Gendlin (1967) and Fromm-Reichman (1974) working with patients in acute psychosis. From the Chinese tradition comes the following:

> The true human nature is the primal spirit. The primal spirit is precisely human nature and life, and if one accepts what is real in it, it is the primal energy. And the great Way is just this thing . . . whoever seeks eternal life must search for the place whence human nature and life originally sprang . . . Only the primal spirit and the true nature overcome time and space. The energy of the seed, like heaven and earth, is transitory, but the primal spirit is beyond the polar differences. Here is the place whence heaven and earth derive their being. When students understand how to grasp the primal spirit they overcome the polar opposites of light and darkness and tarry no longer in the three worlds. But only he who has envisioned human nature's original face is able to do this.
>
> (Wilhelm 1962: 24–25)

This notion resembles the archetype of the Self which Jung refers to as the person's inherent and psychic disposition to experience centredness and meaning in life, sometimes conceived of as the God within ourselves. Buber (1987) was essentially concerned with the close association of the relation to God with the relation to one's fellow men, with the I–Thou which issues from **the encounter with the other you in relationship**:

> The extended lines of relations met in the eternal *Thou*. Every particular *Thou* is a glimpse through to the eternal *Thou*; by means of every particular *Thou* the primary word addresses the eternal *Thou*. Through this mediation of the *Thou* of all beings fulfilment, and non-fulfilment, of relations comes to them: the inborn *Thou* is realised in each relation and consummated in none. It is consummated only in the direct relation with the *Thou* that by its nature cannot be *It*.
>
> (Buber 1987: 99)

It is quite possible that psychotherapists may delude themselves in ways which may be dangerous for them and for their clients if they mistakenly, prematurely or naively focus on the transpersonal and, for example, overlook or minimize transferential or personal phenomena. There are always the twin dangers of 'spiritualizing the psychological' or 'psychologizing the spiritual', as we will see later.

There are in fact many atheists who could accurately be described as practising existentialists or phenomenologists. However, simply because there is an absence of specific reference to the transpersonal in one of its many disguises in a particular author's work does not mean that awe and mystery are not also inhabitants in those spheres. (I've heard tell that the point of a mystery is that the secret it conceals is more important than the truth it reveals.) Some authors such as Heidegger (e.g. 1987), Levin (1985), Merleau-Ponty (1983) and Irigaray (1985) work explicitly with the notion of Physis or *élan vital*. Levin, for example, observes:

> In *Epidemics*, a work attributed to Hippokrates, it is said that 'nature (*Physis*) heals disease . . . Let us not forget that *Physis* is an ancient word for Being . . . What makes such a stride 'ontological' [to do with being], then, is the *openness* of its awareness to the deepest meaning of the ground encountered by motility and the intense *energy* (*physis*) this openness lets burst in . . . From out of its primordial relatedness-to-Being (*Physis*) it determines the principles of our moral life, regulating our comportment (*Gebärde*) and enabling us to sustain the posture, the bearing and behavior – finally, the implicit destiny – of a morally upright being.
>
> (Levin 1985: 258, 269–71)

Levin also comments on how Heidegger saw 'the possibility of experiencing that openness of Being as a field of dancing energy – as, in a word, *Physis*' (1985: 334).

Of course, one of the first and most profound of existentialists, Kierkegaard (1954), had a depth of genuine relationship with a Christian God of poignant and powerful conviction. Marcel (1950), too, is a Christian – a Catholic this time – who presents us with his highly personal reflections of his existence. He claimed that in his philosophical work he was open to Christian and non-Christian. However, a deep and mysterious sense of the sacredness of life permeates all his writing:

> Whatever the metaphors used, there is a persistent sense of Being as enfolding my own being and the other beings who are present to me and to whom I am present, like a mother liquid in which it is my true destiny to remain in solution and my perpetual tendency to crystallize out . . . But salvation has no meaning unless things have really gone wrong; faith in the integrity of the universe, on which hope is grounded, only means something in a world which is rent by real and serious breaks.
>
> (Marcel 1950: 17)

Then there is also for example Tillich, whose truly existentialist struggles with faith, life and despair represent not an easy and simple solution to the exigencies of existence and the anguish of being human, but a more complete engagement. He states, '**The courage to be is a function of vitality**' (1952: 79).

The relation of the *vital élan* [physis] to that which it produces is not conceivable, it is magical. Since the physico-chemical actions of which the organism is the seat cannot be abstracted from those of the milieu, how can the act which creates an organism individual be circumscribed in this continuous whole and where should the zone of influence of the *vital élan* be limited?

(Merleau-Ponty 1983: 158)

Transpersonal psychotherapy

Transpersonal psychotherapy is any approach to psychotherapy or counselling which engages explicitly with the transpersonal therapeutic relationship. It is one of the activities deriving from the discipline of applied Transpersonal Psychology. It can be practised by any psychotherapist (with the appropriate training) from any religious or spiritual tradition – or from none. The same would apply to transpersonal counselling.

Transpersonal psychotherapy needs to be differentiated from **spiritual direction**, which is concerned with helping a person directly with his or her formulated relationship with God: '. . . the most fundamental issue [which the client brings] is that relationship and its underlying questions: "Who is God for me, and who am I for him?"' (Barry and Connolly 1986: 5).

Pastoral psychotherapy is the work that people do, such as Mullahs, clergymen and nuns, who have formal religious responsibilities for the welfare of their people. It is undertaken as a practice explicitly associated with a particular religious tradition or religious organization – '. . . which are reflective and draw effectively on psychological and clinical insights, but which also respect the integrity of religious resources and seek to allow these to shape pastoral counselling work in appropriate ways' (Lynch 2000: 341). In practice there may be some overlap with what has been called psychospiritual psychotherapy.

Psychospiritual psychotherapy also usually tends to be a kind of approach based in certain religious or spiritual traditions such as Wicca, Buddhism, Christianity, Sufism, Shamanism, Paganism and so forth. (There isn't yet, as far as I know, explicit provision for multi-faith or inter-faith or 'trans-faith' pastoral counselling.)

Where priests or religious people are trained as psychotherapists, they may practise any 'brand-name' of psychotherapy (Jungian, Psychosynthesis, Core energetics, transactional analysis or whatever). However some of these professionals with formal religious roles may also call their practice 'transpersonal psychotherapy' to emphasize the **explicit** inclusion of the transpersonal dimensions of psychotherapy.

As always in these issues of boundary demarcations these categorizations are indicative, not definitive. There will be many exceptions. Furthermore, it is very likely that the actual psychotherapy activity in the consulting room (or church annex, or Yoga youth camp or client's home or monastery) might be exactly the same – even though they can be described in different **psycho-languages**.

For those who are interested, 'Beyond schoolism' (Clarkson 1998b) is a paper concerned with further discussion of this issue. It is indeed possible that transpersonal psychotherapy in fact represents the common overlapping area between all such kinds of psychotherapy – certainly many of the skills involved are the same (see for example Hart 1980: *The Art of Christian Listening*.)

Religion, spirit, soul and the transpersonal

> Science without religion is lame, religion without science is blind.
>
> Albert Einstein (1879–1955)

Religion

Another important distinction which needs to be thought about is that between religion, spirit, soul and the transpersonal. William James defined religion as 'the feelings, acts, and experiences of individual men [and women] in their solitude, so far as they apprehend themselves to stand in relation to whatever they may consider the divine' (1985: 50).

Freud has clear negative views about religion:

> The formation of a religion, too, seems to be based on the suppression, the renunciation, of certain instinctual impulses. These impulses, however, are not, as in the neuroses, exclusively components of the sexual instinct; they are self-seeking, socially harmful instincts, even so, they are usually not without a sexual component.
>
> (1907: 39)

Spirit

The word 'spirit' is often used as a synonym for soul or the transpersonal – as in 'spirit of place'. Ani defines 'spirit' as: 'The creative force which unites all phenomena. It is the source of all energy, motion, cause and effect. As it becomes more dense, it manifests as matter' (1994: xxviii).

In the New Age literature and many indigenous practices spirit is taken to mean what Heraclitus meant by *physis* – the healing, creative, growth-producing energy which pervades everything living and dead. Kazantzakis writes that the *élan vital*, the spirit, 'is the breathing of God on earth' (1960: 111).

Every language I have encountered (from Japanese to Ibo) has a word which is used to betoken this aspect of existence. European languages often use the word God, but usually its meaning is much more limited and suffused with transference distortions from organized religion. The originator of Creation-focused Spirituality, Matthew Fox, also equates spirit with life:

> Life and livelihood ought not to be separated but to flow from the same source, which is Spirit, for both life and livelihood are about Spirit. Spirit means life, and life and livelihood are about living in depth, living with meaning, purpose, joy and a sense of contributing to the greater community.
>
> (Fox 1994: 1–2)

Soul

Of the leaders in facilitating the self-creation of artificial life, Hillis says:

> To me there is a soul, but the soul is in emergence . . . The soul is the result of taking simply things that you understand the rules of, and applying this emergent behaviour that is both a consequence of the rules and also not obviously connected to it. That's to me where the soul is. That's a much more interesting, robust place for the soul to be than off in some little corner of science which we just haven't figured out yet.
>
> (quoted in Levy 1992: 341)

Regarding a definition of soul, Rumi answers the question like this:

> What is the soul? A joy
> when kindness comes, a weeping
> at injury, a growing consciousness.
>
> (Rumi 1991: 117)

I do not agree with Hillman's (1985) distinctions between soul and spirit. It seems to me that he is conflating normative or religious universes of discourse with transpersonal or mystical ones.

It may be more useful to consider **religion** as that aspect of human experience which can be subsumed under notions such as the organized church, membership of a sect, loyalty to a creed or a chieftain or a guru, a spiritual practice in some kind of tradition or another or even the avowed values in a person's life such as atheism, Marxism, nationalism, vegetarianism, capitalism, pantheism, and all other such varieties of **systems of belief**.

Religions or values as systems of belief

The systems of values or beliefs may be very vague or be elaborately worked out; rigorously enforced (e.g. Sharia) or only used for special occasions (Humanistic funerals); encoded in oral history or parchments, inscriptions on ancient monuments or preserved as in the millions of volumes in the Vatican Library.

Usually such systems (explicit or implicit) carry certain norms, laws, ideologies, rules or regulations for their adherents, which are followed or broken. For example, think of Kosher kitchens, or Christian baptism, or the genital mutilation of Sudanese young girls (or Freud's female analysands who had their clitorises surgically repositioned in order to achieve male-defined, normal, mature, 'vaginal' orgasms) (e.g. see Bonaparte et al. 1954; Phillips 1998; Gooch 1995).

Whatever one's views on various religions throughout the world and throughout the ages, human beings seem to have had need of them at all times and in all places. Without doubt they have been used to commit much evil; arguably they have also done some good along the way. As Rumi (1991) says:

> Remember this spiritual truth. It is unqualified,
> and unconditional. Though the *before* and the *after*
> are really one. Punishment and clemency, the same.
>
> Did you know that already?
> Don't say **yes**,
> or **no**.
>
> And don't blame a religion
> for your being in-between answers.
>
> (Rumi 1991: 77)

The quotation below from Symington (1990) is representative of the usual psychoanalytic position:

> Roman Catholics, particularly those with a special devotion to Mary, are antipa-
> thetic to psychoanalysis, which favours healthy fruitful intercourse both interper-
> sonally and intrapsychically. Such religious people steer clear of psychoanalysis
> and thereby deprive themselves of opportunities for better understanding of
> themselves. It is also true, however, that psychoanalysts steer clear of religious
> people. I have the distinct impression that many analysts are also frightened of
> religion. I think one reason is that they are afraid to face the religious aspects of
> psychoanalysis itself. Another is that religious devotion, especially in its more
> intense forms, comes from the psychotic area of the personality.
>
> (Symington 1990: 115)

However, our clients come to us, whatever their current views are, with their lives already having been coloured by such normative systems in their families, their schools, their places of worship, their culture's acceptance, rejection or modification of such systems. They are inescapably culturally situated in compliance, defiance, certainty and/or questioning.

The reasons, facts, rationality of the normative domain of ethics and values cannot be solved at **level** five. As Bauman, the postmodernist ethicist, writes:

> Reason cannot help the moral self without depriving the self of what makes the self moral: that unfounded, non-rational, un-arguable, no-excuses-given and non-calculable urge to stretch towards the other, to caress, to be for, to live for, happen what may. Reason is about making correct decisions, while moral responsibility precedes all thinking about decisions as it does not, and cannot care about any logic which would allow the approval of an action as correct.
>
> (Bauman 1993: 248)

In an attempt to be 'scientific' many approaches to psychotherapy have pathologized religious or even spiritual beliefs and practices or ridiculed them in theory and practice. Many black people have told me that they would not go back for a second psychotherapy session to, for example, a white psychodynamic therapist because they just could not find any acceptance of the reality of their religious beliefs – a living aspect of their everyday moment-by-moment existence. Many European psychotherapists and counsellors find the exuberance and passion of syncretistic rituals strange or indicative of serious psychological disturbance – from their own cultural perspective.

On the other hand there is a growing interest in all aspects of the transpersonal in our culture among ordinary people (e.g. astrology, *feng shui*, spiritual healing). More than anything else, the factional division within the 'schools' of psychoanalysis and psychotherapy affects the workings and expectations of therapy with people with religious histories, questions about the meaning of life/death or spiritual yearnings.

> Nasrudin was sent by the King to investigate the lore of various kinds of Eastern mystical teachers. They all recounted to him tales of the miracles and the sayings of the founders and great teachers, all long dead, of their schools.
>
> When he returned home, Nasrudin submitted his report, which contained the single word 'Carrots'.
>
> He was called upon to explain himself. Nasrudin told the King: 'The best part is buried; few know – except the farmer – by the green that there is orange underground; if you don't work for it, it will deteriorate; there are a great many donkeys associated with it.'
>
> (Shah 1985: 86)

On the other hand, if we accept that many – if not all – human beings have a capacity to experience the sublime, the awesome, the peak experience or oceanic dimension, and that this is a capacity that all human beings can enjoy and grow from, then we stand accused to the extent that psychotherapy falls short of enabling people to discover or celebrate in this way. However, human beings are beginning to realize that there is not only one truth about the world – or for that matter about our own experiences – and this paves the way for an **inclusive** perspective on what we may call the transpersonal dimension.

We live in a world in which the authority of previous guides has apparently crumbled. They have become fragments, bits of a particular archive (of Western Europe, of the white male voice), part of a local history that once involved the presumption (and power) to speak in the name of the 'world' (Boradori 1986: 82).

The seven-level model

As a consultant philosopher originally trained in Ryleian and phenomenological/existential traditions, I have been trying to find a way for people to understand the multiplicity of discourses in texts, practices and in our disciplines. Over the years I have noticed a certain pattern emerging and in 1975, after a terrible tragedy – the birth and death of my baby son – I first wrote it down as a complete intuition coming, as it were, from nowhere?

Several individuals and communities of knowledge and practice have effectively used this model to clarify their thinking, their writing, their research and their communications. In my view, it is an implicit ordering principle of all clear-thinking discourse whether or not the speaker or reader is conscious of it. It is, for me, an essential conceptual grid for working with the transpersonal dimensions of human existence. That's why I used it in the 'Transpersonal' chapter of *The Therapeutic Relationship* (Clarkson 1995a: 181–220). If you work with it, you will be surprised to discover it has many, many other uses as well (e.g. in working with moral and ethical dilemmas as in Clarkson 1996c, 2000a).

The Clarkson (1975) seven-**level** model is a tool which has been found helpful in simultaneously holding and handling a multiplicity of discourses and the complexity of our multi-layered human experience. Different, independently developed and quite contrary to Wilber's (1980) **levels**, this model is **not** hierarchical or developmental in the sense of moving from one **level** to another so that one is in any sense seen as being 'higher', 'better' or 'more developed' than another.

It follows the phenomenological rules of '*epoche*' (bracketing off of assumptions and preconceptions), description and 'equalization' (Spinelli 1989). The **levels** of descriptions in this model therefore all coexist as

descriptions of equal value which may even be mutually contradictory at the same time.

In this sense the model is a **phenomenographic** exercise as in the phenomenological nominative domain of discourse, not intended as a 'theory' (**level** 6) or as a 'fact' (**level** 5). As the poet Rilke asked, 'Are we, perhaps, **here** just for saying: House, Bridge, Fountain, Gate, Jug, Fruit tree, Window, – possibly: Pillar, Tower? . . . but for **saying**, remember, oh, for such saying as never the things themselves hoped so intensely to be' (1964: 64). For the phenomenologically descriptive **level** 3, previous knowledge, opinions or values are temporarily 'bracketed off'. The **levels** or **domains** (as Matura in a personal communication prefers that I call them) could equally well be numbered in the opposite way (from the top down.) According to Peat:

> Bohr's complementarity principle states that a single consistent description will never exhaust the meaning of what is happening at the quantum **level**. Rather, what is required are a number of complementary, mutually contradictory descriptions. An electron is described as both delocalized and wavelike, but also localized and particle-like.
>
> (Peat 1996: 264)

This seven-fold archetype of human experience may well be what Bohm (1980) called 'an implicate ordering principle'. I like using the million-year old (or more) ammonite as a natural image of its wholeness. An ammonite is defined as 'a fossil cephalopod . . . with a coiled chambered shell like Ammon's horn'. Ammon was 'the ancient Egyptian ram-headed god, Amun, identified by the Greeks with Zeus' (MacDonald 1972: 43). 'Every organism', said Uexküll, 'is a melody which sings itself' (1926: 159).

> With his knees doubled up under his chin, with his hands spread toward the light, with the soles of his feet turned toward his back, God huddles in a know in every cell of flesh.
> When I break a fruit open, this is how every seed is revealed to me.
>
> (Kazantzakis 1960: 91)

There are different logical criteria – different **kinds** of 'truth values' for each domain (see Copi 1961). **This means that different kinds of knowledge are evaluated by different means**.

It is best **not** to imagine the seven-**level** model as a kind of ladder, but rather as a sheet of paper folded into a circular tube shape where **level** 1 and **level** 7 touch each other. Using it this way could change your perspective on the world.

Phenomenography is the empirical study of the limited number of qualitatively different ways in which we experience, conceptualize, understand, perceive, apprehend etc. various phenomena in and aspects of the world around us. These differing experiences, understandings etc. are characterized in terms of categories of description, logically related to each other, and forming hierarchies according to given criteria.

(Marton 1992)

Generally, but also particularly in terms of the theme of the transpersonal at issue here, the particular usefulness and relevance of this model was pointed out to me by friends, colleagues and students in discriminating and differentiating between different **levels** of experience, conceptualization, literary and clinical phenomena. Thus it may also prove useful to sort **levels** of experience, discourse or intervention in spiritual or emotional psychological crises and to engage in psychotherapy and supervision generally.

These experiences of the transpersonal may range from the boredom of a life well lived but yearning for meaning; to acute 'breakdowns' filled with visual and aural hallucinations; to the visitations experienced by many saints, for example the love affair of the great poet and Sufi teacher Rumi with Shams, the old beggar dervish – which led Rumi's students to be convinced that he was mad and reportedly drove them to murder him. Yet from this union poured forth some 100,000 sublime poetic works on the nature and love of God (Schimmel 1993).

We began
as a mineral. We emerged into plant life
and into the animal state, and then into being human,
and always we have forgotten our former states,
except in early spring when we slightly recall
being green again.

That's how a young person turns
toward a teacher. That's how a baby leans towards the breast,
without knowing the secret of its desire,
yet turning instinctively.

Humankind is being led along an evolving course
through this migration of intelligences,
and though we seem to be sleeping,
there is an inner wakefulness that directs the dream,
and that will eventually startle us back
to the truth of who we are.

(Rumi 1991: 34)

Two domains (or levels) differentiated

'Psychoanalytic theory often appears to have a disadvantage through being formulated in such a descriptive way that the observational and the theoretical **levels** seem confused, at the same **level** of abstraction' (Grinberg et al. 1975: 58). In my view the confusion of logical **levels** of discourse is also ubiquitous in counselling and psychotherapy generally right across all the approaches – thus conveying our confusion to our clients too. Yet there are also examples of clarity in almost every major psycho-language – and we will analyse one of these shortly.

Let's start by distinguishing just **two different levels** in discussing (or experiencing) the transpersonal. At one **level** we find religion or systems of faith or values which tend to be shared by a reference group, has 'holy' texts and ethical prescriptions for how to live. Differences of opinion and values at this **level** tend to be emphasized – and not infrequently lead to vicious wars between people of differing faiths. This could be said to be the **divergent** quality of the transpersonal at a collective **level**.

At another **level**, there is a domain of experience which is transcendent in the sense of being both highly individual **and** universal in some way. This domain is usually only experienced and cannot easily be put into words. At this **level**, from my studies, it appears that the mystical traditions of all the world religions (and then some) seem to share many more similarities than differences. Thus, Jewish, Islamic Sufi, Hindu, Christian and African syncretic mystics seem to have – and point to – very similar experiences. These experiences could be said to have a **convergent** quality. Sectarian loyalties seem to be transcended and transformed. (For a good example, see Rumi's poem 'True Religion' on page 211.)

So, in addition to the religious (or normative) domain of the usual discourses from systems of faith, we can differentiate another 'domain of discourse' or **level** of experience about the transpersonal. So, at one **level** are our experiences and discourses concerning **values, beliefs, cultural norms**; and at another **level** is that which **transcends description**. In the seven-**level** model these are respectively the normative (or **level** 4 domain) and the transpersonal (or seventh **level**). (I see 'soul' as the personal aspect, and 'spirit' as the impersonal aspect of the transpersonal.)

The transpersonal experience or universe of discourse is not **necessarily** connected to or in harmony with the normative **level** (which coexists with it). Essentially the transpersonal by my definition cannot be expressed in language. Simply put: **it goes beyond words**. If it is expressed in words, the discourse has already moved to another **level** like narrative (6) or description (3) – then it is thus, by definition, no longer the transpersonal of the seventh domain or the seventh realm. '**The Tao which can be told is not the eternal Tao**' (Lao Tsu 1973: 1).

The Nobel-prize-winning Russian author Solzhenitsyn makes the point in the following way:

> Not everything has a name. Some things lead us into the realm beyond words . . .
> It is like that small mirror in the fairy tales – you glance in it and what you see is
> not yourself, for an instant you glimpse the inaccessible, where no horse or magic
> carpet can take you. And the Soul cries out for it.
>
> (Solzhenitsyn 1973: 11)

But human beingness (ontology) and human knowing (epistemology) is even more complex than just such a duality. And it is for this reason that I developed the seven-**level** model. ('Ontology is concerned with what there is [being] whereas epistemology is the study of how we know, if we know, and what we know' – Flew 1971: 50.)

Clarifying of definitions and separating out logically different universes of discourse according to the ways we can experience, know and act on them is a sign of 'good thinking' (Clarkson 2000a; Heraclitus, in Kahn 1981). Learning to **recognize** this implicit pattern can thus facilitate self-understanding, interpersonal communication and philosophical clarity. Hopefully it can thus contribute something beneficial to the human condition.

Everyday conversations (and psychotherapeutic texts) are replete with people saying 'at one **level** this' and 'at another **level** that' and 'at yet another **level** that'. Also people who have seriously grappled with the sometimes mutually contradictory but yet **coexisting** realms of human experience or human search for 'what can be known and how we can know it' seem to use it spontaneously. For those who have not experienced this kind of problem yet, and believe there is only 'one truth', the model will be useless.

What I think I have done is to recognize a naturally occurring phenomenon, not to construct another cognitively preconceived 'model' which **has** to be learned and practised in order to be effectively applied. We will also return to it in the final chapter. According to Eigen (in Molino 1997):

> Rather than have war between all these different dimensions of experience, it's
> much more fruitful to keep open the possibility that each has a voice, that each
> has a say in the play of voices, and to see what happens . . . But whatever faith is,
> Bion associates it with opening, with the propensity to become open. To go in
> the other direction, towards *k* [knowledge], would be a premature exclusion of
> one voice in favour of another, as opposed to a plurality and balance of voices.
>
> (in Molino 1997: 108)

To illustrate the seven **level** model as a **multivocal** expression of human transpersonal experiences, here follows a transcript of an interview with the eminent psychoanalyst writer Michael Eigen demonstrating his awareness of the 'primacy of multiplicity'. As far as I know he has never heard of the Clarkson seven-**level** model, yet in his 1997 interview with Molino he spontaneously distinguishes between coexisting domains of experience in relation to the domain of what we have called 'the transpersonal'.

I reproduce below an extract of Molino's interview with Eigen as well as the same extract with the addition of some comments in square brackets in order:

to disprove the common prejudice that no psychoanalyst 'touches on the transpersonal';

to show how Eigen naturally and spontaneously distinguishes the seven domains of transpersonal experience in his own words;

demonstrate in a preliminary way how the different domains can be identified in the work of authors not familiar with the model.

Extract without commentary, to be read first:

What is faith for Michael Eigen?

Different things at different times. I guess there's spiritual faith and there's natural faith. I place a great deal of weight on natural faith. I've nothing against spiritual or mystical faith, . . . but there's an awful lot of faith that springs simply from sensory experience, from how good it feels to be able to walk down a street and move one's limbs and not be in prison . . . It brings up a feeling inside that, while it might be stretching things to call it 'faith', I really do have to call it that . . . It makes one feel good to be alive, it makes one feel that life is good . . . The body seems to have this faith . . . Very often I've been astonished by how a dying animal seems to not know it's dying, by how it acts in the face of death, and seems to live, to be moving or trying to move or live to the last ounce . . . It just keeps going to the end . . . Or even when it stops moving and gets into a dying position, it doesn't seem to be angry or yelling about its imminent end. Somehow there seems to be an acquiescence, a simple ebbing of energy in the direction of death. It's a kind of body faith, a faith the body has.

I suppose one could talk about an affective faith or an emotional faith: the 'Ouch!' and 'Yum!' of things . . .'Ouch! That hurt!' . . . or Yum! That was worth it!' So it's more than pleasure and pain, I think. When one talks about a pleasure or pain principle, one's de-animated it because it's not simply bad or good, it's heavenly, it's heavenly . . . It's wonderful! . . . it feels yummy all through . . . You know, one would have to be totally mad not to have a secular or ironical self and see the limits of things, but I rather like siding with this feeling of good to the last drop in psychoanalysis . . . like a bug that never stops moving . . . There's just a sense of never giving up . . . never giving up on a case . . . not giving up on anyone . . . Who knows better?

All this begs another question. What does Michael Eigen mean by God?
God only knows! I think I have to be honest to say I mean a biblical God, the God of Abraham, Isaac and Jacob . . . But having said that I can step back and say: 'Hey well what I mean by God could be anything, because I don't know . . . In a sense God is a total unknown . . . the very notion ties the so-called biblical, personal God closer to me than I am to myself . . . And then there are times one can just lift up one's hands and say, 'Wow, all this out of nothingness' . . . which feels wonderful . . . to blank oneself out and be totally open to whatever currents pulse this way or that...whether you're into body, or emotions . . . Taoist or Buddhist whatever, it feels good. You know, in the Kabbala, God has . . . is . . . goes beyond names . . . the Ein Sof, the infinite of infinites, the great unknown, the 'I-itself' . . . By the time God gets named! . . .

I had a patient once who, in the midst of a fierce negative transference, blurted out loud: 'I am that I am', without any apparent sense of the phrase's biblical echo. The woman was stating her difference and uniqueness in a rather common-sensical sort of way, but the sheer power of her words was unmistakable.
That's wonderful. I think Ben, in my book *Coming through the Whirlwind*, does something like that at one point. It's what we're doing all the time: we're 'am-ing' . . . and we're 'am-ing' each other too . . . we're enabling each other *to am.*

According to what Eigen says in this interview which bears very close scrutiny, he distinguishes between

– 'a **natural faith of the body**' which is like that of animals (physiological **level** 1) and includes 'a simple ebbing of energy in the direction of death' (ebbing has the connotation of life's rhythms)
– an **affective or emotional faith** expressed (**level** 2) – 'the Ouch and Yum of things'
– a **biblical God with specific names** – 'the God of Abraham, Isaac and Jacob' (nominative **level** 3)
– a **realm of values with moral implications** – 'never giving up on a case', 'not giving up . . . not giving up on anyone' (normative **level** 4)
– an **acknowledgement of (level 5) the rational / positivistic scientific realm** (where he says what many scientists have said before): 'One would have to be totally mad not have a secular or ironical self and see the limits of things . . .'
– the sixth **realm of experience where different narratives (stories, theories or perspectives**) can be used to refer to the transpersonal – Cabbalism, Taoist, Buddhist
– the **experiential realm** where words simply fail: 'where one can just lift up one's hands and say: "Wow, all this out of nothingness" . . . blank oneself out and be totally open to whatever currents pulse this way or that . . .' – the 7th **level** or transpersonal region beyond names.

This example of the natural **emergence** of seven ways of engaging with the transpersonal experience in the spontaneous discourse of someone I have never met leads me to conclude (not for the first time) that the seven different ways of **being** (ontology) and **knowing** (epistemology) constitute an embedded phenomenological shape (or fractal) of human experience and human discourse. (It may be at least as ancient as the ammonite.)

So, now for a re-reading of the extract with added identification of the seven **levels** in square brackets:

What is faith for Michael Eigen?
Different things at different times. I guess there's spiritual faith and there's natural faith. I place a great deal of weight on natural faith. I've nothing against spiritual or mystical faith, . . . but there's an awful lot of faith that springs simply from sensory experience, from how good it feels to be able to walk down a street and move one's limbs and not be in prison . . . It brings up a feeling inside that, while it might be stretching things to call it 'faith', I really do have to call it that . . . It makes one feel good to be alive, it makes one feel that life is good . . . The body seems to have this faith . . . Very often I've been astonished by how a dying animal seems to not know it's dying, by how it acts in the face of death, and seems to live, to be moving or trying to move or live to the last ounce . . . It just keeps going to the end . . . Or even when it stops moving and gets into a dying position, it doesn't seem to be angry or yelling about its imminent end. Somehow there seems to be an acquiescence, a simple ebbing of energy in the direction of death. It's a kind of body faith, a faith the body has [*physiological level 1*].

I suppose one could talk about an affective faith or an emotional faith: the 'Ouch!' and 'Yum!' of things . . .'Ouch! That hurt!' . . . or Yum! That was worth it!' [*emotional level 2*] So it's more than pleasure and pain, I think. When one talks about a pleasure or pain principle [*level 6 theory*], one's de-animated it because it's not simply bad or good, it's heavenly, it's heavenly . . . It's wonderful! . . . it feels yummy all through [*emotional level 2*] . . . You know, one would have to be totally mad not to have a secular or ironical self and see the limits of things [*rational level 5*], but I rather like siding with this feeling of good to the last drop in psychoanalysis . . . like a bug that never stops moving . . . There's just a sense of never giving up . . . never giving up on a case . . . not giving up on anyone . . . Who knows better? [*normative level 4*]

All this begs another question. What does Michael Eigen mean by God?
God only knows! I think I have to be honest to say I mean a biblical God, the God of Abraham, Isaac and Jacob [*nominative level 3*]. . . But having said that I can step back [*move perspective*] and say: 'Hey well what I mean by God could be anything, because I don't know . . . In a sense God is a total unknown . . . the very notion ties the so-called biblical, personal God closer to me than I am to myself . . . And then there are times one can just lift up one's hands and say, 'Wow, all this out of nothingness' . . . which feels wonderful . . . to blank oneself out and be totally open to whatever currents pulse this way or that...whether you're into

body, or emotions . . . Taoist or Buddhist whatever, it feels good. You know, in the Kabbala, God has . . . is . . . goes beyond names . . . the Ein Sof, the infinite of infinites, the great unknown, the 'I-itself' . . . By the time God gets named! . . . [*transpersonal level 7*]

I had a patient once who, in the midst of a fierce negative transference, blurted out loud: ' I am that I am,' without any apparent sense of the phrase's biblical echo. The woman was stating her difference and uniqueness in a rather commonsensical sort of way, but the sheer power of her words was unmistakable.
That's wonderful. I think Ben, in my book *Coming through the Whirlwind*, does something like that at one point. It's what we're doing all the time: we're 'am-ing' . . . and we're 'am-ing' each other too . . . we're enabling each other *to am*.

Commentary

I have seldom found as beautiful an articulation by a psychotherapist of the relational physis as BEING. Bion thought that Transformation in O is something like

being what one is . . . The 'O' of transformation . . . has an unknowable character. The sign 'O' is applied by extrapolation to all that, in other frames of reference, might be called 'ultimate unknowable reality', 'absolute truth', reality, the thing-in-itself, the 'infinite', the 'unknown' . . . Bion says that reality cannot be known by definition, but it can 'be'. He calls this *becoming* O.

(Grinberg et al. 1975: 52)

For Heidegger too: 'The "energising sense" is an experience of *Physis*, as it surges up through our mortal frame . . . This bodily felt sense of wholeness, hermeneutically disclosive of Being, is *necessary* for the unfolding of the Self as an *ontological* being' (in Levenson 1991: 291). Transformation in O is something like 'being what one is'.

. . . Every word I say
is trying to coax a response
from that.
'Lord', I call out,
and inside my 'Lord' comes,
'Here I am,'
a 'Here I am'
that can't be heard,
but it can be tasted and felt
in every cell of the body.

(Rumi 1991: 49)

Transpersonal psychotherapy in practice: some initial guidelines

– Consider that all humans have to make meaning of their lives in some way – or else despair will ensue. When people lose this meaning, their will to live disappears (see Frankl 1973).
– Inform yourself about different religious and transpersonal traditions and be open to experiences which are different from those in your own culture.
– Learn to differentiate between transpersonal or spiritual experiences and psychotic phenomena.
– Learn to differentiate between collective forms of organized religion and the mystical traditions which are very similar in most religious and spiritual traditions.
– Learn to differentiate between the psychologization of spiritual hunger and the spiritualization of psychological problems.
– Investigate and explore your own proactive countertransference issues (negative past experience, ignorance and prejudices) regarding different religious or spiritual traditions.
– Learn to differentiate between spiritual practices which enhance life and cults which can glorify and seek death such as the mass suicide in Jonestown.
– Learn to differentiate between (a) appropriate guilt for wrongs committed ('amends' in AA language); (b) neurotic guilt; and (c) existential guilt.
– Meet your client where they are in these terms – not where you think they should be.
– Become familiar with rituals. For example in the course of a long-term psychotherapy a woman begins to experience deep grief and sadness for the seven foetuses which she aborted without much thought or care some years later. What are your options for helping her?
– Build good working relationships with religious or spiritual leaders who are also psychologically aware and be willing to co-work or to refer to them as appropriate.
– Prepare yourself for answers about your religious beliefs or spiritual practice. How and when will such information be appropriately or inappropriately disclosed?
– Never mix spiritual direction with counselling or psychotherapy unless you are specially trained to do so.
– Make a point of asking about religious beliefs or spiritual background and current practices at first interview.

- Take your cues from your client. Wait until there are clear indications about their needs for the transpersonal relationship to be explicit. It doesn't have to be.
- If you work within a particular tradition such as in a Catholic psychotherapy service or a Jewish old age home for example, be aware of the negative influences (both exaggerated positive or negative transferences) which people may project on to you because of what you may represent to them. Be willing to explore these openly and non-defensively with your clients.
- Just because people are atheists, agnostics, sceptic scientists or humanists, does not mean that they do not have 'awe-some' experiences of life and death, beauty or nature. Allow them to inform you about how such awareness supports and develops them in their lives. There may come a time when you can use their metaphors (of planets, the life of cells or the beauty of garden roses, the roll of history) to assist them in a language which is valuable and 'use-full' to them.
- Cherish the body. It is the first and most vital connection to the Divine.
- Or cherish the body. It is the first and most vital connection to the rest of the cosmos.
- Finally, as a Zen master might say: 'Don't confuse the finger pointing at the moon with the moon itself.'

Chapter 2
Overview of the transpersonal relationship dimension in all psychotherapies

Story-Water
A story is like the water
you heat for your bath.

It takes messages between the fire
and your skin. It lets them meet,
and it cleans you!

Very few can sit down
in the middle of the fire itself
like a salamander or Abraham.
We need intermediaries.

A feeling of fullness comes,
but usually it takes some bread
to bring it.

Beauty surrounds us,
but usually we need to be walking
in a garden to know it.

The body itself is a screen
to shield and partially reveal
the light that's blazing
inside your presence.

Water, stories, the body,
all the things we do, are mediums
that hide and show what's hidden.

Study them,
and enjoy this being washed
with a secret we sometimes know,
and then not.

(Rumi 1991: 29)

41

The excellent and ground-breaking book Persuasion and Healing by Frank and Frank (1993) surveyed Eurocentric psychotherapy outcome studies along with other cultural healing practices in the rest of the world. In a masterly analysis they identify four essential factors for psychological healing to occur:

- the therapeutic relationship
- a dedicated space
- a prescription for action
- a culturally congruent narrative

They also show that there is no significant evidence that theoretical approach is relevant to the successful outcome of Eurocentric psychotherapies – no matter how measured. There is substantial other evidence that it is in fact the **psychotherapeutic relationship** rather than theory, diagnosis or technique which potentiates the beneficial effects of psychotherapy. (See Clarkson 1998b for a review.) I will mention here only three other studies:

a) In 1950, Fiedler had already researched the differences between exponents of three different schools – Freudian, Adlerian and Nondirective. He found that the differences in actual practice between experienced practitioners in different schools were considerably smaller than between beginners and their more senior colleagues in the same school. That is, it appears that their practice was more a function of their experience of the therapeutic relationship than of their theoretical orientation *per se* (Fiedler 1950).

b) More recently, in his paper 'The effectiveness of psychotherapy' – which discussed the Consumer Report study sampling some 3,000 consumers of therapy in the USA – Seligman wrote in summary that:

> Long-term treatment did considerably better than short-term treatment . . . No specific modality of psychotherapy did better than any other for any disorder . . . Patients whose length of therapy or choice of therapist was limited by insurance or managed care did worse.
>
> (Seligman 1995: 965)

c) In discussing what a research expert such as Barkham (1995) has described as 'the pinnacle of research efforts in researching psychotherapy', Elkin concluded that there appears to be no significant difference which can be particularly ascribed to specific differences in approach, and she is now focusing 'on the actual patient–therapist interactions in the videotaped treatment sessions' (1995: 183).

In 1996 Shapiro concluded:

> Many, if not most, of the cherished beliefs of theorists and practitioners of partic-
> ular methods of psychotherapy remain largely unsupported by the kinds of
> evidence preferred by those who control the budgets of health care systems
> across the globe . . . However, 'head-to-head' comparisons among treatments
> differing in the strengths of their respective evidential support show surprisingly
> modest differences. For most of the disorders reviewed here, there is little
> evidence to take us beyond the paradoxical 'Dodo bird verdict' of equivalent
> outcomes from very different treatment methods.
>
> (Shapiro 1996: ix)

Heaton (1999) is unambiguous:

> These systems hide an implicit moral stance under the guise of objective science.
> Self-knowledge is to be discovered in the action of relationship, not by cutting
> oneself off from the flow of life and then seeking an answer to one's problems
> which is conditioned by a theoretical system. That is one type of self-deception.
>
> (Heaton 1999: 60)

In addition to the multitude of studies which have testified to the
overriding importance of the therapeutic relationship, it has further been
found that there are **different kinds** of relationship required for different
kinds of patients, and this factor is more important than diagnosis or
technique in predicting effectiveness of psychotherapy or counselling. My
research (which has been nominated for another PhD) identified **five
modes of therapeutic relationship** which are potentially present in any
so-called 'pure' approach as well as in so-called 'integrative' approaches
(such as the Systemic Relational Integrative Psychotherapy approach
which I have developed and which is summarized in Appendix 4).

I have demonstrated this embedded relational matrix also in Freudian
psychoanalysis, transactional analysis, Gestalt, Jungian, RET and integrative
arts therapy. Dale (in Clarkson in press a) has shown how it is demonstrated in person-centred psychotherapy from the client's and supervisor's
perspectives. Nuttall (2000) has demonstrated how it applies to Kleinian
psychoanalysis. Furthermore, several psychotherapy and counselling
courses – from BACP accredited courses to UKCP and MSc Degree courses –
have been based on the five relational modes themselves as a model for
Integrative Psychotherapy or counselling – including psycho-spiritual
psychotherapy from a Christian perspective. (See the PHYSIS website:
www.physis.co.uk.) It has also informed several practice-based PhD theses.

These findings from my personal, theoretical and practice-based
research are consistent with the experience and research of other workers
reporting that (as long as the explanation or 'narrative' is culturally

congruent) experiences of mental and emotional healing have **always** existed in human societies. Furthermore such healing practices are **right now** helping many people in distress **across the world** through what is sometimes referred to as 'indigenous medicine'. (See Moodley 1998 for an excellent review.)

Perhaps the Eurocentrism of so many individualist psychotherapy practitioners and theories (their racism or cultural **incongruence**) could explain why, for example, black people are so rarely considered 'suitable' for the talking cure in the UK (see Cleminson, in press, for a review). From numerous anecdotal and personal experiences in psychotherapy and training, it is clear to me that the absence of explicit acknowledgement of the transpersonal dimension of human experience in most Eurocentric approaches alienates many peoples from, for example, an African/ Caribbean background, and simply misses the moment-by-moment reality of a lived and living faith.

Furthermore, Kleinman (1988) discusses how every West European psychotherapeutic theory (or narrative) minimizes the radical differences between egocentric Western culture and socio-centric non-western cultures and discloses that **culture exerts a powerful effect on care**. As Helman observes of Kleinman, 'Whether this narrative is short (as in spirit exorcisms) or lengthy (as in psychoanalysis) it summarizes *post hoc* what had happened to them, and why, and how the healer was able to restore them to happiness or health' (1994: 280; my emphasis).

There is also evidence of experiences by which people feel harmed – abuses of relationship. With the exception of sexual abuse, one of the most salient facts here is that the harmfulness seems to have to do with the extent to which a psychotherapist entrenches into a theoretical position (or 'sticks to his story') when challenged or questioned by their client (see Winter 1997 for examples and review).

And just in case one thinks there are not competing stories within stories (theories against theories), let's hear from 'the psychodynamic' or psychoanalytic approach:

> Psychoanalytic theory is replete with dichotomies, intrapsychic/interpersonal, drive/relational, fixation/regression, deficit/conflict, even the hoariest of all, nature/nurture. One is always tempted to say, 'Why not see and use both perspectives?' But these are not different perspectives on the same reality: they are different realities, entirely different pervasive sets about what reality is. They are opposing philosophies of life. Therapists who talk about character and character disorders see patients, psychotherapeutic devices, and outcomes differently from therapists who talk about personality. Just because we are using the same words, we are not using them in the same way. We talk to each other, we must begin with the assumption of difference. I believe that our particular Tower of Babel is

built on the paradoxical illusion that we are all speaking the same tongue . . . Any
reader, not totally committed to one ideology or another, cannot fail to be
impressed – and one might hope, dismayed – by the total conviction with which
prominent analysts proclaim diametrically opposed clinical strategies for what
they diagnose as the very same characterological category.

(Levenson 1991: 244)

Leading teachers of cognitive-behavioural approaches such as Padesky
(1998 workshop in London) stress, before anything else, that the
'approach' can only be effective within a sound therapeutic relationship.
Youngson and Alderman (1994) who are cognitive-behavioural psychologists, report substantial behavioural change **without** the theoretically
required cognitive changes. It only takes one apple **not** to fall, to disprove
Newton's (or Beck's) law of gravity.

So how can we gain clear understanding of ourselves and this our
complex multilingual world? Definitely not by just adhering dogmatically
to one language and only speaking to others who share that language:

The way to attain an integrated concept and practice of knowledge, and conse-
quently to address many crucial issues of our age through a transdisciplinary
approach, does not lie in applying ready-made, 'mechanical' procedures based
on automatic, stereotyped formulas and standardized recipes.

(UNESCO 1998: 7)

As the Oxford philosopher of psychology Farrell pointed out (1979),
participants, 'trainees' or clients are usually considered to be 'cured' or
'trained' or 'analysed' or 'qualified' by one single criterion – they have
adopted the WOT ('way of talking') of the leaders, governing bodies,
examination boards and others of perceived status or power. Rarely if ever
are the **clients** actually asked their opinion about what 'worked'. In David
Winter's and my current research, theoretical orientation also does not
appear relevant from the clients' perspective – but the relationship does.
Even the psychoanalyst Bion (1970) writes:

Walpole's concept of serendipity could be applied to interpretations. This type of
discovery arises when one stumbles on things which throw light on other things.
This allows an understanding of and knowledge about them which was hitherto
absent. The patient's associations and the analyst's interpretations are ineffable.
The analytic session is a type of experience than can only be shared by the
analysand and his analyst, and cannot be transmitted, in its essence to a third
person. This is why communication of a recorded session, be it for supervision,
or in a scientific paper, will inevitably be imperfect. The relation between the
analytic couple is of such a nature, that no mental event in one can be said to be
understood without reference to the state of mind of the other.

(Bion 1970: 75)

Never, as far as I know, does the client's opinion form a significant part of the professional assessment of competency. It is other colleagues who examine the candidate for how well they can describe *post hoc* what they did (or do) in a particular theoretical language. If they can't, they 'fail' – no matter how many clients have been healed in the therapeutic relationship with them. (See for example Clarkson 1996g on accreditation procedures in psychotherapy.)

Of course we remember the old observation that Jungian clients have Jungian dreams, and transactional analysis clients have transactional analysis dreams. They're probably learning the psychotherapist's language (or rhetoric). An empirical study by Silverman, from London University, also found repeatedly that 'rather than being a deviant case, such adoption by clients of the professionals' rhetoric [way of speaking] is common . . . each centre [of psychotherapy] offers an incitement to speak structured according to its own practical theories' (1997: 209).

So perhaps our Eurocentric psychotherapy theories are what Frank and Frank (1993) would call our culturally congruent narratives – our WOTs according to Farrell (1979). In this way each different brand-name **psycho-language** can be spoken well or made into gibberish. However, each unique language ('game') also has its rules of grammar, as well as the potential for poetry. There are in existence 'pure' languages which are no longer spoken, but some are still studied – e.g. classical Greek and Latin. There are people who can speak two or more languages well and others who refuse (or can't) learn any other language than their 'mother tongue'. There are also 'integrative' languages such as Esperanto, Yiddish and Fanagalo. Anyway, most languages in use, like most cultures, are also in a process of constant change.

In their massive and scholarly overview of 40 years of outcome research, Hubble et. al write that 'rather than squeezing the client's complaint into the language and theoretic bias of the therapist's, the data [**level** five facts] suggest the exact opposite' (1999b: 430):

> Each client presents the therapist with a new theory to learn, a new language to practice, and new interventions to suggest . . . the process begins by listening closely to the client's language . . . Speaking the client's language prevents the client from being trapped in and influenced by a particular theoretical view and increases the chances that any change will generalize outside therapy. In addition, speaking and working within the client's language provides the container for learning the client's theory.
>
> (Hubble et al. 1999b: 431)

In any case, the narratives of theory are located in a different **universe of discourse** from that of facts or even research. The Oxford philosopher Gilbert Ryle (1966) again had to clarify for modern (and postmodern) philosophers a kind of thinking error he called 'category confusion'. This is when one class of domain or kind of discourse is assigned a truth value which is logically inappropriate to that domain. (See also Chapter 10.)

Our theoretical psychotherapy languages can be beautiful and useful, but they are actually the preferred words we use to describe experiences, not the experiences themselves. Theory cannot properly or logically substitute for these other universes of discourse nor be conflated with them. And as Edwards et al. (1995), among many others, have pointed out again, method is always and already theory in disguise.

For some years now I have termed the Babel phenomenon in psychotherapy '**schoolism**'. At a 1990 European Conference in Rome, where I shared a platform with the North American Integrative Psychotherapist Norcross, I defined 'schoolism' as **passionately held convictions of being right which fly in the face of the facts**.

The fact that psychotherapy in the UK is formally organized by the UKCP into 'schools' and 'flag statements' is a sad example of this. It implies that one can rarely change one's 'approach' – even in the face of the current evidence that this is not significant for effectiveness as far as the **client** is concerned – without being perceived as disloyal to the 'flag'. Hubble and O'Hanlon even suggest that loyalty to a formal theory and its later impact on the way events are understood and handled in therapy can be understood as 'theory transference' (1992: 430).

An absurd dialogue which really took place

Psychologist: Your patient approached me for psychotherapy, but I am unwilling to see him without your permission.
Psychiatrist: So, which school do you follow?
Psychologist: I have extensive training in all the major approaches and I am a professor of psychotherapy and counselling psychology. I am also a chartered clinical psychologist. Shall I fax you my CV?
Psychiatrist: No, I just want to know which model you use.
Psychologist: My work is based on the therapeutic relationship. The bulk of the research shows that approaches or models are not related to the effectiveness of . . .
Psychiatrist: I don't want a lecture, I just want to know which approach you use.
Psychologist: I haven't even met this person, how can I know which of many models he needs?
Psychiatrist: But you must have a model!
Psychologist: Would you, as a psychiatrist, decide the medication a particular patient needs without even seeing the person first?

Schoolism is sometimes presented (or required) in the form of 'this is my philosophy of counselling (or whatever)'. Now of course we could say with

Humpty Dumpty in Alice's Wonderland something like: 'Words mean what I choose them to mean and nothing else . . . The only question is who is to be master and that is all' (Carroll 1986: 109). However, philosophy is in fact an ancient and rigorous academic discipline. It is not a statement of learned or preferred values. According to Wittgenstein, 'Philosophy is the discipline of thinking about thinking. The object of philosophy is the logical clarification of thoughts. Philosophy is not a theory, but an activity' (1922: 77).

In his *Dictionary of Philosophy*, Runes does admit a popular use of the term which is even more telling: 'private wisdom or consolation' (1966: 235). In this sense schoolism is a dogmatically shared private wisdom or consolation which tends to outlaw questioning and expels dissidents. (A 'shared private' wisdom is an oxymoron.)

Grosskurth, for example, reported how in 1950 Bowlby compared the Kleinian group of analysts to a religious sect (Rycroft called it 'the Ebenezer Church') 'in which, once one had espoused the doctrine, one was welcomed to the fold. If one deviated, if one did not subscribe totally to the doctrine, one faced the terrible threat of excommunication' (1986: 428). Unfortunately recent events in the UK have proved that this is now also true even for GPTI – a UKCP member organization. (For more information see Clarkson 1998b; and the ethics section of the PHYSIS website: www.physis.co.uk.)

> Submitting to the already constructed theory of another by trying to make it one's own is a way of drowning one's ability to fantasize in rationality, or in a rationalization that corresponds to the fantasies or desires of another or to the fantasies and desire other than one's own. One is therefore ignoring one's own fantasies, or repressing them, but more fundamentally, one is ignoring the fact that the other's theory is based on fantasizing; or what I would call in the broad sense delirium. One then slips back into the foreclosure of the subject, essential to [old exclusively positivistic paradigm] scientific productions . . . In order to question analysis [or psychotherapy] one must first stop being fascinated by theory and analyse the fantasies or desires that give rise to it; one must analyse theory as the text of dream or myth.
>
> (Roustang 1982: 57)

It has of course been pointed out many times that it is usually in the interstices, conflicts and liminal spaces where the creative discoveries of any art or science are made. (See e.g. Koestler 1989; Gleick 1989.) According to Beitman:

> The major problem with the notion of 'school' is its relative inflexibility in response to new ideas in psychotherapy. Schools have responded to varying degrees of innovation, but the value of schools has been to preserve good ideas. At this point in psychotherapy's history, these good ideas within schools have been preserved well enough.
>
> (Beitman 1994: 210)

So we babble at each other in our different psycho-languages (from our different 'schools'), often not realizing that we are talking about the same experience or about different experiences in the same language. Eight hundred years ago Rumi wrote:

> There are Indians and Turks who speak the same language.
> There are Turks who don't understand each other.
>
> (Rumi 1991: 18)

In 1999 Norcross wrote:

> Let's confront the unpleasant reality and say it out loud . . . In the dogma-eat-dogma environment of *schoolism*, clinicians traditionally operated from within their own particular theoretical frameworks, often to the point of being oblivious to alternative conceptualizations and potentially superior interventions.
>
> (Norcross 1999: ix)

So here we have a situation in psychotherapy and where we pride ourselves on **listening to the client** – as long as the client learns to speak **our** language. If they don't – of course – it's too often seen as the client's fault. For example: 'He doesn't do his homework'; 'she doesn't have enough ego-strength'; 'he is playing games'; 'she's resistant'; 'he just doesn't want to deal with his feelings'; 'she has a personality disorder'; 'he doesn't keep appointments' (or is always late); 'she expects me to give her answers'; 'he expects me to do all the work'; 'she wants me to give advice'; 'he is not ready for psychotherapy'; 'she thinks God will solve everything'; 'she doesn't want to talk about her childhood'; etc., etc. Are we really listening in such cases? Might it be then that we psychotherapists are not learning our clients' individual languages?

Might it be time we re-dedicated ourselves to listening to our clients?

> The world order speaks to humans as a kind of language they must learn to comprehend. Just as the meaning of what is said is actually 'given' in the sounds which the foreigner hears, but cannot understand, so the direct experience of the *physis* of things [or people] will be like the babbling of an unknown tongue for the soul that does not know how to listen.
>
> (Heraclitus, in Kahn 1981: 107)

Narrative

Narrative means story, myth, history, theory – whatever form the telling of the story takes. Theories are stories because they have not been proved at the rational **level** five. We can tell many stories about any fact (such as statistics) but our explanations or theories are not facts. Logically only when theories or hypotheses are 'proved' at **level** 5 do they become 'facts'.

It is actually hard for me to understand how 'narrative' is considered a new approach to psychotherapy (or is it just another brand-name for the same ancient soap?). Surely all psychotherapies involve the telling of one's story? It is a similar puzzlement for me as when psychotherapists refer to 'body-thera-pists' – as if psychotherapy necessarily excludes the therapy of the body? However, psychotherapeutic approaches which now designate themselves as 'narrative' want to highlight this story-telling, meaning-making **level** of psychotherapy – the **level** six of experience or the sixth domain of knowledge (see Clarkson 1975 and 2000c). It is to be logically and epistemologically distinguished from the consensual realm of facts and probabilities (**level** 5).

However, some of our stories/theories, myths or narratives can be better or worse for our use **depending on commonly recognized criteria for judging a good theory**, i.e. validity, reliability, coherence, lack of internal contradictions, elegance, utility, 'fit' with surrounding theories and already proven facts as well as economy of explanation (e.g. Occam's razor).

It is, for example, a scientifically proven fact that eye-witnesses to a road traffic accident can all witness the same event, but their interpreta-tion, their stories can be vastly different (Cutler and Penrod 1995). Each one (or group) of us can construct our individual varying narratives or stories from the same facts.

> The reflective awareness of one's personal narrative provides the realization that past events are not meaningful in themselves but are given significance by the configuration of one's narrative.
>
> (Polkinghorne 1988: 182)

Furthermore, such stories can be diametrically opposed – as the old example in folk wisdom of the half-full or half-empty glass of beer illus-trates. Perception is all. The great film *Rashomon*, in the hands of an artist such as Kurosawa, also demonstrates how the same event is construed by the different participants in completely different ways. As we watch this film we feel how our perspective shifts on the story as we inhabit the phenomenologically experienced world of each of the characters in turn.

We see and experience the same event through four different pairs of eyes, bodies and aspirations. Through the medium of the film we are also confronted (if we wish to be) with our urgent child-like need for 'knowing the truth'. Yet Kurosawa leaves us with a multiplicity of coexisting narra-tives – and we never know exactly what the 'real truth' is. Could we tolerate the horrifying idea that perhaps the 'real truth' in the realm of narrative does not exist?

Lyotard (1989) defined **postmodernism** as the 'collapse of the meta-narrative'. He says that at this point in history we are collectively experiencing the collapse of the 'big story of stories' which can authoritatively subsume all other narratives.

Postmodernists, like 'existentialists', usually disagree with each other, often don't identify themselves with this brand-name philosophy, and many people can be categorized as 'postmodern' in their approach who have never even heard of the idea. Anyway, another definition by Glass (1993) says that postmodernism is

> a philosophy that has reacted strongly against several assumptions of modernity: those concerning progress, history, causality, system, absolutes, meaning, the unitary self, technological judgement, and conformity. It celebrates difference, change, transformation and flux.
>
> (Glass 1993: 1)

Which 'authorities' can we still trust to tell us 'the truth' without flinching? Capitalism, communism, psychoanalysis, Christianity – all these are meta-narratives attempting to explain all historical and future facts within their own respective universes of discourse. Yet each in its own way has failed many human dreams of finding an absolute rock of infallibility in which we can believe and according to which we can conceptually and experientially organize our lives. (Witness the recent Catalan sculpture of Pope John Paul felled by a rock in the Tate Modern.)

> We live in a world in which the authority of previous guides has apparently crumbled.
>
> (Boradori 1986, cited in Chambers 1990: 82)

We have seen ideological dream after ideological dream flower, and fail to solve the monumental problems facing our world – the impending destruction of the planet, the millions of people dying of hunger and disease, the rise of fundamentalism of an extreme degree. There is a profound sense in which we have become disillusioned, and yet many lack the energetic, courageous despair of existentialists such as Kierkegaard. While they largely conform to the externals, the young seem to listen to authorities now with a built-in scepticism. At the same time there is a 74% increase in suicides among young men in the UK in the last ten years (Pepinster 1992).

> The emergence of postmodern thinking addresses our current, global mode of interaction and our need to attend to issues of diversity. The modernist reliance on the individual as the primary organizing principle of society is replaced in postmodernism by a communal, relational, interactive attention to under-

> standing the social order. In a world where *local* economies depend upon *world* politics and trade and where *world* economies must consider and depend on *localized* governments, an emphasis on self-contained individuals becomes minimally informative.
>
> (McNamee 1992: 191)

The act of **construing** – acknowledging that humans construct/create their realities (each from his or her own localized perspective) instead of finding an infallible source of 'the truth' or discovering an 'objective reality out there' – has led to a variety of philosophical and methodological approaches. One name given to this trend is *post-structuralism*, which 'proposes a subjectivity which is precarious, contradictory and in process, constantly being constituted in discourse each time we think or speak' (Weedon 1987: 32).

It has involved the abandonment of

> one of the deepest assumptions (and hopes) of Enlightenment thought; that what is 'really' available for perception 'out there' is an orderly and systematic world, (potentially) the same for all of us – such that, if we really persist in our investigations and arguments, we will ultimately secure universal agreement about its nature.
>
> (Shotter 1992: 69)

Variously the alternatives to modernist thought have also been referred to as constructionism, constructivism, postmodernism, discursive practice or phenomenology and some brands of existentialism. For the purposes of this book I will use the word 'constructual' to refer to all of these attempts. The central notion is the acknowledgement that we humans 'construe' our versions of reality – each from the particular situatedness in which we have been existentially thrown like a pebble on a beach (see the notes to Heidegger's *Existence and Being* by Brock 1949: 369).

> Our generation is realistic for we have come to know man as he really is. After all, man is that being who has invented the gas chambers of Auschwitz; however, he is also that being who has entered those gas chambers upright, with the Lord's prayer or the *Shema Yisrael* on his lips.
>
> (Frankl 1973: 137)

The narratives of psychotherapy and counselling

According to Lax, psychotherapy 'is a process of continuing to engage in a conversation with the intention of facilitating/co-creating/co-authoring a new narrative with the clients without imposing a story on them' (in McNamee and Gergen 1992: 74). Do we ever 'impose' a story on our clients? What is a 'theory' but a 'story'? And remember that Foucault (e.g. 1967, 1974, 1979) taught us that all stories (and disciplines) impose discourses of values and power. (That means that every theory carries implicit or explicit collective norms.)

> It is not simply that therapists from a given school will ensure that their clients come away bearing beliefs in their particular account. By implication (and practice) the ultimate aim of most schools of therapy is hegemonic. All other schools of thought, and their associated narratives should succumb. Psychoanalysts wish to eradicate behaviour modification; cognitive-behavioural therapists see systems theory as misguided, and so on.
>
> (Gergen and Kaye 1992: 171)

'Much of the therapeutic literature indicates an allegiance to a modernist view of the world . . . The shape and direction of the talk is dictated by models, stages and methods clearly identified in texts and professional journals and books' (McNamee 1992: 190); '. . . nowhere are the wobbly foundations of the therapist's account made known; nowhere do the therapist's personal doubts, foibles, and failings come to light' (Gergen and Kaye 1992: 171; see also Clarkson 1998b).

> Psychological narratives can (and do) claim scientific credentials thus assuring the seal of professional approval. From this vantage point we see that the thera- peutic process but inevitably results in the slow but inevitable replacement of the client's story with the therapist's. The client's story does not remain a free- standing reflection of [their] truth, but rather, as questions are asked and answered, descriptions and explanations are reframed, and affirmation and doubt are disseminated by the therapist, the client's narrative is either destroyed or incorporated – but in any case replaced – by the professional account. The client's account is transformed by the psychoanalyst into a tale of family romance, by the Rogerian into a struggle against conditional regard, and so on . . . by providing the client with a scientific [sounding] formulation, the therapist has played the appointed role in a long-standing cultural ritual in which the ignorant, the failing, and the weak seek counsel from the wise, superior and strong. It is indeed a comforting ritual to all who will submit.
>
> (Gergen and Kaye 1992: 169–70)

> The 'visualist bias of positivism [can be replaced] with talk about voices, utter- ances, intonation, multivocality' in an attempt to shift from models of observa- tion to models of participation in language. A metaphor of sight (gaze) implies distance and thus objectivity. A metaphor of sound implies proximity.
>
> (McNamee 1992: 197)

So the client's problem is not 'seen through' and the client's story is not merely a story to which we as psychotherapists listen. 'It is also a situated action in itself, a performance with illocutionary effects. It acts so as to create, sustain or alter worlds of social relationship' (Gergen and Kaye 1992: 178). **Narrative is a relational act.**

'Selves are only realized as a byproduct of relatedness. It is not independent selves who come together to form a relationship, but particular forms of relationship that engender what we take to be the individual's identity' (Gergen and Kaye 1992: 180). Which version of the story we tell is dependent on the audience (the intermediaries) to which it is told in relationship. Just think of how a CV is rejigged depending on whether you are applying for a practitioner post in a GP practice, a university lecturer's post or to be a yoga teacher at the local educational centre – depending on who is going to hear (or read) the story, and why. (Always assuming that you are not **lying**, that is, falsifying **level** five facts.)

Think of a particularly difficult time in your life. Tell the story from at least four different points of view – yourself as **victim**, yourself as **rescuer**, yourself as **persecutor** and yourself as **bystander** to the drama (see Clarkson 1996d). You will find that this is possible. Then tell the story as if it were a **film** which you were watching and then as an **experiment** you were observing Life conducting with yourself. In narrative psychotherapies 'discursive space is created in which a multiplicity of interpretations and descriptions become viable' (McNamee 1992: 191).

> In this way those turning to us in times of trouble may come to transcend the restraints imposed by their erstwhile reliance on a determinate set of meanings and be freed from the struggle that ensues from imposing their beliefs on self and others. For some, new solutions to problems will become apparent, while for others a richer set of narrative meanings will emerge. For still others a stance toward meaning itself will evolve; one which betokens that tolerance of uncertainty, that freeing of experience which comes from acceptance of unbounded relativity of meaning. For those who adopt it, this stance offers the prospect of a creative participation in the unending and unfolding meaning of life [physis].
>
> (Gergen and Kaye 1992: 183)

Heidegger also writes that 'physis as logos is the poesis of physis – "the ultimate source of thought as well as of language and poetry". The human *logos*, as it shows itself in language and poetry, is merely a response to the *logos* of *physis*' (quoted in Avens 1984: 70). Poetry and art are indeed major ways in which physis both reveals and conceals itself. (Therefore the presence of so much Rumi in this book.)

This again shows remarkable consistency with Groddeck's idea that humankind's insistence on symbolizing – making meaning – was an expression of the It and not of conscious thought; man [and woman] is lived by the It and lived by the symbol from the very beginning. 'While the grown-up has difficulties gaining insight into the interaction between the symbol and the It, the child has this insight spontaneously' (Groddeck 1988: 17).

Narrative approaches 'work with a part of the human psyche that is surprisingly neglected in many schools of therapy – the form-giving, meaning-making part, the narrator who at every waking moment of our lives spins out its account of who we are and what we are doing and why we are doing it' (Clarkson 1990: 137). Perhaps in the end our stories are being told **through** us by life (physis) itself lying in the 'boundless and inarticulable capacity for relatedness itself' (Gergen and Kaye 1992: 181). After all, as Wittgenstein reminded us, '**What cannot be said, cannot be whistled either. Whereof one cannot speak, thereof one should be silent**' (1922: 189).

> A fuller appreciation of the importance of the realm of meaning for understanding human beings will require a different kind of training for scholars in the human sciences. This training will need to include a study of the structures and relations of a linguistically organized reality. It will also require a redefinition of the human sciences: instead of conceiving themselves as natural sciences, the human sciences need to conceive of themselves as multiple sciences. The object of their inquiry, the human being, exists in multiple strata of reality, which, although interrelated, are organized in different ways.
>
> (Polkinghorne 1988: 183)

The transpersonal psychotherapy Babel

Unfortunately a similar Babel phenomenon is happening among the so-called transpersonal or psychospiritual 'schools' – just as it has always happened between different peoples following different religions, apparently different gods and definitely different versions of whatever constitutes the 'bible' for them. And many and wide are the versions of religion created from, for example, the same New Testament of the Bible, along the whole spectrum from fundamentalism to literary metaphor.

So now we have 'transpersonal schools' (or approaches or orientations or models) using Assagioli versus archetypal Jungians (and at least four other 'schools' of Jungians); Buddhist-oriented transpersonal psychotherapy versus transpersonal psychotherapy based on the Kabbalah; the Wilberians versus the Rinzai Zens in the Suzuki/Watts tradition (e.g. Suzuki 1964, 1972); astrological psychotherapy versus Christian psychotherapy; deep ecology approaches versus past-life regression therapy – the examples go on and on.

So our clients (and we also), wishing to explore the transpersonal dimension, are again faced with difficult – if not impossible – choices:

'Which brand of transpersonal psychology do you want?' And the questing client replies: 'How do I choose between them? Which "approach" will be right for me? How can I know this before I have spent several years and much money (more than some £30,000 training to be a psychotherapist) before I might find out, for example, (a) that I have made a mistake, or (b) that the transpersonal "school" is going bankrupt and my training will not be "recognized" (?) or (c) that the guru or sheik I have been following for a decade has been running a harem of underage girls on students' fees all this time?'

> Warriors in battle do like this too.
> A great mutual embrace is always happening
> between the eternal and what dies,
> between essence and accident.
>
> The sport has different rules in every case,
> but it's basically the same, and remember:
>
> the way you make love is the way
> God will be with you.
>   (Rumi 1991: 124–25)

Of course there are no easy guaranteed answers. But does it really have to be so difficult? Is it not more a matter of listening and enabling our clients to find their own way to the transpersonal in a language – a narrative, a myth or a story in whatever idiom which suits them?

Something that might help

Rawlinson (1997), a phenomenologist of religion 'who has learned to live with the uncertainty of *not* adjudicating between inconsistent, ultimate truth claims and alternative transpersonal perspectives' (Schlamm 2000: 2) says that '. . . opposite truths apply to the human condition. The only option to us, therefore, is to come to terms with ambivalence . . . opposites have to be embraced' (Schlamm 2000: 2). Since it is obvious that people choose different kinds of approaches (which may all be equally effective – or not – at the final judgement) to the transpersonal, Rawlinson provides a pragmatic taxonomy (classification) of characteristics of different mystical traditions. Although he may not agree, for me **in practice** this taxonomy is approximate and categories may overlap and interpenetrate.

From the perspective I consider useful here, they can be seen to operate from different 'centres of gravity' and with different metaphorical temperatures. And of course there are numerous varieties within different 'paths to salvation' with people (and teachers) often crossing over into other categories.

Very roughly, in my psychological use of this taxonomy, they correspond to the Jungian personality typology of **thinking** ('cool structured', e.g. Wilber), **feeling** ('hot structured', e.g. Kabbalah), **sensation** ('hot unstructured', e.g. syncretic or African-centred Christianity) and **intuition** ('cool unstructured', e.g. Rinzai Zen Buddhism, of which I consider Suzuki and Alan Watts to be exemplars).

(If you want to read more about Jung's psychological types read his wonderful book *Personality Types* (1944). Kiersey and Bates (1984) created a questionnaire which may help you identify your own type or you could arrange to do a Myers–Briggs test with a certified user who is also a qualified psychotherapist. Another excellent work is *The Many Worlds of Time*; in Clarkson 1997a: 219–43, I take it further into typological aspects of facilitating excellence and 'genius'.)

To return to Rawlinson's typology of spiritualities (or *soteriological* paths – see Table 1), according to him, **hot** is that which is other than oneself; that which has its own life. It is not something that one has access to as of right. It is powerful and breathtaking and is associated with revelation and grace.

Cool is the very essence of oneself; one need not go to another to find it. Hence one does have access as of right. Although I disagree with him at some **levels**, Rawlinson believes it is quiet and still, and is associated with self-realization.

The meaning of **structured** is that there is an inherent order in the cosmos and therefore in the human condition. There is something to be discovered and there is a way of discovering it. A map is required to find the destination.

By contrast, **unstructured** teachings say there is no gap between the starting point and the finishing post. Method and goal are identical. We are not separate from reality/truth/God and so no map is required. Everything is available now and always has been. (Adapted with apologies from Schlamm's summary with addition of some non-Indo-European perspectives and my own experiences of the four types of spirituality.)

Note: It seems to me enough has been said/written about cool structured and essentially there is little or nothing that **can** be said about cool unstructured, so the other two traditions have somewhat more content in this following table.

Table 2.1 Soteriological pathways (adapted from Rawlinson 1997)

Hot Structured	Hot Unstructured
• Emphasizes the numinous, and as other than oneself • Teachings are mysterious • Chogyam Trungpa • Everything that exists in consciousness turns into its opposite – enantiodromia • The more experience of spiritual light, the more we are confronted by our own darkness, the more instinctual, with shadow • Somatically based mysticism • Knowledge granted piecemeal and often miraculously • Emphasis on ecstasy – crazy wisdom teachers, hot magic – the manipulation of the laws of the universe (based on the image of the human body) and the manipulation of the laws of the cosmos in the service of self-transformation • Teleological • Conscious mastery of the ego must submit to a radical regression with an uncertain outcome, a regression that can lead to psychosis as well as transcendence, disintegration as well as higher integration (Washburn 1988: 37) • Conscious mastery of somatically based mysticism, e.g. Tantra • Regression in the service of transcendence, e.g. Jung who emphasizes the conjunction of opposites conjoins prepersonal and transpersonal development and experience	• Emphasizes the numinous as other than one-self, affirming that there can be no gradual or progressive spiritual development at all – 'The devotee ends up at the same point that he or she started from - there are no distinctions in love' • Teachings are mysterious - the Christian mystic experiences ultimate disempowerment in order to eliminate any lingering residue within the soul of desire for personal spiritual satisfaction, which itself prevents union with God • St Theresa (as quoted in Rawlinson 1997) ... there are no distinctions in love, God alone exists and He is unknowable, love is a gift and a mystery, not a right • Ani: 'A cosmic being must be whole. In such a being reason and emotion cannot be experienced as disparate, unconnected and antagonistic. The more "intelligent" such a self becomes, the more it understands language as merely metaphor.' • 'A cosmic self cannot objectify the universe' (Ani 1984: 45). There is no separation between 'self and 'other', mind and body, individual and universe • e.g. Spiritual/religious/Life of the world's first peoples, American Indian and South American practice, Syncretic Christianity, African religions, Sufism, Pure Land Buddhism and Hindu bhakti • Teleological (the future determines the past)

Cool Structured	Cool Unstructured
• Teachings are available - gradual • The source of spiritual liberation lies within oneself • European 'systems' with ascending grades • Needs precise knowledge, dualistic • Developmental, hierarchical. • Higher levels are 'better' than lower levels of being, i.e. women, blacks, animals • Plato: 'it requires a long and troublesome process of education' • Causal • Linear progression • Cartesian dualism • Yoga • Meditation • Preoccupied with 'pre-trans' fallacy, e.g. Wilber (1980)	• Teachings are available everywhere all the time – sudden illuminations, so 'the direct experience of the physis of things [or people] will be like the babbling of an unknown tongue for the soul that does not know how to listen' (Heraclitus, in Kahn 1981: 107) • The practice of meditation is not necessary for the attainment of self-realization – living is the meditation • Neither liberation, nor the knowledge that leads to it, admit any degrees or gradations (Shankara, the founder of Ramana's Advaita Vendanta tradition) • Meditation 'does not consist of sitting or lying down, and until you give it up you won't come near the truth' (p.333) e.g. Rinzai tradition of Suzuki (e.g. 1964, 1972) and Alan Watts (1968) • Pre- and trans-unity.

[God says:]
I have given each being a separate and unique way
of seeing and knowing and saying that knowledge.

What seems wrong to you is right for him.
What is poison to one is honey to someone else.

Purity and impurity, sloth and diligence in worship,
these mean nothing to Me.
I am apart from all that.
Ways of worshipping are not to be ranked as better or worse than one another.
Hindus do Hindu things.
The Dravidian Muslims in India do what they do.
It's all praise and it's all **right**.

It's not Me that's glorified in acts of worship.
It's the worshippers! I don't hear the words
they say. I look inside at the humility.

That broken-open lowliness is the Reality.
Not the language! Forget phraseology. I want burning, burning.
Be friends
with your burning. Burn up your thinking
and your forms of expression!
Moses,
those who pay attention to ways of behaving
and speaking are one sort.
Lovers who burn
are another.

(Rumi 1988: 20)

Transpersonal psychotherapy in practice

A man was telling his friend in a pub about his 'near-death' experience. He said he had died and gone to heaven. His friend asked him: 'Did you get to see God?' 'Yes,' he said. His friend asked: 'Please tell me what he looked like.' The man said: 'She's black.'

Many psychotherapists and others have asked me: 'How do you introduce the transpersonal into a psychotherapy session?' I have always been rather surprised by this question for two reasons: (a) I do not see how any healing can take place without the transpersonal – I surely do not 'do it' myself!; and (b) how can you do therapy of any kind without knowing how this unique person makes sense of their life – and inevitable death?

So at the initial consultation I almost invariably ask the client (or clients) what I have come to call '**the meaning of life question**'. The words may differ depending on whom I am speaking to and their own particular 'language', but the question is essentially very simple: 'What are your ideas about the meaning of your life?' or 'What is your religious or spiritual background?' or 'How do you make sense of what has happened to you?' No one has ever found this question strange or uncomfortable. Even if someone responds by saying: 'I think this life is all there is and we just have to make the most of it', I have been given an answer which is at least as (and perhaps more) important than their GP number or whether they are currently taking drugs or medication. Other examples include the following:

- 'I was just born cursed, unlucky in every way.' This could indicate a fatalism which could be very destructive to our work together – particularly if supported by a belief in a psychologically damaging kind of fatalistic astrology.
- 'The cause of all my trouble in relationships is that my mother died at my birth.' This can indicate her way of understanding life's dilemmas around which we can together begin to build a conversation around the way this particular client construes her world.
- 'You know, I was very devoutly Christian as a child, but after a priest abused me sexually, I completely lost all faith in myself, God and life itself. I just can't see the point of it all.' This client could be indicating a very serious suicidal risk – a vital part of assessment and far more indicative and likely to facilitate a further frank discussion than clinically asking: 'Are you contemplating suicide?'
- 'The devil sent me because God wants me to kill all prostitutes.' The potential danger to self and others along with the disordered thinking mandates extreme caution in continuing to see this person.
- 'The British government has ruled that I cannot take the body of my dead child home to be buried in the ancestral grounds and now I will never rest, because his spirit cannot come to peace.' The cultural background needs to be explored and respected while anticipating serious transferences around issues of racism, colonial exploitation and what the Australian aborigines call 'the stolen generation'.

Why is this 'meaning of life' question so important? In no particular rank order, here are some of the reasons:

1. It identifies which **language** that unique client uses to refer to ultimate issues and important values. I can either join them in the conversation using information from my previous knowledge or inform myself through questions, reading, films, consultation with people who know more about it than I do – and there are always those.

2. It often acts as the very best screening question in the mutual **assessment** of suitability for psychotherapy between therapist and clients. As the examples above show, the psychotherapist can get quite precise indications of psychosis, rigidity, lack of meaning (existential *anomie*), suicidal or homicidal tendencies – in short how the client construes his or her world.

3. It creates a **mutual frame of reference** to which we can both refer in our work in future. For example, if someone uses the *I Ching* (an ancient Chinese form of divination which Jung also used) this information gets logged in the psychotherapist's resources for future use. There may come a difficult time in the psychotherapy where the client has forgotten that they have had good guidance from the I Ching (Wilhelm 1951) in the past – and the psychotherapist can remember and remind the client of this resource in their personal repertoire at a most crucial time.

4. Extensive research from MIND (a mental health organization for people who have been 'users' of the psychiatric system) has repeatedly found that some form of spiritual, religious or transpersonal perspective on life is – according to the people themselves – more important in **recovery and health maintenance** than counselling – and certainly more important than psychotropic medication. To ignore this dimension of human experience or make it 'undiscussable' in psychotherapy is therefore to refuse to use a major source of strength and courage for the individual. I believe this also has ethical implications.

5. Individual exploration of what meanings different names/labels/words have for that unique client at that particular time (and it may change) can reduce **collective** or **cultural countertransferences** of the psychotherapist and aid the process of 'bracketing' off previous assumptions, simplistic understanding, superficial knowledge and so on. (Don't expect your client to 'teach' you, in their time, to correct, for example, your racist distortions; rather, make your own friends in that cultural community.)

   If the psychotherapist has, for example, in the past been personally abused by a Protestant minister, or has 'escaped' from an oppressive Catholic background, or is struggling with an arranged marriage, the psychotherapist needs to work through their real or potential countertransferential distortions (or biases) by means of their own therapy and/or supervision – or spiritual direction. This is part of the psychological cleansing which every client deserves from their psychotherapist.

6. It indicates right from the first session that there is place in the psychotherapist's world view which allows for values, meaning, beliefs

and spiritual practices to be brought into the psychotherapy – if and when the client wants. **The transpersonal dimension of human experience becomes discussable** – whether in art, nature, science, service to others or whatever. This is an extremely important point because so many clients have told me they felt and clearly understood (through the silence of their therapists or analysts on these matters or their ignoring of such subjects when the client brought them up) that such things 'don't belong in psychotherapy'. As I have shown elsewhere (Clarkson 1995a: 170–80), the therapist's imposition of their own values on the client happens as much through what is **not** spoken about and non-verbally conveyed than what is actually said.

7. It helps to establish the psychotherapist's awareness of the **limits of their competency**. This is a requirement in most, if not all, professional ethics codes, and facilitates responsible referral or the need for additional resources. If you are not comfortable dealing with ambiguity, 'unknowing', paradox or simultaneous contradiction, refer the client to people who are. I am not personally in a position to support a mother whose ten-year-old daughter is being taken to have her clitoris and vaginal lips amputated by a Harley Street surgeon. ('Female circumcision' – like 'friendly fire' – is a nominative euphemism which blurs the physiological and emotional impact of the real facts for particular normative groups.)

8. It helps to establish the **need for additional resources** or expert consultation. I am not authorized to conduct an exorcism or to deliver absolution in the confidential safety of the confessional. However, I know psychologically informed people in most religious traditions who are. (Priests for example cannot be forced by the law to disclose information received in the confessional; psychotherapists can and have been.)

9. It frequently is a rich and valuable source of personally **meaningful metaphors** for the client which can be used, or referred to later as the client rewrites or enlivens their own personal life story or myth. Cox and Thielgaard (1987) in their wonderful book *Mutative Metaphors in Psychotherapy* demonstrate movingly and convincingly how the introduction of Shakespearean characters and images can change even the most psychiatrically disturbed criminal inmates of a prison like Broadmoor. The language of astrology or archetypal myths – such as Jamaican folklore or Bolen's (1984) work on the archetypes of Greek Gods and Goddesses in every person – are examples of fine sources of inspiration.

10. Finally, through the meaning-of-life question **death and dying becomes available** in the consulting room – or wherever the

psychotherapy is taking place. All religions and spiritual traditions contain narratives or stories about living and dying – 'the meaning of it all'. When faced with major life decisions (such as abortion, marriage, divorce, forgiveness, 'making amends', emigration, a dementing parent, a genetic heritage of breast cancer or some other kind of fatal disease, the psychological aftermath of natural disasters, involvement in a war, a change of vocation), it is sometimes helpful to ask the client (in whichever language they would prefer) to imagine what they would have wished they had done now if they were on their deathbed many years hence.

And if someone does not have access to, or does not want to avail themselves of, the rich hoard of cultural, religious, artistic or scientific or natural stories of the earth, they will still have to find **some** kind of meaning for their lives to get through the nights when the despair and pain of being human becomes overwhelming.

Chapter 3
Transpersonal
psychotherapy

Two kinds of intelligence
There are two kinds of intelligence: One acquired,
as a child in school memorizes facts and concepts
from books and from what the teacher says,
collecting information from the traditional sciences
as well as from the new sciences.

With such intelligence you rise in the world.
You get ranked ahead or behind others
in regard to your competence in retaining
information. You stroll with this intelligence
in and out of fields of knowledge, getting always more
marks on your preserving tablets.

There is another kind of tablet, one
already completed and preserved inside you.
A spring overflowing its springbox. A freshness
in the center of the chest. This other intelligence
does not turn yellow or stagnate. It's fluid,
and it doesn't move from outside to inside
through the conduits of plumbing-learning.

This second knowing is a fountainhead
from within you, moving out.

(Rumi 1988: 36)

Heraclitus is the spirit who influenced me most in my development as a psychologist and psychotherapist. The extant **Fragments of Heraclitus**, in *The Art and Thought of Heraclitus*, is available in a good translation with the Greek original texts by Charles Kahn (1981). Heraclitus wrote them in Ephesus, on the coast of Asia Minor (north of Miletus), around 504–501 before the Common Era and deposited the book as a dedication in the great temple of Artemis. He was a poet with an interest in perfume.

Why Heraclitus? As a philosopher he addressed himself to the nature of the *psyche*. According to Friedman (1964), Heraclitus was the forerunner of existentialism. He was also the first psychologist who said: 'I go in search of myself' (Fragment XXVII); and concluded that 'You will not find out the limits of the soul by going, even if you travel every way, so deep is its report' (Fragment XXXV).

My searching into the Heraclitean fragments shows this to be true of the fragments themselves: they are inexhaustible – no matter how long and how deeply his work has been studied over the last 2,500 years. Their process and their content **embody** each other, each is a part **and** the whole. Although a multiplicity of languages coexist in which experience can be described, his claims that direct experience is of a different **level** of discourse than what is 'heard' from others also make him the first phenomenologist in the Occidental tradition.

For Heraclitus, self-knowledge leads to the knowledge of what is 'shared by all' – a universal principle of wholeness. There is no part of the whole that does not remain in relationship with every other part which is also a whole. The fragments are concerned with how people live their lives and die – how to make sense of our experience. In the Heraclitean epistemology 'questions of cognition are inseparable from questions of action and intention, questions of life and death' (Kahn 1981: 100).

> Everyone, and every thing, and every action, glorifies
> You, but sometimes the way one does it
> is not recognized by another.
>
> Human beings rarely understand how inanimate objects
> are doing it, the walls and the doors and the rocks,
> those masters of glorification!
>
> We squabble over the doctrines of the Sunnis
> and the Jabris, and all their seventy-two
> different interpretations. It never ends.
>
> But we don't hear the inanimate objects
> speaking to each other, and to us!
>
> How can we understand the praising
> of what doesn't speak?
>
> Only with the help of One whose love
> opens into the spirit's telling.
>
> (Rumi 1991: 84)

Throughout the extant fragments Heraclitus can be seen to differentiate different domains of discourse, e.g. direct experience, passions, rational thought, beliefs, opinions, and the different **kinds of truth** which coexist at individual, collective, human, inanimate and cosmic **levels**. 'The business of scientific inquiry is not to ascribe rationality to men but to study in a rational way the irrational ways of mankind' (Wolman 1965: 11).

According to Wittgenstein, philosophy itself is a medicine (*physic*). Philosophy **is** the discipline of thinking about thinking. 'The object of philosophy is the logical clarification of thoughts. Philosophy is not a theory, but an activity. The theory of knowledge is the **philosophy of psychology**' (Wittgenstein 1922: 77, my emphasis).

Confronted with 'the speed of change, the growing complexity of the world and with the new challenges of history' the 1998 UNESCO International Symposium – 'Towards Integrative Process and Integrated Knowledge' – 'recognized how the nature of reality itself, with its inherent complexity and multiform character, but at the same time with its deep unity, requires transcending the boundaries of single disciplines. It was also observed that the probable reason for these global issues to necessitate a transdisciplinary approach is that they tend to reveal, more than others, the underlying complexity of reality' (UNESCO 1998: 8).

So how can we gain clear understanding of ourselves and this our complex multilingual world? Definitely not by just listening to monolingual authorities (theoretical learning):

> The way to attain an integrated concept and practice of knowledge, and consequently to address many crucial issues of our age through a transdisciplinary approach, does not lie in applying ready-made, 'mechanical' procedures based on automatic, stereotyped formulas and standardized recipes.
>
> (UNESCO 1998: 7)

The philosopher for all ages says that we need to search and search again. Research **means** to search again. Into many things. 'People who love wisdom must be good inquirers into many things indeed' (Fragment IX). Why? Because **'physis loves to hide'** (Fragment X).

Since Plato fractured the original mind/body unity, physis has sometimes been mistranslated (as the Romans did) with the limited word 'nature'. Heidegger is categorical:

> The later concepts of 'nature' must be set aside: *physis* means the emerging and the arising, the spontaneous unfolding that lingers. In this power rest and motion are opened out of original unity.
>
> (Heidegger 1987: 61)

When Heidegger uses the word **Being**, he means **physis** in the original ancient Greek sense. Furthermore:

> The Greeks did not learn what *physis* is through natural phenomena, but the other way around; it was through a fundamental poetic . . . experience of being that they discovered what they had to call *physis*.
>
> (Heidegger 1987: 14)

Heidegger thinks that physis as logos is the poesis of physis – 'the ultimate source of thought as well as of language and poetry. The human *logos*, as it shows itself in language and poetry, is merely a response to the *logos* of *physis*' (Avens 1984: 70).

There are three further themes which, although they overlap and are in relationship each with each other as constantly changing **wholes**, between them embrace perhaps the most important emphases for me as a psychologist and psychotherapist. These are: (1) everything is in relationship to everything else; (2) everything changes; and (3) everything is a whole.

Everything is in relationship to everything else

So, the first theme is process, or dynamic interrelatedness. Colloquially, **everything is in relationship to everything else** – even our relationship with the first *physicians*. Heidegger thought that

> the early Greek understanding of **being as physis** is not one outlook among others. Rather it is definitive of who we are as participants in Western History . . . As a result, any new beginning [turn] will involve recapturing the insights flowing from those initial 'wellsprings' of understanding that set our civilization on its course, the new beginning is 'realizable only in a dialogue *(Auseinandersetzung)* with the first'.
>
> (Heidegger 1959/1987: 27)

And, according to Naddaf (1993), physis is 'the cornerstone of Western philosophy' (personal communication).

The warrior-philosopher Jan Smuts was the founder of the forerunner to the United Nations – and the last South African Prime Minister before 'apartheid'. He bequeathed the word **Holism** to philosophy and wrote that wholes are not closed isolated systems externally: they have their field in which they intermingle and influence each other: 'The holistic universe is a profoundly reticulated system of interactions and interconnections' (Smuts 1987: 333).

The dynamic interrelatedness of all of human life is now a well-established scientific fact. Like quantum physics, the chaos and complexity sciences highlight the importance of relationships (e.g. Lewin 1992). The observer (researcher, clinician) is always part of the field – always affecting and being affected in that relationship. Our current physicists have shown us that everything and potentially everybody is in relationship in a kind of dance. It is impossible **not** to have a relationship with another person **and** we will continue to affect each other's states – even should we never see them ever again (Isham 1995, and personal communication 1999). Pictures showing 'entanglement' illustrate how we physically interpenetrate each other. Everything is in this sense connected with everything else and any separation is therefore theoretical or descriptive rather than actual.

> Epistemologically, the things we see (people, objects etc.) exist only in relation-ship and, when analysed microscopically, they too are best viewed as relation-ships . . . Relationships become the primary source of our knowledge of the world . . . in fact things ultimately are relationships.
>
> (Cottone 1988: 360)

Very recent findings regarding the nature of reality as reported by Crown (2000) in the *New Scientist* indicate that this entanglement – i.e. the relationships between apparent objects – is the primary reality: apparent objects 'have no intrinsic existence – they are defined only by how strongly they connect with each other, and ultimately they disappear from the model. They [the apparently separate objects] are mere scaffolding.'

Cahill is quoted as saying:

> The Universe is rich enough to be self-referencing – for instance, I'm aware of myself. This suggests that most of the everyday truths of physical reality, like most mathematical truths, have no explanation. 'Objects', people, mathematical theorems, new ideas, 'the experience of the present', local connections emerge from a sea of randomness – they owe their existence solely to their relationships with each other.
>
> (Crown 2000: 24)

Examples of 'tele' from psychodrama (Greenberg 1975) or synchronicity in Jungian thought (Jung 1969a) abound in psychotherapy and supervision. They, amongst many other examples, give credence to the notion that there are meaningfully interconnecting patterns in all of human existence – including the parallel process phenomenon observed in psychotherapy supervision (see Clarkson 1998a). You will notice how it is like a fractal – self-similar across time and space.

Repeatedly, many of us experience that, whenever we stop to pay attention to a particular conjunction between events and people, some significance – often profound – is laid bare. One could say that such 'non-local connections' emerge from the sea of randomness which is our everyday world and our everyday consciousness.

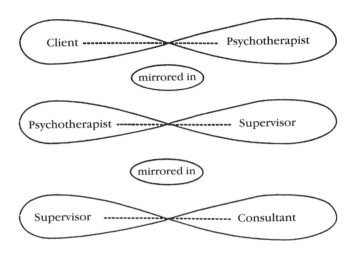

Figure 3.1 Parallel process

So it seems that the Heraclitean notion that everything is in relationship to everyone and everything else forever is in a sense **philosophically**, **experientially**, **scientifically** and **psychotherapeutically** accurate.

Everything changes

Heraclitus was *par excellence* the philosopher of change. The second theme, which I see as a continuous flow around the cycle of awareness from 500 BC to my work today, shows how

> He regarded the universe as a ceaselessly changing conflict of opposites, all things being in a state of flux, coming into being and passing away, and held that fire, the type of this constant change, is their origin. From the passing impressions of experience the mind derives a false idea of the permanence of the external world, which is really in a harmonious process of constant change.
>
> (Hawkins and Allen 1991: 663)

So, Heraclitus postulated that change is the only thing in the whole world of which we can be certain. The nature of this change, according to him, is usually cyclic: 'One cannot step twice into the same river, nor can one grasp any mortal substance in a stable condition, but it scatters and again gathers; it forms and dissolves, and approaches and departs' (Fragment LI).

Structure is slow process and process is fast structure. The unifying force of all life phenomena which is suggested by Heraclitus is Physis. The river water symbolizes the one Physis, or life force. It is similar to Bergson's 'élan vital' but is conceived of as all-embracing – everything.

The coincidence of opposite values in one action allows it to be a symbol of the one Physis. It was conceived of as the healing factor in illness, the energetic motive for evolution, and the driving force of creativity in the individual and collective psyche – and the universe. It is *diunital*:

> The African universe is personalized, not objectified. Time is experienced. There is no infinite abstract and oppressive future; it grows organically from the past and present. Value is placed on 'being' rather than 'doing'. The universe is understood through phenomenal interaction, which produces powerful symbols and images, which in turn communicate truths. 'Diunital logic' indicates that in African thought a thing can be both A and not A at the same time . . . it can be understood as the recognition and affirmation of the ambiguity and multidimensionality of phenomenal reality. What is contradictory in Euro-American Aristotelian logic is not contradictory in African thought. The European *utamawazo* [collective spirit] cannot deal with paradox.
>
> (Dixon 1976, summarized in Ani 1994: 97–98)

However, the Platonically trained Caucasian usually imagines opposites as polarities – two separate polarities or points at the opposite ends of a line. (In a similar way as they/we see the past behind us and the future stretching like train tracks ahead of us into a distant, but different, future.) Heraclitus, other pre-Socratics and most first world cultures see opposites as the outer boundaries of a unitary cycle, punctuation marks in the unrolling story of the universe.

This sense that everything is **changing all the time**, as a result of relationship, is the very heartbeat of the Heraclitean message:

> The ordering, the same for all, no god nor man has made, but it ever was and will be: fire ever-living, kindled in measures and in measures going out.
>
> (Heraclitus: Fragment XXXVII)

Guerrière's translation stresses the auto-poiesis (self-making) of physis even more: 'kindling itself in measures and quenching itself in measures' (Heraclitus, in Guerrière 1980: 97).

Heraclitus suggests, therefore, that the nature of change is intrinsically rhythmic – kindling and quenching. 'The beginning and the end are shared in the circumference of a circle' (Fragment XCIX). Any psychotherapist (any human being too) is familiar with the rhythms of breathing in and breathing out, of eating and excreting, of arousal and orgasm, the seasons, the generations, civilizations. This is the intrinsic and inevitable cyclic nature of human existence.

> The god: day and night, winter and summer, war and peace, satiety and hunger.
> It alters, as when mingled with perfumes, it gets named according to the pleasure
> of each one.
>
> (Heraclitus: Fragment CXXIII)

One of the many corollaries of appreciating the cyclic nature of phenomena is the importance of the void – the abyss space – when physis is in hiding. However, it is from the void that the new emerges; it was in the deepest darkness that Moses found God, and it is when we most truly let ourselves go into the emptiness (of despair or illness) that fullness (and healing) can begin to arise. **Creativity happens at far from equilibrium conditions** (Briggs and Peat 1990). Or in Rumi's words: 'Many demolitions are actually renovations'(1990: 79).

> But there is a cure,
> and individual medicine,
> not a social remedy:
> Sit quietly, and listen
> for a voice within that will say,
> *Be more silent*.
>
> (Rumi 1991: 28)

The recent scientific thrill of discovering evidence that our known world emerged with a 'Big Bang' from the void (for example, Davies 1992) echoes human experience of a sudden insight, a figure/ground shift, a turnaround (or *metanoia*) that obliterates one phenomenological world and brings another into being. Like death, it is inescapable and yet human beings so often try to a-void it. It is my conviction that if we only had time to teach the human race one thing before we self-destruct, it would not be the linear skills of making 'training standards', but rather the cyclic skills of navigating the endless changes in our bodies, our lives and in our worlds.

> With its very coming-to-life every living thing already begins to die, and
> conversely, dying is but a kind of living, because only a living being has the ability
> to die. Indeed, dying *can* be the highest 'act' of living. *Physis* is the self-produc-
> tive putting-away of itself, and therefore it possesses the unique quality of deliv-
> ering over itself that which *through it* is first transformed from something
> orderable (e.g. water, light, air) into something appropriate for it alone (for
> example, into nutriment and so into sap and bone).
>
> (Heidegger 1998: 227)

Everything is a whole

> Graspings: wholes and not wholes, convergent, divergent, consonant, dissonant,
> from all things one and from one thing all.
>
> (Heraclitus: Fragment CXXIV)

A meditation on the meaning and implications of this fragment tends to invite us into feeling how profoundly Heraclitus understood and wanted to communicate the intrinsic one-ness of all phenomena.

It also gives a new and contemporary articulation to the original Heraclitean ideas: for example, Briggs and Peat state: 'The whole shape of things depends upon the most minute part. The part **is** the whole in this respect, for through the action of any part, the whole in the form of chaos or transformative change may manifest' (1990: 75). However, we need to understand that this wholeness includes its **opposite**. 'The name of the bow is life; its work is death' (Heraclitus: Fragment LXXXIX).

Thus cosmic unity includes the notion of *enantiodromia*, a term subsequently used both by Jung (1969b) and by Perls (1969a). This refers to the nature of the unity of polarities. Opposites may have contrary qualities, yet they can turn into each other at their apotheosis. 'The same . . . living and dead, and the waking and the sleeping, and young and old. For these transposed are those, and those transposed again are these' (Heraclitus: Fragment XCIV).

The more fully I configure my anger, the more likely that it can turn into love or understanding – and of course vice versa. In chaos theory a similar phenomenon has become known as the 'flipover' effect (Gleick 1989: 29) – the sudden figure/ground shift from one polarity to another. It appears to apply to both process and content. Rarely can one polarity remain the same for long without calling its diametrical pole into being. 'It is not better for human beings to get all they want. It is disease that makes health sweet and good, hunger satiety, weariness rest' (Heraclitus: Fragment LXVII).

> Although Physis is wont to hide itself, it manifests itself in multiple ways . . . The form in which Physis does manifest itself through phenomena is **their one-ness**. That is to say, it suggests a certain one-ness in multiple things, a certain 'coincidentia oppositorum' (coincidence of opposites).
>
> (Guerrière 1980: 103)

The universe is a whole. The individual and the collective are each a whole too. Heraclitus is sympathetic to the fate of the exceptional individual (and I would add that everyone has such potential). Heraclitus however expresses his contempt for the Ephesians: 'since they drove out their best man, Hermodorus, saying, "Let no one be the best among us; if he is, let him be so elsewhere and among others"' (Fragment LXIV).

Yet he realizes that the individual and the collective are in irretrievable relationship, and conflict is necessary. 'The counter-thrust brings together, and from tones at variance comes perfect attunement, and all things come to pass through conflict' (Fragment LXXV: see Clarkson 2000b).

> Bion states that the new idea contains a potentially disruptive force, which violates to a greater or lesser degree the structure of the field in which it appears. Thus a new discovery violates the structure of the pre-existing theory, a revolutionary the structure of society and interpretation the structure of the personality.
>
> (Grinberg et al. 1975: 77–78)

> An example among the many possible is a group which promotes an individual, who is exceptional in his creative-destructive role, to a position in the Establishment where his energies are absorbed by administrative functions.
>
> (Grinberg et al. 1975: 20–21)

From a Heraclitean perspective, whether defended or concealed, whatever part or particularity is present, the whole is enfolded in that fragment in the same way as a fractal of anything enfolds the whole and a moment of time enfolds all of eternity.

The fractal – a concept from chaos theory – is an immensely fruitful metaphor to draw upon within psychotherapy today. The word fractal was coined by Mandelbrot (1974) to describe this phenomenon of a repeating pattern – the whole repeated in every fragment, and thus spiralling off each other towards creative evolution.

> The final net result is that this is a whole-making universe, that it is the fundamental character of this universe to be active in the production of wholes, of ever more complete and advanced wholes, and that the Evolution of the universe, inorganic and organic, is nothing but the record of this whole-making activity in its progressive development.
>
> (Smuts 1987: 326)

But Smuts speaks only of **progressive development**. Heraclitus' physis is both creative and destructive (de-structuring). So is the *auto-poeisis* of modern complexity theory. Mingers (1995) makes the very explicit connection between auto-poiesis and physis. He postulates that Heidegger practically invented the word auto-poeisis, as in the following quotation: 'Physis also, the arising of something from out of itself, is a bringing forth, poeisis. Physis is indeed poeisis in the highest sense' (1995: 1). Wholes are made indeed, and they also fragment as planets (perhaps even our own) eventually explode in fiery conflagration.

> There is one common flow, one common breathing, all things are in sympathy. The whole organism and each one of its parts are working in conjunction for the same purpose . . . the great principle extends to the extremest part, and from the extremest part it returns to the great principle, to the one nature, being and not-being.
>
> (Jung 1969c: 490, quoting Hippocrates in Precope's translation)

Of course, even – or particularly – in Heraclitus, holism, change and dynamic interrelationship (even between opposites) are also fractals of **one whole**. By extrapolating these themes, I am merely focusing on three different facets of a unity which intrinsically is indivisible, although it is forever changing, and although its parts are forever interrelated, even as they oppose or contradict each other. Using Lyotard's words – except for the last one:

> There are stories: the generations, the locality, the seasons, wisdom and madness. The story makes beginning and end rhyme, scars over the interruptions. Everyone . . . finds their place and their name here, and the episodes annexed. Their births and deaths are also inscribed in the circle of things and souls with them. You are dependent on God, on nature. All you do is serve the will, unknown and well known, of physis, place yourself in the service of its urge, of the *physein* which urges living matter to grow, decrease and grow again. This service is called healing.
>
> (Lyotard 1997: 271)

In summary

Physis (or Phusis) is an ancient Greek word very rich in meaning. It is used to refer to life energy as it manifests in nature, in growth and healing as well as in all dimensions of creativity. Physician or physic (as in medicine) and Physics (as in Quantum and Chaos understandings of the world) are both derived from it. Here it is used as a concept to concentrate some of the most significant qualities and aspirations of my work – in honour of everlasting change, unlearning as well as learning, living as well as dying well, bodysoul, the cycle as potent paradigm for human evolutionary processes, the individual and society, relationship and archetype, the importance of nature as teacher and inspiration, the drive towards complexity, quality and wholeness, the coexistence of contradictions. Whether in individuals, children, couples, groups, organizations or artistic work, the central and organizing theme is simply to have life and to have it more abundantly.

Transpersonal psychotherapy in practice

So where is physis (life energy, soul, spirit) hiding in our consulting rooms – where can we trace the tracks of the transpersonal?

Apparently meaningful coincidences ('synchronicity')

Jung first named the phenomenon of apparently meaningful coincidences *synchronicity*.

A young woman I was treating had, at a critical moment, a dream in which she was given a golden scarab. While she was telling me this dream I sat with my back to the closed window. Suddenly I heard a noise behind me, like a gentle tapping. I turned round and saw a flying insect knocking against the window pane from the outside. I opened the window and caught the creature in the air as it flew in. It was the nearest analogy to a golden scarab that one finds in our latitudes, a scarabaeid beetle, the common rose-chafer (*Cetonia aurata*), which contrary to its usual habits had evidently felt an urge to get into a dark room at this particular moment . . . It was an extraordinarily difficult case to treat, and up to the time of the dream little or no progress had been made. I should explain that the main reason for this was my patient's animus [male archetype], which was steeped in Cartesian philosophy and clung so rigidly to its own idea of reality that the efforts of three doctors – I was the third – had not been able to weaken it. Evidently something quite irrational was needed which was beyond my powers to produce. The dream alone was enough to disturb ever so slightly the rationalistic attitude of my patient. But when the 'scarab' came flying in through the window in actual fact, her natural being could burst through the armour of her animus possession and the process of transformation could at last begin to move. Any essential change of attitude signifies a psychic renewal which is usually accompanied by symbols of rebirth in the patient's dreams and fantasies. The scarab is a classic example of a rebirth symbol.

(Jung 1969a: 31, 438–39)

Since natural laws are (relative) statistical truths, valid only at macrophysical **scales**, the Newtonian notion of causality does not necessarily exclude the possibility of other kinds of connection or relationships in time between events. (Indeed family systems therapists base their interventions on principles of mutually influencing, virtually simultaneous interactions.) However, Jung's notion of **synchronicity** postulates not only that there are meaningful connections between people which are not based on nineteenth-century ideas of causality but **also** that there are meaningful connections between people and events other than systemic human relationships. Rank writes that

There is no longer a fixed position for the observer – that is consciousness – but only the moment-to-moment dynamic relation of the twosome [or more]. This replaces 'historical' with 'immediate' causality, which in the strict sense of the word is causality no more.

(Rank 1989: 113)

So when double meanings, depth significances, correlative events or unusually creative and unusual correspondences emerge in life and in psychotherapy, Jung (and Redfeld's 1994 *The Celestine Prophesies*) advises us to pay special attention to them. So when a man asks the therapist: 'What shall I do?' and a book called *Feel the Fear and Do It Anyway*

(Jeffers 1987) suddenly and unexpectedly falls out of the bookcase, I guess it's as much 'grist for the mill' as anything else.

There's no need illogically to conflate epistemological domains by 'believing' in synchronicity as a **level** five 'fact' for us to notice and use such symbolically rich phenomena meaningfully.

At the nominative **level** three there is also an illuminating linguistic coincidence. Koestler observes: 'It is incidentally, a fascinating example of synchronicity that both physicists and para-psychologists should use the term *psi* to indicate what is still unknown; a curious verbal flash that may serve to indicate common ground between the two disciplines' (1972: 142).

From quantum physics comes an unexpected support for acausal connections, i.e. Bell's theorem of non-locality:

> Bell's theorem proposes that certain predictions made by quantum mechanics are *impossible* in any terms previously understood by physics. If these quantum predictions are *true* we must use whole new categories of thinking about physical events to understand them. It is not good enough to 'fix up' or readjust classical physics [or old paradigm psychotherapy] . . . Classical physics holds that any relationship existing between two or more particles must be mediated by a local force – attraction, repulsion, or at least some signal. Quantum mechanics predicts that two particles can be correlated instantaneously in the *absence* of any such force or signal, that somehow certain particles' properties can be linked nonlocally across space and time.
>
> (Marshall and Zohar 1997: 64–65)

Group / family or cultural experiences of ritual

> Freud's gradual move away from abreactive ritual of a cathartic kind towards associative methods of self-consciousness is entirely consonant with his desire to produce a professional, *scientific* psychology. This is because science, particularly in the late nineteenth century, was deeply hostile to ritual. It even saw itself, on occasion, as self-consciously improving upon those areas of the social which, once governed by 'irrational' rituals, could now be brought under scientific control.
>
> (Stallybrass and White 1993: 286)

Yet people from Malidoma Some (1996) to Bly (1990) to Bani Shorter (1996) now deplore the psychological and spiritual impoverishment which the neglect of ritual has brought to those of us under the ideological influence of Enlightenment scienticism.

> What would happen if ritual died? . . . Singers forget their songs. Storytellers no longer remember their tales. We act out the myths that are telling our lives. Models replace mysteries. Answers take the place of questions. Eventually we lose the thread of significance and are left wandering in a labyrinth of meaning-

lessness . . . [But] ritual does not die though it can be neglected, trivialized, misused and to some extent ignored. Yet, if desacralized and cut off from psychic awareness, its motive force, the image [or experience] of the Holy reverts to unconsciousness, while existing observances become repetitious and sterile.

(Shorter 1996: 117)

What is ritual? An invocation of the transpersonal by synergetic group participation

In my view there are some traumata which are intrinsically community-based and for which one-to-one individual psychotherapy is often inadequate. Sometimes the healing can **only** take place in the context where the injury was sustained – through group or community participation. Sexual, ritualistic or physical abuses by a family group, school or religious community, peer-groups, workplace bullying, being publicly shamed, the experience of being scapegoated, violation of the natural rites of passage (such as first menstruation, getting married, death of a human companion animal), public torture and wartime rape are some such instances.

Because of so many requests to give examples of the use of ritual in psychotherapeutic practice, here follow three rituals (purifying; grief; celebration and protection) which I have facilitated as a group psychotherapist. I do it rarely and only when the time, intuitively and clinically, is ripe. This is in order to illustrate, not 'the right way', but some ways. Since my limited powers of expression cannot possibly do justice to the atmosphere, the group climate, the background knowledge of the person and circumstances, I trust the reader to use their imagination constructively. Ritual is a very powerful form of intervention and should always be done with conscientiousness and reverence. So, firstly some general guidelines.

Principles for the facilitation of ritual in the healing rites of psychotherapy

1. An explicit and sound **working alliance** contract with everyone involved is essential. Only those who want to, participate. No therapist should do it without having had personal experience of the healing power of ritual or who feels in any way uncomfortable with any aspect of such a process.
2. Be aware of possible **transference distortions** or cultural biases which might make the ritual, the words, the objects or the atmosphere distasteful to some participants; or of participants who are not ready or willing to voice their desire to be absent; or participants who may be at risk of distorting potentially **reparative** experiences afterwards – for whatever reasons.

3. Prepare. People should have **time** (10 minutes or many weeks as appropriate) seriously to consider the implications of the ritual for themselves and others so that they can shape and influence or avoid it if they wish. A dedicated **space** should be prepared with both planned elements (taking into account the nature of the requested ritual) as well as space for spontaneity and serendipity

4. Ritual for me is about **concretizing the transpersonal**. Honouring the hidden magic in the everyday – the healing and transformative creative physis in everything (or in Heidegger's words: 'Bringing Being to stand'). Many rituals are conducted with the simplest real or symbolic representations of the four (or five) elements on a low table: fire, water, earth, air (and wood for the Chinese). For example, candles or sparklers; a bowl of water or in the rain; flowers or stones; feathers or incense (and a specially chosen wooden object).

5. A well-performed reparative ritual is **inclusive**. Everybody involved, no matter their age or ability, needs a role or function whether it is to read a poem, light or blow out the candle, play the Tibetan bowl or drums, carry the tray of flowers, actively witness the event or guard the boundary of the **temenos**. A lovely year-ending ritual designed and conducted by one of the members of my training groups, after some impromptu dancing, involved a division of the group into 'chorus' (those participants who were willing to sing) and 'percussion' (those participants who were willing to follow her lead in clashing pot lids, shaking a jar of small change, or just tapping their feet on the ground).

6. **Intentionality**. The intention – the reparative effect – needs to be specified so that all participants understand enough about its objective to **feel** that they can personally energize the intention on behalf of the community or for the individual who has requested the ritual. In an all-Jewish community, some Christian rituals (or words) might be inappropriate, in a multicultural group, universal themes and ordinary words can usually get us there. Alternatively each member can speak in their own language their culture's prayer of thanks before eating food (or going to sleep). I find this extremely beautiful and moving, particularly if I understand nothing of the words. This is because then the sounds and the intentions of a whole world can be felt and imaged more intensely at physical and spiritual as well as all the other **levels**.

7. **Narrative and/or symbolic congruence** is essential. Some people find very elaborate serious and formal rituals 'precious'; others appreciate it. Other people, like myself, often (depending on the circumstances) prefer that a certain kind of lightheartedness, informality and humour also be accessible – if not positively welcomed. (Joy is such a repressed emotion in this culture.)

8. The **facilitator's role** is similar to that of the conductor of an orchestra. He or she is at minimum responsible for the beginning, the tempo, the volume and the appropriate closure or ending of the parts and the whole.

9. The **protagonist** (if it is done for one or more individuals of the group) is responsible for specifying their intentions for the ritual, requesting or refusing certain elements (or roles), and making the very best use of it in their future lives.

10. Finally it is important, despite the best preparation and planning, to **remain open** to sudden inspirations, intuitions and serendipity – including spontaneous improvisation or even the proper abandonment of the work if appropriate. The true skill of the ritual facilitator lies in the blending of personal and professional responsibility with a transpersonal availability for allowing the numinous mysterious to emerge.

Three examples of rituals from psychotherapy practice

The woman whose father died in a far-away land

Benita was an asylum seeker, having fled from her war-torn country of birth. When the news came of her beloved father's death so very far away, she was distraught at the thought that she would not be able to go to tend his body or even attend his funeral. It was neither safe nor legal for her to do so. Fortunately she, as a result of her therapeutic work in the group, had (perhaps) re-established almost regular contact with him by sending cards, letters and gifts which may or may not have reached him. We had decided that it was better to do this, whether or not he received them, than **not** to demonstrate her love for him in such ways.

Bereft of her friends' and family's support, living in fear of having her asylum request refused, emotionally confused, feeling guilty for having escaped soldier-rape like her mother and sister, she felt quite unable to channel her grief in any way. (She was 'not religious'.) Here was a human being desperately crying out for symbolic community. Although we, of course, could not substitute for her real kith and kin, the group could provide a container of a kind for her experience of such a loss. We could publicly witness this event and somehow dignify her father's death by participating with our consciously shared experiential acknowledgement.

She passed around a photograph of her father. Then she vividly imagined her father with us in the group room. Then she introduced each of us in turn to him, telling us details of his early childhood, his individual characteristics and food preferences. She explained to him how important we had become to her and asked his permission to include us in the ceremony. By now we knew his name as well as the clumsy loving way he used to stroke her long black hair with his huge knobbled hands during his rare, but genuine, moments of tenderness. We could virtually feel the human beingness of him present with us, yet so many many miles away.

In 1897, Freud had already stated his 'insight that there are no indications of reality in the unconsciousness, so that one cannot distinguish between truth and fiction that has been cathected with affect' (Masson 1985: 264). So, by the use of what Jung called 'active imagination' (see Angelo 1992), or what Perls (1969a) would call the 'empty chair technique', she opened her heart to her beloved dead father, telling him her rage, her fears, her regrets, her guilt, her memories, her longing, her sadness and her love for him. I encouraged her to speak in her own language which he would understand better. It made no difference. By now many of us were weeping too.

Then she lit a candle. We all followed her out of the house to the river. Each one of us laid flowers and feathers on the water, remembering our own fathers (dead or alive), lamenting for all children separated from their parents and their homeland, but particularly honouring the life of this man, Benita's father, whom we only knew through her shared experience. A poem was read. Several people made their own silent vows of reconciliation before circumstance or death would rob them of the opportunity to say their love and gratitude to living parents.

The fragility of life shimmered in and through us like an English summer's breeze in honouring this one particular death. Benita said goodbye to him. Finally the flaming candle floated downstream while we kept silence until the experiential cycle felt completed in a serene peacefulness.

The Hindu man who bought a new car

Arjuna was the youngest son of a very large and ancient family who had never felt that he 'deserved' the good things of life. His sister was the first female child to be allowed to live in two thousand years. Until his generation, all female children of this ancient family had been killed at birth to prevent them marrying 'out' and perhaps undermining the family's power or possessions. Arjuna had distanced himself from them and come to make a new life on his own terms in Britain, but here had somehow always stopped himself from achieving or enjoying material success.

During his years in therapy he had made substantial progress towards his goals. Despite a physical disability, his self-acceptance was solid under most circumstances. He had brought his temper under control and he had re-connected with a spiritual meditation tradition which was meaningful to him. He had also experimented with being honest in his relationships with different women and he now felt ready at all **levels** for an intimate long-lasting relationship which could lead to marriage and children. But the money issue was the last one to go.

So of course we had been emotionally involved with him for some time in the planned purchase of the shiny brand-new powerful car. He drove it for the first time to come to the group. This act brought him in touch with a deep fear that if he was successful in his own terms, he would also have to die. The new car was a symbol of problems overcome, but it was somewhat spoiled by the fear of being punished for it. Then he told us that 'back home' in his culture the family and community would always ritually 'bless' the acquisition of a new house or a new sculpture or a new vehicle. This would serve both as protection and for celebration. We were now all the family he really had – would we please do this blessing for him?

So we gathered up uncooked rice and sandalwood incense, tinkling Indian bells and pink rose petals from the garden and we all went out to bless the car – which was parked across the street. We had to walk round the shiny new car three times while asking for protection and blessing it as a symbol of the fact that, due to his own efforts, he had the capacity to make his dreams come true. I made sure to place an illustrated copy of the Kama Sutra in the car's cubby hole. It was serious **and** it was fun. Several jokes must have been told, because I can remember the sound of our laughter. Afterwards a woman who had been watching us from the other side of the street came up to me and spontaneously kissed me. She said: 'I have never seen anything so beautiful.'

The nun who had been sexually abused

There was a compliant, obedient and submissive nun who had been sexually abused as a child and then later sexually and ritually abused by a priest. As a result of being in therapy, she wanted to break off this relationship, but he threatened to curse her with eternal damnation. Eventually she was placed in a convent out of his reach. However, now she was suffering nightmares, flashbacks and self-abusing by cutting her breasts and genitals with a Stanley knife. She found she could no longer take comfort and guidance from her prayers. This was the worst.

She said that through what she only now understood were his vile actions, he 'had stolen my prayers'. Furthermore the sight of the cross (which he had used in unmentionable ways) was now physically repulsive to her. She desperately longed for re-union with her experience of God, but she could not use any of the usual ways to connect with her tradition. This wicked priest had defiled all the holy symbols for her by using them sexually in the way that he had done with her. At the moment, she trusted us more than the church. However, she wanted to find her way back. If only, somehow, she could feel cleansed.

It's important to say that the ritual we eventually enacted (during a five-day intensive workshop) was preceded and followed by individual and group psychotherapy from a highly qualified and sympathetic practitioner experienced in such cases supported by consultation with another (decent) Catholic priest.

Suffice it to say that her community of friends received her confession, respectfully heard her shame, helped her to sort her responsibility from his, denounced the abuse of power she had experienced, lovingly confronted her. Upon her request, the community forgave her in a way which she could accept, while still holding him responsible and accountable for his misdeeds. During the course of her therapy she had begun to conceive of protecting herself, but there was still work for her to be done to prevent this man doing similar things to other vulnerable people. Finally she felt she needed to forgive God himself for letting this happen to her. And she did.

Our jointly designed ritual involved her reliving and catharting her suppressed emotions during the incidents and physically experiencing the 'dirt'. This was followed by us washing her gently in clean spring water. We also used perfumed oils, such as Juniper, known for their purifying properties. After the old clothes were communally burnt and the ashes stamped into the earth outside, we clothed her in a clean white linen robe. We had heard all, understood all, and forgave her all. She had wanted this from us. Now she was free to start once more.

Recently I attended a Catholic church service where she sang solo the Lord's Prayer in her exquisitely pure soprano voice. It was vibrantly alive with exultation, devotion and sensuality. Yes, she can pray again. When I heard it, I was moved to tears.

Cooperation of other creatures

I usually work with my small well-trained Shih Tzu dog, Donna, in my consulting room – unless clients or supervisees prefer her not to be there. She usually lies quietly by my side on the couch where I sit. However, there have been several times when she unexpectedly acted overtly as assistant therapist.

On one occasion a man in supervision was telling us, rather unemotionally, how his daughter had been 'glassed' in a pub incident. (This means that someone broke a beer bottle and cut her face up with its jagged edges.) This was supervision, not therapy. But before I had a moment to think, Donna virtually flew across the room (some five or six feet) to sit next to him as if she immediately responded to his pain and wanted to extend her creaturely comfort to him. This is what I call instantaneous visceral empathy.

On another occasion a younger man had reached the apotheosis of his childhood anger at his father who had viciously abused him, his siblings and his mother all during his growing-up years. Physically he was racked with a rage that he had never before allowed himself to experience. He knew that he could use a large cushion to vent his most vicious and abusive feelings towards the father of his childhood and could say to this symbolic representation of his father whatever he wanted to without censoring it himself or experiencing judgement from me. (This was after some years of therapy focused on fear and then grief.)

In any event, after some twenty minutes full-bodied catharsis of what felt like murderous rage, he was finished. It seemed to last an eternity. At one point I wondered what the neighbours would make of the noise and the swearwords, but I didn't care. Not only had he expressed his rage towards his father, he had also experienced the internalized abusive father in himself against which he had always defended himself by excessive niceness – a potentially dangerous combination in any personality. In the silence that followed, with his head buried in the pillow, he wept again: 'Now that I have been that angry, nobody will ever love me again.'

He did not pick up his head until Donna (who had witnessed the whole outburst very quietly) had licked all the tears off his cheeks. When he eventually got up, he was shining and there was nothing left to say.

Creativity in the therapeutic process

According to the Oxford English dictionary, **to create** means '**to bring into being**'.

Before the word 'being' (Eigen's 'am-ing') I feel like the Rabbi who, when he wanted to pray aloud, couldn't bring any words out. He stuttered on the first syllable. The very idea of addressing the Divine virtually paralysed his tongue. And indeed in Judaism, the true name of God is never uttered.

So what can be said?

The notion that psychotherapists are artists of a kind seems to me to be *hubris*. If anything like art, it is an emergent **mutual** co-creation – more like a dance – between the people involved and creative Being itself. (If, for the sake of sense, we accept that at some **levels** there is a difference.) Most great artists know that their creations do not come into being from themselves – but by grace from another source.

This is also my experience of the healing process in psychotherapy. Amazement. Wonder. Awe. Wow! 'How did that happen?' Then I take refuge in Jung's admonition: 'Learn your theories as well you can, but put them aside when you touch the miracle of the living soul' (1928: 361).

There are essentially two major stories about creativity in psychotherapy.

One, directly from Freud, postulates that **creativity is the result of sublimation** (a psychological defence mechanism) against sexual and aggressive drives. So, therefore Leonardo da Vinci was preoccupied with water because he was enuretic as a child. What a pity all enuretics don't become Leonardos! (Many other researchers, for example, Goertzel in his 1965 book, *Cradles of Eminence*, discussing among others Edison, Roosevelt and Einstein, have demonstrated the lack of evidence for predictability between childhood experiences and later achievements.)

The other story about creativity in psychotherapy is that it is the **basic universal energetic drive** which may or may not be used in the enactment or transformation of sexual and aggressive drives. Thus, Physis is considered largely independent as well as **prior** to and **more basic** than Eros and Thanatos. (Just pay attention to how a wound on your body heals.) This story postulates, in contradistinction to the other one, that it is exactly 'the generalized creative urge' which can transform and create meaning from our experiences of life, love and death – and healing. Notice, among all the other treasures, how Koestler uses the word '**level**' in the following apposite quotation from his work:

> The forces through which the basic polarity manifests itself vary on each **level**, but there is nevertheless the same pattern running through the whole gamut. The two faces of Janus: one, that of a proud, self-asserting whole, the other of a humble integrated part, yield a serviceable pair of symbols. It certainly has a wider range of applicability than Freud's pair of Ultimates – Eros and Thanatos. The sex-drive appears in our view as only one among many other integrative forces in both animal and human societies; while aggression and destructiveness appear, not as primary instincts, but pathological flare-ups of the self-assertive tendencies under conditions of abnormal stress. Both Eros and Thanatos appear only relatively late on the stage of evolution: creatures that multiply by fission or budding are ignorant of sex and death. [But not of natural creativity.] The great duet in Freud's metapsychology does not constitute the whole opera.

(Koestler 1972: 114)

Often we simply look at the Janus face in sculptures or other reproductions as an illustration of the double-ness of experience and of life. Polarities gazing in opposite directions. It frequently is as if we relate to the image or the experience or the idea or the myth as if its concretization into a work of art is not a miracle of transformation of 'base' material into spiritual gold.

Too rarely we ask the question: What force **created** it? The experience, the emotion, the image-making, the imagination which transformed this human experience into the idea, the work of art – that is the poiesis of physis. It's like the notion that fish won't recognize water as their element because they live in it and take it for granted. In a similar way we live in and through physis, often not noticing the energy of **transformative process itself.**

Table 3.1 Characteristics of Thanatos, Eros and Physis

Thanatos	Eros	Physis
Death	Survival	Life
Death instinct	Sexual instinct	Life instinct
Destruction	Procreation	Creation/creativity
Destruction/destructuring	Preservation	Transformation
Mortido	Libido (inwardly directed)	Libido (outwardly directed)
Seeks freedom from striving	Seeks pleasure/ gratification	Seeks fulfilment/ realization
Ending	Beginning	Evolving
Expiration	Inspiration	Aspiration

Appreciation to Phil Lapworth for his contribution.

Rank writes:

> To put it more precisely, I see the creator-impulse as the life impulse made to serve the individual will. When psycho-analysis speaks of a sublimated sexual impulse in creative art, meaning thereby the impulse diverted from its purely biological function and directed towards higher ends, the question as to what diverted and what directed is just being dismissed with an allusion to repression. But repression is a negative factor, which might divert, but never direct . . . This leads us to the profoundest source of the artistic impulse to create, which I can only satisfactorily explain to myself as the struggle of the individual against an inherent striving after totality, which forces him [or her] equally in the direction of a complete surrender to life and a complete giving of himself [or herself] in production.
>
> (Rank 1989: 40, 60)

Winnicott stated that creativity 'is the retention throughout life of something that belongs properly to infant experience: the ability to create the world' (1986: 40) – just like the Aborigines. The ideological notion of superiority (**level** 4) in the first story imported by nominations (3) like 'higher'. In Eurocentric cultures 'higher' is of course considered better than 'lower'.

Despite the fact that Heraclitus taught that 'Lifetime is a child at play', and Jesus said 'Unless ye become as little children', *lower* carries many derogatory connotations such as 'immature', 'undeveloped' and 'down below'. (According to Irigaray one of the many meanings of physis is the genitals.)

> The fact that art and discovery draw on unconscious sources indicates that one aspect of all creative activity is a regression to ontogenetically or phylogenetically earlier **levels**, an escape from the restraints of the conscious mind, **with the subsequent release of creative potentials** – a process paralleled on lower **levels** by the liberation from restraint of genetic potentials or neural equi-poten-tiality in the regeneration of structures and functions.
>
> (Koestler 1989: 462; my emphasis)

Even when Ogden (1994) believes that the analytic couple must attempt to understand the experience of their individual subjective realities interacting with the intersubjective realities that they create together and that this reciprocal tension is the motor of the psychoanalytic process, he resorts to an analogy with an automobile, not with the natural unfolding of a fern leaf. (I suppose this is why **some** transactional analysts call themselves ego-mechanics!)

Yet in 1986 already, the president of the International Union of Theoretical and Applied Mechanics, Sir John Lighthill, wrote in the *Proceedings of the Royal Society*:

> We are all deeply conscious today that the enthusiasm of our forebears for the marvellous achievement of Newtonian mechanics led them to make generaliza-tions in the area of predictability that . . . we now recognize are false. We collec-tively want to apologize . . . for spreading ideas about determinism that after 1960 were proven to be incorrect.
>
> (in Prigogine 1995: 7)

The Nobel prize-winner Ilya Prirogine who quotes this adds as a conclusion:

> The future is uncertain; this is true for the nature we describe and this is true on the **level** of our own existence. But this uncertainty is at the very heart of human creativity. Time becomes 'construction' and creativity a way to participate in this construction.
>
> (Prigogine 1995: 7)

What does this mean in counselling and psychotherapy practice?

In psychotherapy we are dealing with a mysterious process to do with the creative life force in which we live and breathe and have our being. Although facts and figures, theories and previous experience can take us close to it, we do not yet (despite all the volumes written on creativity) really understand it. If the work of psychotherapy is restoring **vitality** (or enlivenment) to the person's inherent self-healing capacities, analogies with cars and outdated physics are not particularly helpful. Perhaps the most we can do is prepare ourselves and the space as best we can for the auto-poietic emergence (self-creating manifestation) of healing in the context of the therapeutic relationship. This **whole** book is an attempt to help.

> I began to write when I realized all I had to do was speculate, question, argue, create a model, take a position, define a problem, make an observation, propose a solution, illuminate a possibility to participate in a (continuous) written conversation with my peers . . . not to deliver the Truth.
>
> (Murray 1986: 147)

So I take the position that whatever **medium** we use – words or silence; dance or drama; clay or sand trays; active imagination or role play; guided visualization or tapping meridian points; Shakespearian quotations or dream interpretations; poetry or drawing; intensive breathing or shouting at cushions; explanations about 'the family romance' or wanting to devour milky breasts; images of art or metaphors drawn from nature; myths or mysteries; diagrams about snags and pitfalls or depriving patients of privileges; persuasion or 'empowerment'; progressive relaxation or touching spiders; solitary journal keeping or forceful group confrontation; listing self-critical thoughts or learning self-soothing; prescribing books or insisting on abstinence; DSM diagnoses or philosophy; astrology or biorhythms; conflict resolution or sensory sensitization exercises; encouraging 'solutions' or writing letters giving paradoxical instructions to family members; disciplined meditation or hugging trees, drums or 'chickensoup' – **we are the servants of physis**.

> **About the Sun** (a poem a client gave me)
> This is what I think.
> That one day I shall be whole.
> Not a shadow, nor an excuse, nor a victim of others' grief.
> Their loss has been my pain, because they didn't see how much I cared.
> (Perhaps I didn't show it, or didn't even know it.)
> Now, I glimpse a new way through, Where feeling doesn't mean pain,
> Because it's not my fault.

I shall care; for them too: but most of all for Life and me.
For I am good, and will tread the sunny path I choose.
I will lead, and they can follow,
But they must show they know I care also,
About being whole and me.
And about the sun.

Body/mind phenomena of client and/or therapist

The physical phenomena of a client or therapist and changes in their states of consciousness can also be strong signals of the presence of the transpersonal in the consulting room. Since our bodies are the seat of life, it is important to pay attention to the sense of liveliness of your own body and the vitality of your client as an **ongoing process** throughout every session. Field enquired of his colleagues about such phenomena:

> Quite a few therapists admitted suffering from overwhelming sleepiness, fewer to sexual arousal. There were others who admitted that with certain patients they would have inexplicable surges of physical hunger, stabbing pains in the body, tears, a sudden sensitivity to noises in the street; sometimes even the ticking of the clock became deafening. It was a relief not to feel too abnormal. In time I became increasingly convinced that these somatic innervations were a way of picking up messages from the patient's unconscious. [And body?]
>
> (Field 1996: 38)

Absence of enlivenment in either (or all) means that nothing is happening. This has of course little to do with whether you're talking or not. It has everything to do with breathing. Silences, still generally underused, can be peacefully pregnant with the vital *élan* or dull, boring and uncreative. **Enlivenment** is an **embodied** sense of potentiality where one's life energy is open to all healing and growthful possibilities – ready to act according to 'plan' or ready to surrender to a sudden 'blinding' intuitive inspiration.

In this respect it is vital to distinguish the transpersonal mode of the therapeutic relationship from the **working alliance** going wrong (e.g. female client feels they can't tell you about their childhood sexual abuse by a priest, because you're one); **transference and/or countertransference distortions** of the working alliance (e.g. client is fearing that you also won't believe their story – the way their mother didn't); **reparative or developmentally needed** (information about retreats) and **dialogic dimensions** of personhood (e.g. behaving aggressively in a passive way, or 'sulking' because you were late last time).

Extreme care (and expert supervision) needs to be taken not to confuse these other modes of the therapeutic relationship with the transpersonal mode. (Otherwise it's best ignored. As one of my students said: 'The Divine wouldn't be bothered.') Wishful thinking, grandiose ideas, religiosity, projective identification (or hypnotic trance), collusion, over-identification, proselytizing, envy or skewed admiration on the part of the therapist are only a few of the things that can go wrong and be positively dangerous.

Self-knowledge and self-awareness are essential to minimize counter-transferential distortions or damaging biases (working with countertrans-ference is the subject of a specific chapter in Clarkson 2000c). It is not essential to have any particular religious or spiritual practice yourself – but you will need to find a way to respond to such questions if asked. 'Neutrality' about a dimension that is this important in people's lives is on a par with neutrality about homophobia, misogyny and racism: support for the oppressor.

As a rough guide, if the therapist is by 'first nature' or temperament rather impulsive, it's probably wise only very rarely to act often on urges to share 'images', sudden inspirations or to provide 'intuitively' guided gut-feeling responses. If the therapist wants to develop in this direction and is by 'first nature' inclined to withhold or censor such ideas away, it is probably beneficial, with competent guidance, to risk slightly more.

As always, the rigorous attitude of an enquiring scientific observer aware of his or her situatedness and cultural perspective (*Clarkson 1995c*: 293–94) is recommended. **There are levels at which causality operates and it is logically proper to use these for those purposes**. If something works and there is evidence of increased lively creativity after an interven-tion, do it again; if something doesn't work with a client, try something else. All of us can learn – and need to calibrate again and again – how to manage ourselves in such unexplored waters. And any reputable scientist knows that there is more about the world that we don't know than we know.

Having made some of the most important warnings, I can now say that it's not that difficult to identify the transpersonal dimension in the therapeutic relationship. Firstly, if it feels like you, it's not the transpersonal. If you can explain it, it's also not. If you feel proud of it, it's not.

Secondly, if it feels pure, clean, both clinically right and simulta-neously very different from anything you've done before, it probably is. If you feel the inspiration coming through you instead of from you, it probably is. If you experience a sense of timelessness – as if a minute lasted an hour – it probably is. If you yourself are healthy, well-loved and resourceful, it probably can be.

'By their fruits ye shall know them.' What follows such genuine moments of inspiration, intuition, silence, experiment or laughter in psychotherapy is gratitude, wonder, joy, serenity, increased resourcefulness, peaceful tiredness or enhanced energy, more respect for all living things, a more pervasive empathy, a decrease or disappearance of bitterness or resentment, an intensified physicality, a temporary (it's never permanent) alignment of all seven **levels** of experience like a perfectly tuned chord, a deeper appreciation of the moral complexities of life and our responsibilities to ourselves, others and the world as well as an ease-full congruent determination to have (and give) life and have (and give) it more abundantly. (For what has been called THE most important award-winning Zen book of the last decade of the twentieth century on consciousness, neurology and mystical states, see Austin 1999.)

Dreams

What are dreams?

Psychology does not quite understand dreams. We know from research that everybody shows several periods of REM (rapid eye-movement) during their sleep and that on awakening some people can recall some of their dreams. So, dreams are **experienced** as a series of pictures with concomitant psychophysiological events in the mind of a sleeping person.

Since the dawn of history people have tried to make sense or meaning from their dreams. Many stories are told in the Bible of how dreams were interpreted by people such as Joseph in order to understand current events and in particular to foretell the future. Nowadays it is a controversial point whether prophetic dreams exist.

In the olden days and in the folklore of different cultures, there have been specific meanings attached to certain dream images or ideas. Rather like teacup fortune-telling books of symbols and meanings, there are dictionaries of 'the meaning of dreams' which will say, for example, that dreaming of a wedding signifies some happy event. These dictionaries are available from most self-help or divination shelves in bookshops. But even such dictionaries will usually say that other aspects of the dream and the dreamer's life situation and life history should be taken into account in trying to understand the meaning of the dream for the particular person.

Most people however do recall some of their dreams some of the time. Recurrent dreams or themes are not unusual. Different approaches to psychology, psychotherapy or psychoanalysis have different ways of working with dreams. Freud (1900), for example, suggested that dreams are either about anxieties or about wish-fulfilment. Jung thought dreams brought us existential messages from the unconscious to help us develop as full human beings. Perls (1969a) thought that all the people, objects or places in a dream represent parts of the dreamer himself.

Professional psychologists or analysts would not interpret the dreams of people they don't know or with whom they don't have a contractual professional relationship. However, we can all refer to commonly occurring meanings, such as a snake being a symbol of sexuality or a circle being a symbol of wholeness or healing. Generalized meanings of this kind are often wrong or useless for an individual person, but may give them something to disagree with or think about.

To truly learn to use one's own dreams is usually fun and healthy, but professional psychotherapists who are skilled and experienced in dreamwork can also help. Given their numinous quality it's hard to see how one could work with dreams in the psychotherapy relationship without an appreciation of the transpersonal dimension. In addition to the multitude of other works on the subject, I would also refer the reader to Haslam (2000) for a useful guide to working with dreams.

Although dreams have been written about in almost every major psycholanguage (and then some), generally there are two major ways of using dreams therapeutically – **individualistic** and **collective** approaches.

Under the individualistic approaches dreams can be understood in five main ways. Firstly, they can be seen as biological or neurological mechanisms of the brain to 'work through', so to speak, affective or emotional leftovers of the day's experiences – the so-called day-residue. Secondly, there are creative or problem-solving dreams. Many famous examples concern a scientist who went to bed with a pressing creative problem and then dreamed the answer to their creative problem. Many people use this as a regular problem-solving technique. Thirdly, there are also those kinds of dream which are understood as more of a symbolic enactment of the individual's psychological concerns. Freud's (1900) *The Interpretation of Dreams* is an exemplar and beautifully written work in this genre. Fourthly, some dreams are understood to have a cathartic purpose – if someone dreams, for example, of killing a friend with whom they are angry, the dreamer often feels released and relieved of the emotional pressure, more informed and better able to cope with the perhaps problematic real-life situation. Finally, it is hard to deny that some people do have prescient dreams, meaning that they dream of events before they actually happen. There are of course several competing explanations for this phenomenon, but none have been proved conclusively.

Collective or relational approaches to dreaming include, firstly, **coupled dreams** (between lovers, spouses, friends or therapist and client), and secondly, **social dreaming** (as in the social dreaming groups originated by Gordon Lawrence), where the dreams are understood to be all relating to each other and illuminating something about the group or the human condition. Finally there are ways of understanding dreams which imply that **the world (Life) is dreaming us**. From this perspective all dreams are understood to be the world (or physis) dreaming through the individual(s). For example, during the time we, as inhabitants of this planet, were facing the immediate threat of nuclear war, many people engaged with this theme in their dreams – as if we were collectively trying to solve our common world problem.

Lucid dreaming involves dreaming while semi-awake. It is said (whether true or not) that the Senoi people do 'dream-sharing' in the community every morning. Their children are taught to intervene consciously in their own dreams so as to understand themselves and life better. So for example, if a terrible monster is chasing a person in their dream, the dreamer stops running away (or goes back into the same dream later) asking the monster his or her name, requesting to see their face (or naked body) and often asking for a gift from the previously frightening spectre. In this way, people are encouraged to 'face their shadow' and consciously incorporate all the creative resources at their disposal for development, healing and transformation. Whether or not it is 'true' factually, it is in practice a useful and creative way of working experientially with dreams in a community.

Von Franz writes that Jung 'hated it when pupils were too literal minded and clung to his concepts . . . [and once exclaimed]: "This is all nonsense! The shadow is simply the whole unconscious"' (von Franz 1995: 3). The shadow is that which is not in the light. It may be evil, it may be beautiful. It is always a creative manifestation of physis.

Finally, I learned from Hella Adler that when people don't remember their dreams, it is often equally valuable to tell a part of their ordinary day **as if** it were a dream and to work with it just as if it were in fact a 'real' dream.

Spontaneous silent or intentional spoken prayer

> One of the people at the Windsor Castle Consultation [on Mental Health, Spirituality and Religion in December, 1998] told a story. A person went to a sage and said he had smoked while praying – was that wrong? The sage admonished the person: 'Prayer is very important and should be treated with respect. You should not smoke a pipe while praying.' As the person turned away, the sage continued: 'On the other hand, it is good to pray while smoking a pipe.'
>
> (Tilley 1999: 3)

Almost everybody who faces a serious crisis or gets bad news, whether they believe in the divine or not, exclaims something like 'Oh God!' or 'Oh my God!'. Prayer can be vocal, spontaneous or learned, planned, individual, couple or communal. Some people go to church (or yoga or mosque or garden or Stonehenge or household altar) to pray or chant; some people experience their whole lives as a prayer.

For our purposes we can roughly distinguish five kinds of prayer:

Supplication (asking for something)
Intercessionary (asking on behalf of someone else)
Contemplation (concentrating on a devotional image or mantra)
Ceremonial prayer (as with Bar Mitzvahs, meal times or funerals)
Prayers of gratitude and praise (where there is only affirmation of the beauty and wonder of life notwithstanding the existence of pain and suffering)

Of course every individual can develop their very own versions of prayer. Kazantzakis, in his wonderful book of spiritual exercises, *The Saviors of God*, writes:

> My prayer is not the whimpering of a beggar nor a confession of love. Nor is it the trivial reckoning of a small tradesman: Give me and I shall give you.
> My prayer is the report of a soldier to his general: This is what I did today, this is how I fought to save the entire battle in my own sector, these are the obstacles I found, this is how I plan to fight tomorrow.
> (Kazantzakis 1960: 107)

Astonishing to me is the fact that so many people across the world keep praying in spite of many prayers not being answered. In my view, the appropriate conducting of prayers is best left to those who are theologically and professionally trained to do so. However, if a client should themselves express a wish to pray in a counselling or psychotherapy session, I would think it is both courteous and possibly helpful to respectfully explore their wish, and perhaps be silent and accepting while they do what they believe will be most beneficial for them.

For many people, their relationship with what they consider to be 'God' or 'the Buddha' or 'the ancestors' is as, if not **more** important than their relationships with their fathers, mothers or the therapist themselves. In such cases, the therapeutic task of empathic listening and facilitation is no different than dealing with any other important psychological relationship.

A person's five-dimensional relationship to the divine

A person's relationship with their image or idea of God usually also conforms to the archetypal fractal shape containing five aspects of relationship. A person may have a relationship with their God which is purely functional (the **working alliance**). God, its priests and church ceremonies are there to conduct baptisms, weddings and funerals if and when so contracted.

Until the advent of counselling and psychotherapy as professions, people used to turn to their local priests or gurus, spiritual communities and other ritual practices (such as the Islamic Ramadan and the Jewish Day of Atonement) for **reparative relationships** as well as to understand and **develop** themselves to become 'better' human beings.

> 'May the will of Allah be done,' a pious man was saying about something or other.
> 'It always is, in any case,' said Mulla Nasrudin.
> 'How can you prove that, Mulla?'
> 'Quite simply. If it wasn't always being done, then surely at some time or another *my* will would be done, wouldn't it?'
>
> (Shah 1985: 102)

Some spiritual or religious traditions also explicitly incorporate a direct and unmediated **person-to-person** dialogic relationship to God. Leonard Bernstein's magnificent *Kaddish*, dedicated to the late President Kennedy, is an extraordinarily powerful example.

It is my opinion, like that of Eigen, that the **transpersonal** dimension of a person's relationship with the Divine simply goes beyond words. Sometimes, it doesn't make sense to speak of a personal relationship any more although, as I showed in the analysis of the extract from an interview with him in Chapter 1, a personal relationship which can be articulated may **also** exist at the same time.

The transcendent wordless transpersonal is pure experience of oneness and awe where concepts end in a world which transcends our limited notions of what is 'good' and what is 'evil'. For example, according to the Jewish Hasidim, 'Evil too is good. It is the lowest rung of perfect goodness . . . all the worlds, the good and the evil are comprised in the Divine Presence' (Buber 1962: 90, 91). Jung quotes Dorn approvingly: 'There is nothing in nature that does not contain as much evil as good' (1967: 55).

Jung also reproduces a letter from a former patient which has remarkable resonances with the last letter from one of my former patients reproduced in Appendix 3:

> Out of evil, much good has come to me. By keeping quiet, repressing nothing, remaining attentive, and by accepting reality – taking things as they are, and not as I wanted them to be – by doing all this, unusual knowledge has come to me, and unusual powers as well, such as I could never have imagined before. I always thought that when we accepted things they overpowered us in some way or other. This turns out not to be true at all, and it is only by accepting them that

one can assume an attitude towards them. So now I intend to play the game of life, being receptive to whatever comes to me, good and bad, sun and shadow forever alternating, and, in this way, also accepting my own nature with its positive and negative sides, Thus everything becomes more alive to me. What a fool I was! How I tried to force everything to go according to the way I thought it ought to!

(Jung 1967: 47–48)

However, the aspect which the psychotherapist is most likely to come across as a problem in the consulting room is **transference distortion** of/toward the God which the person has internalized or introjected. However difficult, this is often quite appropriately the province of the therapist.

Marie grew up in a very strict orthodox religious home, going to a Calvinist church several times a week and internalizing a very judgemental punishing image of God. She felt that she was a 'worm in the face of God', an unworthy, sinful creature who deserved nothing but pain, misery and unending unrewarding hard work on earth. Anything else was 'selfish'. Indeed, from when she was 18 months old, her parents used to give her solemnly administered 'hidings' in order to 'beat the selfishness out of her'. Personal desires, or worse, **pleasure** of any kind whatsoever **was a sin** and a sign of her inherent evil nature.

No matter how 'purely' she lived her life or how much good she did for other people through unending guilty self-sacrifice, she could not even be sure of 'getting her eternal reward in heaven after going through this earthly vale of tears'. According to the doctrine of predestination God had already decided her final fate before she even died. The Scandinavian Calvinists in the film *Babette's Feast*, in their dourest moments, were having a bacchanalian orgy compared to her life.

It's a long story and impossible to tell. During her many years in psychotherapy it did involve her in many overt conversations with her projected experience of God – sometimes rage, sometimes tenderness. For her, she had to externalize and communicate with God as if he had also been a verbally, psychologically and spiritually abusive parent. Gradually she released the distortions.

This was not accomplished without considerable opposition from those still in her life who thought psychotherapy was 'un-Christian' and a sign of her rebellion against obedience to God's laws.

She had to (and chose to) rework apparently every single aspect of her experiential understanding of the nature of divinity, its place and function in her life (past, present and future). Eventually Marie found another spiritual narrative with a gentler God and she started living a more human(e) life.

Intuitions and prescience

A client told me that when working on an intensive care unit where staff had to move between two areas at the opposite ends of a very long corridor:

> I just had the feeling that I had to go over to the ward area to have a look, so I left the intensive care unit and went over to the ward – just in time to stop a nurse friend of mine from giving pre-medication to a child via the wrong route. She was going to give the pre-medication via a vein instead of giving an intramuscular injection.
>
> There was also a second checker, but none of them realized what they were doing. One can imagine the shock she had – on the verge of committing a drug error. In fact, what might be worse was that one would not know what effect the drug would have on the child who was not getting any ventilatory assistance . . . he might stop breathing . . . My friend was ever so grateful that I went over just in time to stop her perhaps killing the child.
>
> There was another occasion when I went and checked a baby's blood gas when the baby was so stable that it was not necessary to perform any blood gas measurement. I uncovered the blanket and found that the little leg was rather pale, sometimes the arterial annula could cause obstruction with the implication that if it was left unattended, the circulation to that limb would stop, i.e. you lose the limb. In no time flat I removed the arterial line and the baby's limb had returned to normal by the time our shift was over. I do things without knowing what caused me to make that move.
>
> I often wonder if there was a price I had to pay for telling people things before they actually happen . . . people from my culture believe that you are not supposed to tell others what only Heaven knows. It is in the other's fate and you're not supposed to alter anything. Well. I just could not resist from giving warning to others if I got any strange feelings. For another example, I asked one of the nurses if she was pregnant again and it also came out of my mouth that she was carrying twins. She was, but I diagnosed it without the information going through my rational left brain. Poor Lizzy was shocked when her doctor confirmed that she was indeed carrying twins.

Doing psychotherapy or supervision with people who are naturally gifted 'psychics' presents its own special difficulties and extensive discussion of this theme will have to wait for another publication. Suffice it to say here that many such individuals have reported to me that they cannot mention it in their training or supervision. In personal psychotherapy it is also often either devalued as a sign of some pathology or worse – the psychotherapist treats them with exaggerated deference – as if it isn't just a natural ability. And like most natural abilities, there are some people who are exceptionally gifted, but every person has more or less of it – and everyone can develop their natural abilities.

Dogs can hear frequencies of sound which humans can't. Some dogs can anticipate when a child is going to have an epileptic fit some 15 minutes before it happens and are trained to place the child safely in the recovery position until the fit is over. Many human companion animals appear to 'know' when their people are coming home – no matter how unpredictable this may be (Sheldrake 1988). We know that we see only a part of the colour spectrum. There are, for example, ultraviolet rays which we cannot perceive and yet 'man' has now 'proved' that they exist. Psychology has shown (e.g. the cocktail party phenomenon) that human beings are capable of concentrating on one aspect (such as a conversational partner's voice) in situations where that should be virtually impossible due to the surrounding din. We know that through desensitization soldiers, for example, appear to be able to ignore massive injuries during battle and not feel the pain or amputation of a limb until well after the event.

Koestler explains:

> Our main sense organs are like narrow slits which admit only a very narrow frequency range of electro-magnetic and sound waves. But even the amount that does get in through these narrow slits is too much. Life would be impossible if we were to pay attention to the millions of stimuli bombarding our senses – what William James called 'the blooming, buzzing multitude of sensations'. Thus the nervous system, and above all the brain, functions as a hierarchy of filtering and classifying devices which eliminate a large proportion of the sensory input as irrelevant 'noise', and process the relevant information into manageable shape before it is presented to consciousness. By analogy, a similar filtering mechanism might be assumed to protect us from the blooming, buzzing multitude of images, messages, impressions and confluential happenings in the 'psycho-magnetic field' surrounding us . . .
>
> It is a plausible guess that many of our everyday thoughts and emotions are telepathic or partly telepathic in origin . . . I have long felt that the conventional questions asked about telepathy ('Does it occur, and if so, how?') are less likely to be fruitful than the question: 'If telepathy occurs at all, what prevents it from occurring all the time?'
>
> (Koestler 1972: 131, 130, 132)

Other so-called paranormal phenomena

Freud tried to make explanations for 'the uncanny', but nonetheless psychotherapists still experience phenomena that are not (perhaps yet) fully explicable by either the positivistic sciences or by psychoanalytic theory.

One eminent analyst (who would not want her colleagues to know about it) told me the following:

A patient came to see me and, uncharacteristically, I felt very unsympathetic to her. She seemed hostile and devious and the session did not go well at all. I felt threatened in some way and unable to trust her in her relationship with me. She did not return for the next appointment, so I send her a bill. She declined to pay it. I send her a reminder. Eventually I received a cheque from her, but it was smeared with brown and red dirty substances.

After that I became very anxious, several of my patients started leaving without ending appropriately for less than appropriate reasons, I suffered nightmares and was generally losing weight. Then my husband had a dream in which he saw someone 'evil' having bound me in chains and preparing to torture me. He suggested that I consult a 'white witch' – something I had never even known existed before. I managed to trace one and she turned out to be a very pleasant very ordinary person whom I experienced as both sane and loving.

She explained to me that this phenomenon was psychologically based and that I needed to be 'grounded' again. I found I could accept her explanation and follow her instructions. She thought that I had at some **level** accepted this patient's negative intentions towards me, perhaps because I was not sufficiently prepared for such an occurrence. She conducted several rituals in my consulting room.

One ritual involved taking a very big Spanish onion, cutting it into four quarters and putting the quarters in each corner of the room so that they would symbolically 'extract' the undermining and destructive vibrations which had come into my practice. I did this as she had advised with relaxation and meditation to support the work. After three days, I felt the departure of the disturbing but indescribable elements in my room and in my practice and everything, including my health, returned to normal as my inner peace was restored.

The Cambridge philosopher, Charles Broad, wrote in the journal *Philosophy* that

> paranormal cognition and paranormal causation . . . may well be continually operating in the background of our normal lives. [For example] our understanding of, and our misunderstandings with, our fellow men; our general emotional mood on certain occasions; the ideas which suddenly arise in our minds without any obvious introspectable cause, our unaccountable immediate emotional reactions toward certain persons . . .
>
> (quoted in Koestler 1972: 129)

It's worth quoting at length here from Reed (1988), an esteemed psychologist who set out to 'debunk' supernatural experiences:

> Perhaps the crucial point is that it has become more and more apparent that all our commerce with the world is *constructive, interpretative and tentative*. At all **levels** of cognitive activity we seem to operate by setting up and testing

hypotheses, by problem-solving and by selecting strategies. As we have seen, this applies to attention, perception, imagery and memory as well as to the more conscious weighing of evidence involved in judgement and belief. Once this view is accepted, many of our 'anomalous' experiences suddenly seem much less sinister and inexplicable. For if cognitive processes are constructive, interpretative and problem-solving in nature, then there can be no question of objectively 'correct' or 'identical' perceptions and memories. It is no longer mystifying that our recollections of a place or a person may turn out to be sadly amiss. We need not invoke reincarnation to explain why we 'recognize' something we have not previously encountered. We need not rely upon spiritualism to explain why we occasionally 'see' somebody who is not there or 'hear' our name called when no living person has called it. Our cognitions are dynamic, and each of us is continually constructing his own models and arriving at decisions according to his experiential history and his personal schemata. It is to be expected that discrepancies will occur – both between and within individuals . . . The 'problem-solving' in cognitive activity is not like [intellectual puzzles which lead by the application of formal logic to one correct solution or at least to a finite number of alternative solutions]. The situation [in cognitive problem-solving] is open-ended, the data are seldom sufficient, the criteria are never absolute and there are no ultimate solutions. Most of these cognitive 'problems' are therefore insoluble in any formal sense. Their 'solutions' can only be tentative and relative to the working models we construct. Yet we engage in such 'problem-solving', often at various **levels** concurrently, throughout our waking lives. It is small wonder that our 'solutions' occasionally surprise us or others. What is surprising is that so much of our experience strikes us as being orderly and appropriate, and that our reports of it can be shared or at least [frequently] accepted by those around us.

(Reed 1988: 192–93)

Hands-on or distant healing

I don't know how many psychotherapists or counsellors will admit that they believe in spiritual healing, but many of our clients do. Furthermore an increasing number of hospitals employ healers. In many countries there will be something like the UK's National Federation of Spiritual Healers with a register, accreditation system and ethics code which can be a good resource.

I would recommend that psychotherapists generally **do not** do hands-on healing – unless there is a very explicit contract, special insurance, informed consent and they are specially qualified to do so, for example bio-energetic therapists or Reiki practitioners. This is especially true in touch-phobic cultural environments. Transference distortions in working with someone else's body are difficult to deal with and often cause more problems than they solve. In most cases the symbolic holding of the healing **relationship** is sufficient.

The narrative that I find useful is to admit that there is much we do not know, and that spiritual healing which involves concentrating healing life energy on behalf of yourself or someone else can generally do little harm and may be at least comforting, if not genuinely useful. However, **if** we accept that sometimes something like distance healing can be experienced by some people to occur, it is inevitable that distance damage can also be experienced. Anything that is a force for good (like food or love) can be used in abusive ways.

I say this because I have come across a number of people who sincerely feel and believe that they are being damaged at a distance – sometimes by previous gurus. Whether we call it delusional or not, this is their genuine subjective experience. When this is a presenting problem, most counsellors or psychotherapists should refer to a qualified senior practitioner with knowledge of the spiritual or cultural traditions involved and expertise in this area.

Extremely intense experiences (*jouissance*)

When I published the findings on my researches into transformational processes (in Clarkson 1989b), I identified five major ways in which fundamental beneficial and permanent changes occur in human lives – education, religious or political conversion, crisis, love and healing/ psychotherapy. In further identifying the major characteristics of such *metanoias*, **intensity** – whether of despair or bliss – emerged as a very important and apparently universal characteristic. (The others were: despair, surrender void experiences, relationship, community validation, sense of mission and the appearance of archetypal images of transformation in dreams and in art; Clarkson 1989b: 55–71.)

Bion came to the conclusion that 'Catastrophic change is an inevitable moment in all processes of evolution and growth' (Bion 1970: 31). Mahrer (1985), among several other psychotherapy outcome researchers, has also identified the importance of **intense experience** in order to facilitate profound change. What I think we are trying to describe is a whole seven-**level** experience of intensity – body, emotion, words, values, reason, story **as well as** some indescribable element all together in one moment. In Gestalt it is called 'final contact' (see Clarkson 1989a). So often clients (and ourselves) say (when some undesirable personal pattern is not changing) something like: 'I know it in my head, but not here – in my gut.' Such experienced body/mind splits may reflect the fact that the healing has not been fully integrated. Sometimes it's a stage in the process, sometimes people never get beyond it.

Perhaps this happens because many therapists, as well as their clients, believe that intense experiences are dangerous, manic, delusional, 'too much', devoid of reason, 'will end in tears before bedtime', and so forth. I tell clients who need it that: 'You can get as excited as you like, as long as you keep thinking', and 'Of course sadness will come after joy, but joy will then again come after sadness', and 'You'll be just as disappointed whether you let yourself feel your anticipatory excited hope for the desired event or not'.

Where therapeutic narratives carry moral imperatives (implicit commands or explicit modelling) of 'balance', equanimity, dis-passion-ateness, objectivity, neutrality, detachment (without detachment from detachment), the **exclusive** value of rationality, equilibrium, lack of toler-ance for/the prohibition of fully experiencing (without being labelled 'pathological') the up and down cycles of existence, it is as if they are trying to 'iron out the wrinkles of living'. As if life will let us get away with this for long!

> A monk said to Nasrudin: 'I am so detached that I never think of myself, only of others.'
> Nasrudin answered: 'I am so objective that I can look at myself as if I *were* another person; so I can afford to think of myself.'
>
> (Shah 1985: 54)

The best word I have found to use for such intensities of experience is the invented French term *jouissance* (Derrida 1992: 55–56). It is predictably very hard to define precisely. However, it indicates extremely intense experiences such as the height of pleasure at orgasm. It is like Jung's *coniunctio oppositorum* – the coexistence of opposites. It involves a momentary but complete loss of boundaries between self and other; a simultaneous dying and being born. In French orgasm is even called 'the little death' (*le petit mort*). 'It is the **yes** of re-affirmation, of promise, of oath, a **yes** to eternal recurrence . . . [remaining] unstable, subtle, sublime' (Derrida 1992: 287).

Megill (1987) writes that workers such as Derrida are

> trying to encourage our capacity for *ekstasis* – that imaginative ability that we possess to transcend our own situations, to get outside ourselves in time and space. This is a highly important project, for it is precisely the capacity for *ekstasis* [ecstasy] that enables us to function as moral beings, allowing us to see ourselves in the guise of those upon whom we act. Yet, it is a project that for all practical purposes has been excluded from the domain of the social sciences, and has been repressed within the humanities . . . [These writers] aim to bring back to thought a concern that in the Enlightenment view finds its place, if it finds any place at all, in art and religion.
>
> (Megill 1987: 341–42)

Freud, the nineteenth-century scientist, denied the transpersonal and believed that 'oceanic' feelings in the presence of nature or during meditation have to do with reliving a blissful state in the womb. However, I have had much clinical experience of clients whose womb experiences have been anything but bliss-full. Just consider some examples – sharing a womb with a dead twin foetus; surviving several attempted abortions; and during her pregnancy, a mother who was addicted to heroin and frequently verbally and physically assaulted. (One husband regularly kicked his wife in her stomach when she was pregnant. On the one occasion she miscarried, he forced her to immediately 'clear up the mess' herself.)

However, in his research on highly functioning individuals, Maslow's (1968) descriptions of people's 'peak-experiences' is full of *jouissance*. So is the irrepressible awe and wondrous miracle of witnessing a baby's birth or falling in love. People who have had near-death experiences report similar feelings and the rest of their lives are often profoundly changed as a consequence.

> [The] energising sense is an experience of *Physis*, as it surges up through our mortal frame . . . a dance, I mean, in the sense of a primordial ontological attunement, a deep chthonic intentionality – the very energy of Being (Physis) giving rise to various ontic motions, rhythms such as our working. The earthen ground of Being is such that only my whole body *felt in its wholeness* can 'espouse' its primordial geometry, its transcendental geology. Understood in relationship to the earth, its ground of support, 'dance' is the joyful feeling of an ontological movement, a movement which, by virtue of its guardian awareness, attunes us to the primordial Being of the ground and gathers us into the embracing arc *(arche)* of its ecstatic energy . . . perhaps a thoughtful experience of the hermeneutical round-dance would open us to the possibility of experiencing that openness of Being as a field of dancing energy – as in a word, Physis . . . The round-dance is dealing not only because its *ekstasis* breaks down the defensive rigidity of our culturally acquired ego-body, but because, in so doing, it awakens our ontologically most primordial body – 'my energetic body', as Merleau-Ponty would say. In the *ekstasis* of the round-dance therefore, we are opened to a space whose dimensionality can be experienced in relation to the 'energy' of Being *(Physis)* as a whole.
>
> (Levin 1985: 291, 299, 346)

What is part of the whole, but less spoken of in western therapeutic literature (and rarely admitted in ordinary European life), is the sometimes inexplicable (and almost shameful) sense of transcendence, vitality and alive-ness which people experience even in the presence of death or other 'abysmal' experiences. Danger and death both have the quality of intensifying our sense of vitality . . . 'to take us out of our old selves by the power of strangeness, to aid us in becoming new beings' (Rorty 1979: 360). **It was while he was starving in prison with worms crawling in his flesh**

that St John of the Cross conceived his great poems including the 'Dark night of the soul'. He called it 'Oh, happy lot!' (St John of the Cross 1973: 1).

The writer-director Patrice Chereau admits:

> It's strange how at funerals you can feel the energy change even as you enter and leave the cemetery; how as soon as you're back in the street people start to laugh again and you get this sudden explosion of energy. This sounds awful, but once, a long, long time ago, I made love immediately after a funeral and it was the most beautiful love-making of my life; very strange. But you do get these sudden changes and mixtures of emotion – everyone remembering how much they loved their father, for example, at the same time as recalling how unbearable he could be – and I do think we learn things from that, about ourselves and our relationships, about being more careful and generous with others.

(Interview with Patrice Chereau, Andre 2000: 75)

It was when she was heartbreakingly and uncontrollably sobbing for the first time after many stony years since the suicide of her lover, that my client exclaimed in a voice full of joy from my tear-soaked lap: 'I'm so wonderfully happy that I'm finally crying!' Handing her the Kleenex would have felt so very petty. (If she needs to, she knows where to find them for herself.) At Maori funerals in New Zealand the depth of grief for the departed is demonstrated by whether the grieving person's tear-fuelled nasal mucus stretches all the way to the earth in which the burial is being done (personal communication, Revd Kofler, 1999). Anyway, naturally drying tears are reportedly good for the skin. And it releases endorphins ('feel-good' hormones) so that you often feel some sense of transformation.

With acknowledgement to Chris Jenkins (personal communication, 2000), I should mention another intense experience (perhaps because it is so rare) – that of **silence** in the healing space. Silence can be a few moments to absorb new understanding in the **working allianc**e; hostile and defiant or compliant and submissive in **the transference**; **reparative** (while someone is emotionally working through a triumph or a disaster in non-verbal bodily ways); **person-to-person** (like being with a friend just listening together appreciatively to the rain on the roof); or truly **transpersonal** – no explanation, just the most profound shared experience of 'passing angels' or 'amazing grace'.

Life as the great co-therapist and world events as catalyst or support for the work

> 'The best thing for being sad,' replied Merlin, beginning to puff and blow, 'is to learn something. That is the only thing that never fails. You may grow old and trembling in your anatomies, you may lie awake at night listening to the disorder

of your veins, you may miss your only love, you may see the world about you devastated by evil lunatics, or know your honour trampled in the sewers of baser minds. There is only one cure for it then – to learn. Learn why the world wags and what wags it. That is the only thing which the mind can never exhaust, never alienate, never be tortured by, never fear or distrust, and never dream of regretting. Learning is the thing for you.

(White 1987: 181)

This invaluable advice (or just another story) from the Wizard Merlin to the young King Arthur forms the kick-off point for writing something about the contribution of apparently 'external' events to a person's psychotherapeutic journey. However, I think it applies to all forms of healing and indeed to **getting the most out of any life here on earth**. There may not be an externally defined meaning to life. This is possible.

Certainly we have no **level** five **evidence** for the existence of some such externally defined authoritative and overarching 'meaning'. However, many people (whether from a spiritual, cultural or psychotherapeutic 'school') apparently want to believe that they have found such an incontrovertible and eternal 'truth'. All too often they then try to impose it on the rest of the world through exclusion, domination or even by violence – for example by forcible conversation to Christianity or Islam through torture – as has so regrettably happened in many parts of the world.

I vividly remember my solitary distress as a shuddering child when I heard a radio broadcast by the then South African prime minister, John Voster – a committed Christian. In his heavy accent he intoned with absolute conviction: 'Even in the darkest night, I have never for a moment doubted that I am right.' In my mind I always heard that voice as accompaniment to news of how another black activist, according to the police and the newspapers, 'had committed suicide by jumping out of the window' of one of the most fortified and secured interrogation and torture chambers in the 'civilized' world.

The fact that medical evidence of torture (pliers to the penis, beatings, crushing of toes with chairs or bricks, being made to stand naked and wet in front of a fan until pneumonia set in, electric shock to the genitals, gross brain damage, amputation of nipples, fingers with nails pulled out etc. etc.) was found on the corpse was dismissed as only 'untrustworthy street rumour'.

In the Wall Street Journal of 12 February 1982, the Anglo-American Corporation issued the following statement: 'The very regrettable consequences of events such as Dr Agett's death [in detention] is to invest industrial relations with political tension' (in Coe and Metz 1983: 30). In the Johannesburg Star of 6 May of the same year, Lt Gen. Johan Coetzee pronounced that South Africa's security laws were 'absolutely necessary for the survival of our civilized existence' (Coe and Metz 1983: 28).

There will probably always be crime and violence in the world – particularly in countries who have been, over so many generations, **collectively traumatized**. The fact that such white-led crime and violence was **legal** (and economically buttressed by other 'civilized' countries) at the time, simply obscures the **genuine** statistics. Biko had said that the 'suffering' which the bystanding countries did not want to 'inflict' on the blacks through economic sanctions was as nothing to the suffering his people experienced already: 'We are used to suffering.'

I hope nobody asks what this section has to do with the transpersonal relationship in Eurocentric psychotherapy. Or with the human need to make meaning for their lives (and deaths). Or with the moral responsibility of denying our human relationships with 'others' through bystanding. Or with unquestioning belief in 'truths' propounded by 'authorities'. Or with the very few black psychotherapists in Britain. Or with the fact that a national psychotherapy association won't hold a listing of black therapists so that black people, if they wanted black therapists, could contact them. Or with the statements about how 'unsuitable' so many black people are for 'the talking cure'. Or with the possible utter irrelevance of not only our theories, but also what we actually **do** to alleviate the suffering in the world. Or with the economic interests which sustain our 'professional organizations' and their 'training schools' (see Clarkson 2000a).

Suffering, death, illness, poverty, betrayal and disaster can come to us all. (And then we're likely to ask 'Why me?' or just simply 'Why?'.) These are the times when our clients' and our own beliefs about life's meaning get confirmed, abandoned or transformed. Today I read in a newspaper that Kim Taylforth 'found her marriage, her belief in the legal system and her Mormon faith all challenged by the outcome of the legal cause undertaken [and lost] by her sister Gillian' (Greene 2000: 24).

What about parents of the children who are sexually abused and killed – their little bodies thrown away like so much discarded left-over raw meat? (After the foxes and crows had been at one British little girl, Sarah Payne could only be identified by her fingerprints.) One paedophile in the USA had a 'friend' who came in during the rape, laughed and then went away without intervening. Subsequently this friend asked the murderer salaciously whether the 8-year-old girl had been 'wet' before he penetrated her. The 'friend' claimed (and got) immunity from prosecution – because he had only been an innocent bystander.

Should psychotherapists 'vigorously contest the client's irrational beliefs', give interpretations about transferential disillusionment in the 'Father' or explain early childhood experiences of unsatisfactory attachment in such cases? Or should psychotherapists avoid and ignore ultimate themes – unless they possess an official diploma stamped 'transpersonal'?

> Our answer must consist, not in talk and meditation, but in right action and right conduct. Life ultimately means taking the responsibility to find the right answer to its problems and to fulfill the tasks which it constantly sets for each individual.
>
> (Frankl 1973: 77)

There was a woman who had been so awfully physically abused as a child that she became psychologically/physically desensitized to pain and abuse. So when she was raped, she just 'went out of her body' until it was over. And when the rapist said, 'Are you going to call the police?' she experientially couldn't understand for days why he might have asked her this. Police were there for others, not for her.

So she let people abuse her endlessly without actually noticing it until finally she thought that perhaps it might be a good idea if she learned to 'protect herself'. This was not only an entirely novel thought to her, but one she had hardly even begun to entertain until after many years of intensive psychotherapy. Even then, when burgled, she gaily said to her colleagues, 'Oh, it doesn't matter, it's only earthly goods.' (It is well known that the sheer shock from unprovoked assault or sudden injury takes some time to register even in people with a less traumatized background.)

Only some six hours later (because eventually the therapy had begun to take some effect) she thought: 'I've been burgled. If other people are burgled, they call the police. Other people think it isn't right to be fodder for thieves without making some objection. My therapist says I must object when I am badly treated. I think I will call the police.' The burglary, you see, could be seen as providing her with an opportunity to start putting self-protective boundaries in place, however tentative they may sound.

In these situations, it is possible to consider that Life is the Great Co-therapist.

> 'Mulla, Mulla, my son has written from the Abode of Learning to say that he has completely finished his studies.'
>   'Console yourself, madam, with the thought that God will no doubt send him more.'
>
> (Shah 1985: 4)

Like some Zen master, we don't even have to be falling asleep in meditation (*zazen*) to be rudely awakened by a blow to a shoulder of complacency. As Bauman points out: '. . . the frustration of certainty is morality's gain' (1993: 223). Maybe all events in a person's life (e.g. being diagnosed with HIV) as well as external events in a person's world (e.g. the death of Princess Diana) are providing assistance or at least learning opportunities to that person on their life's journey towards death. Perhaps it's just like Merlin said.

Sudden inspirations/understanding (*satori*)

The Rinzai tradition in Zen Buddhism makes use of *koans* (or riddles). Koans are a kind of mental/spiritual puzzle which are not soluble at a rational **level**. However, sincere and whole-hearted engagement with the puzzle (such as 'the sound of one hand clapping') can sometimes quickly, sometimes over many years, lead to complete enlightenment (*satori*).

Gestaltists call this the '**aha experience**' – the enantiodromic moment when figure and ground interchange. It could be similar to occasions when an 'insight' (or a 'vision') leaves you gasping for breath as your self-world view fundamentally re-organizes itself. At the perceptual **level** 1 almost all human beings can experience this 'figure–ground shift' as we see the vase 'shift' into two profiles (and/or vice versa) of the familiar Gestalt psychology picture.

According to Young-Eisendrath, 'The **effective** therapeutic relationship . . . is like a Zen koan for both participants: it invites and defies old interpretations' (1997: 642). Invites **and** defies.

Any attempt to explain it must, by definition, fail. Like Derrida and his kin would say, it is not irrational, but **non-rational**. Yet it uses a device of reason, by pushing the limits of rationality to its **enantiodromia** where it flips into its transpersonal, transcendent opposite (analogous to the 'flip-over effect' in Chaos science.) This both includes **and** excludes the purely rational **level** 5.

I used several examples in my book on Gestalt (Clarkson 1989a) to fractally and economically encapsulate the meaning of each chapter. Koans tend to be shorter, faster and more effective than any exposition. For an illustration here I like the lightbulb joke.

'How many Zen Buddhists does it take to change a light bulb?'

'I don't know, how many Zen Buddhists does it take to change a light bulb?'

'Three. One to change the light bulb, one not to change the light bulb, and one neither to change the lightbulb nor not to change the light bulb'.

That's it. The end of duality which includes duality. Impossible to explain, but 'getting it' is the best thing. I believe that the greatest Zen master, Life itself, sets us koans which take us to, and then beyond, the limits of our rationality in order to invite us into indescribable bliss and peace while still fully participating in the vicissitudes of existence.

I woke from a dream (which I do not remember) suddenly and fully convinced that I finally had understood what Christ meant by 'Love your enemies'. I felt this very strongly with a sense of elation and excitement at the insight. However, it was certainly not just a rational understanding, it was a 'grasp' of his meaning at all seven **levels**. It simultaneously involved my whole body; what felt like all my emotions; my sense of words and language; my values; my rational faculties; my theoretical narratives drawn from philosophy, theology and psychology – as well as an indescribable experience of opposites coexisting and coalescing seamlessly at a transpersonal **level**.

It was almost as if I felt it as if I had empathically experienced the meaning of this apparently paradoxical instruction as if from the inside of Christ himself. It's impossible to explain properly, but it was like having entered into his inner world in a truly phenomenological sense so that I could 'get it' from the inside. Body, soul and spirit. I don't expect anyone else to understand this experience, but I will attempt to tell it so that perhaps other therapists can also admit to having similar inexplicable experiences. Thus, we may be able to begin to talk about it or at least allow for our clients' experiences of this kind.

There was of course a prepared and enlivened experiential ground for this physical/spiritual illumination. As a white South African I have been in a lifelong engagement with moral and ethical issues. What bothers me (and many other people) profoundly about many so-called organized religions and spiritual dogma about a 'loving God' is the existence of evil deeds.

The suffering and injustice in the world while such things happen exists while those who **can** make a difference deny their own collusion (their human relationship) and 'pass by on the other side of the street', avert their eyes, claim ignorance or wash their hands of the blood of others like Pontius Pilate. (See Clarkson 1996d for further exploration of this theme.)

As a child in church I was told by Calvinist preachers that people (like the Chinese in my imagination) who maybe hadn't even heard of Jesus would go to hell anyway. This did not seem fair to me. Even as a teenager I refused to take communion for myself because of this unjust rule (a possibly trivial but sincere gesture of solidarity and 'passive resistance'). 'Love' seemed to me a very confusing word in the name of which incredible injustice, cruelty, torture and much of the wickedness of the world was committed. (Fred West told his daughter as he tortured and raped her that he was doing it out of love in order to prepare her properly for marriage.)

So Christ's instruction 'to love your enemies' in my simple opinion was neither fair, nor logical. How could you love people who hurt and damage you and others without 'bystanding' or colluding with their damaging conduct? However, Christ himself cursed a fig-tree just because it did not have any fruit on it when he and his disciples were hungry. Furthermore, he got so angry at the money-lenders in the temple that he caused great consternation by throwing them (and their stuff) out.

Later, particularly from Rogers, I learned to differentiate between unconditional acceptance of the human being and disapproval for their behaviour. The Catholics taught me to 'love the sinner, not the sin'. In my way I have sincerely attempted to practise this for most of my life – to the confusion of several people who find such an attempt at congruence 'bizarre'. Yes, I think I have learned to love **the person** at the same time as undertaking what I could to act as responsibly as I knew how in terms of unlawful, immoral and unethical **behaviour**.

But, 'loving your enemies' (even though taught by most great spiritual masters from Jesus to Gautama Buddha to Gandhi, to Rumi and many others) still seemed beyond my conception or capacity. I'd heard a story that the Dalai Lama was welcoming to his refuge one of his students. This student had in the most perilous circumstances fled Tibet and had been captured and tortured by the Chinese. The Dalai Lama said something like: 'I trust you did not face too many dangers on your journey here.' And the student replied: 'The greatest danger I experienced was that sometimes I almost lost my compassion for the Chinese.'

However, as Brandon points out, in his book *Zen and the Art of Helping*:

> I don't see compassion as necessarily 'making people feel better'. It is a much more robust process than this. It does not involve simply being good and pleasant to people. Saying the right or socially acceptable thing is not usually being compassionate. Being nice is a simple ongoing social device to avoid undue disturbance and pain. Compassion accepts the risks and ignores those dangers.
>
> (Brandon 1976: 57–58)

Christ's instruction was simply an unsolvable *koan* for me. Until that morning as I woke up from a dream. And now I feel I understand wholeheartedly what these teachers mean. Without Judas, no crucifixion and no resurrection. Without conflict, still slavery. Without suffering, no joy. Now I've also lived long enough to see and really appreciate how those who have attempted to hurt or damage me and mine have been my greatest teachers and kindest benefactors. (If you want to know more about this, you can check the Physis website and/or ask me about it in person.)

At this time of writing I consult a very rational traditionally trained atheist cognitive clinical psychologist for 'rehabilitation' after my angina attack (under the kind of traumatic circumstances which contributed to the death of one of my dearest seventy-four-year-old spiritual colleagues). I also regularly see (for supervision of supervision and mothering) one of the last surviving students of Jung.

To one, the illumination I took from my moment of unspeakable blessing might be a 'cognitive thinking error' or even a delusion; to the other one I wouldn't even need to explain it. She just smiled her grace at me. Yet, at different levels (the rational and the transpersonal) they are both helping me as the client. The work of holding all levels of my experience and learning (as well as unlearning) simultaneously in its incompleteness remains my own responsibility.

Some guidelines for the transpersonal psychotherapist

Improve your physis-detector (tracking ability)

I think it was Bertrand Russell who advocated a sound 'shit-detector'. I propose alongside this wise advice, the development of our capacities to detect signs of growth or Life – no matter what it may look like on the surface. Heraclitus was one of the first to say that 'Physis loves to hide'. So, as physicians of the soul, is there anything we can do to develop our physis-detecting abilities? I believe it has more to do with **unlearning** and **unknowing** what we have actually learned from our teachers or training institutions – or at least realizing that this 'knowledge' is only one very small aspect of the whole of existence. As Wittgenstein said:

> Mere description is so difficult because one believes that one needs to fill out the facts in order to understand them. It is as if one saw a screen with scattered colour-patches, and said: The way they are here, they are unintelligible; they only make sense when one completes them into a shape – Whereas I want to say: Here *is* the whole. (If you complete it you falsify it.)
>
> (Wittgenstein 1980: 257)

To the Kalahari bushmen, like many other first world peoples, the way to find vital life where to all appearances it is hiding (like water in the desert, buck in an empty field, antibiotics in stones) is to enter into the inner-beingness of that for which you are searching. (The poet Gerard Manley Hopkins's 'inscape'?) I think it is like what we mean by empathy with other humans in counselling and psychotherapy, but the bush people's also includes a lived and felt empathy with all that concentrates life's vitality. By 'being' the tiger or the elephant, you know in all your body's marrow where it has been, how many days it has been fleeing and whether it's been wounded or not.

> In [Indigenous science,] a holistic world in which each part enfolds the whole, it becomes possible to enter into the inscape of the smallest insect, plant, or leaf and zoom outward into the whole universe. Sa'ke'j Henderson has suggested that the People's relationship with plants, animals, rocks, and trees serves them as a kind of electron microscope. By entering into direct relationship with the animals and the Keepers of the animals, the People were able to gain access to the knowledge they have about the world. Native people, Henderson would say, not only have knowledge that comes from direct experience, but access to the knowledge of the birds, insects, animals, rocks, and trees. This sort of process of knowing allows one to enter directly into the perception of nature at many scales and **levels**.
>
> (Peat 1996: 251)

Inter-connect

Give up the notion of being 'separate' from others or from life; this may be true only at some **levels**; at other **levels** we are each part of the great interconnected web of Life. The best preparation is experiencing this interrelationship with all of life and death and transformation at all **levels** within yourself.

A Japanese man once taught me that all the sages are joyful because they have faced reality with all its contradictions and have given up the illusion that things should be different. I have frequently pointed out the surest recipe for unhappiness is wanting other people to change.

Take the next step

Stop wanting the 'perfect solution' or believing that we are entitled to heaven (or anything permanent) on earth – 'if only' some authority would fix it for us. We were never promised a rose garden – even less so a rose garden without thorns. Utopian ideals (and their iatrogenic consequences) have perhaps caused more unnecessary suffering in the world than anything else. If we cannot reach 'perfection' or 'self-realization' or whatever the ideal state is as defined by the guru, people often hate themselves and despair. Every solution to a problem carries the seeds of the next problem within it. Just take the next step.

Remember that just because sometimes we cannot find in ourselves (or see in our clients) Life's creative self-actualizing tendency, it doesn't mean that it's gone. It may just be hiding. **Trust the process only *after* you've done the best technical work you know how.**

See the glory in everyone. From Nelson Mandela's inaugural speech:

Our deepest fear is not that we are inadequate. Our deepest fear is that we are powerful beyond measure.

It is our light, not our darkness, that most frightens us. We ask ourselves: 'Who am I to be brilliant, gorgeous, talented, fabulous?'

Actually, who are we not to be?

You are a child of God. Your playing small doesn't serve the world. There's nothing enlightened about shrinking so that other people around you won't feel insecure. We are all meant to shine, as children do. We are born to manifest the glory of God that is within us.

It is not just in some of us: it is in everyone. And as we let our light shine, we unconsciously give other people permission to do the same. As we are liberated from our own fear, our presence automatically liberates others.

Chapter 4
Prima materia – the opening of the work

An Early Morning Eye
When you start some new work,
give in completely to it.

You're excited
because the Creator keeps you
from seeing what's missing.

Your heatedness hides that,
so you do the work, and then look back
and see the nature of it.

If you'd seen that at first,
you wouldn't have done anything!

Don't worry about repenting.
Do the work that's given,
and learn from it.

If you become addicted to looking back,
half your life will be spent in distraction,
and the other half in regret.

You can live better than that!
Find happier friends.

Say: Show me the faults
of my destructive actions, but don't show me
what's wrong with my good work.
That way I won't get disgusted and quit!

Solomon had a habit of visiting the mosque at dawn,
because then he could see
with an early morning eye
the new spirit-plants that were growing.

Encourage that freshness
in yourself, not what clouds you
with dullness and futility.

                                        (Rumi 1990: 119–20)

As we have seen, myths of all cultures and religions or traditions of all times are concerned with giving meanings to the beginning and to the end; life and death, coming-into-being and passing away. In this chapter we will concentrate on the beginning of transpersonal psychotherapy remembering that in every beginning is also an end. Beginnings are the most important part of any work. How we begin anything (including psychotherapy) contains all the seeds of the middle – and the end.

'The scientists of change also wax poetic over the issue of *sensitivity to initial conditions*' (Briggs and Peat 1990: 73). As Gleick says:

> Tiny differences in input could quickly become overwhelming differences in output – a phenomenon given the name 'sensitive dependence on initial conditions'. In weather, for example, this translates into what is only half-jokingly known as the Butterfly Effect – the notion that a butterfly stirring the air today in Peking can transform storm systems next month in New York.
>
> (Gleick 1989: 8)

Chaos theory and complexity science bring disturbance to our ideas of causality, and intervention into all complex adaptive systems (such as human beings) – for example the possibility that very small interventions or chance occurrences have very large, unpredictable or unknown effects. As the incomparable Nasrudin said: 'Only children and the stupid seek cause-and-effect in the same story' (Shah 1985: 26).

The beginning of the creative relationship which is called healing (or creation itself) unleashes the forces of chaos (see Weinberg 1993). Anything can happen. When a client enters into what could be a transformative or a destructive relationship with a psychotherapist they take a step into the unknown. Old illustrations of the alchemical work (which Jung saw as the symbolic imaging of psychotherapy) vividly demonstrate this.

One lovely picture which I found in my researches (and which has since hidden) shows the transforming, transformative mythological couple together in the preparatory bath as being in relationship with everything else – nature, animals, the wind, the sun and all the elements. A rather typical business man from the City of London said it in his fractal way: 'It's like lifting up the skirt of my soul.'

The philosopher' stone – the lapis – starts off as 'repulsive matter' variously described as filth, cheap, despicable, concealed in dung, the 'vilest of the vile' and paradoxically also 'the highest natural good'. Life emerges from the sexual act in birth covered with blood and faeces. And the references to genitals, the sexual embrace of the couple are not accidental: *physis* – the creative emergence of Life itself – is also a word used for genitals. But of course in psychotherapy the relationship has to remain **symbolic** (not acted out) for the work to be accomplished.

Personally I am touched by the presence of a dog in several of such pictures. The dog has been humankind's most ancient faith-full animal companion. Dogs were regular attendants in the caves of Aesclepius (the Greek god of healing), in the arms of the Dalai Lama, licking the sores of the wounded in the Bible, present in Freud's and Jung's consulting rooms, doing therapy today (as PAT dogs) where the 'talking cure' cannot reach – the elderly, the hurt, the children and old people who have been exiled by our 'society'. In the words of one woman suffering from long-term, and so far incurable, severe mental 'health' problems, who finds human contact too painful to bear: 'I cannot go out of my house without my dog. Without my dog I feel too naked to face the world.' In the unconditionally accepting presence of the dog – the inner animal – we can strip our psyches naked and perhaps survive.

Beginnings from chaos and crisis

People usually (and with best prognosis) come to psychotherapy when there is a crisis in their lives. It may be the shock of a disaster or a bereavement, or the crisis of a lover leaving (or not leaving), a crisis of confidence or a wish to move beyond a steady state that has become boring, predictable and meaningless. Crisis occurs

> when a person faces an obstacle to important life goals that is, for a time, insur-
> mountable through the utilization of customary methods of problem solving. A
> period of disorganization ensues, a period of upset, during which many abortive
> attempts at solutions are made.
>
> (Caplan 1951: 18)

Even though most people, lay or professional, can report anecdotes or personal experiences of how **crisis**, whether personal, environmental, intrapsychic or interpersonal, precipitated changes of a profound and lasting nature to their whole way of living and their view of life, there appears to be a dearth of scientific research into the positive transformative qualities of crisis.

One crisis which has been reasonably documented is the 'near-death' experience. This experience of 'leaving one's body' again appears to be reported in many different cultures in similar ways:

> Near-death experiences are frequently reported as similar to the symbolic death
> of initiating rites in tribal cultures, after which a person returns with a different
> and deeper perspective on life, often with a spiritual consciousness which
> enhances their lives and the lives of those associated with them.
>
> (Lorimer 1987)

In *Life Wish* (1987), Jill Ireland describes her recovery from cancer, and Rachel Charles' book *Mind, Body and Immunity* (1996), which has helped so many suffering people, is the result of her own experience of recovery from cancer. These are only two of numerous autobiographical accounts which document how a crisis ranging from a diagnosis of a life-threatening disease to going blind or being raped to having a child trapped under a car can permanently and positively change people's lives. There are many films which illustrate the possibility of transformation following on the impact of crisis in the person's life.

> Emotional occasions, especially violent ones, are extremely potent in precipitating mental rearrangements. The sudden and explosive ways in which love, jealousy, guilt, fear, remorse, or anger can seize upon one are known to everybody. Hope, happiness, security, resolve, emotions characteristic of conversion, can be equally explosive. And emotions that come in this explosive way seldom leave things as they found them.
>
> (James 1985: 202–3)

In Tennessee Williams' play, *Cat on a Hot Tin Roof* (1959), the protagonist Brick also demonstrates a *metanoia* of a kind. Brick's psycho-emotional movement from a defensive position through anger to sadness, to fear, to a genuine breakthrough is most poignantly dramatized. This may be another case where the novelists and the playwrights tread intrepidly on the terrain which the psychologists have hardly begun to identify.

However, one of the greatest psychologists, William James, wrote:

> But a new perception, a sudden emotional shock, or an occasion which lays bare the organic alteration, will make the whole fabric fall together; and then the centre of gravity sinks into an attitude more stable, for the new ideas that reach the centre in the rearrangement seem now to be locked there, and the new structure remains permanent.
>
> (James 1985: 201–2)

Webster's dictionary defines crisis as a 'decisive' or 'crucial' period, a 'turning point' (Webster 1944: 2440). 'Indeed the Chinese character for crisis combines those for opportunity and danger' (Clarkson 1988).

Of course, crisis intervention theory (Parad 1969) is theoretically based on the assumption that crisis conditions can be used advantageously as transformational vortices in individual lives and in family systems. I have heard therapy referred to as 'a slow nervous breakdown'. The task of the therapist is inducing turbulence into the system which throws it out of a habitual and deadening balance – allowing *second order change* or new and novel forms of self and living to emerge.

First order change is incremental improvement – the step by step building-block version of change which does not re-structure or reconfigure the nature of the system itself. An example of first order change is pressing down the petrol pedal of a car in order to go faster; second order change is changing gears.

Our work could also be described as the facilitation of a healing crisis – as in homeopathy. And indeed, until the psychotherapy client is willing to enter into such a crisis ('lose their balance' so to speak) very little substantial or second order change can take place. Going into the unknown of a psychotherapy relationship with a stranger is a kind of loss of balance – ideally a 'falling in life'. Of course the first Tarot card depicts the Fool starting off on his journey, his dog by his side, his one foot precariously striding into the abyss.

Csikszentmihalyi's (1992) notion of 'flow' corresponds to but is more limited and one-sided than the Heraclitean notion of physis. In my opinion, he tends to **over**-emphasize positive feelings and the almost inevitable surmountability of life's obstacles. However, during an organizational consultation he paraphrased Dante as follows: 'Virgil tries to reassure Dante: The good news is that there is a way out of the dark forest. The bad news is that the way leads through hell' (Csikszentmihalyi 1992: 237).

However, accounts of positive changes subsequent to crisis still mostly tend to be reported in magazines and newspapers rather than attracting funding for serious psychological research. Massimini et al. (1987), as paraphrased in Csikszentmihalyi, is an exception. This study found that 'a large proportion of the victims mentioned the accident that caused [their] paraplegia as both one of the most negative and one of the most **positive** events in their lives' (Massimini et al. 1987: 193).

Perhaps this book may draw some attention to this relatively unexplored, but profoundly exciting aspect of human psychology, and readers are invited to write to me contributing case studies, literary sources and personal experiences.

Initial conditions of the psychotherapy relationship

In science as in life, it is well known that a chain of events can have a point of crisis that could magnify small changes. But chaos means that such points were everywhere. They were pervasive. In systems like the weather, sensitive dependence on initial conditions was an inescapable consequence of the way small scales intertwined with large.

(Gleick 1989: 23)

If perhaps we do the thought experiment I have suggested and we accept (even for a moment) that no field exists without an observer,

no 'me' without the organization around me, no *you* without *us* – how do we effect beneficial changes, who is doing what to whom and why? All the notions of nineteenth-century science which so many psychotherapists devotedly apply to human beings (!) may be outdated or even wrong.

Taking on board some of these new ideas may require that certain established ideas are relinquished or, at the very best, substantially rethought. Sometimes people may find it worrying, sometimes aggravating, and sometimes even an assault on their most cherished assumptions. For example, the commonly unquestioned notion that childhood experiences cause adult disturbance is based on Eurocentric and culturally charged notions from conceptions of a linear, billiard-ball universe. (However, there is no denying that it makes for good – **level** 6 – stories to retrospectively explain current problems!) Such deterministic ideas are however not based on conceptions of living growing wholes in the process of a collective quantum evolution.

If it is true that there are such incredible consequences of initial conditions, what does this mean about our understanding of the psychotherapeutic process? It may dictate a shift in clinical approaches to the treatment of psychiatric disorders; for example, Mandell (in Briggs and Peat 1990: 168) questions traditional models for treating human beings – these most unstable, dynamic, infinitely multi-dimensional, choice- and meaning-making organisms – with linear and reductionist models like hydraulics or motor cars.

Levenson, in a long clinical tradition, but using the new paradigm notion that the analytic relationship – or any part of this relationship – is in essence a hologram (and, I would add, a fractal of the whole), writes:

> Any small piece of the clinical material contains the total configuration. Both past and future. Thus the patient's opening comment in the waiting room or coming in the door as he sits in the chair, will establish the leitmotif that runs through the entire session, that picks up on the last session, and will very likely continue on into the next session. Any ten minutes of a taped session can be explicated to an entire analysis. Any dream of the patient contains implicit in it – literally, enfolded in it – the entire story of the patient's neurotic difficulties.
>
> (Levenson 1976: 2–3)

Compare this with a microscopic perspective on the first three minutes of meeting a new client (Clarkson 1992b: 90–100) **and**, just for fun, with Weinberg's 1993 book on 'the first three minutes' of the universe.

> Simple systems give rise to complex behaviour. Complex systems give rise to simple behaviour. The laws of complexity hold universally. Should this not shake

or at least rumble the accepted psychological paradigms? 'Is is possible that mathematical pathology, i.e. chaos, is health? And that mathematical health, which is the predictability and differentiability of this kind of a structure, is disease?'

(Gleick 1989: 298)

So, chaos scientists have discovered that predictability, 'balance' and regularity can be a sign of illness. In psychological theorizing too there has often been a preoccupation with homeostasis, equilibrium, adaptation. As well as emphasizing the dynamic and chaotically transforming capacities and hungers of human beings, I have also drawn attention to 'stability under stress' (SUS). (See Feltham and Dryden 1993: 181; and Clarkson 1992b: 36, 39, 78–79, 83, 85, 92–93, 100, 145, 187.) By 'stable under stress' I obviously do **not** mean 'staying in some permanent balance' but the ability to respond creatively and effectively to buffeting intra- and extra-psychic forces without permanent disintegration (Clarkson 1995b: e.g. the chapters on diagnosis, Kitbag, and Group Dynamics).

Exploration of disequilibrium, disruption and disturbance has but rarely been conceived of as healthy or creative. Yet 'creativity happens at far from equilibrium conditions', often needing the stimulus of deadlines, emotional turmoil or a change of setting to flourish. All these themes we are considering can have a massive impact on theory, practice and research in all the human disciplines, but not least in therapeutic psychology, psychotherapy, supervision and organizational work.

Potentially the impact of these developments on these fields must be disturbing, disorientating and may perhaps even precipitate disequilibrium. It certainly seems important to me that at least some of us are willing to have our own theoretical experiences and our philosophical constructions challenged by these new and provocative models, conceptions and developments. It is possible that under such stimulus, creativity in psychology can continue to evolve disruptively rather than dogmatically.

Gergen (1990) for example encourages the construction of new and more practical forms of theory as one of the most important tasks of the psychology of the future. Ford, self-proclaimed evangelist of chaos, sees the excitement in the prospect of disequilibrium conditions in organizations: 'Dynamics freed at last from the shackles of order and predictability . . . Systems liberated to randomly explore their every dynamical possibility . . . Exciting variety, richness of choice, a cornucopia of opportunity' (Briggs and Peat 1990: 114–15).

> Until recently, such phenomena as the volatility of weather systems, the fluctuation of the stock market, or the random firing of neurones in the brain were considered too 'noisy' and complex to be probed by science . . . [Chaos theory is] turning our perception of the world on its head; and . . . discoveries in mathematics, biology, and physics . . . are heralding a revolution more profound than

the one responsible for producing the atomic bomb. With practical applications ranging from the control of traffic flow and the development of artificial intelligence to the treatment of heart attacks and schizophrenia, chaos promises to be an increasingly rewarding area of inquiry – of interest to everyone.

(Briggs and Peat 1990: back cover)

Like Quantum physics, the science of chaos highlights the importance of **relationships**. In this way, chaos science has shown us that everything and potentially everybody is related in a kind of dance. Everything is in this sense connected with everything else and any separation is therefore theoretical rather than actual. Along with these fundamental and mind-changing developments in our relationship with our conceptual environment, there are changes in our actual world relationships.

Clouds are not spheres, Mandelbrot is fond of saying. Mountains are not cones. Lightning does not travel in a straight line. The new geometry mirrors a universe that is rough, not rounded, scabrous, not smooth. It is a geometry of the pitted, pocked, and broken up, the twisted, tangled, and intertwined. The understanding of nature's complexity awaited a suspicion that the complexity was not just random, not just accident. It required a faith that the interesting feature of a lightning bolt's path, for example, was not its direction, but rather the distribution of zigs and zags.

Mandelbrot's work made a claim about the world, and the claim was that such odd shapes carry meaning. The pits and tangles are more than blemishes distorting the classic shapes of Euclidean geometry. They are often the keys to the essence of a thing . . . To some physicists chaos is a science of process rather than state, of becoming rather than being . . . But physiologists have also began to see chaos as health . . . With all such . . . phenomena, a critical issue is robustness: how well can a system withstand small jolts. Equally critical in biological systems is flexibility: how well can a system function over a *range* of frequencies. A locking-in to a single mode can be enslavement, preventing a system from adapting to change. Organisms must respond to circumstances that vary rapidly and unpredictably; no heartbeat or respiratory rhythm can be locked into the strict periodicities of the simplest physical models, and the same is true of the subtler rhythms of the rest of the body. Some researchers, among them Ary Goldberger of Harvard Medical School, proposed that healthy dynamics were marked by fractal physical structures, like the branching networks of bronchial tubes in the lung and conducting fibers in the heart, that allow a wide range of rhythms.

(Gleick 1989: 5, 94, 292–93)

Indeed the only time the heartbeat apparently becomes regular (balanced) is just before a coronary attack. (So much for seeking balance!)

Maslow, one of the few psychologists who investigated examples of optimal health, creativity and actualization, was the man who brought the term 'peak experience' into mainstream psychology. However we struggle with the words to describe these concerns we are faced with the necessity for using them. One such word which I like because it corresponds with some of my own convictions and which I think is interesting because of its similarity to Hillman's ideas is the notion of *re-sacralizing*:

> Resacralizing means being willing, once again, to see a person 'under the aspect of eternity,' as Spinoza says or to see him in the medieval Christian unitive perception, that is, being able to see the sacred, the eternal, the symbolic. It is to see Woman with a capital 'W' and everything which that implies, even when one looks at a particular woman. Another example sees its symbolic value, sees it as a figure of speech, sees it in its poetic aspects. One goes to medical school and dissects a brain. Certainly something is lost if the medical student isn't awed but, without the unitive perception, sees the brain only as one concrete thing. Open to resacralization, one sees a brain as a sacred object.
>
> (Maslow 1968: 284)

The relationship – the person of the psychotherapist

Since the client has independently been doing their own preparations for beginning by making or entering this new relationship (considering therapy, searching for a suitable practitioner and making the appointment) the psychotherapist is also preparing him- or herself for the healing encounter. 'Readiness is all.'

In certain parts of Nigeria they tell the story of how the chameleon's eyes popped out. Another animal, a tiny squirrel, was sick and the chameleon helped to keep the fire alive by blowing on it. His eyes popped out from the blowing on the embers. The other animal got well, but the chameleon's eyes stayed popped-out. They say that if you need an explanation of the philosophy, your mother's dowry (*lobola*) must be returned because she made a stupid child. People will pay attention to the sick animal who got well, but they must also look at how hard the chameleon must have had to work because of how far his eyes popped out.

For Heraclitus, flame, fire was the source of physis. I see healing as blowing on the embers of another's person's self-healing life energy. 'Burn-out' is when your own flame goes out (see Clarkson 1992b: 277–83). Caring for the carer is the first responsibility of the healer.

There are volumes written about the ideal preparation that the psychotherapist needs to undergo in order do effective psychotherapy – many of these are contradictory. Personal psychotherapy is usually a requirement for humanistic, psychoanalytic, existential and some integrative approaches; it is not required from clinical psychologists, psychiatrists, cognitive-behavioural psychotherapists and some family and psycho-sexual therapists. Alternatively it may be variously redefined as, for example, 'personal development', for practitioners in neuro-linguistic programming (NLP). Personal psychotherapy, then, is not a requirement for clinical psychologists and psychiatrists.

There is, in fact, no actual scientific evidence that either personal psychotherapy of the practitioner or longer training increases their effectiveness. (See Corney 1997 for a thorough review.) Hogan argues that 'instead of focusing on restricting practitioners from entering the field, we need to embrace the entire range of therapists focusing on a sound disciplinary system and good education of the public' (1999: 1). Furthermore, therapists of all persuasions (and many more from crystal healing to having colonic irrigations) have, without argument, effected 'cures' which, by the criteria of the patients or clients themselves, have resolved their difficulties, alleviated pain and given them courage and skills to continue with full lives.

> It isn't the technique, it isn't the therapist, it isn't the lack of training. It isn't the new wonder drug, it isn't the diagnosis. It is our clients' own inborn capacities for self-healing, and it is the meeting – the relationship in which two or more sovereign or sacred 'I's' meet as 'we' engage with significant questions of existence.
>
> (O'Hara 1995: 30)

Klein's final resort to 'constitutional factors' (e.g. 1984: 67, 115) as an explanatory paradigm is actually very similar to 'inborn capacities for self-healing'. The Protestant theologian Tillich is in accord with this:

> A life process which shows this balance [between fear and courage] and with it power of being has, in biological terms, vitality, i.e. life power. The right courage therefore must, like the right fear, be understood as the expression of perfect vitality. The courage to be is a function of vitality. Diminishing vitality consequently entails diminishing courage. To strengthen vitality means to strengthen the courage to be. Neurotic individuals and neurotic periods are lacking in vitality. Their biological substance has disintegrated. They have lost the power of full self-affirmation, of the courage to be. Whether this happens or not is the result of biological process, it is biological fate.
>
> (Tillich 1952: 79)

So what is the ideal preparation for the psychotherapist? I think this is not the most fruitful question. Different kinds of 'preparation' will necessarily 'fit' with certain kinds of healing 'rituals' and certain kinds of narratives – whether culturally congruent or not. The important point is precisely the fact that **attention** is paid to the preparation of the practitioner themselves.

These preparatory rituals may involve 11 years of five times a week Kleinian psychoanalysis, seven years of study at medical school, a correspondence diploma in hypnotherapy, a meditation before the session, or washing one's hands. They may not make sense to us now. For example, there was a time when a Dr Semmelweiss insisted upon washing his own hands as preparation for delivering babies. He succeeded in greatly reducing the death rate by infection in the hospital where he laboured. Of course some women still died, but he was on the side of Life. Semmelweiss was laughed at, humiliated, ostracized by his colleagues and eventually, in despair, he committed suicide. Yet nowadays careful handwashing before any operation is a necessary preparation for any doctor, acupuncturist and nurse.

Ablution or immersion of the whole or part of the body of the practitioner in water is probably one of the oldest and most prevalent of all preparatory rituals. I know from rebirthers that they bath and change their clothes several times a day. Every day there are hundreds or thousands of holy teachers and other people bathing in the revered Ganges river in India. Yes, now we have 'proved' it is for reasons of hygiene too, but that is only one **level** of its meaning – the rational. (And, as most people who have worked, for example, in organizations, know, the rational layer in human existence is the thickness of one sheet of paper in a metaphorical ream.)

Symbolically, ablution is the cleansing of the body/mind/spirit/self of the practitioner to prepare themselves to receive both the client(s) as well as metaphorically or actually to cleanse themselves of previous 'dirt'. In the Rosarium woodcuts the relationship itself (alchemist and soror figures) even gets in the bath . Practitioners do ablutions also in order to be cleanly receptive to the visitation of whatever names they give the unpredictable aspect of the creative healing force – the grace of God, insight, learning, spirit, the self-actualizing tendency, Reich's (1972) *orgon*, the core energy of Pierrakos (1974, 1987), Being, physis.

I try and describe it practically by saying that we need to cleanse ourselves to meet each client anew, fresh and open to all possibilities – however unlikely – which can emerge in the healing encounter. For this small period (50 minutes or so) I can attempt to bracket off ('epoche') my previous experiences, my ongoing concerns, even my previous opinions about what this person can or cannot achieve. For this brief time I will work from the clearest, best, most holy place in myself. The empty space – where Being breathes through me to metaphorically blow on the smouldering embers of life's fire in the other. Like any performing artist, I have practised and prepared, but when I go into the dance itself to perform the duet or chorus line, I will truly yield to a music I may never have heard in this way before.

So what about all my training, my reading, my research, my 30-odd years of personal analysis and psychotherapy training? Are they to be suspended or denied? Have I not learned anything of value? Of course I have. This has also been part of my preparation. Inevitably those skills of observation, creativity and understanding of the other kinds of therapeutic relationship are also present, but my proactive countertransference, my 'own issues' can be left outside the consulting room – or at least shown the door as soon as they come to awareness.

> In our ordinary activities our mind is often narrow and closed in upon itself; it is very difficult to achieve any goal, to really relate and have an unselfish attitude to others . . . On the other hand, if we diligently try to open our minds, we will naturally have compassion . . . the realization of emptiness naturally provides boundless compassion and pure perception of others. Our practice of the two truths, relative and absolute, must go together inseparably. We must understand from above with the absolute outlook while practising climbing up the spiritual mountain from below with relative practices, according to our individual capacity and inclination . . . understanding according to the supreme view and practising according to one's ability.
>
> (Khenpo and Surya Das, of the Dzogchen tradition, 1995: 53, 54)

The three psychological qualities I have found most essential to being an effective healer are:

1. **Personal experience** of profound change, particularly 'the dark night of the soul', which seems to be a requirement for any creative break-through, whether in art, or in national change.
2. **The willingness to do it again** and again. The recognition that the nature of the change experience is cyclical (or resembles that of a spiral), and the realization that we need to enter the void again and again if we are to emerge more fully and completely.
3. A welcoming positive or at least **enquiring attitude to change** through relationship with ourselves, others and the world, an invest-ment in evolution as well as the willingness to bear disintegrating and fragmenting forces at all **levels** without incapacitating ourselves.

The place

As Frank (1973) showed, in addition to the healing relationship, the **space** where it takes place in all known cultures and throughout history is of vital importance. Gerard Adler (1979) referred to this as the *temenos* (holy space) and all rituals begin, after the preparation of the healer, with a preparation of the space.

This space may be a circle in the sand, a pentagon drawn with chalk on a marble floor, a candle and incense, a river in a township, a makeshift altar in a forest, an ancient circle of stones, the Celtic well over which the cathedral has been built, the confessional box, a luxurious room in Hampstead filled with antique furniture, a bare and clinical hospital room, the presence of books or a notepad, a tape-recorder, a double-door to shut away the outside world, a shabby community college room in a centre for refugees, a room full of floor cushions, tennis rackets and toys; straight upright chairs which silently forbid any spontaneous movement, couches to lie on and blankets for the chill of flesh or spirit, tissues, dried or fresh flowers or the smell of disinfectant or dust.

Both Goodman (1962) and Rowan (1996) point out that furniture in which the psychotherapy takes place tells a story about what is to take place there. One can even deduce from each arrangement what the particular theory (or narrative) is which is being enacted, what they hypothesize has gone wrong with the client, and what 'prescription for action' he or she believes would put this right. I have stressed (Clarkson 1995a) the way in which the apparel (vestments) of the therapist as well as their furniture and location (speech, language use, smells and archetypal shapes) convey a relatively full account of the practitioner's values – no matter how much they claim 'neutrality' or say that they do not 'impose their values on their clients'.

Research by Cowie and Clarkson (2000) into the cultural representations of psychotherapists in late twentieth-century English-language literature found a similar emphasis on **the place** dedicated to healing of the soul. Interestingly enough, in our internet age, we also found that at least two machines were involved. One computer (TAT – The Absolute Truth) worked alone and successfully with the client. (I do remember at least one research result from the psychological literature which indicated that computer therapy was scientifically found to be as good as, if not more effective than, traditional human-to-human psychotherapy.)

An as yet unpublished ground-breaking paper, 'Counselling and psychotherapy online' (Ormay 2000), explores, amongst other things, the nature of the 'space' created by using the medium of the world-wide internet for counselling and psychotherapy (or 'cybertherapy') practice. Ormay cites Steuer (1993) on the notion of 'tele-presence'. This is based on findings that 'presence does not refer to the actual human surroundings, but to a **perception** of them' (Ormay 2000: 4, my emphasis). On this theme it is also important to refer to the Ethical Guidelines for Webcounselling published by the British Association for Counselling and Psychotherapy (BAC 1999).

In studying the theoretical orientations of our sample of psychotherapists, the two cases involving computers actually emerged as having the characteristics usually associated with practitioners from the Humanistic/Existential 'school': for example, personal authenticity, skilful use of the dialogic or **person-to-person** relationship with a focus on personal responsibility for choices in the midst of life's existential givens.

Along with ample literary evidence of the **working alliance**, some form of **bias (or transference)**, and intentional use of the **relationship for reparation**, we also found traces of the **transpersonal relationship** in the novels.

As regards this (last or first) relational dimension, Rivers compares himself, for example, to a witchdoctor, when contemplating his own work as a psychiatrist and a female psychotherapist's traditional Mimi dolls (Alther 1985) in her consulting room. Are these invocations to the unknown Thou? At first the client objected to these, but at the end of therapy she took a Mimi doll away with her – as a 'transitional' object?

In a favourite consulting room, there are all the volumes of the *Mahabharatha* (a Hindu Holy book of which the extract called the *Bagavat Gita* is the crowning jewel), a Minora, the Bible, Zen texts, African, Tibetan and Chinese sculptures, and encyclopaedias of mythology and the world's religions. I know therapists who travel with sandtrays and washing baskets full of crayons and paint to enliven dead surroundings. Others regularly buy flowers to take to work in whichever cold and bare hospital interview room to which they are allocated on a completely unpredictable basis. I try never to teach, supervise or do without the presence of physis – even if I have to bring in a stone, or a leaf or a lonely back-of-the-bed hellebore picked from the university campus. (Sorry!)

On one occasion I was faced with a number of people in a conference centre built from miles and miles of bare concrete, up on the second floor with not a painting, not a touch of green in sight – and no time to go and fetch something. Then inspiration struck – I asked people whether they would be willing, just for the time of our session, to find something about themselves or in their bags which could represent another kind of creativity – the power of transformation even in the bleakest of surroundings. Out came tangerines, a beautiful purple scarf, a favourite notebook, a piece of diamanté jewellery, some pretty multi-coloured pens . . . We put them on the floor in the middle of the circle of hostile chairs and together we created, from our own resources, a *temenos* in a minute or two.

I know of colleagues who do some form of meditation – e.g. the **five relationship dimensions (concerning the process)** and **seven level body meditation (concerning the content)** – to prepare themselves for each day or every session. (See the second edition of *The Therapeutic Relationship* – Clarkson, in press c – for further details.) Others fill a crystal vase with fresh water and an uncut amethyst in their consulting rooms to absorb 'negative energies'; many practitioners consult Feng Shui experts in order to 'balance' the life energies in their room (and so do many international businesses). There are many other ways of organizing 'psychic protection' for the sometimes very dirty work that we do. (See e.g. Bloom 1996.) Others again do regular 'sacred space clearing'. (See e.g. Kingston 1996.)

Nor does this sacred space have to be external. I was profoundly moved when Renos Papadopoulous gave a paper at a 1998 conference called 'Doing psychoanalysis in unusual places'. He was working with hospitalized soldiers and refugees from another country whose language he could speak. He would 'hang around' until one of the men wanted to speak, helping with various tasks around the ward in the mean time. There was no scheduled time for 'the appointment', no couch, no 50 minutes, no therapeutic contract even(!). Yet he formed an internal psychological frame for the therapy which was demonstrated externally by the fact that he wore a tie when on 'duty'. He also put his diary down as marker of the beginning of the session by the patient's bed and removed it again at the end. What people do speaks so much louder than what they say.

The space in which the psychotherapy and/or supervision takes place may also be symbolic or **archetypal** – drawing at some **levels** on our ancient collective experiences of the 'spirit of place'. Here follows a summary table of such an idea which can be adapted at the implicit or explicit narrative **level** 6 to enrich our work metaphorically – and perhaps in other ways too.

So when I hear from some colleagues how clients (especially those from oral cultures and those who do not share our Eurocentric cultural conceptions about time) 'don't keep their appointments', are 'always late', 'don't want to make a contract', 'are not psychologically minded', 'want to go over time' or 'expect me to wave a magic wand', I wonder what we think we are doing? So if they won't speak our WOT, we simply won't make a therapeutic relationship with them? The requirement that the defeated take on the oppressor's language is as old as war.

A culturally congruent narrative

Frank (1973) also showed that all effective healing practices required a culturally congruent narrative. What works is not necessarily 'the story' you believe in, but the client's story – a narrative that 'fits' for the **client**. I have dealt with this extensively in Chapter 2, so I will just share a few comments here.

For example, in the first session, when clients ask me what 'my approach' is, I enquire about their previous reading or learning about psychotherapy and what meanings they have construed from that (in words chosen to fit that particular person and their conversational vocabulary and

Table 4.1 Summary table – the archetopoi of supervision

Nature of the problem	Locale	Type of focal issue in the parallel process	Role	Primary tasks	Theoretical focus – e.g.	Example
Danger	Hunting grounds	Survival	Cerberus – guardian	Minimize/obviate danger	Boundaries	The supervisee reports that her depressed client has threatened to kill her child
Confusion	Home/ Community	Transference Countertransference	Psyche – sorter	Analyse Separate Clarify	Oedipus complex	The client is in an erotic transference with the supervisee
Conflict	Arena	Ambivalence Splitting	Zeus – mediator or referee	Resolve Surrender Integrate Reject or accept	Paranoid-schizoid to depressive position	The patient wishes to terminate analysis. The supervisee vacillates between feeling regretful or relieved at the prospect
Deficit	Academy	Lack (of information resources, technique, experiences, skill)	Chiron – educator	Enable or intentionally supply information resources, techniques, access	Corrective reparative or developmentally needed experience	The supervisee is worried because they 'broke the boundaries' by accompanying to the police station the patient who had been raped on the way to the station
Development	Temple	Avoidance or exploitation – of mystery *Coincidentia oppositorum*	Hekate exploitation Nature/God/ Physis	Allow space for, create a *temenos* or vas, enable, acknowledge, the transpersonal dimension (not make archetypal what is, individual what is archetypal)	Collective Unconscious/ archetypal	As a young girl the patient had been ostracized by her fundamentalist religious community for appearing to have caused the death of a younger sibling. She believes she has the devil inside her and that only God can give her absolution

communication style). Often people will claim that they 'know nothing', but even then they have watched the 'soaps', or they have friends who have been in psychotherapy/training or they will talk about their favourite books or films. Then, quite naturally and spontaneously they tell me in their own words the 'rationale' for their difficulties and the nature of their expectations of me and from the psychotherapy.

If they want to know more (usually these are people in psychotherapy or training), I will explain that I am fluent in several psycho-languages (Freudian, Jungian, Kleinian, Gestalt, Person-centred, TA, Bioenergetics, existential and cognitive-behavioural therapy for example) and I will ask whether they had a particular preference. I explain that research has found that the most effective element in all psychotherapeutic approaches is the therapeutic relationship and that we will need to discover together whether we can build and work within our particular new relationship to accomplish the goals they want for themselves.

If they are lay people, I give them a little booklet which explains the field in ordinary language (see Clarkson 2000a: Appendix 1, 298–304). If they are trainees or veterans in the mental health field I might also give them a copy of the Babel paper ('Beyond schoolism', Clarkson 1998b), and/or refer them to *The Therapeutic Relationship* (Clarkson 1995a), depending on how far they want to go in their exploration. This is all part of the assessment process – and of course we have **already** started working together.

When a client comes to me asking for something which I cannot or will not deliver, I offer them alternatives. An example is when an individual came asking me to cure them of their homosexuality which they believed to be a pathological illness. I explained that I did not share their views on the nature of homosexuality, but some other professionals did.

I was willing to work with her on her feelings and conduct of which she was ashamed. But, I said, in fairness, it would be better for her to work with someone who conceptualized her problem in a way which suited her own theories and beliefs better at that time. I gave her the names of some of my colleagues who would share her deeply held views on this matter. (The initial conditions were not right for me and there were other competent professionals for whom such initial conditions would be right.)

Another example concerned a financially stricken young woman with a very severe psychiatric history who had set her heart on working with me. When I heard about her sudden, frequent and long hospitalizations, her anorexia, drug-taking and the extensive series of previously failed psychotherapeutic relationships, but **particularly** about her forms of 'acting out' against her previous psychiatrists, psychologists, counsellors and psychiatrists (stalking, threatening their children, breaking consulting room furniture, smashing the consulting room windows, physical attacks, and so on) I explained that I did not see how I could responsibly take her on in once-a-week psychotherapy. (This was all I had space for at the time.) She insisted that she believed that I could help her and her sincerity moved me.

I then made initial conditions for her which were **unusually** precise and explicit. I said that I would work with her – if she so much believed I could help her. **But** I would break off the therapeutic relationship at the first sign of her being late for sessions, breaking appointments without proper notice, not paying the full fee at the beginning of every session (I often do substantial reduced-fee work), any form of threatened or actual verbal or physical abuse against anybody including herself, finding out that she was in hospital again and so on and so forth. Was she willing to accept these conditions? Yes.

I then explained that she could **talk** to me about any of her feelings of wanting to do such things and that I would whole-heartedly support her if she felt she needed to be hospitalized again. Then she could **phone me** and we would work together so that she could find a safe 'asylum' if she felt she was 'losing it' in order to make it as planned and beneficial experience as possible for both of us.

You can probably guess the end of the story. She is now, a decade or so later, a healthy, sane, creative professional woman with good friends, a steady loving relationship, a rich emotional life and an apartment in a most desirable city block. She has learned and continues to learn from the ups and downs of existence, growing psychologically and spiritually stronger and wiser with each turn of Life's wheel.

Did she get hospitalized during this time? Yes. As we had contracted, she phoned me one night some six years ago in desperation – she wanted to be admitted to a psychiatric hospital. I said, 'Well done, I'll help.' As luck would have it she couldn't get herself admitted. The local psychiatrists would not accept that she needed admission – because she was sane enough to ask for it! She **did not want** to 'go mad' (her words) or cut herself again or attempt suicide – she was just asking to be contained in her familiar environment to hold her and prevent her doing crazy things. She had no money for a private facility.

All my friendly and understanding psychiatric colleagues were away on holiday or did not have available beds in their facilities. I could not get anybody to help us. This was our foreseeable emergency and I was impotent. Entirely due to her own ingenuity (and considerable verbal skills) she eventually managed to persuade a young registrar on emergency duty late that night to admit her to the psychiatric ward. The next afternoon at about three o-clock she phoned me: 'Petruska I'm coming out, I don't belong here any more.'

Much later she explained to me that all the other psychotherapists always started off being so 'accepting' that she never could really trust them. She **knew** that when she did certain things they'd turn against her and all that acceptance would turn out to have been 'phoney'. She said that because I was so honest and clear about what 'up with which I would not put' in our first session, she trusted me right from the beginning.

> A True Human Being is never what he or she
> appears to be. Rub your eyes,
> and look again.
> (Rumi 1990: 65)

A prescription for action

As Frank (1973) showed, healing practices throughout the world always include some prescription for action – some ritual activity. Apart from (a) my last-mentioned client's undoubtedly strong motivation for change in working with me, (b) my clinical experience in working with patients diagnosed as psychotic, (c) the fact that she was in profound crisis when she came to see me, (d) using **her** language for our narrative, and (e) what one could call the grace of God, we worked out (f) **the healing ritual** between us, by detailing exactly the frame – time, place, setting, fees, conditions for termination, and so on. The prescribed activity for the 'cure' (which she defined for herself) was **talking** about feelings, not acting them out; along with a mutually negotiated agreement for phone contact in specified emergencies.

Some prescriptions for action in Caucasian psychotherapeutic cultures are: 'Lie down on the couch and tell me anything that comes into your head without censoring it'; 'Fill in this depression scale and keep a daily diary of the thoughts which happen just before you feel the compulsion to wash yourself any more than twice a day'; 'Imagine your father in that empty chair as if he's here right now and tell him how his beatings frighten you'; 'Visualize yourself going up the mountain and meeting a wise person there who has a special message for you. What is this person saying to you?'; 'Perhaps you would consider setting aside some private time to think about your child who died. You could bring together his baby shoes, photographs and anything else that reminds you of him. You might even want to light a special candle for his soul'; 'Bring your own tissues' (Masterson 1985); 'Let's make some squiggles on this piece of paper' (Winnicott 1958); Family Therapist: 'Will you answer her?' (Gorrell-Barnes 1979: 84).

Examples of other prescriptions are: 'Follow the twelve steps and come to meetings'; 'Make a no-suicide contract'; 'You could re-decide that script decision'; 'Don't have sexual intercourse with each other until you've completed the sensory sensitivity exercises'; 'You might want to close your eyes as soon as you find your eyelids becoming heavy'; 'Introduce yourself to the group by saying your name and adding: "I am a sex addict"'; conveying by one's conduct (silence) that client questions will not be answered; 'Think of the time you won that marathon, anchor that self-confident victorious state by pressing your flesh between your thumb and your forefinger'; 'Use these puppets to show me what daddy did to you'; 'Let's have a group drumming session'; 'Please tell me your associations to that dream.' A one-session cure for writer's block: 'I think you must keep going downhill and being a bum until you hit bottom' (from *Ordeal Therapy*, Haley 1984: 188).

Another example from a one session cure of enuresis in a hostile eight year old boy by the famed hypnotherapist Erickson: 'Look at those puppies right there. I like the brown one best, but I suppose you like the black-and-white one, because its front paws are white. If you are very careful, you can pet mine, too. I like puppies, don't you?' (1967b: 428; note – the puppies were not **level 5** 'real'). One of my other favourites from Erickson: an enuretic couple were 'told that the absolute requisite for therapeutic benefits would lie in their unquestioning and unfailing obedience to the instructions given to them. This they promised' (1967a: 410). Then:

> You are both very religious and you have both given me a promise you will keep. You have a transportation problem that makes it difficult to see me regularly for therapy. Your financial situation makes it practically impossible for you to see me frequently.
>
> You are to receive experimental therapy and you are obligated absolutely either to benefit or to pay me whatever fee I deem reasonable. Should you benefit, the success of my therapy will be my return for my effort and your gain. Should you not benefit, all I will receive for my effort is a fee and that will be a double loss to you but no more than an informative disappointment to me.
>
> This is what you are to do: each evening you are to take fluids freely. Two hours before you go to bed, lock the bathroom door after drinking a glass of water. At bedtime, get into your pyjamas and then kneel side by side on the bed, facing your pillows and deliberately and jointly wet the bed. This may be hard to do, but you must do it. Then lie down and go to sleep, knowing full well that the wetting of the bed is done with for the night, that nothing can really make it noticeably wetter. [They did it for two 'never-ending' weeks, but the problem then disappeared.]
>
> (Erickson 1967a: 410–11)

Sounds like nonsense to some ears – until you read Erickson's deeply informed theoretical rationale (narrative) which explains why he thinks it worked. (Of course, any transpersonal **level** talk **is** non-sense.) Rumi says: 'You can't understand this with your mind. You must burst open!'(1990: 9).

However some may still think that is actually nonsense or just simply wrong. The point is people are in pain and we as psychotherapists say we want to help. The point is, Erickson's prescription for action worked. It alleviated and ended their suffering. Now I grew up in South Africa where *sangomas* ('witchdoctors' or medicine-people) are consulted for human pain at least as often as (if not more often than) black and white Western-trained doctors. Indeed I heard about a European-trained clinical psychologist who was at the same time a local sangoma in the village where he lived.

When asked how he knew which clients wanted the clinical psychologist's services and which clients wanted the sangoma's services, he replied: 'It all depends on which door they come into my consulting hut. One door is for me as a western clinical psychologist and the other door is for me as a traditional healing medicine-man.' 'So what's different in your practice?' 'Just the stories we tell and the prescriptions I make for them – I work from where each client is.'

Just one more example from Africa: there was a woman who came for healing because she could not fall pregnant. She had tried everything else – including western medicine – and nothing had helped. The indigenous healer prescribed that she washed herself thoroughly. Then she was to go and sit in a particular tree for three days and nights. When she came down she would fall pregnant before her next menstruation. And so she did. **Be careful** in criticizing or looking down from a lofty colonial height on such narratives and such prescriptions.

People get cured of their ills in such ways too – and always have. Furthermore, the best most advanced pharmacological products lead our Western-trained psychiatrists to say: 'Take these pills.' Yet I also have it on the best authority (personal communication from Professor Lader of the Maudsley) that the placebo rate for anti-depressant medication is between 25 and 35 per cent! This means that of people whose depression is cured – by their own criteria – some 35 out of a hundred patients might as well have been taking sugar pills.

At 14, Alexandra Aitken found out her father, the politician Jonathan Aitken, was accused of pimping and dealing in illegal arms; much worse was to come. Alexandra said later in a newspaper interview:

> I know it all might sound strange (when I first started the treatments I was sceptical too) but afterwards you feel as though all your cobwebs have been brushed away. When you look at your face you look different, much clearer and fresher. Also, it helps to take everything in my stride.
>
> (Morgan 2000: 49)

The healer who worked with her explains his work as follows: 'In oriental medicine the body is made up of seven major chakra of energy points . . . In a healthy person this life energy – or bio-energy – should flow freely through the body. Bio-energy healing simply corrects the energy flow' (Morgan 2000: 49). Western medicine practitioners are beginning to recognize the notion of the energy field within and surrounding the body, as the Scientific and Medical Network organization and its publication *Network* continues to attract more and more members. Recent reports, in the *Lancet* for example, provide increasing medically tested evidence that homeopathy 'works'.

It helps if the client or patient has a rationale (a theory or story) for why the prescription for action would work. In interviewing some patients about their experiences of psychotherapy in the NHS, one person reported that after having suffered a most traumatic medically induced trauma, she had spent the following 13 years in agony and rage. One of the things that she found most helpful was that her psychotherapist had encouraged her to write letters (which she never posted) to express (or cathart) her rage and disappointment directly to the people who had so abused her and let her down in her reasonable expectation of competent care from them. This prescription for action really helped her.

In the same group was another person whose therapist advised him to write a letter to his dead father, go to the cemetery and read the letter out loud to his father. He said he felt like he was just going through the motions – as if he was reading dead words 'to the nettles'. The prescription for action (which under other circumstances may have been helpful) lacked an appropriate story – a rationale or theory which was culturally acceptable to this man, and so the intervention failed. Indeed it set the therapy back in an unfortunate way. The working alliance was not appropriately established for it to work.

Prescriptions for action need to be carefully tailored to suit each individual in relationship with the therapist at that time and for that particular place in their journey. On the other hand, there is, according to most spiritual traditions (and Jung's notion of the collective unconscious), deep and ancient wisdom in each being which may need no theory or rationale except the trust in the therapist's conduct of the healing process.

Don (1996), a psychotherapist, writes about a patient, Wendy, who had no knowledge of yoga, meditation, Jungian or metaphysical writings; he had, therefore, no reason to believe that she knew about the Kundalini serpent, the uroboros, which Yogic traditions visualize as an energetic force going up (and down) the spine:

> I next saw Wendy after a three-week break because of my summer vacation. She
> related a dream to me. In the dream, she and her friend Steve were walking and

unexpectedly came across my Saint Bernard, with whom Wendy had a very affectionate relationship. Upon seeing the dog and feeling its love and acceptance for her – an acceptance 'no real person would ever give me' – Wendy felt that in 'one simple step' energy could rush up her spine. This would actually lift her physically as well as energetically, thereby making her a 'real person'.

[Later, Don writes] I think, however that if we are willing to look more deeply, we can see man in terms of his descent from the cosmic. In the process of this descent, it is the unfolding of his lower order systems which occurs . . . The higher **levels** of the self, which are completely ignored in the mainstream of Western psychotherapy, are intact at birth and before.

(Don 1996: 366, 373)

So, a last word on 'expectancy effects' (see Aspy 1974; Tausch and Tausch 1998; Clarkson 1995a: 36–40, for review). Yes, believing that something will work improves a prognosis immeasurably. But when you're in dire need and your child is dying, you'll try anything – whether you believe it will work or not. (At least I would.)

According to Rumi: 'A drowning man reaches for anything! The Friend [God] loves this flailing about better than any lying [or sitting] still' (1991: 58).

I think we know from many anecdotes that people don't have to believe in something for it to work. Recently a person told me that the first time a therapist suggested to her that she hit a cushion, she thought the therapist more in need of psychological help than she was. Did she eventually do it? 'Yes, but I thought it was a rubbish idea.' 'And then?' 'Oh, it was a turning point for me in my therapy and I've never looked back.'

Case study: part 1

Preparing the *vas* – initial conditions and the working alliance

Jeder came to see me because his wife could not stand his depression any more. He had seen his GP who recommended that he take anti-depressant medication, but he did not want to start the course, since he felt it would be a sign of 'weakness'. He had built an internationally renowned business and was well respected in the City of London. After selling his company for many millions of pounds, he 'retired', but continued to be active as a director on the boards of several charities. He lived in a beautiful country mansion, with luxurious apartments in Cannes, the West Indies and a *pied-à-terre* in London.

At first impression, Jeder looks like many other men of this class and background in the financial sector, young for his years. His hair and nails are meticulously groomed. However, he has stopped going to the gym since his depression had left him feeling completely unmotivated. He comes in a suit whose cut I recognize and is very formal, addressing me as Professor Clarkson. The atmosphere reminds me of being an inadequate shop assistant dealing with a customer who already knows in an impatient and cross way that he won't get good service from this shop. But he has to go through the motions anyway so that he can say to his wife that he did actually try.

I ask him whether he always obeyed his wife's wishes. No, it's been a marriage in name only for many years now for the sake of the children, but the family was getting worried. It was all just too much effort and now they were also pestering him to take the drugs. They had stopped making love many years ago. His wife was a difficult woman, but a good mother to his children and he wouldn't want to hurt her. That's why he has always used prostitutes before. However, in recent times he couldn't even get an erection – and this had happened several times. So now he doesn't even bother with that any more. He just has not got the energy.

What makes you feel alive? What gives you pleasure? He answers with a question accompanied with a cynical laugh: What's pleasure? Nothing really, even things I used to enjoy like playing golf or going to the theatre seem silly and childish. Do you have any friends? Yes, there are some business associates from the old times and a couple of months a year we used to meet for a business lunch. Other people have died, some I never see any more. How do you get on with your children? My sons are a waste of time – I've set them both up in the business, but the one is a heroin addict in Manchester and will probably do himself in any day. We have no contact. The other one is running the business, or rather walking the business downhill. The new Board will probably get rid of him soon – but at least he has the network and can easily get another job more suited to his abilities. My eldest daughter did not get on with her mother and is now living in Australia. She won't even speak to me on the phone if her mother is in the house. I haven't seen her for years. The other daughter married some small-time farmer and lives in the country with my two granddaughters.

Have you faced other problems since your retirement? There's a long-standing legal battle about my parents' estate which has been going on for years. But frankly, I can't be bothered fighting that any more. Let the rest of that family do what they want.

Tell me about the best times in your life. I really can't think of anything. My life seems to have just passed me by and I was too busy building the company to spend much time with the children. So I don't really know them. But, I always went to their graduations . . . I remember though when I was a teenager I used to go to church and Christian youth events regularly to meet the girls and that was a very nice time. What else? Well, I once won a national swimming championship and I was very happy about that. I trained very hard for several years and I think I was a little attracted to my coach. It was day after day of being in the pool at daybreak and doing miles of laps every single day – even on weekends. (Sigh.) But that was a long time ago.

When he paid me, it was an irritation, not an expense. I asked him whether he wanted to come again and he said I had a nice room and he might as well, so we made another appointment.

Analysis

The work

In the initial session with Jeder, I judged that he was very seriously depressed and had been so for a long time. He'd lost the self-esteem and meaning in life that his business activities had given him or that had kept him too busy to realize the emptiness inside. At his point now he couldn't see the point any more – a possible suicide indicator.

The culturally congruent narrative

The sale of his company was perhaps the devastating loss that had affected him most, but he was quite unable to talk about his feelings. There is a psychological condition called *alexithymia* – the inability to put feelings into words. Degrees of this are quite common among the men of some cultures. All 'that kind of thing' came under the heading of 'depression' for Jeder.

The relationship

Jeder was probably too de-energized to commit suicide at the moment and he had some consideration for his family. He'd mentioned a Christian background. He had had virtually no social support. The people he mentioned as his friends were patently not what I would have called friends. Rather typically for males of that generation and culture, he still clung to some idea that he could recover without showing the weakness of 'having to take pills'. But basically he did not believe in me, in himself or very much else. Thus there was only the vaguest possibility of an effective working alliance.

Anyway – would I want to work with him? Could I let go of my prejudices and biases and see him as a unique individual 'with an early morning eye'?

The place

He did say the room was 'nice'.

The prescription for action

I was quite uncertain whether he would take it up, but I did offer him the very limited option of 'coming again'.

Chapter 5
Nigredo – disillusionment in the therapeutic relationship and in life

Dance with the Bandage Torn Off
Dance, when you're broken open.
Dance, if you've torn the bandage off.
Dance in the middle of the fighting.
Dance in your blood.
Dance when you're perfectly free.

Struck, the dancers hear a tambourine inside them
as a wave turning to foam on its very top, begins.

Maybe you don't hear that tambourine,
or the tree leaves clapping time.

Close the ears on your head
that listen mostly to lies and cynical jokes.

There are other things to hear and see:
dance-music and a brilliant city
inside the Soul.
Stretch your arms and take hold the cloth of your clothes
with both hands. The cure for pain is in the pain.
Good and bad are mixed. If you don't have both,
you don't belong with us.

Today, like every other day, we wake up empty
and frightened. Don't open the door to the study
and begin reading. Take down a musical instrument.

Let the beauty we love be what we do.

There are hundreds of ways to kneel and kiss the ground. (Secret)

(Rumi 1988: 55)

> We read in the psalm: 'If I ascend up into heaven, Thou art there; if I make my
> bed in the netherworld, behold, there Thou art.' When I consider myself great
> and think I can touch the sky, I discover that God is the faraway There, and the
> higher I reach, the farther away he is. But if I make my bed in the depths, if I bow
> my soul down to the netherworld, there, too, he is with me.
>
>   (Buber 1962: 104)

Freud dismissed the idea of Physis in an innate developmental urge as 'a pleasing illusion', but in the work of Jung it appears quite frequently. For example, Jung approvingly quotes pseudo-Democritus: "**Physis rejoices in physis, physis conquers physis, physis rules over physis**" (1966: 262).

Extensive investigation of Jung's use of the term however reveals contradictions and paradoxes that may be illuminated by study of the notion of Physis throughout history and in the contemporary practice of psychoanalysis and psychotherapy (Clarkson, unpublished PhD thesis, University of Kent).

It is postulated that his (and Hillman's) ambivalence about Physis reflects the dualistic splitting of the concept of Nature which first occurred in occidental thinking with Plato. This was subsequently perpetuated by, for example, the Juliani (see Ronan 1992) until it became enshrined in occidental philosophy through the work of Descartes and in physics through to the work of Newton. This effort has been so successful that the Caucasian mentality almost cannot conceive of mind and body as **different aspects of a unitary phenomenon** and results in all of what Ryle (1966) called the logical fallacies of 'the ghost in the machine'.

Heidegger's convoluted language is trying to say the unsayable:

> Being in the sense of *physis* is the power that emerges. As contrasted with
> becoming, it is permanence, permanent presence. Contrasted with appearance,
> it is appearing, manifest presence. The phenomenological correlation became
> the 'alethiological correlation' where physis was associated with the ultimate *a
> priori*, the first of everything about the human world and thus (for those with the
> sensitivity for it) the most obvious fact of all. Yet it is generally overlooked, not
> primarily because of some human defect but above all because it [physis] 'prefers
> to hide' (Heraclitus Frag. 53) in the sense of being ultimately unfathomable.
>
>   (Heidegger 1987: 125)

One of the hiding places is in different cultures. As Holdstock (1990) points out: 'The ensembled individualism of Africa extends beyond the concept as discussed by Sampson (1988). It transcends the **level** of inter-personal relationships and reaches into the realm of the spiritual. Not only humans, but all things are imbued with "seriti" (force, energy, spirit). It is as a vital force, which is part of a larger vital force, that the individual participates in the world. In fact, the human being is not only vital force, but vital force in participation.' Druids hold very similar beliefs.

Sereti is Physis by yet another, perhaps even older name. Other African countries use the word NTU, the Japanese talk about Ikiru-Chikara; Ancient Egyptians referred to Ka; Hindus to Prakriti. Another hiding place is in the frontiers of the Eurocentric sciences of chaos and complexity where the notion of auto-poiesis shockingly accurately duplicates the earliest pre-Socratic understandings of **life's self-creation**.

Complexity science refers to the same phenomenon as those aspects of auto-poiesis which are still mysterious, the 'physis' which makes systems and organisms emerge and self-develop out of unpredictable circumstances – auto-poietic emergence itself.

Saturn tax

In ancient Rome they held great Saturnalias, which were feasts of food and drink and licentiousness. During this feast there was the extremely important ritual of passing to each other (and beneath the table) a skull – *memento mori*: remember death. The purpose of this ritual was to remind each other that no matter how abandoned and intense their experiences of life would be, it is also important to remember that death and suffering are always with us.

It has often been pointed out to me that people complain that as soon as they have, for example, the perfect marriage, or have arranged the perfect party, that something happens to 'spoil' it. Being human, as we are, we then tend to focus on this negative aspect, somehow feeling that it detracts in some way from the perfection of the moment and reminds us that nothing is perfect, balanced, or stable for long.

It's not like the saying 'There'll be tears before bedtime', with its silly prohibition or inhibition of joyous excitement. It's that laughter follows on tears and tears on laughter and laughter on tears *et secula et secula*. No amount of curtailing our laughter will prevent the cycles of Life from manifesting. No amount of 'not getting too hopeful about something' will prevent the feelings of disappointment when the anticipated (job, mate, opportunity) does not materialize.

> I tell you this story to remind you
> that the loss of the body and the loss of material wealth
> is good for your spirit.
>
> Buy discipline and service to others with your life,
> and if discipline comes without your asking for it,
> bow your head and be grateful.

When that happens,
God is paying special attention to you,
is holding you close,
and whispering in your ear
the original word,
BE!

(Rumi 1988: 28)

Another way of speaking about this is that we can prepare ourselves through an *amor fati* (a love of one's fate). This involves looking out for, anticipating and giving thanks for that flaw. For the thirteenth wicked fairy, the fly in the ointment, the tears, the suffering, the disappointment, the betrayal, the 'crack where the light comes in' – according to the Leonard Cohen song.

> This is our epoch, good or bad, beautiful or ugly, rich or poor – we did not choose it. This is our epoch, the air we breathe, the mud given us, the bread, the fire, the spirit! Let us accept Necessity courageously . . . God is never created out of happiness or comfort or glory, but out of shame and hunger and tears.
>
> (Kazantzakis 1960: 114, 111)

Necessity (*ananke*) is another name for Physis. It is through our disappointments that we are able to keep our appointments with our destiny. These disappointments, disillusionments and disruptions can be seen as the necessary psychological 'tax' that everyone must pay to Saturn, the disciplinarian, the stern taskmaster of the Zodiac – time itself in its personification as Chronos. Orthodox Jews leave a corner unfinished in a newly painted room – because 'only God is perfect'.

It also reminds me of the Taoist symbol that always keeps a germ of light in the deepest darkness, and a germ of black in the clearest whiteness. And we can learn from Taoist as well as Heraclitean sources the wisdom of *enantiodromia*. This is the likelihood that when anything becomes most fully and completely of itself, it starts changing into its opposite. In Gestalt this is referred to as the paradoxical theory of change. There is no stasis in nature, no final arrival point while we are alive (and maybe not after we are dead, either).

Figure 5.1 Tao

The Tao that can be told is not the eternal Tao.
The name that can be named is not the eternal name.
The nameless is the beginning of heaven and earth.
The named is the mother of ten thousand things.
Ever desireless, one can see the mystery.
Ever desiring, one can see the manifestations.
These two spring from the same source but differ in name;
this appears as darkness.
Darkness within darkness.
The gate to all mystery.

(Lao Tsu 1973: 1)

The cycle

We are all familiar with the Gestalt Cycle of experience which is a conceptual image of eternal recurrence, the inevitable cyclical nature of human life from birth to death, the inexorable progression from spring to summer, to summer to autumn to winter and then to spring again. (Like the ancient wisdom of the Chinese Book of Changes – the *I Ching*: Wilhelm 1951.) The cycle encapsulates the rhythm of breathing in and breathing out, the essential pattern of gestalt formation and destruction. Being coming into being and passing away. It is perhaps the only notion which carries some security – things will change and change again and again, they will begin, they will come to some kind of peak, climax or apotheosis and then they will decline again to some kind of ending whereafter it begins again.

The healthy, uninterrupted flow of experience is the natural state of a healthy animal or a spontaneous, healthy young child. It is a natural expression of life energy and the drive for actualization of the self or well-being. A need arises, is satisfied, and arises again. The Zen master asks, 'Everybody has a place of birth (origin or beginning). Where is your place of birth?' The adept answers: 'Early this morning I ate white rice gruel, now I am hungry again.' A dominant figure emerges from the background, claims attention, and fades into the background again as a new, compelling figure emerges. This is the cyclic, pulsating nature of human experience. Although it may be temporarily or chronically inhibited, it will re-assert itself again.

(Clarkson 1989a: 27)

Heraclitus saw the flow quality of this experience and the way in which the cycle moves through its opposite poles. 'The cycle is the compact experiential reconciliation of permanence and degeneration' (Guerrière 1980: 88). The Gestalt concept of organism flow is represented by the healthy flow of alternating gestalt formation and destruction, which can be likened to the natural breathing pattern of inhalation and exhalation, of eating and defecating, of arousal and orgasm, of life and death.

Every form of life appears with a specific unfolding in time, as well as in space, followed by a folding in again. The rhythm of plants growing, blossoming and seeding is time-bound. Indeed, according to von Franz (1978), the meaning of time is that in it shapes of growth and decay can unfold in a clear sequence.

The cycle could equally well be represented in a wave-like diagram to show its rhythmic, pulsating quality. I often prefer the cycle in order to emphasize systemic circularity, inter-relatedness and wholeness. I also like it because it echoes the archetypal intuition of a cyclical time in many spiritual traditions, where the cosmic rhythm consists of the periodic destruction and re-creation of the world. Modern physics has revealed that every sub-atomic particle not only performs an energy dance but also *is* an energy dance: a pulsating process of creation and destruction (Capra 1983).

In psychology, as in physics or astronomy, larger or macroscopic cycles mirror smaller or microscopic cycles. For example, the atom bears a structural resemblance to the solar system. Larger units of experience mirror smaller units. The impatient sigh which lasts a moment can mirror a life lived in frustrated impatience. In this holographic way the whole is represented in each of the parts and the parts each contain a holographic representation of the whole. The Gestalt experience cycle in microcosm (such as in the wave-like pattern of breathing in and breathing out) is a natural process. Depending on what task is at hand, be it running or relaxation, the healthy organism will regulate its breathing to maximum efficiency.

The larger macroscopic cycles, for example the sequences of adult developmental stages, may take a lifetime. Larger or smaller cycles can be managed creatively and satisfactorily if the natural processes are allowed to reach their organismic conclusions. This simple but also profoundly subtle paradigm represents healthy organism functioning.

Phylocryptia (the love of hiding)

In the words of Heraclitus: 'Physis loves to hide' (Kahn 1981: 105). (Hiding is a game that lovers play.) Following my thread experientially and academically, I have lost it many times – sometimes for years. Then suddenly it emerges with a psychic call patterned on the first chords of Beethoven's Fifth Symphony – only to disappear from my view again. It also apparently disappears from scholarly investigation – sometimes for short periods, sometimes for decades or centuries. Currently there appears to be only one book in print which deals primarily with physis – in Canada – in French (Naddaf 1993).

Where do we find the original traces – where does Physis hide? In the first treatises of Greek alchemy, 'the divine water is said to effect a transformation by bringing the "hidden nature" to the surface' (Berthelot, quoted in Jung 1968: 101). Sometimes in the creative descent into, sometimes imprisoned in 'the dark of matter' (Jung 1951: para. 308), sometimes it is the king and queen, 'gone back to the chaotic beginnings, the *massa confusa*' (Jung 1966: para. 457), sometimes it is told that 'Beya [the maternal sea] rose up over Gabricus and enclosed him in her womb, so that nothing more of him was to be seen. And she embraced Gabricus with so much love that she absorbed him completely into her own nature, and dissolved him into atoms' (Jung quoting the Rosarium, 1966: para. 457).

> This self-concealment is not imposed upon [Physis] from the outside, but is the manner in which [Physis] itself 'does itself' . . . Physis – the logos in and of things – is wont, that it might be or remain itself, to conceal itself.
>
> (Guerrière 1980: 100)

The Hasidim say:

> God hides in two ways. One way is that God hides so that it is very difficult to find him and yet who knows that God is hiding from him can advance toward him and find him. The other way is that God hides from a man the fact that he is hiding and, since the seeker knows so little about God, he cannot find him. It is this that is referred to in the words: 'I shall hide, hide.' God hides the fact that he is hiding, and those from whom he is hiding do not know him – the hidden one.
>
> (Buber 1962: 15)

Here is a little story which is well-known and repeated in many traditions: A man was struggling in terrible torment across the desert. He prayed to God to accompany him and God answered his prayer. When looking back he saw two pairs of footprints in the sand – except for the worst part of the journey. There he saw only one pair of footprints. Outraged, he accused God, saying: 'I had asked you to accompany me and there, in the worst part, you abandoned me! Don't play one of your tricks on me. I know that you left me then because I can see there is only one set of footprints over that most terrible area.' God answered calmly: 'My son, the time when you can see only one set of footprints is the time I was carrying you.'

According to the Gnostics, as Jung reads them, the god which hides in matter *(deus absconditus)* also conceals itself in the symbolism of the loving embrace between Nous and Physis and the foundations of alchemy. The absconded god is cloaked in the divine or lustrous water and is seen again in the symbol of the uroboros. In this small passage below, already all the main themes of this work are powerfully condensed as if in a homeopathic, infinitely minute dose. However, the analysis of this Physic (medicine) for the world soul may have to reply not only to the intuitive grasp, but sometimes also the scholar's analytical devotions in making obeisance to the *obscurata* (the obscure).

> In spite of the not always unintentional obscurity of alchemical language, it is not difficult to see that the divine water or its symbol, the uroboros, means nothing other than the *deus absconditus*, the god hidden in matter, the divine Nous that came down to Physis and was lost in her embrace. This mystery of the 'god become physical' underlies not only classical alchemy but also many other spiritual manifestations of Hellenistic syncretism.
>
> (Jung 1967: para. 138)

Our ordinary vision may blind us to the goal of alchemy begun by nature and perfected by our own work – it is invisible. 'The stone is that thing midway between perfect and imperfect bodies, and that which nature herself begins is brought to perfection through the art. The stone is named the stone of invisibility (*lapis invisibilitatis*)' (Jung 1968: para. 243).

> There is a spirit hidden in the *prima materia*, just as there was in the Nile stone of Ostanes. This spirit was eventually interpreted as the Holy Ghost in accordance with the ancient tradition of the Nous swallowed up by the darkness while in the embrace of Physis – with this difference, however, that it is not the supreme feminine principle, earth, who is the devourer, but Nous in the form of Mercurius or the tail-eating Uroboros . . . In other words, the devourer is a sort of material earth-spirit, an hermaphrodite possessing a masculine-spiritual and feminine-corporeal aspect . . . The original Gnostic myth has undergone a strange transformation: Nous and Physis are indistinguishably one in the *prima materia* and have become a *natura abscondita*.
>
> (Jung 1968: para. 447)

In this way we find Jung (as in the paragraph above) describing as 'strange' the many transformations or even coexistences of forces, traditions and archetypes into their opposites. Elsewhere he writes:

> The *lapis*, understood as the cosmogonic First Man, is the *radix ipsius*, according to the *Rosarium*: everything has grown from this One and through this One. It is the Uroboros, the serpent that fertilizes and gives birth to itself, by definition an *increatum*, despite a quotation from Rosarius to the effect that 'Mercurius noster nobilissimus' was created by God as a 'res nobilis'. This *creatum increatum* [creature which was not created] can only be listed as another paradox. It is useless to rack our brains over this extraordinary attitude of mind.
>
> (Jung 1966: para. 527)

At a Psychology Conference where I was presenting a paper on 'Narrative approaches in, and the therapy of, psychotherapeutic narratives' (the fractal of this book), someone in the audience said: 'I feel like I am eating my own tail.' The physian image of the uroboros rose like an archangel over his words. But I left it unspoken.

Coincidentia oppositorum (the coexistence of opposites)

'Of course, it not only hides itself but, in and as things, it reveals itself as well' (Guerrière 1980: 101). The hiding is thus also the revealing. 'Although physis is wont to hide itself, it manifests itself in multiple ways . . . all suggest a certain oneness in multiple things, a certain *coincidentia oppositorum* (coincidence of opposites)' (Guerrière 1980: 102).

That physis contains the opposites is by now already obvious. Heraclitus wrote, 'The way up and down is one and the same' (Guerrière 1980: 75) and 'The one matter shows itself in the *coincidentia oppositorum*' (Guerrière 1980: 104). According to Jung: 'The antinomial development of the concepts is in keeping with the paradoxical nature of alchemy.' 'Opposites may be one in their cyclic recurrence: they come around to and replace each other' (Guerrière 1980: 105).

Although Physis is concerned with life most fully, it always also implies its opposite – even its perfection – in death. That is why I do not agree with Murray that Heraclitus denies Lethe. Heraclitus suggests that psyche naturally has to die to attain the highest form of life (Kahn 1981: 251). In the midst of living, we are dying. Although 'the name of the bow is life; its work is death' (Kahn 1981: 65).

> Thabritius is the masculine, spiritual principle of light and Logos which, like the Gnostic Nous, sinks into the embrace of physical nature (Physis). Death therefore represents the completion of the spirit's descent into matter.
>
> (Jung 1968: para 436)

For Dylan Thomas, too:

> The force that through the green fuse drives the flower
> Drives my green age; that blasts the roots of trees
> Is my destroyer . . .
>
> The force that drives the water through the rocks
> Drives my red blood; that dries the mouthing streams
> Turns mine to wax . . .

The lips of time leech to the fountain head;
Love drips and gathers, but the fallen blood
Shall calm her sores . . .

And I am dumb to tell the lover's tomb
How at my sheet goes the same crooked worm.

(Thomas 1980: 8)

Guerrière interprets and explains the Heraclitean gnome using again the image of this water: 'One phenomenon – river water – is *at once* the "same" or identical . . . *and* "different" or other . . . The opposites (sameness and difference) are one; a single phenomenon manifests itself in opposite characteristics (identity and otherness). The river water symbolizes the one physis' (Guerrière 1980: 104).

Jung repeatedly emphasizes and grapples with the inescapable tension between the opposites – the uroboros or 'serpent as allegory of Christ as well as of the devil . . . the strongest polarity into which the Anthropos falls when he descends into Physis' (Jung 1951: para 390):

> the stronger tension between *anthropos-rotundum* and *serpens* [serpent] on the one hand, and the lesser tension between *homo* [man] and *lapis* [philosopher's stone] on the other . . . the descent into Physis and the ascent towards the spiritual . . . The *lapis*, however, though of decidedly material nature, is also a spiritual symbol, while the *rotundum* [cycle] connotes a transcendent entity symbolized by the secret of matter and thus comparable to the concept of the atom.
>
> (Jung 1951: para 391)

As an inheritor of the Christian Gnostic tradition, Jung's struggle comes across in the passage below where he tries to lay claim to a psychology – nay, a **therapy** of the psyche – which has bearing on life and can help to fit people for life. However, here he perpetrates the European split between nature and spirit. He sounds as if he feels he should be able to do that which is impossible – give appropriate psychological explanations for this paradox of the conflict between nature and spirit and their everlasting interchanging:

> . . . we might be tempted by the modern brand of nature philosophy to call energy or the *élan vital* God, and thus to blend into one spirit and nature. So long as such an undertaking is restricted to the misty heights of speculative philosophy, no great harm is done. But if we should operate with this idea in the lower realm of practical psychology, where only practical explanations bear any fruit, we should soon find ourselves involved in the most hopeless difficulties. We do not profess a psychology with merely academic pretensions, or seek

explanations that have no bearing on life. What we want is a practical psychology which yields approvable results – one which explains things in a way that must be justified by the outcome for the patient. In practical ways we strive to fit people for life, and we are not free to set up theories which do not concern our patients and may even injure them. Here we come to a question that is sometimes a matter of life and death – the question whether we base our explanations on 'physis' or spirit. We must never forget that everything spiritual is illusion from the naturalistic standpoint, and that often the spirit has to deny and overcome an insistent physical fact in order to exist at all. If I recognize only naturalistic values, and explain everything in physical terms, I shall depreciate, hinder, or even destroy the spiritual development of my patients. And if I hold exclusively to a spiritual interpretation, then I shall misunderstand and do violence to the natural man in his right to exist as a physical being. More than a few suicides in the course of psychotherapeutic treatment are to be laid at the door of such mistakes. Whether energy is God or God is energy concerns me very little, for how, in any case, can I know such things? But to give appropriate psychological explanations – this I must be able to do . . . The conflict between nature and spirit is itself a reflection of the paradox of psychic life.

(Jung : paras 678, 679)

So at least in several passages in his work, Jung denies that spirit is inherent in matter.

The poet, Kazantzakis – like the African-centred Ani (1994) I quoted before on page 13 – has another idea:

My heart breaks open, my mind is flooded with light, and all at once this world's dread battlefield is revealed to me as an erotic arena.

Two violent contrary winds, one masculine and the other feminine, met and clashed at a crossroads. For a moment they counterbalanced each other, thickened, and became visible.

This crossroads is the Universe. This crossroads is my heart.

This dance of the gigantic erotic collision is transmitted from the darkest particle of matter to the most spacious thought.

The wife of my God is matter; they wrestle with each other, they laugh and weep, they cry out in the nuptial bed of flesh.

They spawn and are dismembered. They fill sea, land, and air with species of plants, animals, men, and spirits. This primordial pair embraces, is dismembered, and multiplies in every living creature.

All the concentrated agony of the Universe bursts out in every living thing.

(Kazantzakis 1960: 123–24)

Finally, it must be acknowledged that the ancient sources are also not indicating a simplistic thesis–antithesis–synthesis solution with a neat and tidy dialectic formula such as Hegelians sometimes want it to be. There is a separation, a tension, a conflict, an important war. As Heraclitus pleaded around 500 BC: 'Let us not concur casually about the most important matters' (Kahn 1981: 33). It is an *enantiodromia*, a violent and sudden shocking transformation from one thing into its total opposite, a passionate and dark embrace, a churning of the stinking waters of the green lion, which 'lets the many emerge'; 'It is the primordial settling-of-accounts, the fundamental ordering, the primitive bringing-forth. This war is the father and king of all . . . it allows [the many] to come forth as what and how they are' (Guerrière 1980: 91).

In Bion's language, transformation in O always has a disruptive character, a kind of '*catastrophic change*. This term links in constant conjunction events characterized by *violence, subversion of the system* and *invariance* in the relation to container-contained' (1970: 53).

'Strife *(polemos)* is the father of all things' (Heraclitus).

(Or nothing happens in psychotherapy until something goes wrong.)

A client writes:

Dear . . . [psychotherapist],

I want to apologize for the way in which I have been behaving in therapy. I have been abusive and hurtful to you. And underneath all this childish, manipulative behaviour, I have felt so frightened – because I've known, in my heart, how unfair I have been and I've not known where it would lead.

When I am into my 'angry child feeling mode' I treat you as a 'witch/monster/bad father figure' and I am furious inappropriately.

When I am into my 'thinking, calm, Adult mode' I know that you are a gifted therapist – skilful, intelligent and caring. I think that as well as being a very proficient therapist, you bring many 'extra's' to your work. I think of you as having a very warm, open heart, which you share with me.

I consider myself blessed by the Universe and by the Gods that put us together and I firmly believe that we are working well and that my 'acting out' was necessary. I'm sorry I was so hurtful during what seemed to me to be an explosion of myself.

I have made great strides because of you and I am deeply grateful. I would never have left my abusive marriage, be living alone successfully, have a loving relationship, realize and transform some of my self-defeating behaviours, if I didn't have you. I would be either in a state of deep depression or high anxiety and I would have to have left my job as I would have been found incompetent.

Even in my most 'angry child' states I know that you are a brilliant therapist. I am so sorry I said all the things I said. I do realize I didn't mean them for you. I will never do that again. THANK YOU FOR BELIEVING IN ME.

With love from,

. . . [client]

The function of the alchemical therapeutic *vas* is to contain the war which rages inside. Instead of living out the conflicts, contradictions and struggles by drinking, chasing after casual sexual encounters, working oneself to burn-out, the psychotherapy place and relationship becomes **the container**. It is indeed like a battleground (like an inner Kurukshetra in *The Mahabharata*: Vyasa 1990) where the opposing armies confront each other. The inner child against the critical parent; the persecutory object against the fragile self; the id against the ego; real self against ideal self, the client against the rules of the psychotherapy frame; ruptures in the working alliance, projective identification – whatever psycho-language you want to speak.

The containing of the therapeutic relationship is the breeding ground for transference and countertransference – when all the biases come out. (For extensive overviews and exploration of these phenomena, see Clarkson 1995a: 62–107; Clarkson, in press d.) In short, whether from client or psychotherapist, or in-between-them, such distortions of the working alliance can potentially **destroy** the therapeutic relationship. However, well used in the service of **transformation**, it can provide invaluable information about what is wrong and what might help – and how.

Sometimes the war is violent and loud as people oscillate between outbursts of rage and grief. Sometimes the distortions can become psychotic. Sometimes the therapist 'breaks down', 'burns out' or succumbs to unethical behaviour such as sexual misconduct. (See e.g. Hedges et al. 1997.)

Sometimes the war is a long siege – a deepening descent into depression or despair. This is the first sign of health – **physis rising**. To the extent that a person can confront and tolerate the opposing forces in themselves, they are usually psychically strong enough to bear it. The monsters gradually – or suddenly – come out.

Some examples are a psychotic 'inner parent', a history of childhood sexual abuse, confessions of abuse perpetrated, e.g. 'I used my baby daughter's gumless mouth to masturbate many years ago and I still blame myself that she is now anorexic'. To the extent that a psychotherapist can contain these disruptive forces, accept them and empathically feel into and with them, the container – the relationship – strengthens.

> The universe is warm, beloved, familiar, and it smells like my own body. It is Love and War both, a raging restlessness, persistence and uncertainty.
>
> Uncertainty and terror. In a violent flash of lightning I discern on the highest peak of power the final, the most fearful pair embracing; Terror and Silence. And between them, a Flame.
>
> (Kazantzakis 1960: 124)

To become empathically attuned requires the greatest discipline. It means that for the period of being with that unique individual the therapist 'brackets' off their own concerns, their own complexes and attempts with the utmost sincerity and respect to 'tune' their instrument (self) to the frequency, tempo and volume of the client. It means 'walking in their moccasins'. It means being like a harp played by a wind.

It means listening not to what you think their words mean, but phenomenologically yielding to their experience of their world. It is visceral empathy. This means the therapist feels it in their viscera – their own muscles. If you do this with a client who is psychotic, you may end up feeling crazy or drenched in sweat. This is diagnostic – as I had to explain to a supervisee who was assigned such a client without having had the necessary experience or competent supervision. Another word for empathy is resonance. Rumi as always says it beautifully:

> Poles apart, I'm the color of dying, you're the color of being born.
> Unless we breathe in each other, there can be no garden.
>
> So that's why plants grow and laugh at our eyes
> which focus on distance.
>
> (Rumi 1988: 17)

Some less poetically inclined people call it 'entering the client's frame of reference' and stick to a kind of cognitive understanding and scientific formulation. It's certainly less messy that way. It also depends on which 'school' you went to – or perhaps even on what your client needs from you. Counselling or psychotherapy of some kind is probably the very first time someone has respectfully listened to the client's story without hurrying them on or interrupting to tell their experience of similar events.

The intimacy which can therefore develop in the therapeutic relationship is sometimes greater than between lifelong spouses. But you are there to do the work together, not to defile the sacred space. The therapist who is too vulnerable, needy of helping or affection, feels unappreciated or under the weather, understimulated or too stressed is in danger of breaking or modifying the boundaries in unhelpful ways (e.g. Hedges et al. 1997).

In my own black time when my best friend had died, it was important for my therapist to be able just to bear my distress and pain unremittingly, week after week, month after month, until finally the healing, like a skin graft, began to 'take'. Somewhere I must have thought, if she can bear it, so can I. As a therapist myself, I knew this must have been a hard and unpleasant time for her, but she proved herself strong and wise enough to stand it – me.

The descent into 'the blackening' (the Nigredo phase of the alchemical work) does require 'getting your hands dirty', sometimes so dirty that they experientially discolour the sun. Jung writes:

> The first state is the hidden state, but by the art and the grace of God, it can be transmuted into the second, manifest state. That is why the *prima materia* sometimes coincides with the idea of the initial stage of the process, the nigredo. It is then the black earth in which the gold or the lapis is sown like a grain of wheat . . . It is the black, magically fecund earth that Adam took with him from Paradise, also called *antimony* and described as 'black blacker than black (*nigrum nigrius nigro*)'.
>
> (Jung 1968: 313)

In Don (1996), the psychotherapist describes in the story of Wendy how his client made a statement at the beginning 'The sun is black, the sun is black' (Don 1996: 362). In the magnificent set of images called the *Splendor Solis*, there is one which illustrates this universally recognized human experience as follows:

Along with many others, Perls (1969a) called this 'the void'. He wrote that void experiences can be futile or fertile.

The **futile void** is when someone goes through this experience of emptiness, alienation, meaninglessness, lack of purpose, lack of confidence, despair and even terror, and emerges unchanged, untransformed or simply bitter and cynical.

Kazantzakis asks:

> How can you reach the womb of the Abyss [like the seed of man in the womb of a woman] to make it fruitful?

> This cannot be expressed, cannot be narrowed into words, cannot be subjected to laws, every person is completely free and has his [or her] own special liberation.

> No form of instruction exists. No Savior exists to open up the road. No road exists to be opened.
>
> (Kazantzakis 1960: 129)

The **fertile void** is when someone emerges from such experiences changed, transformed, more resourced with a greater sense of their own resources and respect for the healing forces of nature. It is a natural part of the creative cycle and most creative people know it only too well. Jung called it the 'night-sea journey'. Sometimes it's referred to as writer's block, sometimes as 'resistance'. (Of which more later.)

But the void seems to be a necessary period of stagnation and putrefaction before the lapis (the golden philosophers' stone) can be created.

There has to be winter for spring to come. People die and people are born who will also die. Often there is pain at a birth – whether a baby or a symphony. Secretly, I sometimes think that the longer or more intense this period is, the greater is the work which is eventually done.

I think of the famous German poet Rilke (1964) who also burst into the exquisite long poems of the *Duineser Elegien* after a very long and painful period of despair and unproductivity:

> Who, if I cried, would hear me among the angelic
> orders? And even if one of them suddenly
> Pressed me against his heart, I should fade in the strength of his
> stronger existence. For Beauty's nothing
> but the beginning of Terror we're still just able to bear,
> and why we adore it so is because it serenely
> disdains to destroy us. Every angel is terrible . . .
> Many a star was waiting for you to perceive it . . .
>
> (Rilke 1964: 60)

However, it is important to remember that the void can last a few minutes as well as many months or years. The experience when you're inside 'the belly of the fish' like Jonah is that it lasts and will last **for ever**. If you can 'see the light at the end of the tunnel', you're not in the void yet.

Physical preparation, as in martial arts, tennis or Tai Chi in particular, teaches people to 'go with the blows', not to find a rigid position, but to flex the knees slightly and centre one's energies in the power-chakra (or hara point which is said to be located four fingerwidths down from the navel). This lowers one's whole centre of energy and then the person is prepared for assaults (or waves or tennis balls) coming at you from any side. Skiers also have to do it in order to be able to 'ride the waves of snow'. I think the same skills apply in riding the waves of life. If you're all in your head, you'll fall over at the first blow which unbalances you. (You could find a partner who can help you experiment with this.)

Many cultures create void experiences as rituals for re-emergence. Vision quests, sweat lodges, the sun dance, initiation rituals of being left with a bleeding circumcised penis in caves, the list goes on and on. In Western cultures the Eleusinian mysteries are said to have enacted this despair; the people in a darkened temple would collectively weep and weep until daybreak when the most wonderful and mysterious visions came to them. These are said to have been so wonderful, that although thousands of people participated for hundreds of years, their secrets are still elusive.

Perera's inspiring book *Descent to the Goddess* explores the myth of Inanna-Ishtar and Ereshkigal from the Goddess point of view. In this

ancient story Inanna, the Sumerian Goddess of heaven and earth, decides
to descend to the netherworld – the land of no return – where her sister
Ereshkigal, queen of the Great Below, lives. Inanna is ritually humiliated,
brought 'naked and bowed low . . . Ereshkigal kills her. Her corpse is
hung on a peg where it turns into a side of green, rotting meat' (Perera
1992: 10). There it hangs for three days. Inanna's trusted female executive,
whom she left on earth, becomes concerned and appeals to two father
gods for help. They both refuse. Finally Enki, the god of waters and
wisdom, responds to the plea and through his creatively empathic invention Ereshkigal finally releases Inanna to life. Perera shows how the two
sisters are in a profound relationship of bi-polarity – the opposites
coexisting and needing and co-creating each other.

The story of Christ also tells of the terrible despair and death of Jesus
after which his corpse was put in the sepulchre – but that he rose to live
again after three days and nights. (See Appendix 2.) Egyptian mythologies,
for example, have very similar themes. Attending the midnight mass of a
Greek Orthodox church at Easter can give an experience which I imagine
was somewhat like the Eleusinian mystery ritual. The emphasis is on the
glory of the **resurrection** and people leave the church, each holding a
burning candle, into a transformed world.

These are myths or symbolic truths enacted in the large collective scale
which mirror the individual's experiences psychologically – replicating the
fractal on a physically smaller scale. But the catch is that the individual who
wants to reach their full potential has to do it again, and again and again.

May writes as follows about the healing power of myth:

> First, the myth brings into awareness the repressed, unconscious, archaic urges,
> longings, dreads and other psychic content. This is the *regressive* function of
> myths. But also, the myth reveals *new* goals, *new* ethical insights and possibilities.
> Myths are a breaking through of greater meaning which was not present before.
> The myth in this respect is the way of working out the problem on a higher [or
> deeper] **level** of integration. This is the *progressive* function of myths.
>
> The tendency has been almost universal in classical psychoanalysis to
> reduce the latter to the former. And to treat myths as regressive phenomena,
> which are then 'projected' into ethical and other forms of meaning in the
> outside world. The upshot of this is that the integrative side of myths is lost.
> This is shown in the great emphasis on *Oedipus Tyrannus* in psychoanalytic
> circles while *Oedipus in Colonus* is forgotten.
>
> (May 1991: 86)

It is less known that the ancient texts also say that once the philosopher's
stone emerges at the 'end of the work', the work starts again – as if from
the beginning. Heraclitus said: 'The cycle is the compact experiential
reconciliation of permanence and degeneration' (Guerrière 1980: 88). It's

a circular work *(opus circulatio)* on all scales – **micro**, **meso** and **macro**. Since it is therefore probably going to happen again and again, we might as well get good at it. Rumi said:

> Here is the mystery
> of *Die before you die*. Favors come
> only after you develop the skill of dying
> and even that capacity is a mystical favor.
>
>   (Rumi 1990: 57)

Transpersonal psychotherapy in practice (distortions, disappointments, disillusionments)

So, how can we 'get good' at it, at being in the void? Is there anything we can do to give help to our clients for these times in their lives? The phenomenological experience of being in the void is always as if for the first time. No matter how often you've been there, every time might feel worse.

It's almost as if, as soon as you've learned how to jump one hurdle, Life gives you a bigger one. As soon as you've changed your 'attitude', 'pattern', script, narrative, meaning or story, there's an unforeseen and unprepared-for twist in the plot. There's an old joke which goes: 'Do you know how to make God laugh?' 'No. How does one make God laugh?' 'You tell him your plans!'

Emergency instructions

In no particular order, here are some tips I have learned from my own and others' experiences which may help in such times:

1. **Normalize** the ups-and-downs of life. Emphasize the circularity of breathing, of all living things, of eating and defecating, of the sexual act or organizational histories, or the stock market, or civilizations. Teach (and live as much as you can) the eternal cycle, the recurrence of patterns which are similar, but not the same. Every night you go to sleep, practise dying. Every morning you wake up, practise being reborn. These rhythms of physis occur many times in every psychotherapy session. It's always inviting us to learn them. It's the natural coming-into-being and passing-away of everything.
2. **Make time** to be safely alone in Saturnian times. *Care of the Soul* by Thomas Moore (1992) is a wise guide-book. There are lessons to be learned and we can't concentrate if we are constantly distracted or assailed by well-motivated but unwise people who want us to 'pull

ourselves together' and feel better quickly – usually so that they can feel better. Hillman and Ventura (1992) called this 'the hygienic approach' to psychotherapy – here's a bad feeling, so we want to brush our soul's teeth and floss it away immediately. Who knows what priceless oysters are to be found in your grit?

3. **Trust the wisdom of your body**. Treat yourself gently. You may want to sleep more, but wake up every four or five hours wanting some milk and cookies. Keep them by your bed. Eat frequent small meals. Listen to your favourite music. Weep if you want to. Wear soft, natural and comfortable clothes. Expose the soles of your feet and walk on grass – or snow. Avoid toxins. And toxic people. There was a popular psychology book by Lesley Hazleton called *The Right to Feel Bad*. (Read it if you can find it – it's unfortunately now out of print. Imagine what the author would have said.) Spiritual flu is at least as incapacitating as the 'real' thing. If you have to attend to daily life (and big decisions are best postponed) as the Zen masters advise: 'Just do the next thing.' Be with loving people whom you know do not have some agenda for you continuing to feel bad – or arrange for a massage. Go with the rhythm. Life is dancing you. Sometimes it's a *tarantella*.

4. If you do the opposite, and instead become tired from **staying active**, prepare for some days (or longer periods) of recovery after riding the storm. In particular, periods of achievement (completing a marathon run or having a baby), intense concentration (exams) and creativity (completing a book) are usually and **normally** followed by downtimes. Psychiatry knows that if people don't kill themselves, depression will remit. Collapse till you feel physis rising again. It will.

5. **Keep a journal** or write an autobiography (e.g. Progroff 1975). Reflect on your life in transition. The manual by Bridges (1980) is excellent. Read it. Look at old photographs and make them into albums. Read the loving or appreciative letters from people which you've learned to keep safely stored away for just such times. Meditate if you can and if you can't, write poetry. As mentioned earlier, when St John of the Cross around 1578 wrote the magnificent, original *The Dark Night of the Soul* he was in prison and his flesh was crawling with worms. He (but remember he was a saint) wrote that it was a 'happy lot' (St John of the Cross 1973: 1).

6. **Give in and give up**. Breathe out. Completely. Paul Tillich (1952) called faith 'a leap into the abyss'. Well-managed breakdowns are breakthroughs. Do thought experiments on the theme of how you or your life needs to be different. Practise turning everything you think you believe on its head. What kind of life do you **really** want? – let yourself think it. A Dorothy Rowe book (e.g. *Depression: The Way Out of Your*

Prison, 1983) can help. Suppose Life is the great co-therapist in all psychotherapy (and I believe it is), what does Life want you to learn at this time? From the death camps of Auschwitz, Frankl wrote:

> We had to learn ourselves, and furthermore, we had to teach the despairing men, that it did not really matter what we expected from life, but rather what life expected from us. We needed to stop asking about the meaning of life, and instead to think of ourselves as those who were being questioned by life – daily and hourly.
>
> (Frankl 1973: 77)

7. **Get help**. Don't hurt yourself or anybody else. Don't be ashamed to take medication, but be careful and inform yourself all about its side-effects before you take it. Make sure you monitor all changes meticulously (e.g. Padesky and Greenberger's 1995 depression inventory). Sometimes medication has unpredictable and unfortunate side-effects. Try natural remedies. Try healing. Try prayer. Consult an oracle, the *I Ching* (Wilhelm 1951), a psychologically informed astrologer, a Tarot-line – whatever has worked for you in the past. Or try something new.
8. Take a **wide perspective** on your life in time and space. Moses only found God in the 'deepest darkness'. Check out Grof (1985). Read astronomy or go to the planetarium on your own. Surround yourself with beauty. Read the philosophers. Huxley's *Perennial Wisdom* (1970) is exactly that. Watch fractal images on your computer screen. Read science books or meditate on the age of an ammonite.
9. Learn from other cultures or the ancients and make your own version of **a ritual passage** journey. Remember the previous times you emerged from the void. Is it an Odyssey or more like Orpheus in the underworld? Is it more like Isis after the dismemberment of Osiris or more like in the Gilgamesh epic? How can you tell or enact it as '**your story**'?
10. Rumi's (1990) advice:

> Be silent and wait,
> and when the clear green fore-head stone is given,
> wear it.
>
> (Rumi 1990: 57)

Footnote

But always remember, like the Persian king who wanted an inscription small enough to go inside a finger ring which would both support him in times of great unhappiness as well as be good advice in times of great happiness: '**This too will change**'. (By the way, after the philosophers had all tried and failed, it was a gardener who came up with the answer.)

Case study: part 2

The *nigredo* phase – transference and the dark night

Are you willing to be sponged out, erased, cancelled
made nothing?
Are you willing to be made nothing?
dipped into oblivion?

If not you will never really change.

(Lawrence 1992: 258)

For a long while, Jeder and I were apparently getting nowhere. He would come in and complain that the therapy was not helping – but he kept coming. I really doubted whether I could help, but grew to respect the tenacity in him. I also begun to feel a visceral compassion for his despair. At the fifth session he reported a dream where his old coach congratulated him on getting to the end of one lap of the swimming pool. That was funny because he was a long-distance swimmer.

He told me that he has had many recurrent dreams over the years of struggling in an overwhelming tide, never reaching the shore; this dream was slightly different. Did he attach any meanings to dreams? No, nothing, probably indigestion, but he knew that psychotherapists were interested in dreams. I said from a psychological perspective it was a 'good sign' – something like shares increasing in value at some **level**.

He wanted me to be explicit about whether I thought he could be helped. I said I really could not know for sure, but I had been with other people who had come through these kinds of experience and actually become much stronger people afterwards – like gold being formed in fire. I explained that it was somewhat like the potential of a crisis for a business. As someone who knows that language, we discussed how much easier it is to turn a company in a financial crisis around than to dramatically improve the performance of a company that is just doing OK.

As a consultant to such an organization, I would have a better chance of accomplishing the stated objectives of increasing shares for the stockholders for the company in crisis, rather than trying to bring about a radical culture change towards excellence in a company that was doing 'just well enough'. Often then, as he knew, managers and employees would be reluctant to make drastic changes. Perhaps he too was just doing OK. Holding himself together and yet still managing to function.

Some weeks afterwards I had a telephone call, full of excuses for bothering me out of hours, but he now felt even worse. He wouldn't have phoned if it wasn't really urgent. He had even thought of 'ending it all'. I scheduled an emergency appointment. He said he kept thinking from which high building he would like to jump and these thoughts would not go away – no matter what he did to distract himself. He hadn't told anybody else, he was so ashamed. He could not do it to his family, but he really, really wanted to.

We talked about the betrayal of a business associate – someone he'd known for many years as a partner and had trusted implicitly. This man had made off with most of his money and crashed their joint effort causing him much 'loss of face'. He had never trusted his judgement of other people since then.

He was also plagued by very vivid memories of a young woman he abandoned when she fell pregnant as a teenager. His family would never have accepted her as his wife. He also had never grieved for the death of his parents. They were distant figures for him since he was sent to boarding school at six and they had no time for listening to 'any little boy of theirs' whingeing about the beatings and the bullying and the sodomy committed by the prefects and some of the masters at the school.

I asked him whether he was angry or disappointed in me, in that he must feel that I had not been able to 'cure' him of his depression. He said, 'No,' and then slowly, 'I suppose so, I must have had some hope to feel so let down now'. He felt worse now than when he had started with me. I said I was truly sorry that he felt that way, but it was quite understandable if he felt that psychotherapy had just made things worse. Perhaps like the external but for him meaningless trappings of his life, the let down was even more shocking since it was just so hard to believe that everything he had valued now seemed so empty. Lawrence wrote that: 'It's a terrible thing to fall into the hands of the living God, but it is a much more terrible thing to fall out of them' (1992: 17).

We discussed various options for action, such as medication or going into a private clinic, but none seemed to be right for him. Eventually I offered to increase the frequency of his sessions and he thought that would at least help to know he could see me more often. There was no one else he could tell just how terrible he felt. His descent into the under-world – the void – was an agonizing experience for both of us. The unattended pain of a lifetime was buried there. It seemed to last forever and it was like watching a drowning man from a ship too far away to rescue him.

Had I not known my way around hell from my own experiences, I could not have borne it. Eventually, in one session, the skin around his weary eyes started crinkling up and moistening. He was swallowing quickly and uncharacteristically fiddled with his cuticles. Silently I waited.

He suddenly he caught his breath and let out some whimpers. I did not look at him, nor pass the tissues.

Just sitting, being there while the painful sobs racked the body of this man until, after an endless twenty minutes of eternity, they subsided like an outgoing tide; according to Eigen's words quoted earlier – just 'enabling each other to am'. He was tired and fell asleep on the couch where I covered him gently with one of the blankets. Near the end of the session I softly woke him with instructions to go home and directly go to sleep after having a biscuit and some milk. He could phone me later if he wanted to.

Chapter 6
Albedo – getting better – the reparative or developmentally needed relationship

Snyder et al. (1999) provide 106 references regarding **hope** as a psychotherapeutic foundation for anyone who is not persuaded by Yalom's (1975) findings that of all factors, hope is perhaps the most important. They also point out that four decades of working from the assumption that a psychotherapist's approach must produce client outcomes superior to non-specific factors, placebo or high-expectancy control comparison groups in order to be considered effective, given **the facts** from the research, is tantamount to testing the nonsensical question, 'Is change superior to change?' (Snyder et al. 1999: 187). They further suggest that:

> Hope may be understood in terms of how people think about goals. Thinking about goals is defined in two components. First, there are the thoughts that persons have about their ability to produce one or more workable routes to their goals [pathways thinking]. And second, there are the thoughts that people have regarding their ability to begin and continue movement on selected pathways toward those goals [agency thinking] . . . Both types of thinking must be present for a person to experience hope . . . In this model of hope, stress, negative emotions, and difficulties in coping are considered a result of being unable to envision a pathway or make movement toward a desired goal.
>
> (Snyder et al. 1999: 180–81)

I read this as another way of speaking about the despair of the characteristic of the *nigredo*. Applied to psychotherapy, this means that clients feel blocked in their efforts to find new goals and/or in their ability to become mobilized to achieve their goals. In addition, there are clients who lack the skill(s) or knowledge (pathways) which they need to accomplish their goals. Thus, therapists may need to assist clients in the identification and exploration of their **desires** and the provision of some reparative or developmentally needed **deficit**. However, Snyder et al. also warn that if the therapist does not listen carefully (attune) to what the client is saying, therapeutic goals (their kind, vagueness or absence) can be more to help 'the helper than the helped' (1999: 191). Furthermore, along with many other contemporary writer-practitioners, they have come to the conclusion that:

> ... another potential problem arises with therapists who are wed to a particular paradigm. Specifically, they may conceptualize clients in one way, using only the techniques associated with their favoured approach. Thus, driven by one's theoretical and technological predilections, the helper may not entertain other paradigms should the preferred approach fail to facilitate positive change. Hope theory suggests that there are many technologies [practices] for helping clients to pursue their goals [desires]. To the degree therapists can be flexible in their interventions, then they have a more powerful set of tools . . . sometimes because of theoretical or technological chauvinism, psychotherapists may be unwilling to accept the fact that their approaches are not working . . . From the perspective of hope theory, any and all roads should be explored to find those that are most suited to help clients . . .
>
> (Snyder et al. 1999: 191–92)

Well, that's unusual, given the current situation in the UK where statutory regulation of psychotherapists is still being determined by 'scholiasts'. Despite my previous work in this area (and probably because I am multi-lingual in 'psychotherapese') I still frequently get requests to support research to 'prove' such-and-such an approach is an effective therapy!

Extrapolating from the research on state-dependent learning (which is discussed more fully in Clarkson 1995a: 150, 324) the ethics of providing a 'safe containing/holding' relationship or supervision or even management (!) could look distinctly questionable. Do the notions of 'holding' or 'containing', or even 'supporting', have an **inevitable** relationship to helping people develop resources, skills and competencies or 'states' in dealing with real life? Real life takes place in different archetypal spaces, and effective therapy, in my opinion, needs to enable clients to live more effectively in such different kinds of spaces. (See Table 10.3 in Chapter 10.)

Might it not encourage dependency and the notion of a false hermetically sealed container for a relationship which is intrinsically abusive (see e.g. Masson 1989), full of false or misunderstood promises and pointing but to an adjustment of compliance, adoption of the language of the more powerful partner in the exchange, and ultimate submission to the cultural status quo with its intrinsic prejudicial and disempowering illusion of protection under the guise of infantilization?

How does it help someone facing death as result a of medical negligence or criminal intent to consider their early infantile feeding patterns?

Being understood is such a joy!
When a person is with people
That he or she cannot confide in,
It's like being tied up.

(Rumi 1991: 18)

We learn from chaos and complexity science to allow for another disturbance to our ideas of causality and intervention into human, organizational or natural systems – for example, the possibility that very small interventions or chance occurrences have very large, unpredictable or unknown effects. As I have shown (Clarkson 1995a), it is by no means clear or established that there is a linear or causal relationship between childhood experiences and adult lives – or (despite the fact of its retrospective value in constructing our life narratives) whether this is necessarily useful in psychotherapy.

A man of 40 had the view of himself as having been abandoned as a baby, spending many hours alone crying and feeling desperate and anxious about being 'left' again. He lived this narrative in his relationships with his parents, his psychotherapists, his friends and his female partners. An opportunity arose when he questioned his mother in detail. Was this true? She apologetically explained that she once left him for a couple of hours with his grandmother when he was a baby and that she also felt very guilty for leaving him as a three-year-old with his father and grandparents when she had to go to hospital. Was he ever left alone? No, apart from those times. She was very sorry about that. He also checked with the rest of the family. No, her facts were accurate. He told us that strangely he felt very much stronger in himself now, less fearful and much more resourced now that he no longer had this (really false) idea about his early childhood abandonment and 'insecure attachment'. All his relationships and his attitude to life improved. What had changed? Just the story he believed about himself.

> 'What is Fate?' Nasrudin was asked by a scholar.
>   'An endless success of intertwined events, each influencing the other.'
>   'This is hardly a satisfactory answer. I believe in cause and effect.'
>   'Very well,' said the Mulla, 'look at that.' He pointed to a procession passing in the street.
>   'That man is being taken to be hanged. Is that because someone gave him a silver piece and enabled him to buy the knife with which he committed the murder; or because someone saw him do it; or because nobody stopped him?'
>
> (Shah 1985: 74)

Once we accept that no field exists without an observer, no me without the organization around me, no *you* without *us*, no investigation of child development without the prejudices of the 'observers' – how do we study what has happened, can we indeed effect beneficial changes, who is doing what to whom and why? All the Newtonian notions of causality which so many psychotherapists devotedly apply to human beings (!) may be outdated or even wrong.

> Nasrudin tried to get a calf into a pen, but it would not go. So he went to its mother and began to reproach her.
> 'Why are you shouting at that cow?' someone asked.
> 'It's all her fault,' said Nasrudin, 'for she should have taught him better.'
>
> (Shah 1985: 41)

For one example, Gergen et al. (1990) comment:

> . . . conceptions of the child may depend on a host of factors uncorrelated to the actual nature of the child. Beliefs about the child vary markedly as a result of history, culture and personal disposition; yet the genetic make-up of the actual child seems to remain relatively constant. Perhaps the most radical view within this domain is that of Kessen (1979). As Kessen proposed, 'the child is essentially and eternally a cultural invention and . . . the variety in the child's definition is not the removable error of an incomplete science' (1979: 815). From this perspective the concept of the child is essentially a social construction, and no amount of observation will provide the basis for an unconstructed or interpretation-free account of the child's nature. Yet is this process of enquiry, learning and re-evaluation of perception in itself not also research?
>
> (Gergen et al. 1990: 108)

There is further discussion on using development clinically in Clarkson (1992b; 1995a: 108–38); and some of the debates about the relevance of our Eurocentric developmental notions of child development for effective psychotherapy are reviewed by Clarkson (1995a: particularly 139–45). Burman's thought-provoking work *Deconstructing Developmental Psychology* (1994) provides excellent arguments to show how much of what passes for developmental psychology (a) abstracts human development from historical and socio-political conditions, (b) pathologizes those individuals and groups who fail to meet its idealized models, and (c) imposes a normalizing ideology which is not willing or able to deal with differences except as inferiorities. Costall et al. (1997) provides further essential reading.

I do **not** mean to say, suggest or imply that our theories may not have their uses sometimes in some places with some people and for some tasks. However, perhaps we might also be willing to consider that sometimes in some places with some people they may not only be ineffective and racist, but also damaging and destructive. All **level** 6 theories are narratives and usually have implicit, if not explicit, value connotations imposing some cultural norm. There is nothing wrong with this. What is wrong (in the sense that it is a logical category error) is to treat as 'theory' what are in fact 'norms', or to deny the fact that all narratives carry value implications.

The therapeutic relationship as research

In an earlier paper (in Clarkson 1998e) I suggested that perhaps the end of the divide between clinical supervision and academic research can begin to be made as the work of doing and reflection becomes integrated. What would be required is a reconceptualization of the primary task of supervision as also that of a consultant or co-researcher in every case or situation brought for disciplined reflection. (See Appendix 5 for a transcribed example of supervisory coaching in this method.)

> The practice of the clinic should not be separated from rigorous and constant research borne from and bearing theory. For example, a qualitative research project such as a disciplined and methodologically informed case study is not something to be done once for a dissertation or a paper – I believe it needs to be conducted with every client, every session, for as long as a clinician/supervisor thinks and works in the profession.
>
> (Clarkson 1998e: 13)

The purpose here then is to record a simple method of self-supervision and describe an attitude of scientific interest and ethical experimentation in the everyday practice of psychotherapy psychology which many students, practitioners and supervisors have found helpful. It is not intended to **be** science, but to explore the use of a kind of scientific metaphor to serve as a guide through the vagaries and vicissitudes of every day clinical practice.

It is probably a truism that people who feel intelligent, resourceful and encouraged learn more efficiently and enjoyably than people who feel stupid, limited and constantly criticized. Practitioners in the helping professions tend to be conscientious, well-motivated and often hypercritical of themselves. Concerns about 'doing damage', saying or doing 'the wrong thing', and appearing in an unfavourable light to colleagues, trainers, supervisors or peers seem to be on the increase. Frequently, on training courses, and in the privacy of the bedroom, the worst criticism does not come from trainers and supervisors, but from the inner supervisor, critic, professional superego or internal parent figure.

Naturally, early in training the prohibitions against what **not** to do outweigh the fund of knowledge or skills about what to actually do that may be helpful. (It is only later in a professional training that it frequently becomes very clear why one should not treat friends and family, for example.) It is not unusual in the learning cycle that this concern about the normative aspects of our work sometimes can interfere with the open curious non-judgemental attitude which is most conducive to learning. This is of course more true once the warnings, cautions and dangers have been taken on board. When learning energy becomes, so to speak, tied up in avoiding mistakes, learning is impeded and creativity and innovation halted.

A metaphor or research paradigm for psychotherapy and practice

So what could replace schoolism in counselling and psychotherapy? No doubt there will be other answers (pathways). Also, because of the often unfortunate connotations that 'learning' and 'teaching' (e.g. giving up your own mind to 'pass') have for many other people, I have come to prefer the idea of **enquiry** or research.

So, I would like to suggest ye olde experimental, empirical (which properly means 'experiential') way: Look, listen, do something you think might work and take extremely careful note of what happens next. If it works, do it some more; if it doesn't work, try something else.

An attitude modelled on the ideal of a scientist practitioner has advantages which can overcome many problems and enhance reflective learning as well as creative unfolding of one's functioning. (There is an extended verbatim transcript of a supervisor using this paradigm in action in Appendix 5 of this book.)

The elements of a model or metaphor for self-supervision seem to be the following:

• An idea or goal, purpose, contract, direction or outcome measure
• A scientific paradigm of some kind
• Units of analysis or attention
• An attitude of interest, curiosity about one's skills and process
• A desire to make a contribution to the common stock of clinical knowledge

An idea or goal, purpose, contract, direction or outcome measure

There has to be something that the client wants in order to have some idea of whether they got all or half or none of what they wanted or not. (This is a requirement of evidence-based practice.) How the objective will be defined (and by whom) will obviously depend on the values, the epistemology and conceptualizations of whichever theory (narrative) is being learned, practised, integrated, questioned or expanded.

For theory, too often, read 'introject'. Theory is always someone else's idea or your idea with which someone else agrees. Every such outcome measure carries, implicitly or explicitly, values, epistemologies and ideologies, as Foucault (e.g. 1974, 1979) and others have shown. In one model the goal may be **insight** into childhood roots of a disturbance (Symington 1986), in another **symptom relief** (e.g. Beck 1976), in another **congruent self-statements** (Rogers 1986), in another authentic expression of feeling in a **fully felt cathartic release** (Lowen 1976), and so on and so forth. We can proliferate examples indefinitely. But you or the client may have some idea, that if the person does *x*, something desired has happened. This is perhaps physiological at a fundamental **level** – am I, the client, getting something that I want?

This of course needs to be differentiated from the therapist 'having their own agenda' in a proactive countertransferential way, such as, for example, when we want our clients to get better so that we can protect ourselves against feelings of inadequacy, to impress our supervisors or to avoid getting into trouble with the agency. Research shows that effectiveness in psychotherapy by the client's assessment correlates strongly with an emphasis on focus (see Clarkson 1995a: 31–52).

There has to be a goal, and ideally an explicit goal on both sides. Ethical issues to do with, for example, clarity of contract, consensual agreement, exploitation, need to be explored.

A scientific paradigm of some kind

Ethically, I think there has to be some way in which we judge what's going on. There has to be some epistemological paradigm. At the simplest **level**, how can we **know** whether anything useful is happening as a result of our professional work? There is, therefore, I believe, good reason for a commitment to 'evidence-based practice'. Of course this implies specifying what we shall call '**knowledge**' and having clear criteria for it.

Controlled experiments are often conducted using the notion of a null hypothesis. This exemplifies the notion that the intervention, or the experiment, or the manipulation of variables, and so on, will not make any difference greater than chance (for example the random results of flipping a coin).

According to formal statistical methods, a five per cent or one per cent probability region can be identified where the difference potentially attributable to the experimenter intervention is likely to be due to such intervention rather than random chance fluctuations. (Although, of course, mere correlation does not 'prove' a causal relationship.) Percentages expressed in terms of the region of probability are a statistical measure of likelihood. One way of saying this is that the chances are that 95 per cent of what the experimenter (or psychotherapist) does has little or no influence on what would have happened anyway.

If we translate this as a **metaphor** for clinical practice we could say that the null hypothesis states that nothing the therapist does or does not do will make more than a chance difference to the problematic situation of the client. The experimenter **attitude** then requires careful observation of the client in order to judge whether an intervention actually does make a difference or not. (An intervention may of course be **active**, such as an interpretation or empathic comment, or **apparently passive**, such as looking away or not answering a question while a silence grows in the room.)

The use of the null hypothesis here is obviously meant as paradigm and metaphor to help the practitioner to be more objective about their own work, less judgemental, but more discriminating. It is not meant as exact or exemplary positivistic science, but as an aid to more effective psychotherapy.

The intention here is primarily to serve the client and to resource the clinician, which may or may not eventually be translated into single case design or other more conventional blending of applied and scientific practice. Hopefully the importation of an open, expectant, but largely unbiased interested attitude can foster the abilities as well as the desire to grade such a practice to conventional scientific standards.

There is in fact not that much scientifically acceptable evidence that 'undoing retroflections' or 'empathic reflection' or 'making interpretations' makes that much difference to the problems that people bring. This goes well against the grain, particularly of 'acceptable attitudes' in trainings that are based on theoretical compliance instead of scientific enquiry, logic and constant methodological enquiry (see Clarkson 1998f).

I think we have an **ethical** and **moral** obligation to pay very precise attention to what we do and what happens, moment by moment in the consulting room and session by session over time in disciplined reflection – with or without the aid of another researcher (or supervisor). A research attitude is: 'Did it make a difference or did it not make a difference? How can I find out if it did? Was it indeed a result of something I did? Was it in the desired direction?' This is a legitimate and responsible experimental attitude, **not** like, 'Am I following the rules I learned on my last training seminar?'.

Obviously we are not talking about laboratory work in the exact, exemplary or classical sense. Yet there is a sense in which the consulting room is always a laboratory. **It matters what we explore, test or discover in this clinical laboratory**. If we only see what we have been trained to see, we may never discover what we're doing well – or improve on it. The intention of using the null hypothesis metaphor offered here is to help the clinician to be less judgemental, less driven by ideological theory, and to be more open, more discriminating, more questioning, more accountable.

Units of analysis or attention

These units can be stimulus–response pairs, transactions, interpretation and the next dream image, identification of the five dimensions of relationship, and so on. There has to be something that we're looking at. Such clinically relevant methodologies have developed rapidly and excellently recently in psychology. It may or may not be translated into a single case design. There are not very fine examples of how one case is conducted as an experiment. Working with one case within a paradigm of enquiry is already possible and may well be adaptable to your work. In order to do this, one needs units of observation – even if these are phenomenological self-reports.

This contrasts with some recent examples where trainees build their competencies on demonstrated adherence to theory – i.e. meeting the requirements of the training or accrediting organization (see e.g. Clarkson 1996g). The training organization naturally exists to further its own theoretical, ideological and, in particular, financial purposes, and the case study often becomes a way of getting the approval of the people who designed the curriculum.

Then it does not meet the criterion of **measurable difference in the direction that people are wanting** attributable to what the practitioner has done or not done. I am not suggesting that this is easy or can comfortably be imported into traditional ideologically based models. I am pleading for an importation of these very serious questions and aspirations to pre- or trans-theoretical rigour and discipline in every piece of work we do – whatever 'orientation' we prefer.

In other words, just because you are not a PhD laboratory-trained scientist does not mean that you should not be thinking, adapting and improving on the scientific method in ways to suit your clinical work. In this way the locus of evaluation is shifted from outside to inside.

Instead of worrying about 'Am I doing Gestalt?' or 'Am I doing proper Freudian analysis?', it becomes 'I did this with that person and this is the evidence I am adducing to indicate that what I did was within this region of probability related to the outcome this person desired.' (Of course the psycho-language you want to use is up to you.) So when you go for examination or accreditation it is not a case of 'Do I meet your subjective compliance criteria?', but more 'This is the way I conceptualized and thought about and judged my work and I would like to share it with you.'

Competence is here defined as **having the internal confidence to meet external criteria in a consistent way as well as knowing the limits of competence and the areas of development** (Clarkson 1994).

Is therapy and therapy training perhaps primarily a 'social influence process'? As we have seen, there has been for the last 100 years a proliferation of theory in therapy. Comparatively recently there are many very intelligent and excellent professionals throughout the world who are questioning the very theory of theory.

Too often what is called 'theory' is conflated or confused with facts, opinion, feelings or linguistic usage. Too often what passes for 'theory' is the vehicle for achieving submission, compliance, decisions about who shall have certification, recognition, status – essentially a vehicle for the establishment and maintenance of power relations. Many authors have addressed these issues, but they are rarely, if ever, on the list of 'prescribed' texts. According to Simons, professional rhetorics

> . . . include a rhetoric of affiliation by which the profession aligns itself with higher status groups and distances itself from lower status groups; a rhetoric of special expertise that includes claims to valid theories and distinctive methods; a rhetoric of public service that simultaneously plays down careerist motives; a rhetoric of social passage that identifies and justifies credentialling requirements; a rhetoric of self-policing that defends against 'interference' from others . . .
>
> (Simons 1989: 117)

There are probably no easy solutions for this. These are the problems. We have seen how 'objective' experimenters influence outcomes of rat experiments even in the most stringently controlled laboratory conditions (e.g. Feather 1982). We have discussed how observers affect physics experiments in the best, most controlled laboratories in the world. I don't think it is as simple as 'having a control group' or 'following theory'. Of course it does not mean that theory is without value. It is our responsibility to be curious about what is going on. And about what other people think. And what we **don't** want to pay attention to as well.

The fact that we probably can't find out fundamentally for sure and for always should not absolve us from the effort of trying. I would like for us to work consciously knowing that we are active in a problematized area. The story goes that Pasteur 'discovered' penicillin because the woman who worked for him neglected to clean some cultures he had left in a dish. It did **not** come from where his attention was directed, but from him becoming curious about an apparently insignificant and even irritating phenomenon. If we only look to see what we already think there is, we will always see what we've always seen. If we sometimes work with what Zen masters call 'soft eyes', we might see something new.

An attitude of interest, curiosity about one's own skills and process

This means a willingness to engage in a genuine self-feedback exercise untrammelled with transferential distortions – self-reflexive in the best way. I perceive that professionals in training are not curious enough about what happens in their consulting rooms. I've heard a man of 50 saying how worried he is about saying something to his patient because of what his supervisor might think about it.

The Oxford philosopher of psychology, Farrell, after intensive research on four training groups, concluded that a group leader helps to produce material that fits in with his WOT (Way Of Talking). Farrell's work suggests that (perhaps always) the person, the organization, the training group is therefore declared 'cured', 'mature', 'competent' to the extent that they have adopted the WOT of the trainer or leader. 'Therefore, the insight and understanding etc. that the operator helps his groups to acquire are not only dependent on this own perspective; they are also dependent on the very method [and thus theory] he uses' (Farrell 1979: 108).

You will notice that if you are **curious** about something, you are not trapped within such questions as 'Is this good WOT or is this bad WOT?', 'Am I doing it right?' or 'Will my supervisor "like" it?'. Curiosity means asking the question: 'What will happen if . . . ?' I submit that this is the appropriate attitude for the practitioner scientist – actively to question the WOTs. In this way we may develop the ability as well as the desire to upgrade our practices to exemplars of enquiry **and** competence.

It is probably important to realize that every piece of research will always be contestable now or later. There are always faults to be found in any method or piece of human enquiry. There is 'no place to hide' even behind the scientific paradigm. The most 'respected' and 'accepted' statistical methods are coming under increasing attack. Many different languages are suitable for many different purposes and are legitimated by many different communities of practice. But what is really going on?

A desire to make a contribution to the common stock of clinical knowledge

Such a contribution can be initiated by sharing observations and experience, by questioning and writing, and by contributing to conferences and the development of the discipline overall. (I suppose this is the old desire to 'save the world' in another one of its multitude of guises.) At the very least it is 'I will write this down so that other people – even one client – may benefit from it.'

Transpersonal psychotherapy in practice

To do this on a [session-by-session and] day-to-day basis requires careful monitoring of the client's reaction to comments, explanations, interpretations, questions and suggestions. It also demands a higher measure of flexibility on the part of the therapist and a willingness to change one's relational stance to fit with the client's perception of what is most helpful. Some clients, for example, will prefer a formal professional manner over a casual or warmer one. Others may prefer more self-disclosure from their therapist, greater directiveness, a focus on the symptoms or a focus on the possible meanings beneath them, and or a faster or perhaps a more laid back pace for therapeutic work (Bachelor and Horvath 1999).

Clearly the one-approach-fits-all strategy is guaranteed to undermine alliance formation. Combining the findings on both client, extra-therapeutic and relationship factors, this conclusion follows. Therapeutic success depends on enabling and confirming the client's resources in a partnership informed by the client's goals and perceptions (Hubble et al. 1999b: 418).

And

> The questioning involved here is not our interrogation of the data, but its interrogation of us.
>
> (Williams 1979, quoted in Cox and Thielgaard 1987: 249)

Case study: part 3

The *albedo* phase: getting better – the reparative relationship with a man who has come through

> . . . What is the knocking?
> What is the knocking at the door in the night?
> It is somebody wants to do us harm.
> No, no it is the three strange angels.
> Admit them, admit them.
>
> (Lawrence 1992: 76)

Within weeks Jeder was a 'new man'. We hardly ever again referred to his crying. He developed an interest in growing a rare kind of orchid. He said the colours of the world seemed brighter to him now than they ever had. With great excitement, he told me this dream:

'I had been having various dreams about seeing my reflection in the mirror, about my glasses not really fitting my face any more. I have been wearing the same pair of steel-rimmed square shaped glasses for many years. Recurrently in my dreams, I would see that my glasses were either falling apart, or that they had become too large and did not suit my face any more, or that I was taking them off, because I really did not need them any more.

'One night, I dreamed of looking again at my face in the bathroom mirror, which was the recurrent locus of my dream state reflection. In the mirror, I would see my face featureless, as if covered by a tight cloth, or a gypsum mask. I had the feeling that I looked good enough, or at least that people considered this to be the case. However, it was quite obvious to me that my face was lacking my particular characteristics. Gradually, I felt a suffocating sensation, a need to break free and like Oedipus in reverse, I punched with my own two fingers holes in the place of the two eyes. I sensed the 'mask' being ripped open and could hear the material tearing. Then I acquired a better vision of myself in the mirror. I could see much more clearly through the two holes. I also had a sense that the mask itself would come off any moment.'

His life energy returned to his body although he reported that he was now much more sensitive to pain and had to have an injection when he went to the dentist – something of an indulgence, but OK. He took up the piano again. He went on a sculpting course – something he had always wanted to do, but for which he never had the time. He had the good fortune of finding an excellent and undemanding teacher who simply helped him materialize his inner visions into marble. Winged fishes.

This was a great period. He started reading books related to his history and present circumstances: *The Making of Them*, an excellent book on boarding school 'survivors', Jungian books on 'mid-life' (e.g. Stein 1983), biographies – even Goleman (1999) on Emotional Intelligence. He could concentrate and read again. Time had become very precious to him and he started wearing his watch again. He started a Tai Chi course after having seen a film of how the ancient elders of China can be found in the early mornings in the gardens and parks doing this graceful body meditation. He tried to trace the teenage girl he had abandoned, but all his efforts were in vain. He even went into couples psychotherapy with his wife to re-ignite their sex life but this was only partially successful. He made peace with one of his sons by writing a letter to that son's possible future children, explaining how he had brought up their dad, and what he wished would be different for their future. We were preparing to end our work together since there was actually little to report except good things, everyday stresses well handled and an eagerness to free up the session time so that he could fit in all his involvements – especially his swimming.

Oh but the water loves me and folds me,
Plays with me, sways me, lifts me and sinks me, murmurs:
Oh marvellous stuff!
No longer shadow! – and it holds me
Close, and it rolls me, enfolds me, touches me, as if never it could
touch me enough.

(Lawrence 1992: 36)

Chapter 7
Citrinitas – the existential person-to-person relationship

A Necessary Autumn Inside Each
You and I have spoken all these words
but as for the way we have to go,

There is no getting ready,
other than grace.
My faults have stayed hidden.
One might call that a preparation!
I have one small drop of knowing in my soul.
Let it dissolve into your ocean.
There are so many threats to it.
Inside each of us, there's continual autumn.
Our leaves fall and blow out
over the water. A crow sits
in the blackened limbs and talks
about what's gone.
Then your generosity
returns: spring, moisture, intelligence,
the scent of hyacinth and rose and cypress.

Joseph is back!
And if you don't feel in yourself
the freshness of Joseph,
be Jacob!

Weep, and then smile.
Don't pretend to know something
you haven't experienced.

Very little grows
on jagged rock.
Be ground.

Be crumbled
so wildflowers will come up
where you are.

You've been stony for too many years.
Try something different.
Surrender.

(Rumi 1991: 61)

The *citrinitas* phase in psychotherapy has to do with the 'stuck places', the 'impasses', the disappointment, disillusionment – and difficulties, the yellowing or maturing of the *albedo* phase.

It has also earned the epithet 'the greater dark night'.

> Accepting that common factors account for much of the change does not mean, however, that suddenly a 'model*less*' or technique*less* therapy is being advocated. As part of the family of curative factors shared by all therapies, models and technique have something to offer. A therapy informed by an understanding of the common factors, therefore, incorporates and actively uses all of the elements or ingredients that have been found to facilitate change.
>
> (Hubble et al. 1999b: 408)

Since comparisons of therapy techniques have not demonstrated differential efficacy, it follows that theories, techniques and models can obstruct effective therapy or they can inspire confidence, hope and credibility. (Witness the claims made for eye-movement desensitization.) According to Kottler: 'That the procedures are not in and of themselves the causal agents of change matters little' (quoted in Hubble et al. 1999b: 418).

The research literature shows considerable evidence that hope and positive expectations – being 'possibility focused' – in one's clinical work enhances the likelihood of clients changing in beneficial ways (Frank and Frank 1993). I have referred to this as creating a 'conceivable self' (Clarkson 1995a: 118). When clients can describe themselves in the **future**, de Shazer (1985) points out, it facilitates achievable changes in the **present**. It is of course not necessary to ask directly – usually the client will spontaneously bring out their hopes for the future. Then the therapist can join in and support this theme within the client's frame of reference and in the client's language.

'Resistance'

The title of a book by Anderson and Stewart, *Mastering Resistance – A Practical Guide to Family Therapy* (1983), encapsulates most of what I feel about the notion of 'resistance' as it is commonly used. It suggests that 'resistance' is something the patient does in order **not** to get well, whereas I believe that healing is a natural process which cannot be 'resisted', as little as a well watered tulip bulb would want to 'resist' becoming a beautiful tulip or a broken bone 'resist' mending.

The notion of 'resistance' in this sense imports at nominative **level** 3, through the use of the word 'mastering', value connotations which suggest that resistance ought to be 'mastered' and that such resistance ought to be mastered within a patriarchal and warlike idiom. Perhaps it even implies that some kind of 'force' is required to get the patient or the family to 'submit' to the 'master therapist' – who knows, in his or her infinite wisdom, more about what is better for the client than the client can ever possibly know.

Of course they have an illustrious precedent in Sigmund Freud who frequently used military metaphors in describing psychic life – defences, resistance, repression, and so on and so forth, and whose authoritative hold over (or punishment of) his patients (and members of the Institute) has hardly ever been doubted. From Irigaray, a critique of Freud on this point:

> Analysis would 'end', then, in the subjectification of all men and women, who now tautologically become subject(s) – without any real difference between the sexes – to (of) an order bringing their needs–desires in line with the desire, the ever-invisible desire, of a Master. Might I suggest to them that he is no more than a Master of their own making, the unconscious made School, a sort of micro-culture which is at once primitive in its magical components and decadent in its imposition of the cult of a Truth whose power to terrorize is proportional to its ability to mask ignorance.
>
> (Irigaray 1991: 84–85)

In my view, when a therapist calls a client phenomenon 'resistance', that therapist has just run out of patience, imagination or respect for the wisdom of the Life process. (It is much more likely that it is the therapist herself or himself who is 'resisting' being an appropriate **servant** of the client's journey.)

As I show in Appendix 5, the transcribed extract of a supervision session, too often what we as therapists experience as the client 'resisting' us (or our 'interpretations') is probably their self-protection against our bad therapy – some form of coercion, manipulation or invalidation. When the client is strong enough, the healing will happen. If it doesn't, it's usually for a very good reason. Such reasons, whether we understand or agree with them or not, deserved at least our respect. I think it was Pascal who said: 'The heart has reasons which reason knows not of.' I therefore treat therapeutic phenomena which many others would call 'resistance' as simple feedback that I am doing something unhelpful. I look for where the life energy is, nourish that, and then get out of the way.

Time after time I have witnessed that psychotherapists in supervision, when alerted to the subtle individual, collective and professional power issues in wanting to 'overcome client resistance, are surprised and delighted by how their clients change as soon as they stop trying to change their clients against their will and against the natural flow of life and its own healing rhythms.

> Readiness for change is inseparably tied to motivation or what might be called motivational readiness. Nevertheless, for decades, clients' motivation has been dichotomized – either they were motivated or not.
>
> (Hubble et al. 1999b: 413)

> As it turns out, the idea of an unmotivated client is not true. All people, all clients have motivation: only the dead are plausibly unmotivated. It is more correct to say the motivation of 'unmotivated' clients may not match the therapist's goals and expectations (Duncan et al. 1997a). Further, no longer is motivation for change understood strictly as some trait, or stable personality characteristic, that passively tags along with clients. Instead, it is a dynamic process strongly influenced by others' contribution to the interaction. In short, motivation is as much or even more contextually as it is personally determined.
>
> (Hubble et al. 1999b: 413)

> . . . the customary rejection of the common factors is an indulgence the field can ill afford. If the professions will not come to terms with the knowledge it now possess and continues to promote assertions rich in bombast but bereft of fact, others will surely define a reality for us. All signs indicate that the emerging reality in 'behavioural health care' is an unpleasant one for many . . . Though this may be equally subject to criticism, payers and consumers deserve to know what works. Should the profession not tell them, they will decide for themselves. One moment's reflection, asking whether therapists can deliver the goods as promised is hardly presumptuous. If transference interpretations, finger waving, desensitization hierarchies, miracle questions, cognitive restructuring, narrative re-storying, and all of the other methods available are said to have special curative properties, then they should show it convincingly. This is equally true of the theories underlying such interventions.
>
> (Hubble et al. 1999b: 407)

I believe that psychotherapy, psychology and all their associated disciplines need to take on the challenges of the new contexts – not to be learned by rote, but to be held in the mind as a constant resource. Otherwise they may become a symptom of those conditions which called them into being. Can it be that the other professions have not fully responded to the call of our time, since no one else, including any established church, seems fully to have answered it?

A discipline such as psychology in its particular British shape does not appear to be responding to the fragmentation and chaotic complexity of our postmodern era, which is moving at exponentially increasing speeds. The problems facing the world on a macroscopic scale, as well as psychologists on a microscopic scale, have become too complex for psychologists or counsellors to have unbridled faith in singular solutions, or to insist on imposing such singular solutions on their trainees or colleagues. We must learn to listen to each other, no matter what our differences of opinion or seniority. There are three requirements for all associated helping professions: that we be willing to move with our times, we move with our art/science, and move with each other.

In the turbulent and troubled psychological waters at the beginning of this century, communication may become more important than certainty, effectiveness more important than positivistic elegance for its own sake, and intellectual and moral questioning of our basic assumptions more important than adherence to a single way of integration.

> Believe it or not, the existing ethical codes of the three largest non-medically oriented health provider organizations [in the USA] . . . mandate that therapists neither practice effectively nor even subject their practices to any systematic or ongoing assessment of outcome . . . Instead all that is required is that therapists practice, 'within the boundaries of their competence and experience' . . . As strange as it may sound, however, a therapy can be administered competently and still be ineffective.
>
> (Hubble et al. 1999b: 438)

Furthermore we all know people whose years of experience consist of practising the same mistakes over and over again! Another strand of this incredibly rich tapestry of changing paradigms and collapsing realities is the momentous event which MacPherson reported happening in April 1992: '. . . a robot spacecraft "heard" the very birth pangs of the creation of the universe from almost unimaginable depths of space and time' (1992: 17).

Evidence has now been found that galaxies and stars, and ultimately humans therefore, condensed from a violent explosive fog of radiation and elementary particles more than 14 thousand million years ago. The universe was thus born from an infinitesimal point – out of nothingness. Even as the boundaries of our knowledge expand in this way, many more scientists are acknowledging some form of ultimate consciousness which can be understood as God. I like to think of this as *physis* (Murray 1955). First named by the pre-Socratic Greeks, it is defined as a generalized creative force of Nature which eternally strives to make things grow and to make growing things more perfect. It was conceived of as the **healing** factor in illness, the **energetic** motive for **evolution,** and the driving force of **creativity** in the individual and collective psyche.

Concerning the Big Bang evidence, Davies (in MacPherson 1992) suggests that there is a purpose and design to the universe and that we, as intelligent and conscious human beings, are necessary to the functioning of the universe. Perhaps we are more intelligent than we know in continuing to try to make sense and meaning of a seemingly chaotic universe – often with too few or too many clues. And perhaps this is why we continue to try to make sense and meaning of our own lives, and live them to a fulfilment that goes beyond the mere satisfaction of physiological, even psychological needs, but that reaches towards the transcendent, the transpersonal, the ultimate wholeness. I believe that psychology, psychotherapy, counselling, supervision and organizational work needs also to acknowledge the final mysteries – the end of our knowledge and the beginning of nothingness.

The playwright Tom Stoppard explains:

> If you knew the algorithm and fed it back say ten thousand times, each time there'd be a dot somewhere on the screen. You'd never know where to expect the next dot. But gradually you'd start to see this shape, because every dot will be inside the shape of this leaf. It wouldn't *be* a leaf, it would be a mathematical object. But yes. The unpredictable and the predetermined unfold together to make everything the way it is. It's how nature creates itself, on every scale, the snowflake and the snowstorm. It makes me so happy. To be at the beginning again, knowing almost nothing. People were talking about the end of physics. Relativity and quantum looked as if they were going to clean out the whole problem between them. A theory of everything. But they only explained the very big and the very small. The universe, the elementary particles. The ordinary-sized stuff which is our lives, the things people write poetry about – clouds – daffodils – waterfalls – and what happens in a cup of coffee when the cream goes in – these things are full of mystery, as mysterious to us as the heavens were to the Greeks. We're better at predicting events at the edge of the galaxy or inside the nucleus of an atom than whether it'll rain on auntie's garden party three Sundays from now. Because the problem turns out to be different. We can't even predict the next drip from a dripping tap when it gets irregular. Each drip sets up the conditions for the next, the smallest variation blows the prediction apart, and the weather is unpredictable the same way, will always be unpredictable. When you push the numbers through the computer you can see it on the screen. The future is disorder. A door like this has cracked open five or six times since we got up on our hind legs. It's the best possible time to be alive, when almost everything you knew is wrong.
>
> (Stoppard 1993: 47–48)

Changes in our scientific context

Another important change in our conceptual environment is, of course, in the area of science, particularly quantum dynamics and human systems of psychoanalysis and psychotherapy. The scientific context is particularly concerned with quantum dynamics in human systems on the one hand, and chaos theory on the other. Zohar describes the process in modern physics thus:

> Quantum field theory takes us even further beyond Newton's dead and silent universe, giving us a vivid picture of the dynamic flux which lies at the heart of an indeterminate being. Here, even those particles which do manifest themselves as individual beings do so only briefly . . . [It gives a] graphic picture of the emergence and return, or the beginning and ceasing, of individual subatomic particles at the quantum **level** of reality [which] holds out deep implications for our way of looking at the nature and function of individual personalities or the survival of the individual self.
>
> (Zohar 1990: 13)

Rumi says:

> This
> that we are now
> created the body, cell by cell,
> like bees building a honeycomb.
> The human body and the universe
> grew from this, not this
> from the universe and the human body.
>
> (Rumi 1991: 22)

What is often referred to as the new physics (being already almost an octogenarian, it is not so 'new') has hardly been addressed in any of the major systems of psychoanalysis and psychotherapy. Apart from the Jungian literature, there is only an occasional paper in Jungian and Gestalt journals. The implications of quantum physics for psychology are potentially enormous. For example, the Cartesian dualism between mind and matter is called into question in a radical and fundamental sense. (It is only from such a dualistic and causal perspective that *vitalism* can be so termed or criticized: '. . . the notion that life cannot be any sort of function or characteristic of exclusively material objects' – Flew 1971: 161. It is thus obviously based on an untenably strict division between the living and material.)

Such simplistic dualisms have virtually been transcended in modern physics. With it has disappeared many *pseudo-problems* such as trying to find the means whereby 'the body' influences 'the mind' or vice versa and what was the 'first cause'. Perhaps the notion of causality itself is limiting. In the mean time, most recent findings from physics and artificial intelligence (as well as the most ancient myths) show something like the following that **life is self-causing**. That is the meaning of *auto-poeisis*, i.e.

physis. Such findings have already potentially invalidated the classical or positivist ideal of an 'objective' description of nature; the goal of traditional academic psychology. But, for all practical purposes, it seems many psychologists and psychotherapists have not quite noticed these seismic tremors to our conceptual universes yet.

As in postmodernism, the new physics makes it untenable to consider an objective or value-free scientific approach. It also postulates the coexistence of apparently contradictory views of reality; for example, in the words of Sir William Bragg, 'Elementary particles seem to be waves on Mondays, Wednesdays and Fridays, and particles on Tuesdays, Thursdays and Saturdays' (in Zohar 1990: 10).

The whole idea of uni-directional causality (that past conditions cause future conditions) is thus also up for rethinking. For example, many of our psychological theories are based on the idea that early childhood influences affect adult life choices and patterns. This could mean that, if we consider the human being as a quantum system, such an idea of past causes may become quite invalid and unhelpful in effecting changes for the future. It is equally possible according to the new paradigms that we live in a **teleological universe** where the future is determining the present (see, for example, de Chardin 1966). I do not think we should rule out the possibility of a Copernican revolution in psychotherapy and I do think we should pay attention to the almost automatic knee-jerk mental reflex by which we may reject such revolutionary and 'upsetting' ideas.

Quantum dynamics in human systems

Quantum physics is 'the physics of that tiny micro-world within the atom; it describes the inner workings of everything we see, and at least physically, are' (Zohar 1990: 4). Naturally, human beings also 'contain' such micro-worlds and at some **levels** will obey different laws than the ones that rule the macro-universe. Quantum physics is also an invitation for the psychologist to think about possibilities.

There are aspects of quantum physics that operate, according to some theorists, only at certain quantum **levels**. Others (such as the controversial author Zohar) believe that human beings also operate on psyche and soma **levels** (or many more), and that these constitute quantum systems. Their smooth interaction is health – on all **levels** and quantum dynamics.

> The whole world of matter, including our own bodies, is made up of atoms and their even smaller components, and the laws which govern these tiny bits of basic reality spill over into our daily lives. A single photon, or 'particle' of light, affects the sensitivity of the optic nerve. The uncertainty principle that rules the behaviour of electrons plays a role in the build-up of genetic mistakes that contribute

to the ageing process and the development of certain cancers, and the process of evolution itself is thought to be similarly influenced.

(Zohar 1990: 4)

Playwrights and novelists have long exploited this fractal effect, by which the whole is fully present in any fragment of it (Atlas 1992). Psychotherapy, in common with some art forms, is the art and craft of promoting growth and/or healing in human beings. However, our most usual paradigm for it is that of client and therapist in a one-to-one, individual relationship. Group or even community therapy is less popularized. (See, however, Clarkson and Clayton 1995.)

In 1948 Foulkes, arguably the father of group analysis, was already writing that:

> From a mature, scientific point of view . . . each individual – itself an artificial, though plausible, abstraction – is basically and centrally determined, inevitably, by the world in which he lives, by the community, the group, of which he forms a part. Progress in all the sciences during the last decades has led to the same independent and concerted conclusion; that the old juxtaposition of an inside and outside world, constitution and environment, individual and society, phantasy and reality, body and mind and so on, are untenable. They can at no stage be separated from each other, except by artificial isolation.
>
> (Foulkes 1983: 10)

At one **level** one can differentiate these artificial opposites, at other **levels** they cannot be differentiated in any sense-able way. From scientific biology, some decades later, new information and new models for human behaviour, particularly the relationship between individuals and the community, are being discovered and developed which continue to support Foulkes' views. Studies of slime moulds (Elliott and Williams 1991) are being used as analogies to human communities. Cellular slime moulds are a group of soil inhabitants that live as single celled amoebae. When conditions are adverse, however, they aggregate to form a cellular collective based on mutual communication, specialization of tasks, and coordination.

As in postmodernism, the notion of the individual as separate from others as an aspect of received consciousness may bite the dust, and what seems to be remaining are the encodings of life in terms of relationships. Zohar, for example, doubts that this perspective has yet been adequately addressed:

> Klein, like Freud, Sartre and Heidegger, has no model for genuine two-way relationship of the sort that leads to intimacy. None can discriminate between the way we relate to other people and the way we might relate to a machine because for them all both machines and people share the quality of being objects.
>
> (Zohar 1990: 113)

Interestingly, as Rogers (1986) pointed out in the 1960s, an emphasis on groups, genuine encounter and mutuality of relationships tends to be construed by right-wing governments and right-wing climates as revolutionary and subversive. This is, of course, not unusual since the group is the most powerful fulcrum for individual or social change. It is the family or cultural group which sometimes appears to create most benefit or to do most damage. It is the group that scapegoats the Jew, the crowd that crucifies Christ, and the mob that lynches a black man in Alabama. It is also a feature of the time at which I am writing that right-wing governments and neo-Fascist or fundamentalist groups are in the ascendant in many places, for example, in Asia, Africa and Europe.

After much analysis of separate parts, relativity and quantum mechanics have brought scientists to the inescapable acceptance that the world cannot be analysed into separate and independently existing parts. Every whole is a part. All parts are wholes. Each part involves all the others in some way, contains or enfolds them (Bohm 1980). The implications of this, taken seriously, could herald the end of empiricism or, at the very least, give equal weight to other possible perspectives such as phenomenology.

> Freudian psychoanalysis, too, largely influenced by Descartes and Newton and in turn so responsible for the way so many ordinary people see themselves, has no conceptual framework for interpersonal relationships . . . As the author of the *Dictionary of Psychoanalysis* puts it: 'This is because psychoanalysis is a psychology of the individual and therefore discusses objects and relationships only from the point of view of a single subject' [Rycroft 1968: 101].
>
> (Zohar 1990: 112)

The fact that there is, in some senses, no 'other' to observe or with which to interact has remarkable implications for psychotherapy and supervision. For example, I would question whether a traditionally understood uni-linear causality limits and restrains rather than enhancing our understanding of and our effectiveness in the therapeutic and supervisory relationship. (For more on the latter, see Chapter 10.) From the perspective of the new physics and particularly from complexity science unidirectional causality becomes a highly dubious notion in explaining physical (or psychological) illness or many comparatively ordinary phenomena (whatever psycho-languages are used to describe them) in the therapeutic relationship. According to Field:

> I think we must recognise that projective and introjective identification, especially in its embodied form, has all the characteristics of a paranormal phenomenon. The fact that it occurs routinely in the therapeutic situation does not make it any less extraordinary.
>
> (Field 1996: 41)

From these additional perspectives, it becomes very difficult, if not impossible, to determine for certain whether the client, frightened of being harshly judged by the therapist, seeks out a therapist who judges him- or herself harshly, or interacts with such a therapist in such a way that brings about, or at least obviates, the resolution of a similar pattern in the client. How come sometimes our clients bring us the very problems which we now need to deal with in our own personal work? We have all noticed occasions when, after dealing with, say, a parent symbolically in therapy, the real life parent changes. There is much unexplained. Or as a client recently observed: 'There is more that we don't know than we know.' **In particular, complexity science and the new physics underlines again the vitality of the relationship field and its crucial importance for of the future.**

> Walking one evening along a deserted road, Mulla Nasrudin saw a troop of horsemen coming towards him.
>
> His imagination started to work; he saw himself captured and sold as a slave, or impressed into the army.
>
> Nasrudin bolted, climbed a wall into a graveyard, and lay down in an open tomb.
>
> Puzzled at this strange behaviour, the men – honest travellers – followed him.
>
> They found him stretched out, tense and quivering.
>
> 'What are you doing in that grave? We saw you run away. Can we help you?'
>
> 'Just because you can ask a question does not mean that there is a straightforward answer to it,' said the Mulla, who now realized what had happened. 'It all depends upon your viewpoint. If you must know, however: *I* am here because of *you*, and *you* are here because of *me*.'
>
> (Shah 1985: 2)

Relationship

> Epistemologically, the things we see (people, objects etc.) exist only in relationship and, when analysed microscopically, they too are best viewed as relationships. It is no secret in physics (Capra 1976, 1983) that the closer we analyse some 'thing' the less it appears as a thing and the more it appears as a dynamic process (things in relationship). Consequently, relationships become a primary source of our knowledge of the world. This can be taken to the ontological extreme by stating that things do not exist . . . that, in fact, things ultimately *are* relationships.
>
> (Cottone 1988: 360)

The development of technology and communications has led to a situation where 'For the first time . . . all humanity has the technological means to sit round the same planetary hearth and listen to each other's stories' (O'Hara 1991: 73). The ecological connectedness of our world has been dramatically brought to our attention by the way in which, for example, the damage to the ozone layer can affect people in all parts of the world. In the same way, the fallout of Chernobyl can affect sheep in Wales. According to Chaos Theory (Gleick 1989), even the fluttering of a butterfly's wings in South America can affect weather conditions in Europe.

There are many thinkers whose work more and more supports the notion that the planet Earth is a whole. One of the most ingenious of these is Lovelock (1989), who postulates the idea that the life of the Earth functions as a single organism which actually defines and maintains conditions necessary for its survival. It has become famous as the 'Gaia' hypothesis.

It can no longer be said that one part of the planet can be said to exist separately from any other part. Our planet is moaning from the assault of pollution in the seas, the deforestation in South America, and the extinction of rare and beautiful species of animals, all of which add up to the equivalent for the planet of cancer in a body. For too long man has attempted to control nature, as opposed to connecting or cooperating with nature and yet, according to Rinzler:

> Our human malaise of disconnection from natural sensation, our symptoms of violence on all **levels**, our lack of compassion for our home, the earth, our incomprehension of the connectedness among all the things of the earth, of the universe, are curable – if we are willing.
>
> (Rinzler 1984: 236)

A relational ethics

The coexistence of what we experience as evil and what we experience as beauty (or good or truth) is the relational nature of *ananke* (necessity). The virus which attacks our immune system shares the same life force as the blood cells which overcome or become defeated by it. They are also always in relationship. I love the following illustration as a stimulus to feel, empathize and imagine about this.

I explored our moral interrelationship with 'our others' and our world in *The Bystander* (Clarkson 1996d). Bauman (1993) was a major inspiration for it. For example, he writes:

> The excuse 'I did not know', 'I did not mean it', is not an excuse which moral responsibility at whatever **level** would accept . . . Whether inside the circle of proximity or beyond, I am morally responsible for my ignorance – in the same way and to the same degree in which I am morally responsible for my imagination, and for stretching it to limits when it comes to acting or refraining from action.
>
> (Bauman 1993: 230)

As we have seen, it has become more and more difficult to 'know for certain' what is 'good' and what is 'bad' in any permanent way. The foundations of our moral certitudes are constantly being challenged, undermined and sometimes shaken to the core. **Therefore, moral and ethical behaviour** can no longer be formulated and prescribed in stone tablets: **it is more like a continually renewing creative co-engagement in our relationships.**

> There is a need for new relations between man and nature and between man and man. [And woman and man.] We can no longer accept the old a priori distinction between scientific and ethical values. This was possible at a time when the external world and our internal word appeared to conflict, to be nearly orthogonal. Today we know that time is a construction and therefore carries an ethical responsibility.
>
> (Capra 1983: 312)

Five ethical relational modes

My book on working with ethical and moral dilemmas in psychotherapy (Clarkson 2000a) brings together a variety of ways of appreciating that a relational ethics affirms that no one can act or not act without mutually affecting and being affected by other people, creatures, the planet itself. Neither can there be an end to this engagement. It is possible to distinguish five ethical relational modes:

- In any encounter, the **working alliance** dimension specifies, overtly or not, what can be reasonably expected from one another and carries an implicit warning about what would constitute a violation of these expectations.
- In any encounter, the **transference/distorted** relational dimension refers to the multitude of ways in which the working alliance can be distorted, often to the detriment of all concerned. However, such distortions always contain information from which valuable learning about self, others or life can come.
- In any encounter, the **developmentally needed** or **reparative** relational mode refers to the multitude of ways in which ethically sound relationships can heal previous relational wounds or develop us as persons or as a collective.
- In any encounter, the **person-to-person** or **dialogic** aspect of relationship can strengthen bonds of affection and respect and/or can bring individual needs into uncomfortable and painful, but authentic conflict with self or others. This may sometimes mean that choices have to be

made which have implications for all the other aspects of a relationship. However, from such conflict, different and perhaps more
complex kinds of ethics can arise.

• In any encounter, the **transpersonal** is the relational mode which
  emphasizes our ultimate values, knowing that the human condition
  often falls short of our dreams. We appear to be forever entangled with
  each other and the world in the quantum sense of relationship. An
  ethical questioning of the transpersonal aspect of a relationship is
  concerned with our ultimate ideals and even notions such as grace. It
  implies that ethical relationships are in essence inspirational and
  aspirational.

I believe Physis is the name people have been looking for to describe the life
force. It's what I believe is a phenomenon of growth and healing prior to
Eros and Thanatos. Life and Death there are, yes; but really, between those
boundaries lies the wonder that we grow, we develop, we evolve, we
connect, we strive for greater and greater perfection, we move towards 'the
good'. Perls, Hefferline and Goodman were in agreement: 'man does not
strive to be good; the good is what it is human to strive for' (Perls et al. 1951:
335). In these words they are articulating a philosophical position similar to
that of the Stoics who were grappling with this idea thousands of years ago:

> A good bootmaker is one who makes good boots, a good shepherd is one who
> keeps his sheep well, and even though good boots are in the Day-of-Judgement
> sense entirely worthless and fat sheep no whit better than starved sheep, yet the
> good bootmaker or good shepherd must do his work well or he will cease to be
> good. To be good he must perform his function; and, in performing that
> function, there are certain things that he must 'prefer' to others, even though
> they are not really 'good'. He must prefer a healthy sheep or a well-made boot to
> their opposites. It is this that Nature, or Physis, herself works when she shapes
> the seed into a tree or the blind puppy into a good hound. The perfection of the
> tree or the blind puppy is in itself indifferent, a thing of no ultimate value. Yet the
> goodness of Nature lies in working for that perfection . . . For the essence of
> Goodness is to do something, to labour, to achieve some end; and if Goodness is
> to exist, the world process must begin again . . . Physis must be moving upward,
> or else it is not Physis.
>
>   (Murray 1955: 43)

> We are part of an Order, a cosmos, which we see to be infinitely above our
> comprehension . . . But in the rest of the world, we can see a moving Purpose. It
> is Phusis [Physis], the word which the Romans unfortunately translated 'Nature',
> but which means 'growing' or 'the way things grow' – almost what we call
> Evolution. But to the Stoic it is a living and conscious evolution . . . The direction
> was towards the perfection of each thing or species after its own kind . . . If a man
> is an artist, it is his function to produce beauty.

> Or if one is a bootmaker – to make good boots. On the Day of Judgement it hardly matters whether you made good boots, or you're chic, or fat or starving. But it matters that you were doing it well.
>
> (Murray 1955: 126)

And the same goes for counsellors, psychoanalysts and psychotherapists.

Transpersonal psychotherapy in practice

Sad to say, clients have not been highly regarded in most therapeutic systems. Called maladjusted, disturbed, regressed, neurotic, psychotic and character-disordered (to name just a few) a reasonable person might conclude that therapists have nothing good to recount about the very people who support their livelihoods. This is no fault of therapists, but it does strongly speak to the professions' traditions. As Held (1991) pointedly observed: 'most theories of therapy are, in reality theories of psychopathology . . . No matter how many unfavourable ways clients are classified in professional discourse, the practice of therapy is not about nosology. It is about change' (cited in Hubble et al. 1999b: 409).

Building on and applying the wisdom of therapy's most influential scholars, Hubble et al. (1999b) view the client's theory as containing most, if not all, of the trappings of any psychological theory. It encompasses aetiology, treatment and prognosis, and includes clients' thoughts, attitudes, and feelings about their problems and how therapy may best address their goals. They view the client's theory of change as not only having the values that most affect the client's participation in therapy but also as holding the keys to success despite the method or technique used by the therapist (1999b: 427).

There is a story of a Zen master who was found scrabbling on the pavement under a streetlight in the dirt. 'What are you looking for master?', asked a passer-by. 'I'm looking for my key', said the teacher. Many more passers-by joined him in looking for his key. After some hours someone asked: 'Are you sure you lost your key here, Master?' The Master said: 'No, I lost it in my house.' 'So why are you out here looking for your key?' The teacher said: 'Because there's more light here.'

> Just as the discovery of Deinonychus [a dinosaur] dramatically changed how dinosaurs were viewed, converging empirical evidence – regarding the importance of clients and their perceptions to positive outcome – is transforming how clients are treated and therapy is conducted. Specifically, the shift is encompassing changes in perspective from (a) clients are slow-witted plodders (or pathological monsters) to resourceful motivated hunters of more satisfying lives; (b) the clinician as the leading character in the drama of therapy to the client as the star of the therapeutic stage; and (c) the omnipotence of the therapist's theory of therapy to the prominence of the client's theory of change.
>
> (Hubble et al. 1999b: 425)

Ask the person who had the key to tell you where he lost it.

The following list of possible questions adds to and has been adapted from those in Hubble et al. (1999b: 410, 412, 432):

- What brought you here?
- Did you notice any changes before making your first appointment and our first session?
- How do you understand your problem?
- What do you think will help?
- What ideas do you have about what needs to happen for you to get through this stuck place?
- Tell me about previous times when you've succeeded in getting through stuck places?
- What ideas do you have about what needs to happen for further improvement to occur?
- Many times people have a pretty good hunch about not only what is causing a problem, but also what will resolve it. Do you have a theory of how change is going to happen here?
- In what ways do you see me and this process being helpful to attaining your goals?
- How does change usually happen in your life?
- What do you and others do to initiate change?
- What was happening at those times? (Obtain a detailed description of what is helping.) What difference will that make to you tomorrow?
- How will your day go better? The day after that?
- What have you tried to help the problem/situation so far?
- Did it help?
- How?
- What's your idea about why it didn't help in the way you wanted?
- Please tell me about a time when you felt confident and secure in yourself?
- Who or what helped you then?
- How did you do that?
- What was different then that you used those resources?
- Which people, places or situations do you use to comfort yourself when things are rough?
- What will be different when (your anxiety, drinking, feuding with your spouse, etc.) is behind you?
- What would be the smallest sign that the (_____) is getting better?
- What will be the first sign?

- When you are no longer (e.g. fighting, in trouble with the law, drinking, etc.) what will you be doing more of instead?
- Who will be the first person to notice that you have achieved a victory over this?
- What will that person notice different about you that will tell him or her that the victory is achieved?
- Where do you suppose you will be when you first notice the change?
- What will have happened just before those changes that will have helped them happen?
- What will happen later that will help maintain them?
- What do you think may go wrong once you leave psychotherapy?
- What could we do to prevent that or cope with it in a better way than you did in the past?

Case study: part 4

The *citrinitas* phase: 'the greater dark night' – the I–you encounter

Then tragedy struck. (Whereas *nigredo* is characterized by the disillusionment, *citrinitas* is characterized by the loss of illusions.) During his annual medical check-up, prostrate cancer was suspected. At first he just couldn't believe it and denied it by not making another doctor's appointment – until I made it a condition if he wanted to keep coming to see me. He was angry with me. Surely it was his right to make decisions about his own life. He should have committed suicide while he was still in control. I was a psychologist. It wasn't me that was dying. Anyway he didn't trust doctors. I held my ground. We started arguing in sessions as often as we did other good work together. But this was also 'good' work. He challenged me about my views on various matters that came up – British intervention in Bosnia, a modern art exhibition, whether adult children should live at home.

The cancer was malignant and fast spreading. He was sinking. Emotionally he became even more depressed than during the *nigredo* period, but now he was also angry, irritable and full of rage. Why had God let this happen to him? Just as he was truly ready for a fulfilling life during his autumn years, a life which had meaning and joy, just as he was feeling that he could cope with almost anything life could throw at him. He couldn't cope with this. He felt betrayed. Why now? If he hadn't changed, then perhaps this wouldn't have happened. Or it wouldn't matter so much. Years ago he would have welcomed death – any death. **Now was the wrong time**.

He was struggling in quicksand. The more he fought, the deeper he sank. Everybody was to blame – including himself. He should have done this, done that: these were the coils of a big snake which was suffocating the life out of him. He knew it was unreasonable but couldn't help feeling that I should have warned him. Why had I not warned him? Periods of intense rage interspersed with paralysing depressions – just like Churchill's 'black dog'. Treatment, chemotherapy and radiation was attempted, but failed – although he lost all his hair and several stones in weight. I was angry too and told him so. Alternative therapies were tried and found ineffective. All our good work threatened by death. How cruel life can be. How helpless I was.

The Bible says: 'It rains on the just and the unjust.' It's just not fair. I remembered an old Chinese acupuncturist I once knew. He stuck needles in sick people's bodies, but he was actually a famed spiritual healer in his region – often achieving miraculous cures. But even for him, there were some people he couldn't cure. So, every morning between 4.00 and 7.00 he would burn incense, meditate and offer them up by name to the Divine, yielding the healing and decisional power to whence it came. But I am not that holy all the time. It's only sometimes I feel like that.

Then I remembered Job and the unreasonableness of the Old Testament God. But Isaac, Job and Jonah were delivered in the end! My supervisor told me that in Islam they say: 'Allah has a thousand hearts.' Apparently it means that God can answer our prayers or not – it's a mystery why some get favoured and others not, some prayers get answered and others not. Why? Surely after all the pain and suffering and healing Jeder had gone through, he deserved to live, not die.

I told him a joke: There was a man hanging by his fingernails over a terrible abyss. He could not even look down, it was so terrible. So the man shouted: 'Is there anybody out there?' And God answered: 'Yes, my son.' So the man said: 'Please tell me what to do!' And God said: 'Let go, my son.' The man considered this for a minute, then he cried out: 'Is there anybody else out there?' Jeder laughed.

Chapter 8
Rubedo – death and rebirth: the transpersonal relationship

Put This Design in Your Carpet
Spiritual experience is a modest woman
who only looks lovingly at one man.
It's a great River where ducks
live happily, and crows drown.

The visible bowl of form contains food
that is both nourishing and a source of heartburn.

There is an Unseen Presence we honor
that gives the gifts.

You're Water. We're the millstone.
You're Wind. We're the dust blown up into shapes.
You're Spirit. We're the opening and closing
of our hands. You're the Clarity.
We're this language that tries to say it.
You're the Joy. We're all the different kinds of laughing.

Any movement or sound is a profession of faith,
as the millstone grinding is explaining how it believes
in the River! No metaphor can say this, but I can't stop pointing
to the Beauty.
Every moment and place says,
'Put this design in your carpet!'

Like the shepherd in Book 11,
who wanted to pick the lice of God's robe,
and stitch up God's shoes, I want to be
in such a passionate adoration
that my tent gets pitched against the sky!

Let the Beloved come
and sit like a guard-dog
in front of that tent.

When the Ocean surges,
don't let me just hear it,
Let it splash inside my chest!

(Rumi 1990: 128–29)

In the Jewish tradition it is a compliment to be called a *Mensch*. The word means very much more than the literal translation of 'person' or 'human'. Houston (1982) gives some of the definitions of a Mensch:

'A Mensch is a full person.'
'A Mensch is not a hero. A hero is a one-shot deal while a Mensch is for ever.'
'A Mensch loves to take his children to the zoo and doesn't mind doing the income tax.'
'A Mensch can give with grace and receive with the same. When a Mensch scrubs the toilet bowl, he's cleaning up the world.'
'When you are with a Mensch, you grow a little.'
'A Mensch celebrates life.'
'A Mensch has leaky margins.'
'A Mensch loves to learn, loves to laugh, loves to listen.'
'A Mensch knows how to cry.'
'A Mensch, when the Nebbish comes to the door, tells him a joke.'
'A Mensch sees the Mensch in you.'
'A Mensch lives on all levels.'

(Houston 1982: 120–21, my emphasis)

Houston also quotes Ortega y Gasset: 'So many things fail to interest us, simply because they don't find in us enough surfaces on which to live, and what we have to do is to increase the number of planes in our mind, so that a much larger number of themes can find a plane in it at the same time' (Houston 1982: 60).

There are moments (or sometimes longer periods) when we humans (whatever our 'stage of 'spiritual development') are blessed with this realization right throughout the body/emotions/language/values/reason/story/soul/spirit in perfect alignment **whatever** the external events are, whether they be painful, such as grief, or pleasurable, such as when awed by the sublime beauty of nature.

Another way of saying this is that it is the experience of all seven **levels** of our experience in perfect harmony in the middle of, for example, making love or balancing your accounts or witnessing the birth of a baby or at the end of another sacred ceremony. The 'experiential reconciliation of permanence and degeneration' in the everlasting cycles of our lives and Life.

Living on all levels at once

Living on all **levels** (let's say seven) at once means that we live with our full humanity:

Level 1: This includes both our **amoebic**;
Level 2: and our **animal** selves;
Level 3: within the **language** communities in which we participate or those we create;
Level 4: constantly, minute by minute engaged in the inescapable freedom of making **moral choices** in our actions and inactions within or against our normative communities;
Level 5: living with the best that reason, **rationality** and positivistic sciences can offer us and we can use at that time;
Level 6: construing our stories, or sharing our **narratives**, our theories and myths about our lives and about life and death generally
Level 7: as well as with a transpersonal dimension of **spirit** which is always and also unavoidably part of the whole of everything we feel, think and do.

Rarely will we experience the bliss of all of these **levels** in harmony resonating like an exquisite chord of seven true musical notes all in perfect attunement. These are the elements of what Maslow (1968) termed 'peak experiences'. My body, my feelings, my words or images, my values, my reason, my meaning and my sense of inexpressible awe all together in tune. No conflict, no confusion, no displacement, no conflation. Each note clear. All the notes creating a music which is divine as well as deeply and profoundly personal.

Such privileged experiences can happen in moments of love, sacrifice, worship, sex, creating a painting, grieving, birthing, dying, doing therapy, running a race, organizing your finances or doing the washing up. Anything at all. Permeated with 'jouissance' – whatever the external circumstances. Green and moist all through. Alive. All of a piece. Abundant. Fully human.

In these states we also vividly experience our connection, the experiential reality of our interrelationship with the rest of the universe. We knowingly feel our kinship with the **earth**, its seasons, plants and fruits; our shared existence with all **other creatures**; our interrelationship with other **communicating beings** through words and images; our belonging within our **cultural** groups (and our chosen families or other normative communities); our share of the **consensual reality** of our situations; a **meaning** for it all which for that moment is adequate or beautiful; as well as a participation in the wonder of all that falls in the **region beyond words**.

We do not have to study to achieve these states. They come to anybody at any time. Look at a baby playing, with all its concentration focused like a laser beam on whatever is at hand – a sunbeam in a dusty room, the space left in the middle of a spill of milk on a table. Children are experts at this. The best teacher of my life taught me: 'Life in small measures may perfect be.'

We can if we want to, but we don't have to meditate to experience such states. They can come to a city stockbroker in the heat of a noon-day crisis in the international financial markets or a parent having a jelly bath with the children.

We do not have to be 'civilized' or 'first world' to feel this relationship with all of ourselves and all of the universe. It is a natural state for many people throughout the world, whether weeping and wailing during a natural disaster or dancing on mine dumps for the delectation of tourists.

We do not have to avoid being 'new age' or 'feminist' or 'fundamentalist'. Life does not discriminate in granting its blessings. 'It rains on the just and the unjust.'

We do not have to be 'spiritual'. Agnostic concert pianists or atheistic surgeons can know this state.

We do not have to be 'emotionally balanced', 'well-adjusted', 'genitally mature' or 'having constructive sexual fantasies' to experience this human condition. Neither do we have to have 'dealt with our issues'. Issues, like the poor, will always be with us.

We do not even have to be 'intelligent' or 'all there'. Many people, for example, who are diagnosed as having Down's syndrome or who are dementing experience this way of being. As one of my friends said: 'As long as they keep me fed and warm, I don't see why I should die just because I've gone senile.' We can learn so much from them.

Not according to my deserts, Lord, but according to thy mercy.

Always we return refreshed, nourished or cleansed from such experiences. Yet it seems we cannot hold on to them, just as we cannot hold a butterfly in our hands for a long time without it being crushed. Life moves in rhythms. Tides ebb and flow. Physis loves to hide. Except perhaps for a few people, permanent bliss in this life is not on the menu. Striving after it is a sure recipe for despair, disillusionment and tragedy. The wrinkles of life cannot be ironed out like a crumpled shirt. You cannot step into the same river twice. Encouraging or deluding others into wanting heaven on earth or permanent 'happiness and peace' may be irresponsible and unhelpful. What will they do then when the dark nights come? And they will come, as sure as dawn will come again.

What is possible? Learning (if we need to), unlearning (which many of us need to) and **celebrating the way Life is**. Then we can attempt to make the most of it and authentically engage in making the world a somewhat better place for us having been here. This is possible and, I think, achievable. For whatever reason we want to believe – 'karma', 'biological constitution', 'original sin' or whatever, each one of us has been given a metaphorical set of cards with which to play the game of Life. **How** we play the individual cards we've been dealt is what makes the difference. Anyway, being yourself is the only thing at which you will ever be perfect. 'When you accept what you are now you become free to be what you are now, and this is why the fool becomes a sage when he lets himself be free to be a fool' (Watts 1968: 180).

Buber advises us that

> It is impossible to tell men what way they should take. For one way to serve God is by the teachings, another by prayer, another way by fasting, and still another by eating. Everyone should carefully observe which way his heart draws him, and then choose that way with all his [or her] strength.
>
> (Buber 1962: 54)

Betrayal

Men and women take many different ways, some good, some evil. It is much more likely that we all take ways with some admixture of the two. Hopefully, most of the time, good will mostly prevail. But rarely for ever. Frequently it is also very hard to judge from the outside at the time what the final verdict of history will be.

Mores, values and information change over time and circumstance. What looks like good, for example, getting the trains on time in Italy, may subsequently prove the platform for Fascism and the persecution of the Jews. What looks like evil, such as the betrayal of Jesus by Judas, may be an essential part of the Christian story without which it might not have been able to unfold in the way that it has – without that betrayal.

Betrayal is part of life and part of loving. It hurts. Sometimes the scars never heal. **And** it is a ticket to transformation. Even so, this does not make it right.

> For we must be clear that to live or love only where one can trust, where there is security and containment, where one cannot be hurt or let down, where what is pledged in words is forever binding, means really to be out of harm's way and so to be out of real life. And it does not matter what is this vessel of trust – analysis, marriage, church or law, any human relationship.
>
> (Hillman 1990: 278)

Neither (as I hope I have shown in this book and others) can we easily hide behind the claim that we are just 'innocent bystanders' (e.g. Clarkson 1996d). When we as individuals or communities witness evil, cruelty, injustice and persecution while choosing to 'do nothing' (hiding behind any of the many excuses or reasons human beings make up for themselves and others out of fear or gain) we are actually complicit in supporting the atrocities of the oppressors. We may for **good** reasons choose to do this, but the moral and ethical consequences of bystanding are our responsibility all the same. As someone very wise once said: 'All that is necessary for evil to triumph is for good people to do nothing.'

I have mentioned many betrayals in this book, for example, the betrayal of children by their parents and the betrayal of black people's trust throughout some of the most gruesome chapters in the history of our world. Someone from an African state told me that when the white settlers first landed in their country, they welcomed them with gifts and hospitality. When, eventually, war broke out (as it invariably did) the male members of the tribe were too shocked to really fight back. This tribe of 'uncivilized savages' was finally virtually wiped out. Why were they so shocked? They were horrified by the fact that the white men actually **killed** their enemies. (Perhaps we're too desensitized by now to imagine or empathize with those black people's surprise.)

You see, in those countries for countless millennia, one would never kill the people with whom you were at war. Killing human beings meant killing **Life**. These peoples considered that that would be a very dishonourable thing to do. It would be like destroying the Life spirit. The point in their wars was to **dis-able** your opponent so that he couldn't fight any more – usually using machetes. That way battles could be won, but Life would be preserved.

Read the following extract before looking to see who the authors are:

> First, that an Advocate shall be allotted to the accused. Second, that the names of the witnesses shall not be made known to the Advocate, even under an oath of secrecy, but that he shall be informed of everything contained in the depositions. Third, the accused shall as far as possible be given the benefit of every doubt, provided that this involves no scandal to the faith nor is in any way detrimental to justice, as will be shown. And in like manner the prisoner's procurator shall have full access to the whole process, only the names of the witnesses and deponents being suppressed; and the Advocate can act also in the name of procurator.
>
> As to the first of these points: it should be noted that an Advocate is not to be appointed at the desire of the accused, as if he may choose which Advocate he will have; but the Judge must take great care to appoint neither a litigious nor an evil-minded man, nor yet one who is easily bribed (as many are), but rather an honourable man to whom no sort of suspicion attaches ... We convened in solemn council [learned] men ... and having diligently examined and discussed each circumstance of the process and maturely and carefully considered with the said learned men everything which has been said and done in this present case ...
>
> (Kramer and Sprenger 1971: 217–18, 261)

Sounds quite fair and reasonable doesn't it? Except for the fact that the names of the witnesses are kept secret. However, even this has been acceptable practice by UKCP member organizations of the twenty-first century (e.g. see GPTI on the Physis website: www.physis.co.uk) where anonymous letters against colleagues are accepted as 'evidence' for expulsion of members although no ethics charge could be made. The issue was an enquiry into the unjust and flawed process of a colleague's sanctions under a Code of Ethics which did not even exist at the time.

People who are interested in the oppression and pathologization of women could also read the rest of the text (particularly pages xxxix and 41–48). Note that a learned man, the Revd Summers, writes in the foreword of this text that: 'There can be no doubt that Sprenger was a mystic of the highest order, a man of most saintly life' (Kramer and Sprenger 1971: ix).

What is the lesson? Beware the cloak of reason. The above extract – and many more could be added – is the reasonable, rational sounding rationale for the torture, hanging and burning of thousands, if not millions of medicine women, children and men as witches or 'wizards' in Europe. (Homosexual men were used as the 'faggots' to light the fires on the stakes.) Recent scientific research suggests that the victims were in fact suffering from ergot-poisoning with its symptoms very similar to 'bad trips' on LSD.

The original book from which this extract was quoted is called *The Malleus Maleficarum* – the Witches' Hammer. It was written by two leading theologians to justify this persecution which still lies like an archetypal scar across our history in the relations between men and women. I could have used any number of other texts – at the time prominent and respectable – which have been used to justify similar or worse persecutions in the past and in the present, for the best 'reasons' and also in consultation with so-called 'learned' men (and women).

Such things do not 'announce' themselves at first in the world as astonishing wicked or **evil at the time**. Their justifications must be made to sound reasonable, rational and often based on 'democratic' principles. Just think of McCarthy's witch hunts in North America, the fact that millions of Germans voted for Hitler. The philosopher Hannah Arendt (1964) has vividly demonstrated 'the banality of evil' in her coverage of the Eichmann trial.

It is my opinion that when ever one **level** of human experience alone is used to the apparent exclusion of the others, or privileged to be 'above' or 'higher' than the domains, similar atrocities are likely to result. Human beings are not very rational – as anyone who has ever been to a meeting might testify. It seems more like that people do things for complex sets of multiple reasons, of which rationality is, in proportion, about the size of a sheet of typing paper held horizontally in a ream. And, as we have seen from Bystander research, the more people support the decision, the more likely it is that individual rights will be sacrificed.

Perhaps if we consider all seven **levels** as coexisting and even sometimes contradictory, our human decision-making might improve. We might also become somewhat more suspicious of 'following the orders' of 'authorities'. Holding our individual and collective multiplicities might just allow for somewhat more different voices to be heard and slightly more humanity to permeate our lives and institutions.

Physis as logos

> Existentialism, that is the great art, literature and philosophy of the 20th century, reveals the courage to face things as they are and to express the anxiety of meaninglessness. It is creative courage that appears in the creative expressions of despair. Sartre calls one of his most powerful plays *No Exit,* a classical formula for the situation of despair. But he himself has an exit: he can *say* 'No exit', thus taking the situation of meaninglessness upon himself.
>
> (Tillich 1952: 143)

This is the working – the **poiesis** – of **physis**. As I have written before: 'Without physis suffering is just suffering, and pain is just pain' (Clarkson 1995a: 107). **It is that we create meaning from our life experiences which makes them enjoyable or bearable**. And it is **how** we create meaning that makes it possible to transcend and transform them. And one of the names for this meaning-creating is physis as logos. Not an avoidance (or sublimation) of our aggressive and sexual drives, but as the potential for creativity in everything – including our hate and our love.

But as Heidegger said: 'Just as there are people blind to colors, so there are people **blind to physis**' (Heidegger 1998: 202, my emphasis). By definition, words fail me. I should only talk of animals and dreams. However, like Rumi, 'just for the sake of saying something' . . .

This phase in psychotherapy is like another rebirth, but instead of the disillusion and disappointment which accompanies Nigredo, and the great optimism of Albedo, the emergence from Citrinitas ('**the greater dark night**') is accompanied by a giving up of illusions *(maya).*

You give up wanting it to be different from the way it is, and yet keep **doing** the right thing without counting the cost. Even if you can't be sure what the right thing is. The world (and the self) is seen clearly and experienced directly, with all its pain and suffering and beauty and love and ambiguity and contradictions and paradoxes. The realization that saying something like I actually heard a colleague say – 'I have integrated my shadow' – is just another shadow (see also James 2000). A claim like 'I have no ego' has the autograph of the ego all over it.

The hurt and broken figure of Christ on the cross (after crying 'My God, My God, why hast thou forsaken me!') symbolizes the hope of resurrection – the *coincidentia oppositorum*. In the representations of Kali Durga (the great Hindu Goddess of the terrible face) with her multiple arms holding dangerous weapons, dripping blood and a necklace of skulls, often shown treading on corpses, there is always one hand with its palm turned up towards the devotee. The message of this hand is: 'Do not be afraid. It's OK.'

Three practice examples of transpersonal psychotherapy

Here follow three vignettes of psychotherapy. (You will have noticed again that my current position is that the transpersonal relationship dimension cannot be divorced from any type of healing.) See if you can recognize how it works in each.

Bethlehem is still a place

Cox and Thielgaard (1987) use the following example to illustrate what they call 'the Aeolian mode'. They define this as the release of creative energy potentially freeing an individual from the restrictive legacy of the past through the use of, and listening to, image and metaphor rather than the formulation of reductionist explanations:

> Toward the end of the last therapeutic group in Advent, with its wide-ranging reflections upon the meaning of life, the word becoming flesh, the words spoken by 'the voices', and the pros and cons of various religious beliefs, one patient turned to the therapist and said:
> 'It'll soon be Christmas in Broadmoor.'
> 'Just in Broadmoor?'
> 'Yes . . . Bethlehem is still a place . . . isn't it?'
> Whatever a formal psychodynamic appraisal would make of the patient's 'mental state', there was no doubt in the therapist's mind that 'concrete thinking . . . psychotic evasion' would be a cynical reduction. The concreteness of precise location 'Bethlehem is still a place' could also be seen as a 'disturbed' patient's way of cutting through layers of irrelevant philosophical abstraction, which distracted her attention from the one fact of which she needed to be certain. She knew that Broadmoor was still a place. That Bethlehem was also still a geographical location (interpret this how we will)

was what mattered. Historically and theologically, the first Christmas was indeed remarkably localized. She exemplified the forceful words by Robert Graves which press towards an overall coherence:
> 'There is one story and one story only
> That will prove worth your telling.'

Graves ends this stanza with the following lines: 'That startle with the shining/Such common stories as they stray into.' Hopefully, for this patient, the Aeolian Mode had enabled her to recognize and tell part of the one story which, for her was worth the telling. Though from a technical point of view it should be noted that the Aeolian Mode helped to tune the therapist's listening, rather than to influence what he said. In this instance, it was important to recognize that 'Bethlehem is still a place' was existentially significant for a patient who wandered, in mind and body, and needed a fixed point of reference. 'Bethlehem in Broadmoor' could be regarded as a clang-association or as evidence of psychotic confusion and dislocation. But it can also sustain prolonged reflection on the location of epiphany and apocalypse.

The story which the patient tells differs from the story which the therapist might tell. Indeed, it would be a travesty of the whole process if this were not so. But both will find that their story falls within the range of *parable;* the story-containing-story of how things are.

(Cox and Thielgaard 1987: 247–48)

A body therapist lies on his back to touch a soul

> I sing the body electric,
> The armies of those I love engirth me and I engirth them,
> They will not let me off till I go with them, respond to them,
> And discorrupt them, and charge them full with the charge of the soul.
> Was it doubted that those who corrupt their own bodies conceal themselves?
> And if those who defile the living are as bad as they who defile the dead?
> And if the body does not do fully as much as the soul?
> And if the body were not the soul, what is the soul?

(Whitman 1955: 98–99)

Boadella, a student of Lowen of Bioenergetics bodywork fame, who calls himself a *biosynthesist*, writes as follows:

> In a totally out of character session, I stopped all attempts to work on energy flow or bodily contractions. I gave up even sitting face to face with Caroline and trying to work directly with her expression. I lay down on my back and began to talk to her about my feeling that at the deepest **level** she did not trust anyone to reach her. Nor did she trust that there was a deep enough self to reach. I admitted defeat in trying to reach the inside of her experience by touching her on the outside, through working with the body. With many people the body work opens the way to deeper contact and opens up the inner glow that Reich describes. With Caroline it was the other way round. Her experience of the session was that for

the first time in her life her soul had been recognized. She had remembered who she was. She had come into the room to listen to what I had to say and to begin to answer from a usually withheld dimension of herself. The session was a turning point which resulted in a progressive thawing out, over the next few months, of her bodily withdrawal signs. She became much warmer. Her breathing became more lively. These changes happened spontaneously, from inside out, because of the quality of touching that happened when physical touch was abandoned as too great a source of threat to her.

(Boadella 1987: 162)

Miscarriage and birth

The clouds weep, and then the garden sprouts.
The baby cries, and the mother's milk flows.
The Nurse of Creation has said, Let them cry a lot.
This rain-weeping and sun-burning twine together
to make us grow. Keep your intelligence white-hot
and your grief glistening, so your life will stay fresh.
Cry easily like a little child.

(Rumi 1990: 80)

Psychotherapist: Usually, feeling 'flat' has to do with keeping feelings that we might otherwise express, in – with flattening feelings.
Client: Yeah.
Psychotherapist: I notice you've almost stopped breathing.
Client: mm . . . I don't know. (*Crying*) I feel as if there's a sadness, that's bigger than any of the things I've spoken about, which I can't identify. Just . . .
Psychotherapist: Well, you're feeling it. You feel your sadness. I suggest you stop trying to identify and simply allow yourself to feel and show me how sad you feel rather than flattening yourself . . . or trying to be explanatory about it.
Client: (*Long pause*) . . . mm . . . feels uncomfortable. I feel as if I'm wallowing in . . . (*Laughs apologetically*)
Psychotherapist: . . . And I hear and see that you're uncomfortable with doing so. Sound's like there's some kind of message about wallowing. I know I responded quite strongly inside me when I heard you saying wallowing. My response was, um . . . sounds kind of self-deprecating.
Client: . . . I think the guilt gets to me . . . I can almost hear my father sort of saying you know, you haven't got any problems, a sort of recurring theme really, that I ought

	to put my imagined problems out of the way . . . be aware of the very real problems of the world . . . Part of me hears that and says, you know, my problems are not imagined, my sadness is not imagined, but it's a lesson that's gone very deep, I think . . .
Psychotherapist:	You're touching your chest.
Client:	mm, I can feel quite a (*Sighs*) – I've got to make an effort to breathe.
Psychotherapist:	Experiment with taking your breath to the centre of where you're feeling you're making an effort, and as you breathe out, letting yourself know what it is you're breathing from there.
Client:	. . . mm, a sort of scream . . .
Psychotherapist:	Take your breath to the centre of where you felt your scream, as you breathe out, you can make a sound, you can scream, let out what you want to let out.
Client:	(*Breathes in and out several times, making small sounds as she does so on out-breath*) . . . (*Breathes some more, deeply, sighing on out-breaths*)
Psychotherapist:	What are you doing now?
Client:	It's odd. I'm just remembering all the times I've not been able to scream when I've wanted to. In childbirth.
Psychotherapist:	You never did?
Client:	Mm. I always felt as if I shouldn't. (*Sighs*)
Psychotherapist:	Sounds like you kept a lot of screams and shouts in there.
Client:	. . . Yeah, the first still-born baby (*Crying*) . . . Just didn't believe anyone would hear, however loudly I screamed.
Psychotherapist:	. . .You were lying there with your legs strung up . . .
Client:	And people were talking to each other and ignoring me . . . When I did make a noise, a very unsympathetic midwife told me it was only a small baby, not to be ridiculous.
Psychotherapist:	Uh, that's outrageous.
Client:	And it was, telling me it was dead, not allowing me to see her.
Psychotherapist:	(*Heavy out-breath*)
Client:	Needing a heck of a lot of stitches actually.
Psychotherapist:	That's terrible, that's really, really terrible, Annie.
Client:	I still have a nightmare about that every now and then. (*Crying*)
Psychotherapist:	Mm . . . So, imagine that these are those people who

	were there then, and this time you're not going to be quiet because they give you silly messages about being quiet or whatever. Actually honour what's going on in You.
Client:	Yeah, pain's pain and I, I'm real.
Psychotherapist:	Yeah, you are.
Client:	It's as though you are denying that I'm real . . . and yes, the baby's going to be dead, but it's mine. (*Crying*)
Psychotherapist:	Mm. It's your baby.
Client:	My baby and I've a right to hold him. (*Crying*) I want to . . . Part of the problem is time. The way one loss has overlapped another, so that . . . got to give time to each loss in a kind of way, perhaps in trying to deny those losses . . . they've added together perhaps. You do need to be able to face them, acknowledge them. Life isn't neat. Can't necessarily tick them off the list . . . exactly what I complained about in those professionals – that first nightmarish still-birth. They just went into efficiency mode. They ticked off the list the things they had to do.
Psychotherapist:	Is that what you think Annie in the past also tried to do too?
Client:	Yes, I think so. But never again.

The following week she reported this dream which I have published before, but never in the context of the full story:

I was in the presence of two older women. One of them seemed to be my 'difficult' grandmother. But she faded into the background immediately. Both women were engaged in religious and spiritual pursuits. But the stranger definitely was more **level**-headed. She suggested I should do an 'exercise'. I was puzzled. She called it 'shedding of the skin'. As she was explaining it to me a young woman was in fact performing the exercise. She put her head on to her chest. And it disappeared into her body. That's all I saw. Although I was slightly scared and apprehensive I told the woman I wanted to do the exercise. So I put my head on to my chest . . . it entered my body. And from then on I had to completely trust the woman. I felt her hands curling my skin across my bones. I was completely soft. Even my bones. She proceeded to peel me, turn me inside out. I felt like a sausage, with an unsavoury skin. I felt this as I was 'peeled'. I remember thinking, 'How nice to get rid of that skin.' But at the same time I still didn't know if I'd ever get out of this very awkward position! I could get completely stuck half-way through . . . Those fearful thoughts crept through my mind as I felt my skin being pushed on my outside. I was still inside. It was awfully dark . . . And then I felt hands quite hard pushing at my head. And I saw light. I saw it from the inside of my own vagina. And I realized I was actually born from myself. I saw the shed skin and even the umbilical cord, which had been cut off. I can't remember how I got 'out' – but when I was OUT I had a new skin and felt VERY fresh all over. And glowing.

Physis

Here I would just like to publish the last paragraph of my paper on Physis (1992b: 202–9) which the Editorial Board of the *Transactional Analysis Journal* required to be deleted. Perhaps they were right.

> To see a person change, to see that flame sputter into life, to see hope rise where once there was despair, to see the laughter at absurdity bubbling over from confusion and self-deception, to see a new child born from an adult who never was one – this is the excitement and this is what makes our work worthwhile. Every day I understand that we are given this small handful of life-energy for this day – this day's quota of sand in the endless timer of life measured on the grand chronologies of eternity. I walk every day into life with this my treasure to waste, to spend, to reduce to ashes, to squander on worthless activity and toxic people, soluble or insoluble problems, my destiny and my freedom; to suppress in some petty way, to free with tender nurturing – this is my life energy, the precious *élan vital* which Bergson (1965) wrote about. Every day I have my share, and every day it is mine to spend and there is no way I can save it up to use another day. I am repeating these things over and over again since I can only now begin to understand it – life is an everyday affair. The energy I save today (in resting, in squandering, in suppression) will not be available tomorrow. I must have to do it today, now, to take my energy as it rises, every moment. Every single moment because it cannot and will not come again, I cannot bank energy, life's energy, to be available to me at another time; just this portion, this little bit is mine today. Everyone else also has only their day's allotment to spend on love and care and creation and celebration – this is only this handful of mine today against the dawning of mortality.

Transpersonal psychotherapy in practice

Consider the dammed-up creativity in your own heart before you diminish the achievements of others. Be gentle with yourself in your creativity as you are gentle with those who create. In psychotherapy we are the servants of physis. Our work is to nurture the flame of healing in the other from the in-between. We do the therapy, physis heals. The muse is never 'broken in'. Creativity only happens at far from equilibrium conditions. Welcome turbulence and chaos so that something new can come.

Fertilize not only your own field, but also the furrows of others. Live bravely and die well as you can, but love life. Enjoy the good times. Laugh a lot. Practise gratitude. Love your enemies – they are your most generous teachers. Accept that you cannot avoid benefiting them. Normalize conflict and learn to transform it – again and again and again. There are no innocent bystanders. Live with the opposites without falling (permanently) into the simplistic dialectic dualisms of good and bad, life and death, individual and 'other'. Everything passes into its opposite. Pain hurts. Weeping is the price we pay for the gift of love. This too shall pass.

Commit arbitrary acts of kindness and random acts of beauty. Work from your wounds, but don't bleed all over your clients. Consider the cycles of life, death in the large and in the small scale. **Do not seek meaning, make it**. Never has there been a time when the world has needed our creative individual and collective physis more. We are all part of the whole and the whole is us. Both good and evil. All of it.

> Religion in this sense is not the goal of life; it is [or can be] the entrance to it, and in freedom of the spirit man has the most glorious instrument of creation that he could desire. For he has discovered God not only in thoughts *about* God, but also in thought itself, and knows himself to be thinking God even when his attention is absorbed in worldly affairs. To those affairs he brings a new power, zest, and spontaneity, for he can give himself to them unreservedly in the knowledge that spirituality is by no means confined to thinking about 'spiritual' things. Thus he can devote himself to thoughts of people and things, of business, music, art, and literature, of science, medicine, and engineering, of eating and drinking, of walking, breathing, and talking, of swimming, running and playing, of looking at the stars and of washing his hands; he has the freedom of God because he is free to think of everything and anything. For if it is true that the innumerable objects of the universe are the thoughts of God, this is what God himself [or herself] is doing.
>
> (Watts 1968: 189)

Case study: part 5

The *Rubedo* phase (death and rebirth)

The last time I saw Jeder was in hospital. His skin was almost transparent, I could see the blue veins through it. All his bones stuck out and I could clearly see the skull beneath his finely drawn features. His wife was there, massaging his feet with a sweet-smelling oil – Neroli. The rest of his body was too sore to touch. He was floating in and out of consciousness, but smiled weakly when he saw me coming near. I'm taking the pills now – morphine, but just enough. Look at this pump on my arm, I can still control the dosage myself. I smiled.

That's wonderful, I said, you screamed. Yes, he said. It's OK now. It's fine. I've surrendered, but I haven't lost. He was proud and serene. Around him on the walls (as I had suggested to the family) were enlarged photographs of his children, letters of appreciation from old employees, pictures the grandchildren had drawn for him on their brightly coloured get well cards. They'd smuggled in his little dog who was peeking out at me from under his bedsheets.

There was also a large poster of a NASA picture showing how our earth would look some billions of years from now when it explodes in a billion fragments to return formless again to the universal void. His much-beloved daughter had buried her feud with her mother and flew to be at his side. She was playing her flute with tears slowly dripping down her lovely face. I did not recognize the melody, but it sounded like birdsong. 'Thank God I lived before I died', he breathed. He started the hacking cough that signals the onset of a soul's departure. The smell of death and opened bowels announced the end. It was very still, like a small boat's mooring rope being cut and moving off into the great flood.

I was amazed by how his death felt like a birth. Lawrence's words came to me: Yes, Jeder had built his ship of death and it was furnished with food, with little cakes and cooking pans and wine for the dark flight down oblivion. He was willing to die, and yes his dead body emerged like a worn sea-shell – strange and lovely. There was a flush of yellow and rose as the dawn begun to glow through the windows of the hospital room. His wife slowly and carefully closed his eyes, crossed his arms and laid some of his own orchids in them. I left them quietly.

> . . . Swings the heart renewed with peace
> even of oblivion.
>
> Oh build your ship of death. Oh, build it!
> For you will need it.
> For the voyage of oblivion awaits you.
>
> (Lawrence 1992: 254)

Chapter 9
The continuation of the work – eternal return

True Religion
What is to be done, O Moslems? for I do not recognize myself.
I am neither Christian, nor Jew, nor Gabr, nor Moslem.
I am not of the East, nor of the West, nor of the land, nor of the sea;
I am not of Nature's mint, nor of the circling heavens.
I am not of the earth, nor of water, nor of air, nor of fire;
I am not of the empyrean, nor of the dust, nor of existence, nor of entity.
I am not of India, nor of China, nor of Bulgaria, nor of Saqsin;
I am not of the kingdom of Iraqain, nor of the country of Khorasan.
I am not of this world, nor of the next, nor of Paradise, nor of Hell;
I am not of Adam, nor of Eve, nor of Eden and Rizwan.
My place is the Placeless, my trace is the Traceless;
Tis neither body nor soul, for I belong to the soul of the Beloved.
I have put duality away, I have seen that the two worlds are one,
One I seek, One I know, One I see, One I call.

He is the first, he is the last,
He is the outer, he is the inner.
I don't know anything except 'Ya Hu!' and 'Ya man Hu!'
I'm drunk on Love's wine, the two worlds
have spun right out of my orbit;
I have no occupation except revelry and wild living.

(Rumi 1994: 217–218; 1952: 7)

Ultimately, no organism can survive without assimilating something from the environment or the surrounding field, growing, discharging something into the environment, and then dying. Psychologically and physiologically, this periodic cycle of emergent need (hunger, urge to excrete, to sleep, to compose a symphony) initiates the excitement of the figure/background process and progress, in the healthy organism, towards completion of that particular cycle and the commencement of another one to attend to the next emergent need of the organism.

> If we accept that the mind and body cannot be absolutely separated, and that the body and the environment cannot be absolutely separated, then we are left with the apparently absurd yet logically consistent conclusion that: consciousness and the environment cannot be absolutely separated.
>
> (Pepperell 1995: 182)

The need arises, flowers to satisfaction and dies away or arises again at a later phase. This healthy, uninterrupted flow of experience characterizes the healthy animal or spontaneous, undamaged young child. In Gestalt psychological terms, it can be understood that a dominant figure emerges from the background, claims the attention and then fades into the background again with the emergence of a new compelling figure in an ever-changing rhythm. This is the same for the whole world and all of time.

Kazantzakis, the poet, says:

> Our profound human duty is not to interpret or to cast light on the rhythm of God's march, but to adjust, as much as we can, the rhythms of our small and fleeting life to his.
>
> (Kazantzakis 1960: 100)

Endings

> With its very coming-to-life every living thing already begins to die, and conversely, dying is but a kind of living, because only a living being has the ability to die. Indeed, dying *can* be the highest 'act' of living (*physis*) . . . is the self-productive putting-away of itself, and therefore it possesses the unique quality of delivering over to itself that *which through it* is first transformed from something orderable (e.g. water, light, air) into something appropriate for it alone (for example into nutriment and so into sap and bones).
>
> (Heidegger 1998: 227)

Once more (see also Clarkson 1995a: 161–66), I will address the question of endings or the termination of psychotherapy – by whatever means. In what by now must be a familiar scenario, different theories prescribe different ways of terminating psychotherapy. **And**, as usual, there are massively wide divergences in theory and practice even among those who claim to be speaking the same psycho-language.

Many psychodynamic practitioners in the UK currently work towards a complete and final ending – when the patient has been 'thoroughly or completely analysed'. Yet Freud (1937) himself considered that psycho-analysis may be 'interminable'. Some psychoanalysts consider it ethical for a sexual relationship to commence with a previous patient six or twelve months after the ending of therapy. Others claim that one should never have a sexual relationship with a previous patient – and furthermore should avoid interacting with them for the rest of time. In practice, these rules are frequently breached, such as when the client becomes a trainee going to meetings with them, voting for them as 'chair' of some particular professional association or needed to speak at a Conference on the 'efficacy' of psychoanalysis.

Sometimes these very previous analysands sit on ethics committees judging their previous analysts! As I have shown (Clarkson 2000a), these gross conflicts of interests are rarely – if ever – addressed in terms of ethics and professional conduct, to the severe detriment of the profession and the public whose welfare is claimed as the justification for such organizations.

As far as I know, Humanistic/Existential/Integrative psychotherapists and counsellors have no unified view either. Cognitive-behavioural therapists often work to short term contracts, so not surprisingly, results are often achieved in much shorter periods. Perhaps its best to 'quit while you're ahead'. All large-scale meta-analytic studies of client change indicate that the most frequent improvement occurs early in the treatment process, after 6 to 8 sessions (Howard et al. 1986; Smith et al.1980).

Some proponents of time-limited therapy see it as a one-off intervention, others as an open-door opportunity for the client to come back again and again throughout their life for another helping hand as the stiles of life re-evoke the old problem or present new ones. So to which theoretical ideological rule should one be faithful? To whatever your own therapist did – or your current supervisor or clinical manager demands?

I so agree with Frank and Frank that 'ideally therapists should select for each patient the therapy that accords, or can be brought to accord, with the patient's personal characteristics and [the client's own] view of the problem' (1993: xv). Surely, the same should apply to how we conduct endings? What is good for the lion may be poison for the lamb.

At a Mind Conference some years ago I was deeply moved when a participant poignantly expressed his bitterness and pain at what he perceived as his previous therapist's unethical behaviour towards him: 'He saw me on the street, and wouldn't even greet me. I felt that I had just been used, I never was a real person for him. I've never gotten over it. It destroyed all my faith in psychotherapy.'

There are so many possibilities: working towards a clear and final ending; reducing the 'dosage' gradually to fortnightly and then three-weekly and so on; leaving the door open for the person to return for one or six more sessions, or to take the work further again for years; using a series of one-off sessions with long periods in between; doing 'one-session cures' as Berne (1971), the father of transactional analysis, advocated; psychotherapy by Internet; developing more and more of a person-to-person relationship where the human 'thrownness' of both (or all) people is acknowledged and celebrated with all its pain, confusion, outrage and joys. I think the most important question is: **What does this client need now?**

I know of many clients who are reluctant to 'get well' in case their relationship with the therapist has to end and if their 'issues' which have taken on, for example, an adult developmental focus or the problem had disappeared. A client asked me, 'If my depression is better, does that mean I can't see you any more?'. Another client and I agreed that she had been 'cured' and was predictably 'stable under stress' (Clarkson 1992b: 81–84). She had ended 'psychotherapy' in her view, but she wanted to continue seeing me professionally as long as I was available. We decided together that her therapy indeed was finished, but she could come and see me from time to time for **life-mentoring** at regular intervals. (Generally I prefer this for such clients so that they don't have to have a 'crisis' before they approach me again after some time for an' emergency' consultation.)

> . . . the Hopis – like the other Pueblos – believe their ancestors to be fertilizing clouds, bringers of rain who will nourish the crops upon which the living subsist. The necessity of death . . . becomes even more accentuated, therefore . . . Death brings into existence the ancestors, who turn into clouds and kachinas that bring rain; moisture feeds the corn and other foods that in turn nourish the Hopi people themselves, and in the eternal cycle, death feeds life.
>
> (Abrams 1997: 219)

The cycles never end

But pain is not the absolute monarch. Every victory, every momentary balance on the ascent fills with joy every living thing that breathes, grows, loves and gives birth.

> But from every joy and pain a hope leaps out eternally to escape this pain and to widen joy.
>
> And again the ascent begins – which is pain – and joy is reborn and new hope springs up once more. The circle never closes . . .
>
> What is the purpose of this struggle? This is what the wretched self-seeking mind of man is always asking, forgetting that the Great Spirit does not toil within the bounds of human time, place or causality.
>
> The great Spirit is superior to these human questionings. It teems with rich and wandering drives which to our shallow minds seem contradictory; but in the essence of divinity they fraternize and struggle together, faithful comrades-in-arms.
>
> (Kazantzakis 1960: 93)

Some clients never want to see you again – perhaps you would remind them of a painful period in their history and they want to move on independently. Some clients want **and need** to feel some connection with you – even in writing you the occasional letter to say how they're getting on with a Christmas card. Some indeed can (and do) become friends or at least professional colleagues. Some become enemies – often retrospectively 'making bad' the previously good therapeutic experience in order to feel 'equal' or 'superior' in some way (negative therapeutic reaction). As Klein wrote:

> the former idealized person is often felt as a persecutor (which shows the origin of idealization as a counterpart to persecution), and into him is projected the subject's envious and critical attitude. It is of great importance that similar processes operate in the internal world which in this way comes to contain particularly dangerous objects.
> ... creativeness becomes the deepest cause for envy.
> ... a particular cause of envy is the relative absence of it in others.

> (Klein 1984: 193, 202, 203)

Freud and Klein are only two of many examples of such a relatively common experience. Anticipation, understanding and working through of the twinned transferences of idealization and demonization can prevent or ameliorate this in many cases. Roberts and Clarkson, for example, defined supervision as only 'a temporary inequality' (1996: 17).

In her outstanding and thought-provoking paper, 'Free will and psychotherapy: complaints of the draughtsmen's daughters', Mary Gergen asks: 'Should enlightenment about the powers of exercising free will, self-determination, [autonomy, self-control, individualism, independence] and personal responsibility be the ultimate goal of therapy?' (1994: 16). She explores the feminist perspective that such constructions of reality are prejudiced in favour of the inscribed masculine identity – 'the result of the [mostly white] male domination of cultural meaning systems' (Brodribb 1992: 16).

Mary Gergen further points out that if we accept the independent individual as the

> most perfect form, many relational losses, most prominently, perhaps, those of intimate personal connection are sustained by women as well as men ... [Unlike in many parts of the two-thirds world,] community, as defined and established by men, serves as an artificial union of separated individuals, not a network of interdependent members, for whom this association is a prerequisite to personal identity ... because of its revolutionary potential, postmodern feminists who favor the disruption of hierarchical ordering practices are often more sanguine about the possibility of 'chaos' than those who benefit from sustained order. [See also, e.g., Foucault 1979; Hekman 1995: 17.]

> (Gergen 1994: 18, 21)

From such a perspective the expert-based power relations between therapist and client, individual and group, men and women become more equalized to form mutually interacting and interdependent relational systems which are auto-poietic (self-producing) with the 'capacity to create new ways of being . . . [finding] new and more satisfying forms of identity and action for clients [and therapists] within their various relationships' (Gergen 1994: 20).

> The Western conception of the person as a bounded, unique, more or less integrated motivational and cognitive universe, a dynamic centre of awareness, emotion, judgement and action, organized into a distinctive whole and set contrastively against other such wholes and against a social and natural background is, however incorrigible it may seem to us, a rather peculiar idea within the context of the world's cultures.
>
> (Geertz 1973: 229)

As we have seen, astonishing support for the 'relational self' is however now accumulating from those archetypal models of rationality and scientific objectivity – the physicists and complexity scientists. For example, we now have evidence from (post)modern physics about *entanglement theory*, which shows that even individual bodies interpenetrate each other. Not only that, but it demonstrates that when two so-called individuals have met once, they are **in effect of each other** at least for the rest of lived time – even should they never meet again. Their changing states continue to influence each other – for ever. Just like atoms in a laboratory. Rumi, of course, knew this 800 years ago:

> Anyone that feels drawn,
> for however short a time, to anyone else,
> those two share a common consciousness.
>
> (Rumi 1990: 90)

In their state of the art government-funded laboratories, our (mostly) white men have known for some seventy years (albeit reluctantly) that the observer is *always* part of the field. That is, 'objective observation' as is commonly understood is scientifically impossible. **The world's first peoples have always known this**. (Of course, twentieth century constructionists, constructivists and postmodernists had their philosophical doubts about it too.)

Yet it was Freud's dearest aspiration to be 'scientific'. 'Objectivity' is still the 'gold-standard' held out to be the (admittedly probably unachievable) ideal in psychotherapy outcome research (Parry and Richardson 1996). If these findings from current physics indeed are **facts** in the consensually accepted rational domain 5 (and it appears that is so), classical notions of self and other, objective and subjective, individuality and autonomy, individual and group, inside and outside, beginning and end, the very nature of psychological knowledge and what we as psychotherapists think we do with it, needs to come under very serious review. (Or we can just keep ignoring it.) Is it indeed beneficial to individuate? Is it humanly possible?

> You are not a single You,
> good Friend, you are a Sky and an Ocean,
> a tremendous YHUUUUUU, a nine hundred times huge
> drowning place for all your hundreds of yous.
>
> As when you fall asleep and go
> from the presence of your self to the Presence
> of your Self. You hear that One and you think,
> 'Someone must have communicated telepathically in my sleep.'
>
> (Rumi 1988: 49)

Jung distinguished between the personal individual self and the transpersonal Self which is 'both circle and circumference'. 'We are only apparently a unity, a stream of innumerable selves following one another like a series of cinematographic pictures, so quickly that they seem one continuous whole' (Blyth 1960: 101).

Many writers have drawn our attention to our multiple selves (see Clarkson 1992b: 175–203; and in press, c). Different theoreticians focus (as usual) on different domains of discourses in relation to the plurality of selves, as I will show further in Chapter 10.

Some cultures don't have the notion of an individualized separate 'self' at all. They think that 'self' is an absurdity – as if it makes any sense to say that a person can be separate from others – or from the rest of the universe. The 'names' we use for people or things are just ways of abstractly referring to a particular concentration of spirit in a particular place and time. It's only one **level** of talking about the distribution of consciousness. According to workers in neurophysiology associated with notions such as 'the connectionist mind', such as Greenfield (2000), consciousness should be seen 'as a means for coordination and communication between brain and body' (Greenfield 2000: 183). She also questions the notion of 'self', particularly in states of intense emotion and concludes, 'We have no idea at all as to the nature of the explanation' (180).

The importance of the group or family system in many cultures as the matrix for learning, resolving conflicts and facilitating healing is sadly contrasted with the individualistic (if exclusive) Western conception of the individual as separate from their culture, their family, their ancestral roots, their ongoing living communities, their one-ness with the fabric of their living spaces and with all of nature. The fact that one-to-one counselling, psychotherapy and psychoanalysis has such relative hegemony in the UK and in the British training schools, curricula and practice is a sad reflection of a profession perhaps wedded to exclusively too this rather limited paradigm of human-beingness.

The reluctance of many people from the less dominant cultures to engage in a form of individual psychotherapy which violates the very ground of their existence is thus also quite understandable.

Greenfield's notion of losing the 'self' in states of intense emotion (or *jouissance*) was anticipated by Koestler, who writes of the 'self-transcending emotions' (1972: 119), for example, love, devotion, empathy, identification, hypnotic rapport and trance states, which are a 'craving to surrender to something that is larger than society and transcends the boundaries of the self' (1972: 118–19).

> All concepts setting boundaries to what we term the self are arbitrary. In the systems view, we consist of and are sustained by interweaving currents of matter, energy and information that flow though us interconnecting us with our environment and other beings. Yet, we are accustomed to identifying ourselves only with that small arc of the flow-through that is lit, like the narrow beam of a flashlight, by our individual subjective awareness. But we don't have to so limit our self-perceptions . . . It is as plausible to align our identity with [the] larger pattern, interexistent with all beings, as to break off one segment of the process and build our borders there.
>
> (Macy 1991: 17)

'Quantum entanglement' (Isham 1995) now also indicates that **scientifically**, self and other are inseparable, that is, at some **levels** we always exist in interrelationship – affecting each other – for ever. Yes. **For ever**. At **level** 7 there is no self and no other – or we are all each other – and the universe.

Classical physics and quantum physics see human states differently. In the one domain the concept of causality makes sense, in the other domain, it collapses into something that cannot be sensibly spoken of. In the classical physical world, we and our clients are separate when we separate. In the seventh domain – the arena of quantum physics and complexity science – we can never be separate or free from influencing each other for ever. We continue mutually to interpenetrate our changing 'states' **for ever**.

> Ordinarily, we regard separate objects [and people] as independent of one another. They live on their own terms, and anything tying them together has to

be forged by some tangible mechanism. Not so in the quantum world. If a particle interacts with some object – another particle, perhaps – then the two can be inextricably linked, or entangled . . . In a sense, they simply cease to be independent things, and one can only describe them in relation to each other.'

(Isham 1995: 27)

In 1935 Einstein recognized that if two particles were entangled, doing something to one could immediately affect the other, even at a great distance. As a result, Einstein doubted that entanglement could be real. But since then, experiments have provided strong evidence that this 'non-local' linking of distinct parts of the world really happens. Might this explain how clients not infrequently arrive at the next session quite improved after the therapist had some good supervision or a particularly fruitful turning point in their personal therapy?

Sometimes I think that 'entanglement' is another word for 'inter-subjectivity' (see Clarkson 2000c). From a transpersonal point of view, there can **never** be an ending to the mutual influences – the relationship – between psychotherapist and client. (At one **level** 'divorce' is also there-fore not possible.)

For some decades I have used the notion of *the principle of inner–outer equivalence*. It means that what happens 'inside' the human being is mirrored in what happens outside in society. If we consider the great expanses of history – human beings on this planet for some billions of years – we will notice that this small packet of atoms arranged for the brief period of our mortal lives and given a personal name is but an eye-blink in the face of eternity.

Imagine speeding the whole process up in the way that we can with film on video. Consider then how the molecular arrangement of this person called Freud coming together and dispersing again within seconds as it again becomes part of the vast fabric of the seething mass of chaos and order we call life-and-death. This thought experiment shows that structure is slow process, and process is fast structure. The so-called individual is a moment in eternity. It is not a concept familiar to all cultures and came relatively recently to the Europe of the Enlightenment.

We have slowly come to understand from 'object relations' theory that 'we **are** our others'. Relationship psychology confirms this (Clarkson 1995a, 1996b). It has also been suggested that the World Wide Web can be seen as a huge neural system connecting every part of the planet (and potentially every individual on the planet with all the others, so that metaphorically and even quite literally we have become one organism). We cannot offend the body of the earth without causing damage to our part/whole body/mind/spirit too. It has been suggested that the whole planet is one living organism – Gaia (Lovelock 1989). **These are also ancient (and currently held) ideas of the world's first peoples** (see, for example, Peat 1996).

Intersubjectivity

In recent years the term *'intersubjectivity'* in Eurocentric psychotherapy and psychoanalysis has come to be promiscuously used to cover a multitude of meanings – all characterized by the fact that they refer to the **relationship** between people. In that loose sense, all books about the therapeutic relationship are books about intersubjectivity. This point may be so obvious as to escape comment.

Trevarthen (1979) applied the term to developmental psychology to indicate the way in which the infant is always in relation as well as its awareness of other beings in his world. Stern (1985) explains that affect attunement is a qualitative state that goes beyond the basic definition of intersubjectivity as he understands it. However, it is not the original sense of the word and is used by developmental theorists in his wake out of its epistemological context to indicate a specific quality of relating sometimes found between caretaker and infant and extrapolated to the relationship between analyst and analysand. This has the implication that intersubjectivity is a 'good thing' – a praxeological notion.

Careless use of the term intersubjectivity could land us back in a similar mess to where we came from – unless we define the meaning of the concept as we are using it and specify the domains in which we are using it to constitute our different kinds of therapeutic knowledge about the practice of psychotherapy.

'There has been a certain incompatibility in some contemporary writings that attempt to combine a theory of intersubjectivity with a brand of psychoanalytic thought, presuming a sharp demarcation between inner world and external reality . . .' (Diamond 1996: 303). Wittgenstein, in his Cambridge Lectures of 1930, said:

> The simile of 'inside' or 'outside' the mind is pernicious. It is derived from 'in the head' when we think of ourselves as looking out from our heads and of thinking of something going on 'in our head'. But then we forget the picture and go on using language derived from it . . . We can only use such language if we consciously remember that picture when we use it.
>
> (in Lee 1980: 43)

Intersubjectivity is, of course, a philosophical term used in the first place by Husserl and then by Merleau-Ponty. In the philosophical branch of phenomenology, it has a rather precise meaning as a condition of human existence of primary interrelatedness. It connotes a philosophically necessary view of the world, contrasted with – and completely different from – that posited by Kantian style idealism on the one hand and positivistic scientism on the other. Intersubjectivity is ontologically different from object relations theory which, although based on the primacy of the individual's desire to be in relationship with others, does not emphasize the a priori and omnipresent nature of the interworld that we all occupy. As Diamond puts it:

> A notion of intersubjectivity which derives from phenomenological perspectives challenges any a priori distinction between individual and social world. There is not division, only primary relation . . . Intersubjectivity implies different ontological premises, a different model of human existence, which is fundamentally incompatible with a psychological theory which begins with the individual. It cannot be a matter of supplementing an individual-based approach with an intersubjective approach. Intersubjectivity involves an entire reworking of founding principles.
>
> (Diamond 1996: 308)

> Classical analysis construes the core of mental life as a discrete entity that can be relative interpretively captured as such. In contrast, the intersubjectivists construe core psychic processes as inseparable from a relational matrix . . .
>   Interpersonal interactions and enmeshments of interacting subjectivities are conceptually closer to the way such mental experiences and images are structuralized in the mind.
>
> (Dunn 1995: 723, 728)

Heimann's broadening of the classical Freudian countertransference formulation also stressed 'that it is a relationship between two persons . . . the degree of the feelings experienced and the use made of them, these factors being interdependent' (1950: 82).

> But attention to countertransference, no matter how totalistic, does not require an intersubjective perspective in the strict sense of the term. The most sensitive account of the analyst's subjectivity may still be considered solely a reaction to (rather than necessarily an active constructing force of) both the patient's transference and the analytic material as a whole. A totalistic formulation of countertransference may be used as a positivistic vehicle to determine what is *in the patient's mind* that made the analyst respond in this or that particular way.
>
> (Dunn 1995: 727)

Ogden (1994) postulated that the analytic couple must attempt to understand the experience of their individual subjective realities interacting with the intersubjective realities that they create together and that this reciprocal tension is the motor of the psychoanalytic process.

Unfortunately, who is influencing whom more is still not clarified by this formulation. Even an empirical cognitive scientist such as Gudjonsson (1997), in his study of members of the British False Memory Society, concludes:

> While many of the respondents in the present survey blamed the therapists for the recovered memories, this may not give a complete picture of the problem in all cases. In some cases the patient may have gone to the therapist with the belief of having suffered abuse already in her or his mind, but without having any memory of abuse. The real question in these circumstances is who is shaping the responses of whom? A patient may be well able to shape the interpretations and comments given by the therapist in an attempt to find an explanation for his or her distress and psychological problems. Therefore, placing the responsibility for the recovered memory phenomenon exclusively on the therapist may be unfair.
>
> (Gudjonsson 1997: 17)

Of course we know from scientific studies of the importance of client motivation to effective outcomes from psychotherapy that it is unfair to place the responsibility for recovery **exclusively** on the therapist! Indeed, having watched patients improve with unethical, untrained and abusive therapists and patients deteriorate with ethical, well-trained and empathic therapists, I am currently phenomenologically convinced that this is 'true'.

> The success of the treatment is not determined by what we prescribe, according to our lights, but by what the It [physis] of the sick man [or woman] makes of our prescriptions. If this were not so, every broken limb that was correctly set and bandaged would have to heal. But that does not always take place. If there were really so great a difference between the doings of a surgeon and those of an internist, a neurologist or a quack, one would rightly boast of one's successes and be ashamed of one's failures. But one has no such right. We do it, but we have no right to do it.
>
> (Groddeck 1988: 225)

However, intersubjectivity in the quantum sense means that there are not dual worlds, but that we all interpenetrate each other. From complexity theory, we also learn that out of such relational fields new properties emerge, not attributable to one or the other but from the interrelated whole. 'Not **how** the world is, is the mystical, but **that** it is' (Wittgenstein 1922: 187).

Few exponents of the current panacea of empathic attunement take into account the possibility that that very attunement can be iatrogenic (where the therapeutic agent actually exacerbates or even causes the problem). If attunement is good and non-attunement is bad, then it follows that bad attunement could be disastrous. Yet some world-famous psychotherapists such as Ellis (e.g. in the 'Gloria' film) hardly display empathic attunement – and yet appear by consensual evidence to be successful in many cases.

Some theorist-clinicians for example consider that a story of being raped as a child told to the therapist encodes the patient's experience of being psychologically raped by (for example) over-intrusive interpretations or breaks in the analytic frame. This may be 'true knowledge' at the symbolic narrative **level** of discourse – verifiable by the verbal or physiological response to the interpretation. But what if they are intentionally deceiving themselves or you are being hypnotized (e.g. projective identification) or they are manifesting what is commonly called 'multiple personality disorders' or dissociation as a result of abusive trauma?

> In these states of dissociative pathology, where the unity of consciousness (always illusory) is sharply breached, we are faced with another puzzling question. Who is remembering? Who has forgotten? Is it a matter of memory at all? One state of consciousness seems to know something (or fantasize something) which another part does not know. Perhaps it is better to think of this as a kind of epistemological pathology.
>
> (Mollon 1996: 198)

And might the pathology lie in our professionals and the expressions of our professional thinking itself?

In the occidental tradition Heraclitus said 2,500 years ago: 'From all things one and from one thing all' (Kahn 1981: 85, CXXIV). Yet, the more we try to explain it, the more we fail, ending up only too frequently (and despite Descartes' objections) **delightfully** in a state of awe.

> . . . There is an excess
> in spiritual searching
> that is profound ignorance . . .
>
> A deep silence revives the listening
> and the speaking of those two
> who meet on the riverbank.
>
> Like the ground turning green in a spring wind.
>
> Like birdsong beginning inside the egg.
>
> Like this universe coming into existence,
> the lover wakes, and whirls
> in a dancing joy,
>
> then kneels down
> in praise.
>
> (Rumi 1991: 93)

Bystanding others, bystanding the world

As was shown in the studies of Greek torturers (Haritos-Faroutos 1983), the first step for making a raw recruit into a fully fledged torturer appears to be training them in bystanding. Novices were usually required in the first instance to act as guards – observers – while other soldiers inflicted the torture. A lengthy process of desensitization was built on this foundation, from supervising prisoners forced to stand for very long periods, until they eventually participated completely in the atrocities. It is implicit in Williams's description that bystanding can be the training ground for moral corruption:

> Having acquiesced in **watching others** torture prisoners, or in beating prisoners, or in **denying them** sanitary facilities or blankets, it is difficult suddenly to protest the use of electrical torture. The recruit has been corrupted by **tacit acceptance** of earlier examples of torture, and it becomes difficult to backtrack and question its use.
>
> (Williams 1992: 306–7; emphasis added)

Our appalling capacity as human beings to inflict damage, death and torture upon other people, animals, trees and plants, and natural systems in general, I believe, has its roots in a profound and terrifying disconnectedness from ourselves as physical organisms.

> We feel and act as if we are in fact disconnected physically, spiritually, emotionally, ecologically and morally, from ourselves and from the universe. We behave *as if* we were each isolated and separate. We cut ourselves off from the roots and springs of life within us – our sensations – and therefore from each other and from all else that is.
>
> (Rinzler 1984: 231–33)

GM food, the ethics of cloning from sheep or human embryos, BSE, pollution, the ever-present danger of nuclear waste, the extinction of species, the poisoning of drinking water, superbugs immune to antibiotics, destruction of the rain forests, the holes in the ozone layer, global warming, the melting of our planet's ice-caps, the exploitation of first world peoples and their resources. This is but a short list of some of the legacies man has created in comparatively recent times.

Apparently, if a plant is injured in the presence of another plant, the survivor resonates with the distress of its injured neighbour and subsequently even appears to recognize the aggressor (Watson 1974). In human beings this phenomenon is referred to as *visceral empathy*, which means people feel with the pain of others in their own bodies. Black South Africans have a word for this – *ubuntu*. It means fellow human feeling –

being able to feel with as if the experience were happening to your own body. It means I hurt when you're hurt.

> In indigenous science the healing power of a plant should not be studied simply in terms of some molecular component that acts on cells in the human body according to a particular mechanism; rather, the plant becomes enveloped within ceremony and story. The plant possesses a spirit. It may be collected and used in a certain way. Within Indigenous science the whole meaning of the plant, and of healing, can only be understood within a wide multilevel context, Meaning is always context-dependent, rather than absolute and context-free as in Western science. However, the idea of a context-dependent meaning and interpretation is now being forced on Western science as well by quantum theory.
>
> (Peat 1996: 263)

Peat further comments on the remarkable similarity between these ideas and Bohr's notion of complementarity (discussed in Chapter 1). It is unlikely that only two domains of description will do anyway. Too often scientists like Oppenheimer have had painfully to realize this. (Having worked on the atom bomb scientifically, neutrally and creatively, he was subsequently found guilty of treason for refusing to work on the hydrogen bomb.) He had noticed from his own experience that all science is value-laden, no matter how 'objective' we claim it is. What about the electrons which melted the eyes of the people of Hiroshima?

Providing they have not become desensitized, as experiments show human beings can be, this visceral experience of pain in the presence of another's pain is an organismically healthy response. Babies can cry if other babies do. We can 'feel for' one another in community. The Kleinians call this 'projecting' feelings, phantasies 'into' the psychotherapist and the resulting process is called 'projective identification'. The mechanism for this has never been described. Sometimes I think the hypnotic trance we as clients and psychotherapists are suffering from is the notion that this is **not** absolutely the way the world actually is. Perhaps entanglement science is another way of speaking about (or pointing to) our inescapable relationality.

> It is not simply that we can enter into states of merger, but that we already exist in a state of merger. From the viewpoint of consciousness we appear separate individuals with a regrettable tendency to lapse into fantasies of fusion; but if we look through the other end of the telescope we will see that the fact of our connection is primary and that our sense of separateness is sustained by a system of defences that differentiates us from one another.
>
> (Field 1991: 97)

Rinzler (1984) writes that knowing and seeing – because the world is now in one communicative network – so much pain, so much hunger, so much violence can eventually cause a moral bluntness, a coarsening of our sensibilities and a heightening of our threshold for outrage in a similar way to the training of torturers (Peters 1985; Williams 1992). I call this phenomenon 'the normalization of the obscene'.

It seems that in order for us to be able to inflict indifference to injustice as well as pain and torture on others, we only first need to experience it ourselves. And even then, this may not be necessary. Experiments at Stanford University showed how quickly and comparatively easily middle-class students could become dehumanizing and dehumanized in a mock prison experiment. This study, by Haney et al. (1973), revealed the power of social institutional forces to make good men engage in evil deeds. It was a woman's tears at the arbitrary humiliation she witnessed that brought this experiment to a premature but conclusive halt.

> The myth of interiority is over, or rather, the idea that interiority is confined to human persons is over. If we kill off the world-soul we actually kill off ourselves, since our souls do not exist independently of the world-soul. This is what true ecological sense is all about. The Australian Aboriginals knew that *only* by keeping the song-lines and the Dreaming tracks of the ancestors alive, could they keep themselves alive. Today, in secular and practical ecology, we are learning that what we do to the world we do to ourselves. This reciprocal, interdependent view of 'physical' reality is the very first stage in an awakening of eros that will ultimately lead us toward a new cosmology and to an entirely new conception of the relationship between self and other, individual and the world.
>
> (Tacey 1993: 281)

> The land itself is the primary text through which Aborigines are educated. It is encoded with information about every dimension of existence, so to learn the secrets of the land is to learn everything worth knowing. Since the Aborigines believe that the land actually participates in the actions and adventures of the Ancestors, they have dissolved the distinctions between culture and nature, between the human world and the cosmos.
>
> The songs and the songlines are so important because they are the musical embodiment of the properties of reality. They are at once the equations they describe and the forces that make it work . . . The Aboriginal view of reality appears strange to us because we are accustomed to thinking in Newtonian terms. In our system, objects are separated from one another and only become connected when force is applied to them. The Aboriginal system rejects our separation of the visible world into discrete objects, just as it denies that matter is the primary **level** of reality. Ironically, it is encountered in a world that exhibits traits found in Aboriginal epistemology. The quantum world view suggests that objects are somehow interrelated without any force acting on them or any communication between them. Moreover, it appears that, in experimental situations at least, 'matter' relies on an observing consciousness to dictate where it should materialize. A proton in an otherwise empty box has the potential of being everywhere or anywhere

in that box until someone takes a look at it. Only then does it occupy a specific position.

These mysteries have led some physicists like David Bohm to argue that there is an overarching order responsible for the manifested order that we observe. Bohm, in his notion of the enfolded order, suggests that on one **level** of reality everything is attached to everything else, whereas on our plane objects appear dispersed and autonomous. Thus the phenomenal world, which we take to be so firm and real, is actually unstable and always changing, spending most of its time as potential. Bohm's theory of reality is continual fluctuation, where partial material properties are never as important as the overall system that includes all the possibilities, all the connections. In many respects, this theory sounds like a paraphrase of the Dreaming. Aborigines seek to define identity in terms of the connectedness of the disparate features of their world. The people, animals, rocks and trees that fill the landscape are all subordinate to the power of the Dreaming that while constant, is unstable – for it must be cared for and maintained if the phenomenal world is to endure. The observation made by both Bohr and Heisenberg that one cannot draw a dividing line between the observer and the observed is fully endorsed by the Aborigines. They imagine a world that was sung into existence by Ancestors and continues to need this maintenance. But in their identification with the land, they are at once objects and subjects, the singers and the song . . . We can no longer assume, if we are fortunate enough to live in one of the 'developed' countries, that our way of life represents the most advanced stage of progress and that other societies have simply been less successful than ours in attaining it. Instead we now know that other societies have made other choices, followed different paths in search of different destinies. This knowledge opens up new vistas on the richness and variety of what it means to be human.

(Maybury-Lewis 1992: 201–2)

The fractality of time

. . . for too long there appeared a conflict between what seemed to be eternal, to be out of time, and what was in time. We see now that there is a more subtle form of reality involving both time and eternity.

(Capra 1983: xxx)

Emotionally we know that eternity can be experienced in a single clock-time minute of bliss or horror. **Clock-time and calendar time** (which many cultures agree on) is different from body time, for example, the intricate rhythms of our hormones, our waking sleeping cycles. Boredom goes very slowly – just think of the last ten minutes of a tedious lecture from which you can't escape. Pain, like in childbirth, often seems to last for ever while it's happening; but the painful time can seem quite short once it's over. Pleasure, too often, is fleeting. Over too quickly.

Emotional time is different from **cultural ways of measuring time**. (The community norms may prescribe a one-year period of mourning. Emotionally it may already be over, or it may take a lifetime.) Hall, for example, describes two broad categories of culturally biased time – monochronic and polychronic.

> **Monochronic time** . . . [is] the increasingly dominant world view of the 24-hour day in which only that time system for measurement exists, e.g. 'the train leaves at 9.35 a.m.' or 'Come to dinner at 8.00 p.m.'
>
> **Polychronic time** . . . [is] for example the time of the Hopi Indians in the United States who have a belief in each thing, each person as having their own time. This concept is therefore very rooted in an individual's own experiencing.
>
> (quoted in Lago and Thompson 1996: 42)

In many Eurocentric training group cultures, the people who are frequently late tease and get teased about 'African time' or 'Jamaican time'. There is a difference between 'vital time' and mechanical time.

> In the African conception, sacred, cyclical time gives meaning to ordinary lineal time. The circle/sphere adds dimension to the lines as it envelops it . . . sacred time is not 'past' because it is not part of a lineal construct. The ancestors live in the present, and the future lives in us. Sacred time is eternal and therefore it has the ability to join past, present and future in one space of supreme valuation . . . Rituals that express sacred time, connecting it with ordinary experience and punctuating life, restate and affirm values, beliefs and symbols, thereby placing daily existence in a meaningful sacred context. African societies do not need an abstract European concept of the future to give their members 'hope'. The European idea of progress is not a universal statement of meaning.
>
> (Ani 1994: 60)

On a rather mundane level, when I started teaching in Italy, I was still rather predictably concerned at the way people just drifted into sessions whenever (it seemed). So I asked the psychotherapists how they could, for example, do group therapy with people arriving at such different moments during the session and hardly ever anybody being there for the time the group is supposed to start?

One member was pleased to explain to me 'that there are **some people** who are more bothered about time than about the quality of the human relationship'. I swallowed hard and adjusted my cultural time clock. It continues to be worth it.

The Greeks had the notion of *kairos* (the right time) which many Christians have adopted as a term for describing a certain kind of spiritual readiness. Most human beings have experiences of 'time standing still' or subjective feelings of having experienced Blake's 'eternity in a moment, and heaven in a grain of sand' – a **transpersonal** sense of being 'beyond time'.

How we construe time, our theories of time and our stories about time can also be very various. Yet again, all these different **levels** of time coexist in every person and every community and in the multifarious rhythms of our universe.

Heraclitus said: 'Lifetime is a child at play, moving pieces in a game. Kingship belongs to the child' (Fragment XCIV). As Groddeck writes:

> And now I was confronted with the strange fact that I was not treating the patient, but that the patient was treating me; or to translate it into my own language, the It [physis] of this fellow being tried so to transform my It, did in fact so transform it, that it came to be useful for its purpose . . . I take pains to free myself as quickly as possible from any unconscious opposition to the It of the patient and its wishes; in so doing I feel happy. I see results and have myself become healthy . . . it seems to me that the hardest thing in life is to let oneself go, to wait for the voice of the It in oneself or another, and to follow that. But it is worth while. One gradually becomes a child again, and you know, 'Except ye become converted and become as little children, ye shall not enter into the Kingdom of Heaven.'
>
> (Groddeck 1988: 228)

I have often said that psychotherapy is possible because psychic time or 'lived time' is phenomenologically and subjectively '**elastic**'. We can move backward in it (regress) or forward (visualize a future state). We can be fully in the here-and-now while doing both of those – or time can stand still.

The transpersonal relationship is characterized by **timeless**ness. Or perhaps it is even better to say that all kinds of time, including timelessness, are embraced and included in the transpersonal.

According to Minkowski:

> It is by means of the *élan vital* that the human personality can unite all of life's various projects into a unified whole, thus creating a life history. The development of the 'personal élan' [physis] signifies a further extension of the personality. Here, again, two aspects of the human personality are held together within this factor. The 'personal élan' is what makes it possible for a human being to affirm his own individuality as well as live and act in harmony with the environment. The harmony with the environment is achieved by virtue of the 'superindividual factor' through which we transcend our own individuality. Our individual personality, on the other hand, is guided by the 'dimension in depth', which is the source for our conscience and our basic tendency toward the good.
>
> (Minkowski 1970: xxv)

This theme is so enormous, it will have to wait for another publication to begin to do it justice. Suffice it here to ask if we could just experiment with the idea that perhaps all kinds of time coexist even if often they subjectively seem to contradict each other? Perhaps every moment is a fractal of all of our existence?

> There are some mysteries that I'm not telling you.
> There's so much doubt everywhere, so many opinions
> that say, 'What you announce may be true in the future, but not now.'
>
> To your minds there is such a thing as *news*
> whereas to the inner knowing, it's all
> in the middle of its happening.
>
> To doubters, this is a pain.
> To believers, it's gospel.
> To the lover and the visionary,
> it's life as it's being lived.
>
> The rules of faithfulness
> are just the door and the doorkeeper.
>
> (Rumi 1991: 69)

Beginning of the work – again

According to Hehaka Sapa, or Black Elk, of the Oglala Sioux:

> Everything the Power of the World does is done in a circle . . . The Wind, in its greatest power, whirls. Birds make their nests in circles, for theirs is the same religion as ours. The sun comes forth and goes down again in a circle. The moon does the same, and both are round . . . Even the seasons form a great circle in their changing and always come back again to where they were. The life of a man is a circle from childhood to childhood and so it is in everything where power moves.
>
> (in Abrams 1997: 186)

> People no longer search, they know the thing exists, they have experienced it for a moment. Thereafter the opus [the work] has a goal, that of finding this moment again . . . People sometimes suddenly discover they are right at the beginning again, they have not even learned the ABC of the shadow problem or something like that, and they say now at last they understand the problem, for hitherto they had only understood it partially . . .
>   This goes on constantly with psychological understanding; there are many layers and something can always be understood on a new and deeper **level**. You understand it with a part of yourself and then the penny drops deeper, as it were, and you realize the same thing but in a much more living and rich way than before, and that can continue indefinitely until it becomes completely real. Even if you feel you have realized something you should always have the humility to say that that is how you feel for the time being; a

few years later you may say you did not know at all before but now can understand what was meant.

That is what I find so beautiful about this work – it is an adventure which never comes to an end, for each time you turn a corner a completely new vista of life opens; you never know and have it all settled, even in the case of things which for the present you feel are sorted out.

(Von Franz 1980: 169, 258)

Hillman (1996) writes that our symptoms, our troubles, our life circumstances are clues to what our souls need to do. These issues in our lives, including the images, fantasies and impulses of childhood, are the metaphorical 'blueprints' that give direction to biography and shape our lives most meaningfully. He points out that the oak tree is **implicit** in the acorn, at least as significantly as the oak tree has an acorn in its history – perhaps more so. He points out that the most prevalent Eurocentric myth which prevents us fulfilling what I have called our 'first nature' (our inherent physis) is the notion that childhood history determines our future. Perhaps the teleological idea that our future determines our past can be held at the same time – just the same as physics has now taught us that light can be both a particle and a wave simultaneously.

If any fantasy holds our contemporary [Western] civilization in an unyielding grip, it is that we are our parents' children and that the primary instrument of our fate is the behaviour of your mother and father. As their chromosomes are ours, so are their mess-ups and attitudes. Their joint unconscious psyche – the rages they suppress, the longings they cannot fulfil, the images they dream at night – basically form our souls, and we can never, ever work through and be free of this determinism. The individual's soul continues to be imagined as a biological offspring of the family tree. We grow psychologically out of their minds as our flesh grows biologically out of their bodies . . . The acorn theory suggests a primitive solution. It says: Your daimon [soul] selected both the egg and the sperm, as it selected their carriers, called 'parents'. Their union results from your necessity – and not the other way around.

(Hillman 1996: 63–64)

In *The Mahabharata* (Vyasa 1990), when Yudishthira, the eldest of the Pandava brothers in the great Indian holy saga, decided to leave this world, he did so with his brothers and a dog for a companion. (Look out in this extract **for the refusal to give up** on those who are 'solicitous of life', thus echoing Eigen's convictions in Chapter 1: 35–38, across the centuries and continents.) I reproduce a section here to encode much of what has been said so far.

After Yudishthira's brothers had fallen down, he refused to enter heaven without God's assurance that they would be there. It had been ordained that he would ascend to heaven in the flesh like it is said Elijah did – 'in this very body of thine'.

But then Yudhishthira said, 'This dog, O lord of the Past and the Present, is exceedingly devoted to me. He should go with me. My heart is full of compassion for him.'

Sakra [God] said, 'Immortality and a condition equal to mine, O king, prosperity extending in all directions, and high success, and all the felicities of Heaven, thou hast won today. Do thou cast off this dog. In this there will be no cruelty.'

Yudhishthira said, 'O thou of a thousand eyes, O thou that art of right-eous behaviour, it is exceedingly difficult for one that is of righteous behav-iour [Yudishthira's himself] to perpetrate an act that is unrighteous. I do not desire that union with prosperity for which I shall have to cast off one that is devoted to me.'

Indra [also the name of God] said, 'There is no place in Heaven for persons with dogs. Besides, the (deities called) Krodhavasas take away all the merits of such persons. Reflecting on this, act O king Yudhishthira the just, do thou abandon this dog. There is no cruelty in this.'

Yudhishthira said, 'It has been said that the abandonment of one that is devoted is infinitely sinful. It is equal to the sin one incurs by slaying a Brahma [Hindu holy man]. Hence, O great Indra, I shall not abandon this dog today from the desire of my happiness. Even this is my vow steadily pursued, *viz.*, that I never give up a person that is terrified, nor one that is devoted to me, nor one that seeks my protection, saying that he is destitute, nor one that is afflicted, nor one that is solicitous of life. I shall never give up on such a one till my own life is at an end.'

Indra said, 'Whatever gifts or sacrifices spread out, or libations poured on the sacred fire, are seen by a dog, are taken away by the Krodhavasas. Do thou, therefore, abandon this dog. By abandoning this dog thou wilt attain to the region of the deities. Having abandoned thy brothers and Krishna thou hast, O hero, acquired a region of felicity by thy own deeds. Why art thou so stupefied? Thou hast renounced everything. Why then dost thou not renounce this dog?'

Yudhishthira said, 'This is well known in all the worlds that there is neither friendship nor enmity with those that are dead. When my brothers and Krishna died, I was unable to revive them. Hence it was that I abandoned them. I did not, however, abandon them as long as they were alive. To frighten one that has sought protection, the slaying of a woman, the theft of what belongs to a Brahmana, and injuring a friend, each of these four, O Sakra, is I think equal to the abandonment of one that is devoted.'

. . . Hearing these words of king Yudhishthira the just, the dog became transformed into the deity of Righteousness, who, well pleased, said these words unto him in a sweet voice fraught with praise.'

Dharma [the divine law] said, 'Thou art well born, O king of kings and possessed of the intelligence and the good conduct of Pandu [his virtuous father]. Thou hast compassion for all creatures, O Bharata, of which this is a bright example. Formerly, O son, thou were once examined by me in the woods of Dwaita, where thy brothers of great prowess met with an appear-ance of death. Disregarding both thy brothers Bhuma and Arjuna, thou didst

wish for the revival of Nakula [his stepbrother] for thy desire of doing good
to thy (step)mother. On the present occasion, thinking the dog to be
devoted to thee, thou has renounced the very car of the celestials instead of
renouncing him. Hence O king, there is no one in Heaven that is equal to
thee. Hence, O Bharata, regions of inexhaustible felicity are thine. Thou hast
won them, O chief of the Bharatas, and thine is a celestial and high goal.'

(Vyasa 1990: 5–7)

Transpersonal psychotherapy in practice

Everyone must have two pockets, so that he can reach into the one or the other,
according to his needs. In his right pocket are to be the words: 'For my sake was
the world created,' and in his left: 'I am dust and ashes.'

(Buber 1962: 106)

Consider that you are responsible for little or nothing

Just for a week listen to everything your clients say about themselves and
their lives as if they're speaking and feeling your life. Keep a very honest
diary and see what you learn not only about yourself, but about them –
and all of us.

We are one. From the blind worm in the depths of the ocean to the endless arena of
the Galaxy, only one person struggles and is imperilled: You. And within your small
and earthen breast only one thing struggles and is imperilled: the Universe . . . we
set out from an almighty chaos, from a thick abyss of light and darkness tangled.
And we struggle – plants, animals, men, ideas, in this momentary passage of
individual life, to put in order the Chaos within us, to cleanse the abyss.

(Kazantzakis, 1960: 105–6; 43)

Consider that you are responsible for everything

Look at every client's issues as if they are bringing the suffering of all of
humanity, the pain of our whole planet, the history and future of
humankind to your door. See them, for that session, wholly in their
context as that fragment (or fractal) for whose welfare you are totally
responsible.

Love responsibility. Say: 'It is my duty and mine alone, to save the earth. If it is not
saved, then I alone am to blame . . . You have a great responsibility. You do not
govern now only your own small, insignificant existence. You are a throw of the
dice on which, for a moment, the entire fate of your race is gambled . . . behind
your fleeting mask of clay, a thousand-year-old face lies in ambush. Your passions
and your thoughts are older than your heart or brain.

(Kazantzakis 1960: 68, 15; 72, 18; 73, 22)

Look at every client from the perspective of eternity

From the perspective of eternity, all these important and significant human problems are simply moments in a great unfolding of which you are just a passing witness. Experience the enormity of time and the planetary universe and yield all notions that you can do anything at all about it.

> Train your heart to govern as spacious an arena as it can. Encompass through one century, then through two centuries, through three, through ten, through as many centuries as you can bear, the onward march of mankind. Train your eye to gaze on people moving in great stretches of time . . . Immerse yourself in this vision with patience, with love and high disinterestedness, until slowly the world begins to breathe within you, the embattled begin to be enlightened, to unite in your heart and to acknowledge themselves of brothers.
>
> (Kazantzakis 1960: 78)

Celebrate difference

There was a man whose colleague asked him one day about his daily routine. 'Well', he said, 'in the morning I wake up with my alarm clock and then I vomit. Then I bath and brush my teeth and then I vomit. Then I get dressed and catch the bus and when I arrive at work I vomit again.' His colleague exclaimed: 'You mean to tell me that you've already vomited three times since you woke up?!' 'Yes', said the man unconcernedly. 'Doesn't everybody?'

> The ultimate most holy form of theory is action.
>   Not to look on passively while the spark leaps from generation to generation, but to leap and to burn with it!
>   Action is the widest gate of deliverance. It alone can answer the questionings of the heart. Amid the labyrinthine complexities of the mind it finds the shortest route. No, it does not 'find' – it creates its way, hewing to right and left through resistances of logic and matter.
>
> (Kazantzakis 1960: 99, 1–3)

Allow yourself to see physis at work in each of your clients

Do so, whatever is going on with them. Do so without judging whether it is good or bad, healthy or unhealthy, sane or insane. Do a thought experiment which attempts the conviction that, whatever their situation and condition, it is the very best human that they can be right now – **and that they are already now perfect** just as they are.

> I am not good, I am not innocent, I am not serene. My happiness and unhappiness are both unbearable, I am full of inarticulate voices and darknesses; I wallow, all blood and tears, in this warm trough of my flesh . . . Imperilled,

moaning and staggering in darkness, I strive to shake myself free from sleep and to stand erect for a while, for as long as I can bear.

(Kazantzakis 1960: 66)

Look for each soul's code

Imagine turning the microscope of child development into a telescope where the client's entire history is seen as laying the groundwork for the person they will become – their 'soul's code' in Hillman's (1996) words. Instead of using the past as an explanatory principle, try just for a week to **use the future as an explanatory principle**. What have they learned from Life and what are they learning now? What is the task for which life has so equipped this person? What necessary training have they already undergone in order to fulfil their own unique destiny?

What is meant by happiness? To live every unhappiness . . . What is our duty? To raise our heads from the text a moment, as long as our lungs can bear it, and to breathe in the transoceanic song . . . Out of an ocean of nothingness, with fearful struggle, the work of a human rises slowly like a small island.

Within this arena, which grows more stable night after day, generations work and love and hope and vanish. New generations tread on the corpses of their fathers, continue the work above the abyss and struggle to tame the dread mystery. How? By cultivating a single field, by kissing a woman, by studying a stone, an animal, an idea.

(Kazantzakis 1960: 79–80)

'Fortunate, unfortunate – who knows?'

There was a man who lived on a farm with many livestock. One day a terrible plague broke out and all his cattle died. The neighbours said: 'How unfortunate!' The man said: 'Unfortunate, fortunate – who knows?' Then the government paid him out a large subsidy and the neighbours said: 'How fortunate!' The man said: 'Fortunate, unfortunate – who knows?' Then bandits came by and robbed him of all his newly acquired wealth. The neighbours said: 'How unfortunate!' The man said: 'Unfortunate, fortunate – who knows?' Then his daughter married a handsome and rich young man who came to help him on the farm. The neighbours said: 'How fortunate!' The man said: 'Fortunate, unfortunate – who knows?' Then there was a war and the army conscripted the young and energetic bridegroom who was helping the farmer. The neighbours said: 'How unfortunate!' The man said: 'Unfortunate, fortunate – who knows?' Then news came that the young man had broken his leg on the battle-field and was being sent home. The neighbours said: 'How fortunate!' The man said: 'Fortunate, unfortunate – who knows?'

The story goes on and on like this in many versions throughout the world. The point is that we never know if what looks like good fortune to the world is indeed fortunate or whether what looks like misfortune to the world is indeed not perhaps very fortunate.

Today I read in some newspaper report of a young boy who broke his arm and it had to be put in plaster. Very unfortunate. Then he fell down a deep well and would have drowned were it not for the fact that the plaster cast acted as a buoy to keep him afloat and alive. Very fortunate. Often bad luck is good luck in disguise and frequently what appears like good luck can carry a curse. We can never tell until the story ends – and even then many things, like posthumous fame and the gratitude of generations to come – carry the story on and on . . .

> Life is good and death is good, the earth is round and firm in the experienced palms of my hands like the breasts of a woman.
>
> (Kazantzakis 1960: 58, 30)

Read the great myths from all over the world

You are living them. Attempt to see these emergent shapes in the lives of your clients (and your own). Myths are the mirrors in which we can study human life. If an elderly man resigns control from his company and leaves it to his three children to dispose of his assets while still alive – does it remind you of King Lear? If a healer-priest attempts to play God – does it remind you of Friar Lawrence? If a woman has large breasts and a well-developed maternal function – does it recall the world-threatening grief-stricken depression of Demeter when she lost her daughter? Is a hare in a race with a tortoise?

What happens in the end of the story as it is usually told? – is there anything to learn to avoid a predictable ending – or to prepare to embrace it as one's chosen (as opposed to inflicted) destiny?

> The cry is not yours. It is not you talking, but innumerable ancestors talking with your mouth. It is not you who desire, but innumerable generations of descendants longing with your heart.
>
> Your dead do not lie in the ground. They have become birds, trees, air.
>
> You sit under their shade, you are nourished by their flesh, you inhale their breathing. They have become ideas and passions, they determine your will and your actions.
>
> Future generations do not move far from you in an uncertain time. They live, desire and act in your loins and your heart.
>
> (Kazantzakis 1960: 69–70, 1–3)

Remind yourself that physis does not ask our permission

A rich and mighty Persian once walked in his garden with one of his servants. The servant cried that he had just encountered Death, who had threatened him. He begged his master to give him his fastest horse so that he could make haste and flee to Teheran, which he could reach that same evening. The master consented and the servant galloped off on the horse. On returning to his house, the master himself met Death, and questioned him. 'Why did you terrify and threaten my servant?' 'I did not threaten him; I only showed surprise in still finding him here when I had planned to meet him tonight in Teheran', said Death (Frankl 1973: 56).

> You are not free. Myriad invisible hands hold your hands and direct them. When you rise in anger, a great-grandfather froths at your mouth; when you make love, an ancestral caveman growls with lust; when you sleep, tombs open in your memory till your skull brims with ghosts . . . We run. We know that we are running to die, but we cannot stop. We run. We carry a torch and run . . . Our bodies shall rot and turn to dust, but what will become of Him who for a moment passed beyond the body?
>
> Yet these are all lesser concerns, for all hopes and despairs vanish in the voracious, funnelling whirlwind of God. God laughs, wails, kills, sets us on fire, and then leaves us in the middle of the way, charred embers.
>
> And I rejoice to feel between my temples, in the flicker of an eyelid, the beginning and the end of the world.
>
> (Kazantzakis 1960: 70, 76, 94)

Welcome ecstasy

> You shall never be able to establish in words that you live in ecstasy. But struggle unceasingly to establish it in words. Battle with myths, with comparisons, with allegories, with rare and common words, with exclamations and rhymes, to embody it in flesh, to transfix it!
>
> God, the Great Ecstatic, works in the same way. He speaks and struggles to speak in every way He can, with seas and with fires, with colors, with wings, with horns, with claws, with constellations and butterflies, that he may establish his ecstasy.
>
> (Kazantzakis 1960: 94–95, 52–53)

Chapter 10
Transpersonal training, supervision and continuing education

Dervishes
You've heard descriptions
of the ocean of non-existence.

Try, continually, to give yourself
into that ocean. Every workshop
has its foundations set
on that emptiness.

The Master of all masters
works with nothing.

The more nothing comes into your work,
the more God is there.

Dervishes gamble everything. They lose,
and win the Other, the emptiness
which animates this.

We've talked so much. Remember
what we haven't said.

And keep working. Exert yourself
toward the pull of God.

Laziness and disdain are not devotions.
Your efforts will bring a result.

You'll watch the wings of divine attraction
lift from the nest and come toward you!

As dawn lightens, blow out the candle.
Dawn is in your eyes now.

(Rumi 1991: 122)

Searching for the transpersonal in counselling and psychotherapy supervision

Over the last ten years or so there has been a great emphasis on training in supervision, and supervision of supervision, with a concomitant growth of checklists, grids, matrices, models and competencies. Yet it appeared as if everything could be 'known' and the experiences in supervision which were of a transpersonal nature were absent, deliberately excluded or simply not considered important enough to pay attention to in the wider scheme of 'training standards', accountability and so on.

So we (Clarkson and Angelo 2000) set about doing a specific, more disciplined research study to explore the place of the transpersonal (the unknown or unknowable, the practical effect of the new physics and complexity sciences and spiritual aspects) in supervision. We asked senior supervisees (and supervisors) who had been on supervision training courses to list what they considered to be competencies which a good enough supervisor should have.

We found that supervisees listed supervisory competencies very much like the many lists of supervisory competencies that proliferate in supervision textbooks (and training courses) of many kinds. We subjected this to thematic analysis of the items mentioned. Familiarity with the material and with qualitative research methodology probably led to 100 per cent inter-rater agreement between the two of us in sorting the items into the five categories of relationship.

Most items had to do with the **working alliance**; some had to do with some **distortion** of it (transference and countertransference); a few had to do with **the reparative or developmentally needed supervisory relationship** and the least number of items were concerned with the **person-to-person or dialogic encounter** between supervisor and supervisee.

Similar findings appear to apply to North American sources. For example, in the indexes of two otherwise excellent books (Ponterotto et al. 1995; Pope-Davis and Coleman 1997) neither 'God' nor 'spirit' can be found.

Neither in the published lists, nor in the 'listed' responses of the supervisees, did we find any acknowledgement of the transpersonal relationship. In our experience, this is reflected in the lack of vitality or 'jouissance' which so often emanate from such lists.

There are fake satisfactions that simulate passion.
They taste cold and delicious,
but they just distract you and prevent you
from the search. They say, 'I will relieve your passion.
Take me. Take me!'
Run from false remedies

that dilute your energy. Keep it rich and musky.
(Rumi 1990: 16)

However, when we asked the supervisees to describe their most significant experience in supervision, the **transpersonal relationship** emerged as highly significant. For most of our respondents this was without doubt the most important aspect of the supervisory relationship. **Yet this is the dimension which is practically excluded from all textbooks on supervision used on most Supervisors' Diploma courses**. I therefore decided to spend some space in this book to discuss how the transpersonal both is, and can be, integrated into counselling and psychotherapy supervision on a regular basis.

I am not in favour of the kind of 'transpersonal' which **excludes** all other **levels** as meaningless. I am referring to the kind of thing which emerged in the ethics research (Clarkson and Lindsay, in Clarkson 2000a) where one respondent wrote to the effect that they were not at all concerned with ethics in psychotherapy because the transpersonal supersedes such considerations in their psychotherapy practice.

It should be clear by now that I am concerned to make a place for the transpersonal alongside all the other dimensions of our knowledge and experience as well as alongside all our other kinds of relationship. So in this chapter the seven-level model is taken further to be applied to advanced practice, supervision, training – and, of course, continuing education. A brief review of the material covered in Chapter 1 is followed by an opportunity for advanced understanding of the kind of category errors which limit and damage our capacity for thinking and acting well in our work and in our lives.

Using the seven-level model for advanced practice, supervision and training

> We will have to come to terms, as we stagger into the postmodern era, with the hard-to-avoid evidence that there are many different realities, and different ways of experiencing them, and that people seem to want to keep exploring them, and that there is only a limited amount any society can do to insure that its official reality is installed in the minds of most of its citizens most of the time.
>
> (Anderson 1990: 152)

As I have explained earlier, another major reason for the prevalent confusion in psychotherapy is, in my opinion, a philosophical naiveté of some psychologists, psychotherapists and psychoanalysts who make *category errors* in their experience, understanding and conceptualization of this relational dimension. It is worth remembering that Ryle actually defined philosophy as **'the replacement of category-habits, by category disciplines'** (1966: 10).

A category error happens when people conceptually confuse apples and houses (metaphorically speaking). When we do that, it is clear that an apple is an inadequate house – an apple lacks a solid foundation, rooms to live in, a roof, etc. (We are not talking of Magritte's apples!) On the other hand it is quite difficult to live by eating houses – unless you're Hansel and Gretel! We have to distinguish between the words and the meanings of apples and houses by properly defining them, and to recognize that the meaning of the words and the values we attach to them in terms of, for example, a 'good apple' or a 'good house' is judged by different criteria.

However, in the same way, as I have shown earlier, people often confuse different conceptual categories and thus make logical and philosophical mistakes. This has endless further negative ramifications and leads to endless disputes and misunderstandings of communication between people. What she **means** when she says she loves him is that she wants to marry and have babies with him; when he says he loves her what he **means** is that at the moment he is in love with her, but not interested in making a long-term commitment.

When the therapist says something like: 'I wonder if, perhaps, there is some way you can take some personal responsibility for your cancer, rather than just handing it over to the medical professionals', the client may feel this as a statement of truth that they have 'brought the cancer upon themselves'. Or the therapist may say something like: 'Your dreams seem to indicate your unconscious desire to murder your mother, so that you can have exclusive sexual possession of your father.' That may be experienced as devastating, and completely different from the way the therapist meant the interpretation. Another way of saying this is that they were in *different universes of discourse.*

Their 'talk' was from different worlds of meaning. For each of the individuals in these examples, their words might have been genuine, sincere and well-meant within their own 'world of talk'. It makes perfect sense within the one person's world of talk. However, the other person is hearing and talking from another world of meaning and experience which is perhaps also genuine, sincere and well-meant, but completely different from the other person's.

As Derrida says: 'No, that which is other is what is never inventable and will never have waited for your invention. The call of the other is a call to come, and that happens only in multiple voices' (1992: 342).

Unless they both (or all in the group) explore quite precisely and deeply what their differences of meaning are and are willing to acknowledge their different meaning universes and create a common world (in Heidegger's German – a *mitwelt*), there is little hope for restoring the integrity of the working alliance and developing the relationship further. Then it might just flounder on the rocks of mutual misunderstanding and confusion. We have probably all been in relationships or attended meetings where we could see this happening and felt helpless to sort it out.

One way in which people colloquially and intuitively try to separate out different universes of discourse is to use the word 'level'. In everyday conversations we often hear (or say), 'Well, at one level this, and at another level that'. For example, when someone asks 'How are you?' it is sometimes quite difficult to tell the truth (whatever that may be!) – I feel fine and terrible, I'm worried about my friend, I am hopeful about the future of my children, my husband and I are arguing a lot, work is wonderful, etc., etc., etc. **But how are you really?** And how can one answer if you really want to tell the other person the fullness and sometimes the contradictions of our experience?

So one person could give quite a full answer, for example, 'Well, my health is quite good, but at an emotional **level** I am still grieving very much for the loss of my home, my family and for having to leave my country during the current Fascist regime. I wake up during the night and scream and scream. At the same time I also feel good about having done the right thing in working here now with other refugees. It is good and important work and I feel I am doing something for other people who have gone through similar experiences. I have worked at the trauma clinic for six months now and have seen some two dozen clients for psychotherapy.

'I am myself in therapy and supervision on a weekly basis. I still have tremendous difficulty in making any sense of it all. The meaning of my life is shattered. I try to find comfort from reading the ancient books of wisdom of my culture and sometimes I think that the doctrine of reincarnation can help me find my way through this terrible tragedy – perhaps we are just here to learn in the Great Cycle of Being. Sometimes during my meditations, for brief moments, I even have a sense of peacefulness amid it all. It is almost as if there is a river bed that is still and solid and a kind of container for the great river of life. There may be calm periods as well as rapids, crocodiles and dangerous waterfalls. But they are also part of life. When I can contact the river bed – which is not often – it helps me. Perhaps it's about eternity in a way. It's about God and not about God. I don't really have words for it. It's just a feeling, but without those moments, my life would not be worth anything to me now.'

To the question, 'How are you really?' from an interested other person such as a supervisor, this man is distinguishing seven 'levels' of experience. These **levels** of talk are all coexisting – and sometimes quite contradictory. Here I am further developing the 7-**level** model described in the first chapter for enhanced understanding and particular application to the supervisory relationship. If you read the extract above again, you will notice that he is talking about seven different kinds of universes of discourse (although he may not know that he is doing this at all). If we asked him, he would perhaps say he is just differentiating different 'worlds' of his experience.

However, the seven **level** model has no value at all for anyone who believes that they have 'the truth, the whole truth and nothing but the truth' as far as other people or approaches to other disciplines are concerned. It is a philosophically grounded way of tackling difficult experiential and intellectual problems. It is a particularly useful tool for dealing with issues such as how apparent contradictions can coexist and even sometimes all be true, but in different worlds of 'talk'. It is especially useful for distinguishing between what philosophers call different kinds or categories for talking about the 'truth values' of statements and what psychoanalysts and psychotherapists may call different **levels** of experience as I have showed in Chapter 1.

By way of a reminder, the **five dimension relational framework** is concerned with the **process** of human relationships; the **seven levels** are concerned with the **content** (see Table 10.3: 258).

The Clarkson seven **level** model can be used to differentiate phenomenologically many different coexistent layers of **human subjective experience**. This application is **ontological** in that it is concerned with realms or **'being'** (or 'am-ing' to use Eigen's word).

The Clarkson seven **level** model can also be used to differentiate many different coexistent discursive realms, or **different universes of discourse**. This application is **epistemological** in that is it concerned with different kinds of **'knowing'** and the different kinds of logical criteria appropriately applicable to different domains of knowledge.

The methodological approach to supervision discussed here is also both **ontological** in that it is concerned with existence or being as well as **epistemological** in that it is concerned with knowledge, what and how we can know and the methodologies we use in distinguishing varieties of truth values between different domains.

Some notes regarding the seven level model

1. As with the discussion of the ammonite on page 31 there is no intention of hierarchy. All these **levels** of experience and domains of discourse can be seen to coexist at least from the beginning of time and at least from the birth of the human infant.
2. Different domains of discourse or experience of 'knowing' coexist (e.g. to believe that abortion is a morally wrong murder of a foetus and yet

to assist such an abortion when it is the result of rape of an eleven-year old girl).

3. Certain domains may be figure at any one moment and others may be in the background – or the *field* within which they have their being. Although people may believe that they can concentrate completely on several things at once, this is not true. They might quickly oscillate between different items, but at any one moment one **level** is likely to be dominant, the others less compelling (see Perls 1969b: 60, for examples).

4. It is important to notice from the start that different *epistemological* **levels** (**levels** of knowing) may or may not contradict each other (e.g. parents may be loved and hated as well as honoured or acknowledged by the use of their surname).

5. It is possible to differentiate between the different domains when we differentiate the criteria for evaluating what kind of 'knowledge' or logical 'truth value' can be assigned to the different domains. For example, no one can assess the subjective **level** of pain experienced by another individual or establish for certain whether the sensation of red that I experience is exactly the same as the sensation of red which you experience when we are looking at the same traffic light. It is, however, extremely unlikely that reasonably sane people from the same period in history and a similar culture will disagree about the number of people physically present in a specified room.

6. People can write or talk with different degrees of clarity about the different domains – whether they have ever come across it by name or not. However, it is actually quite rare for people who are not philo-sophically trained to be as clear as is Michael Eigen in the extract I used in the first chapter (pp.35–38) without having learned to use the seven **level** model.

Angelo (1997) points out that each of the Clarkson seven 'universes of discourse' is also a conceptual doorway to a whole cosmos of tradi-tional image, symbol and narrative. When linking the seven **levels** (or domains) with the five relational modes, she develops an archetypal patterning set out as a Tree of Life, mapping on to the Kabbalistic Sephirot. Remember that the way is not only up the tree of life, but also down. (Just as the 'dragon's breath' in Yoga can raise the Kundalini – serpent-shaped vital force – up and down the human spine and up and down again in an endless cyclic motion.) Figure 10.1 attempts to give imaginal shape to the idea (which is being used by both of us for therapy, training and supervision and will be further explored in future publications).

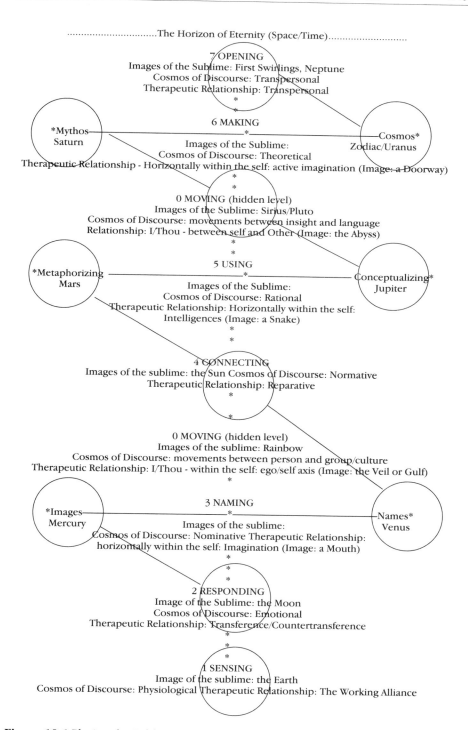

Figure 10.1 Placing the Sublime. *Source*: Angelo 1997:37

Category errors between different domains in psychotherapeutic discourses

Common category errors in psychotherapeutic speech and writing occur, for example, when different epistemological categories (or domains of discourse) are confused, or contaminate each other, or when it is assumed that different categories of knowledge can't coexist despite apparent contradictions, and when there is cross-**level** displacement.

So the first communication and philosophical problem is when discussants, writers and practitioners confuse these universes of discourse, do not distinguish between them, conflate them or overemphasize one at the expense of the other. **I consider it the supervisor/teacher's primary overall responsibility to 'think and act well'** – and to model this and educate others to do so too.

Domain confusion

A form of category confusion indicating a wrong identification of domains, for example, is when a statement that expresses a group norm is taken to be rational definition or fact – something like, 'Because we think it is good therapy to believe our clients, what they say must be true.' (I'm aware that these examples are simplified – but not much!)

Taking the metaphorical phrase 'the body doesn't lie' literally or concretely is another form of confusion between different universes of discourse. If what is meant by the statement is to pay attention to the language of the body in therapy as having its own kind of visceral truth – it is good clinical advice. When it is taken to mean that the traces of our experiences are accurately laid down in our physiology to correspond with the actual events of observable reality – it is nonsense.

Bodies do lie – they respond physically, vicariously attuned with the emotions of others, as anyone who has been to a rock concert or the funeral of a public figure could testify. Bodies show blisters when they have not been burnt under hypnosis. Bodies register physical trauma when only a word or a look has passed. In some parts of the world, people die from no known physical cause when they are 'hexed' by their communities.

Imprecise language supports many domain confusions in theory and practice. **Domain confusion is a form of category confusion indicating a wrong identification of domains – for example, when a statement that expresses a group norm is taken to be a rational definition or fact. It exists if a statement such as 'All psychotherapy should be evidence based' is read as a definitive statement of fact,**

rather than as a postulation of an evolving theory. Domain confusion exists, similarly, when a theoretical hypothesis or possible explanation is treated as a proven fact, e.g. Freud's statement that 'only those children are predisposed to fear whose sexual instinct is excessively or prematurely developed, or who are exigent in manner as a result of pampering' (Freud 1938: 616). Another example is: 'One says rightly that the Oedipus complex is the nuclear complex of the neuroses, that it represents the essential part in the content of the neuroses. It is the culminating point of infantile sexuality, which through its after-effects decisively influences the sexuality of the adult. The task before each new human being is to master the Oedipus complex; one who cannot do this falls into a neurosis' (Freud 1938: 617). (As a matter of fact Freud is frequently clear about the distinction between theory and fact – especially when read in context.)

Domain contamination also happens when one or more domains is impaired by the controlling influence of another domain. One example would be: 'If the effectiveness of psychotherapy cannot be proved by double-blind random controlled trials like psychotropic drugs, it is useless.' This suggests that one domain (that of current consensual reality proven by laboratory-type trials) is the only way of establishing or 'knowing' the effectiveness of psychotherapy.

There are several other domains in which people claim that what has been effective for themselves is judged by their own criteria. It may currently be the favoured 'objective' way of achieving scientific results – but quantum physics, for example, shows alternative 'objective' facts such as the fact that objects are somehow interrelated even though there is no evidence of any causal connection between them. Furthermore, this kind of statement needs to be read in the context of what has been 'proven' about psychotropic medication – for example, that the placebo rate for commonly used anti-depressants has been 'proved' by such laboratory criteria to be between 25 and 35 per cent.

Quantum theorist Erwin Schrödinger invented his now famous cat to illustrate the apparently impossible conundrums associated with quantum physics. The cat lives in an opaque box with a fiendish device that randomly feeds it either food, allowing it to live, or poison, which kills it. But 'in the quantum world, all possibilities coexist and have a reality of their own, and they ensure that the cat is both alive and dead, simultaneously' (Marshall and Zohar 1997: front cover flap). It is only by measurement (a nominative **level** 3 operation) and opening the box that the state – alive or dead – of the cat can be determined.

Domain Conflicts exist when one or more **levels** are experienced in opposition. An indication would be a phrase like: 'I should not feel anger because my spouse died. I know it wasn't their intention to abandon me, but I also know how I feel.' Extensive studies of bereavement substantiate that some kind of anger toward the dead person is felt alongside *knowing* that such a feeling is 'unreasonable'.

At the extremes, the same can be said by most people suffering from obsessive compulsive disorders or phobias, but anecdotal evidence (and some self-reflection) will probably support the notion that there are very few human beings whose feelings and thoughts are always in accord, e.g. New Year resolutions, getting up on a cold winter's morning, only being sexually attracted to socially approved or 'suitable' partners. Too often at a phenomenological or experiential, subjective **level**, people find that 'The spirit is willing, but the flesh is weak,' or patients say, 'I know one thing in my head, but my heart (or guts) just can't accept it.'

Conflict between epistemological domains also exists when one or more **levels** of language are in opposition, and in fact they usually are. There is a world of difference between a client saying 'Daddy was just messing around' and 'Daddy raped me'. Another indication from a psychotherapist would be a phrase like: 'Because my physiological countertransference indicates that the client is telling the truth, I will testify that the event actually happened.' That is taking 'knowledge' from my own body – which is a kind of physiological/emotional knowledge – and equating that with the kind of knowledge (or truth) that judges and police officers are trained to evaluate. It is a different kind of truth and the domains (the court, the consulting room, the imagination, the dream) where these truth values can be enacted are different.

It is argued that rigorous definition of terms and conscientious specification of domains of discourse would be of inestimable help to clinical and supervisory practice, the courts, our profession and particularly our patients, who already suffer from enough confusions of feeling and thinking, moral values and fact, fantasy and phantasy, observation and trance induction, truth and lies. It is also held that this thesis requires this kind of epistemological clarity in order to achieve its task.

At the metaphorical heart of much of the confusion and conflicts in the field of psychoanalysis and lies the unresolved mind–body problem. If a dual world is posited in which 'a ghost in a machine' pulls the levers of the body (to use Ryle's famous phrase) it becomes logically impossible to make valid 'scientific' statements about the psyche. Psychotherapists often write or speak as if we can observe someone objectively and as if we can also sample their subjective experience through our own psycho-physiological and symbolic experiences through empathic identification with their subjectivity. There is a major problem with the notion of objectivity and a minor one with the notion of subjectivity.

The minor problem is the assumption that we can ever know another person's world subjectively through empathy. The research of the social psychologist Abrams, for example, questions 'the egocentric assumption of a shared perspective' (1997: 287). What kind of knowledge is based on empathic attunement and how could we ever know if their experience of being burnt with cigarettes is the same as mine – or what I imagine theirs to be? Also, we usually assume that the 'attunement is one-way' – but intensive countertransference studies from people such as Searles (1955), Langs (1976), Casement (1985) and Smith (1991) have other narratives which are persuasive and have clearly been used to conduct effective therapy in many cases.

> We see our interpersonal relationships as collaborative efforts in constructing [lived] values. We see education as, among other things, a training in the skills of moral reasoning – morality not merely handed down but learned and created and re-created out of experience. And when there is conflict about that, as there inevitably will be, we accept conflict also as an arena for expressing and creating values.
>
> (Anderson 1990: 258)

Cross-level displacement between domains occurs when a condition pertaining to one level cannot find expression on that level and manifests on another level in symbolic form, perhaps as a symptom.
An instance of this is when, for example, notions such as ego or id or 'the unconscious' are reified – treated as a factual entity or place instead of as a theoretical construct or as names given by certain communities of discourse to refer to common meanings shared by definition by members of that community, e.g. all Freudians, all Jungians, all Aboriginals.

When psychological or emotional problems are displaced or treated by means more suitable for religious or spiritual development, we get the ineffective and perhaps damaging effects of the spiritualization of the psychological. Equally destructively, when spiritual issues are reduced to the **level** of emotions or psychology, we get the psychologizing of the spiritual.

The reality of my feelings is no less real than the reality of the fact that this glass will fall if I drop it, and no less real than the fact that this chair upon which I sit is a whirlpool of molecules in motion – yet they are **different kinds of realities** – to be judged or evaluated by different means and measures. It is no good discarding apples because they do not meet the criteria for aeroplanes. It is epistemologically appropriate to use different criteria for different kinds of knowing. Just because some things about it cannot be put into words and we don't currently know why positive change occurs in psychoanalysis does not automatically mean 'we will never know'.

Domain conflation

The commonest form of logical category error in terms of universes of discourse is domain conflation. This involves simply the denial of different kinds of coexisting realities or discourses. It frequently takes the form (along the whole continuum from conscious to unconscious) of trying to fit the complexities of our experience of being and our talk about our world into a **simplistic monistic 'one-truth' which must be true for everybody all the time**.

A rather typical example is when someone says, 'Yes, it's all very well that we are energy fields of sub-atomic structures existing in relationship, but you can't deny that when I drop this glass it will fall on the floor!'. (As if that proves anything but that different experiences and different kinds of knowledge are present simultaneously in our world.) Another classic is the simplistically interpreted adage: 'Nobody can "make" you feel something.' Well, let someone kick you very hard on the shin, and if they can't make you feel the pain, you should probably very quickly consult a doctor. If someone has that degree of numbness in their body (or their heart) they have lost one of its most important protective alarm systems.

The next most frequent logical category error in terms of domain conflation is the adoption of a **simplistic dualistic paradigm**, i.e. body/mind; male/female, true/false, etc. I am proposing that we consider at least a septuality of coexisting experiential and discursive realities. It seems a far better fit with the complexity of human beingness and human knowledge.

Let's take as an example the highly contested concept of 'self' which may occur in therapy, training and supervision.

Firstly, we need to distinguish between the **ontology ('being') of self** and the **epistemology ('knowledge discourses') about self**.

In Table 10.2 the **experience** of self and its phenomenographic manifestations are indicated in the first column under 'aspect of self'. Column 4, 'Theorists', gives some examples of writer/practitioners who have concentrated in their discursive approaches on different **levels** of the self – therefore also somewhat different universes of discourses about the 'self'.

Some writers are very clear about at which **level** they apply their thinking, others are conflated or confused or even conflate different realms of 'self-hood'. You will notice how, by differentiating different domains of discourse and experience, many apparent irreconcilable contradictions between different theorists disappear and the possibility for constructive dialogue and mutual enrichment is enhanced.

The point is that they may each have something very useful to offer us – as long as we know that each 'story' or 'theory' may be focusing or concentrating on one or only some features of the 'metaphorical elephant' of self. By holding and containing all of them together, we may be able to (a)

Table 10.1 The seven level model

Level 1

The Physiological, concerns the person as an 'amoeba' or 'body' with biological, physical, visceral and sensational experience, temperament, body type and predispositions.

It concerns body processes, psychophysiology, natural sleep rhythms, food, physical symptoms of disease, the physical manifestation of anxiety and general sensory awareness, proprioception, 'first nature'. Physiological processes may be 'measured' in some instances such as brain wave patterns on EEG but it is probably impossible ever to know at a physiological level whether another person's sensation of the colour red is similar or different from one's own.

Level 2

The Emotional, concerns the person as 'mammal'.

It is essentially a pre-verbal area of experience and activity. It concerns those psychophysiological states or electro-chemical muscular changes in our bodies we talk about as feelings, affect and/or emotion in psychology. Emotions are essentially subjective, experiential and felt states. Our knowledge concerning emotions seems to be essentially existential, phenomenological and unique.

Level 3

The Nominative, concerns the person as 'primate'.

Under this heading are included the awareness and labelling of experiences and the valisation of experience through naming. It represents the verbal part of communication. Since at least the earliest biblical times, people have known that the 'giving of names' develops 'dominion', ownership and the feeling of mastery over the existential world and the transformation of human experience. There can be some agreement or disagreement within groups, within dialect or language or disciplinary groups for example about 'what things are called'. Within any common set of language rules the fact that certain kinds of words are known to stand for certain kinds of objects can be agreed, debated or disputed.

Level 4

The Normative, concerns the person as social animal.

It refers to norms, values, collective belief systems and societal expectations. This level tends to deal with facts, knowledge of attributes and practices regarding people as 'cultural beings' – the tribe, the group, the community, the church, the political party, and the organizations. Values, morals, ethics are not always subject to logical tests of truth or statistical rationality – it is a realm of questioning or knowing.

Level 5

The Rational, concerns 'Homo Sapiens' – the person as thinker.

This layer of knowledge and activity includes thinking, making sense of things, examination of cause and effect, frames of reference, working with facts and information of the time and place. It covers science, logic, statistical probabilities, provable facts, established 'truth' statements and consensually observable phenomena.

(cont'd)

Table 10.1 (cont'd)

Level 6
*The Theoretical, throws into relief the person as 'storyteller' – as meaning-maker,
making sense of human experience through symbolism, story and metaphor.*
This is based on the notion of theoretical plurality and relativity. Theories can be seen
as 'narratives' – stories that people tell themselves – interesting, exciting, depressing,
controlling, useful and relative, but no one forever true. 'Theories' are in a different
logical category from that of facts. Both in psychological theory and individual experience, it is important to separate these where possible. These are the hypotheses, explanations, metaphors and stories that humans have created in order to explain or test
why things are as they are and why people behave as they do are included at this level.
Theories e.g. can be more or less elegant, economical, valid, reliable, explanatory or
practical. If a theory becomes fact it enters into the more disputable level 5 area.

Level 7
*The Transpersonal, refers to the epistemological area or universe of discourse
concerned with people as, for example, 'spiritual beings' or with the world soul.*
Beyond rationality, facts and even theories are the present regions of dreams, 'direct
knowing', altered states of ecstatic consciousness, the spiritual, the metaphysical,
'quantum chaos', the mystical, the essentially paradoxical, the unpredictable and the
inexplicable.

Source: P. Clarkson (1995) *The Therapeutic Relationship*, London: Whurr.

experience **and** (b) talk about the experience and the discourse of self in a
much more enriched and practically useful manner.

Notice that the only **level** about which there is little dispute is **level 5**
(the factual or rational **level**). Most people of a particular time will agree, for
example, that age is calculated by counting years, months and days from a
particularly designated moment of birth. But, of course, commonly agreed
'facts', such as whether the earth is round or flat, can change over time or
according to different cultural beliefs. Remember that **different criteria for
truth values** at each different ontological or epistemological **level** apply.

Unexamined domain contaminations, conflicts or confusions are likely to
have a negative effect on the clarity and efficacy of applying the concepts of
authors who focus on different aspects of the self clinically in psychotherapy.
The examples given are not meant to be conclusive, but indicative. Consider
for yourself whether and when these examples will help you or your clients
to differentiate among, to be more clear about, and to be more effective
regarding the issues on which you concentrate in your work.

To start this off, here follows a not-untypical summary of one person's
self-experiences. You will notice how they are occurring at different **levels**.
See if you can identify them by using Table 10.2 of self-experience and self-

concepts. Do not be concerned if there is not an **exact** fit. It's more important to use your visceral empathy, imagination and clinical intelligence to discern that there **are** different **levels** of self-experience (being) and that there are a number of different **levels** of discursive practice about 'the self' with different theoreticians focusing or concentrating on different **levels** of knowledge and different ways of intervening (or not).

My name is Judith. I am a white middle-class middle-aged woman. (Sounds like an AA meeting I know.) I have two adult children – my daughter is at a well-known university, my son, although he is 27 years old, still lives at home. He seems very undecided about what to do with his life. I am still married after 30 years to a GP, but there's very little left in our relationship. We speak to each other about the house, the children, the dogs, but we never talk about our feelings (if any) for each other. Our sex-life ceased years ago. I work as a psychotherapist in private practice.

I grew up in a home where my family were considered pillars of the Jewish community, but behind closed doors my two brothers and I were frequently physically and verbally abused by my father. He was what you could describe as a 'tyrant'. His will ruled everything and every minute – whether he was in the house or not. His moods were the moods of the family and completely unpredictable. My mother was therefore down-trodden, always anxious, in bad health with intermittent hospitalizations for various ailments. In fact, she lost a baby daughter before I was born, and I've always felt that she would have preferred the other daughter to have lived rather than me. I've since discovered that she was in a psychiatric hospital for depression for many months after I was born. I think I have inherited her tendency to depression – two of my aunts have committed suicide.

I just don't see the point of living any more. Our friends would be horrified to know, but there seems little . . . Except my work with patients. If it wasn't for the fact that I would let them down . . . When I'm with my patients I feel valuable – as if I'm making some difference to their lives. But outside of the consulting room I just feel flat – going through the motions somehow, a cardboard cut-out. I don't exist as a person for my husband or even my children. They see me as 'wife' or 'mother' always failing them, no matter how hard I try. Of course I get blamed for everything that goes wrong.

Several times recently I have lost my temper and screamed at my son because he just lies on his bed watching TV and won't put any energy into looking for work. That worried me and is the main reason why I've come to see you. I just wasn't myself for days afterwards. He wants to go to Israel to join the army, but I have real problems with what is happening there. I wouldn't want him to get involved in all that.

Perhaps it's the menopause – that's what my husband said, but I don't want to take HRT. I seem to be putting on a lot of weight anyway and no amount of telling myself I mustn't eat, takes the sugar cravings away. This doesn't help either, because I feel so bad about how I look – especially when I know my husband is surrounded with young and nubile nurses and secretaries. Perhaps he's having an affair, but frankly, even if I knew the truth,

what could I do? I'm stuck in my lovely house and couldn't be on my own in
my later years. Who would want me now?

I know this may sound rather self-indulgent, whining away like this. In
many ways I am very fortunate – there are so many people worse off than me
– I see them when I do voluntary work at the Cyrenians. Then I feel guilty
complaining and that makes it even worse. Do you think you could help me?

Obviously, by synchronizing the client's self-experience with the narrative
discourse or theoretical framework which is most suitable to that kind of
experience, it is likely that our clients are more likely to be understood
and understand. For clinicians too, it offers choice and opportunity in a
sea of possibilities and uncertainties which can be clinically and theoretically justified.

When things get unhelpfully stuck or go wrong in therapy and/or
supervision it is often because we are conflating, confusing, displacing,
conflicting or overvaluing experiential and/or epistemological **levels**. A
careful **level**-check – which can take only a minute – is often all that's
needed to restore 'the flow' on the micro, meso and macro-scales. (Like
taking a few minutes to retune – or attune – your instrument.) Skilful and
experienced supervisors are probably already using some multiple-**level**
framework, but being precise and articulate about how and when and why
can be of inestimable value to their supervisees and the clients they serve.

What does this person/these people **sense** about their self? How do they
feel about their self/selves? What do they **say** 'self' means for them? What are
the **values** about, embedded in and acted out in terms of self? How does this
correspond with the '**facts**' about self? (Classical psychiatric tests for sanity –
e.g. consensual reality – ask the name, the place, the date, the name of the
prime minister, etc.) What are **meanings**, the multiple self-stories – or is
there only one? Finally, does this person/these people have a sense of
Self/Nonself – the intricate interconnection with all of life and death?

Are the therapist and supervisor drawing from a theoretical discourse
which is **appropriate** to the client's self-experience and their narratives about
it? As we've seen, the fractal of the parallel process brings the whole of all the
kinds of therapeutic relationships (and their absence) into the supervision.

Power is abused, people can feel misunderstood and the work goes
nowhere (or worse) when any one of them is trying to impose one **level** of
discourse upon any of the others or assume that another's experience is
the same as theirs. Fine-tuning is the work of the therapist and of the
supervisor. **The seven-level model is only a tuning fork**. (Nobody needs
to know if, or how often, you use it.) How you play your instrument of
course depends on your practice, your talent and your concentration –
and your willingness to yield to the greater forces of healing and creative
change that eternally breathe in and out through our universe.

Table 10.2 Self table

Aspect of Self	Example of disturbance/pathology	Foci for therapeutic attention	Theorists, for example
The moving sense of self **Level 1:** Physiological	Exclusion Contamination Interruptions Sense of self as continuity over time	Awareness of organism/environment Contact event Volition Choice	Perls et al. (1951) Berne (1961) Postmodernists (e.g. Anderson 1990) Phenomenologists (e.g. Merleau-Ponty 1983)
The true self/false self duality **Level 2:** Emotional	Adaptation/Limitation Desire to change/grow Developmental or traumatic arrest	Redecision Work with type 3 impasse – first nature? Conceivable self work	Winnicott (1986) Masterson (1985) Sometimes i.t.o. Borderline Patterns
A multiplicity of selves **Level 3:** Nominative	Impoverishment Disassociation Disownment	Awareness/abundance Identification Responsibility	Rowan (1990) Assagioli (1971) Walker and Antony-Black (1999)
The relationship with self **Level 4:** Normative	Other not internalized Splitting Internalized bad object Inadequate other/self structures	Transference Interpretations Provision of developmentally needed self-object relations	Masterson (1985) Stern (1985) Kohut (1977) Sometimes i.t.o. Narcissism
Culturally defined self-identity **Level 5:** Actual, statistical (e.g. as in 'equal opportunities forms', birth certificates according to gender at birth, family names, socio-economic strata, class, accent, country of birth, and all other ways self is classified by others)	Identity disturbance as result of mixed 'race', cultural or religious background disability sexual orientation or gender change age class biography, etc.	Clarifying internal and external locus of definitions (level 4 and 5) from personal experience (1, 2 and own narrative – level 6) Investigation of the meanings of descriptive terms or classifying words at level 3	Breakwell (due 2001) and other writers on these themes.

(cont'd)

Table 10.2 (cont'd)

Aspect of Self	Example of disturbance/pathology	Foci for therapeutic attention	Theorists, for example
Narratively constructed self **Level 6:** Narrative or Theoretical	Life-stories or biographical constructions of life 'script' in damaging or limiting ways (e.g. karma, 'bad genes', early irreversible trauma etc.)	Re-storying 'Rewriting the script' Changing the ending Multiple coexisting narratives with freedom and flexibility to choose between them	McLeod (1997) Berne (1972) Steiner et al. (1975) Erickson (1967a) Systemic approach (e.g. Simon et al. 1985) and some CBT therapists as well as other authors who focus on choice and responsibility in creating one's own life-story or authoring one's life.
Self as organizing principle of physis **Level 7:** Transpersonal	Alienation Despair Defence against awe and wonder Overidentification with 'Self', narcissism, anomie, psychosis	Development of core as well as detachment from notion of self-hood, interpenetration with all of life/death	Pierrakos (1974) Jung sometimes (e.g. 1951) and Savary (1977) Clarkson (e.g. 1992b) Heraclitus (in Kahn 1981)

Transpersonal psychotherapy supervision in practice

- Supervision which is inclusive of the transpersonal relationship is a **physian co-creation** between all the people and the field of environment and world events at that particular moment.
- Supervision which is inclusive of the transpersonal dimension is characterized by a climate of openness and experimentation, uncertainty and paradox – but most of all by love.
- Supervision which is inclusive of **level 7** experientially and ontologically is marked by **spontaneity, humour, conflict, emergent ethics – and beauty**.

- In any supervisory situation which makes space for the transpersonal there **is room for awe, mystery, poetry, beauty, comedy, tragedy, and silence**.
- Transpersonal psychotherapy supervision is based on a constant awareness or frequent recall of **all the peoples of the world and the planet itself**.
- Psychotherapy supervision which is integrative (or the newly fashionable term 'integral') in the sense that there is room for the transpersonal or spiritual dimensions of human experience is also based on a constant awareness or frequent recall of all **the world's history and all our possible pasts, presents and futures**.
- Supervision which is inclusive of spirituality frequently deepens and widens into experiences which are felt **as going beyond, over or beneath** 'ego' or individual boundaries.
- Transpersonally conscious psychotherapy supervision is perhaps best conducted in groups where the group matrix itself becomes the **alchemical *vas* with a seven level awareness** of all individuals, the group and the atmosphere as a whole resonating with information. Perhaps there is a beneficial correlation between the diversity in the group and the emergent creativity and healing power generated for those who are absent.
- Psychotherapy supervision which honours the hidden curriculum of spirituality knows and **loves embodiment** where the sensations and feelings of participants are valued indicators of meaning, nutrients for the ground of being and the source of all healing.
- Finally, I'll just paraphrase the Zen sage Basho in applying his advice to psychotherapy supervisors:

> . . . **you must leave your subjective pre-occupation with yourself**. Otherwise you impose yourself on the person and do not learn. Your supervision issues of its own accord when you and the other learner have become one – when you have plunged deep enough into the person to feel something like a glimmering there. However well phrased your supervision may be, if your feeling is not natural – if the person and yourself are separate – then your supervision is not in the service of true healing but merely your subjective counterfeit.
>
> (in Nobuyuki 1966: 33)

Table 10.3 provides an indicative example of how the **content** of the seven ontological **level**s or epistemological domains can be mapped across the five-dimensions of the relational **process** in psychotherapy and supervision.

Table 10.3 Matrix of relational type vs relational process in psychotherapy and supervision

Relationship type	Level 1 Physiological	Level 2 Emotional	Level 3 Nominative
Working alliance	re. mutual trust at physiological levels, prerequisite for cathartic expressive work, bodywork of any kind or touch, degree of temperamental similarity or difference i.t.o. colour, sexual orientation, shared history of abuse or addiction, etc. – recognition factors, time, physical location, animal sense of danger/safety, atmospheres of scarcity, abundance, etc. smells, physical appearance, conditioned/learned prejudices. Sensory awareness techniques.	re. boundaries, limits, willingness to bear/survive empathic failures, establish trust at an emotional level, for the therapist not to feel too 'used up' to stay available, not so frightened of client's envy that they avoid healing interventions, for example. Desensitization techniques. Classical conditioning. Breathing and relaxation. Reichian and bioenergetic processes and techniques.	Diagnosis and identification of preferred perceptual learning or personality styles. NLP, renaming in Gestalt, and behavioural uses of TA and the naming of ego states or personified introjects. Shared meaning Definitions Strategic and systemic parameters and interventions
Transference/ countertransference	re. potential for psychophysiological retraumatization of client e.g. re-enactment of abuse, destructive or idealizing expectations, psycho-physiological reactive or proactive countertransference reactions including harmartic acting out through suicide, homicide or psychosis, inductions or projective identifications such as victimizing, neglect, etc.	re. feelings of like or dislike for the client/therapist, historical psychological or cultural emotional echoes of client and/or therapist's past, feelings and avoidances or resistances in terms of affect and feeling expression or suppression as determined or influenced by their individual or cultural past.	'Button words'

Reparative/developmentally needed	re. provision or withholding of touch, containment or challenge, play or art materials for creative enactments, suitable space and staff for regressive or cathartic work, bodily feelings in the therapist of when and how to respond to different development stages, strain or trauma; need to differentiate proactive issues from reactive information and choice of intervention.	re. probably all the most important aspects of this kind of therapeutic relationship are emotional or to do with affect or feelings, attachment and loss, pattern identification and replacement procedures (cf. Winnicott, Bowlby and Miller). Rechilding and redecision, rebirthing, peri- and pre-natal work.	Mantra, affirmation, mnemonic Reflective process The awareness continuum of Gestalt, for example; the description, naming and labelling of experience. The provision of language reframing or re-naming by categories or developmental stages, or identification of danger, confusion, conflict, deficit or development area.
Person-to-person	re. mutual authenticity and congruence of contracting for safety, for work, for responsibility; visceral empathy, physiological resonance, physical sharing of existential vicissitudes – physical vulnerability to accidents, death, loneliness, embodiment, temperamental or physical similarity, individual uniqueness.	re. empathic attunement, emotional resonance, feeling recognition or revulsion.	Person's name 'Genuine words' Mutative interpretations (Cox and Theillhard) Phenomenology
Transpersonal	re. mutual physical/sensory and experiential participation in a co-creating universe; in effect of natural forces which appear contradictory and paradoxical if not impossible such quantum fields (Schrodinger's cat), chaotic and complex cultural and scientific, synchronistic, real events as they impact therapy, life, (the storm-causing butterfly), e.g. Jung's patient and the chameleon, parapsychological effects, past-life regression?	re. spiritual emotions: devotion, awe, ecstasy.	Paradoxical words Games Koans Jungian archetypes, myths, symbols and creative artefacts.

(cont'd)

Table 10.3 (contd)

Relationship type	Level 4 Normative	Level 5 Rational	Level 6 Theoretical	Level 7 Transpersonal
Working alliance	Shared values Cultural dimension Social justice issues	Agree facts, RET, decontamination of the Adult ego state, strengthening the ego or objective ego, CAT, behaviour rehearsal, homework, research which focuses: on contracting, the working alliance, compliance, etc.	Getting client to 'open up' – tell their story, dreams. Cognitive behavioural therapy (Skinner, Beck – the provision of a working language).	Spiritual attainment Openness Willingness to work through
Transference/countertransference	Inherited values/prejudices	Confront projections with true facts	Beliefs based on past experience; the way of talking derived from drive theory, ego psychology, object relations and/or self psychology.	Collective unconscious
Reparative/developmentally needed	Re-evaluation counselling, parent ego state work in Transactional Analysis, cultural therapy, feminist therapy, Alcoholics Anonymous, reality therapy, reparenting approaches, and perhaps the work of Peck. Values Clarification, affirmation work, logotherapy. Comparative and integrative focus on approaches to the self – e.g. the true and false self of Winnicott, the active self of Ferenczi, Fromm-Reichman, Shapiro	Information, CAT, cognitive techniques, provocative therapy, RET.	Reframing the story, learning sharing and creating life narrative, myths, stories, fairy tales, and finding meaning through identification, participation or transformation of individual or collective patterns.	Absolution

Person-to-person	Understanding, issues of differentials in norms, power, values, socio-economic pressures – e.g. sexual orientation, gender, physical appearance, race, class, age, abilities, bystanding.	Presence of signs of real relating	Sharing life stories, humanistic approaches which person emotional mode of 'being'	community of like spirits
Transpersonal	Organized forms of religion, culturally agreed values	Anecdotal evidence, logical argument and/or quantitative or qualitative research which explores transpersonal aspects of psychotherapy, for example, astrology, synchronicity, telepathy, intuition, and aspects of the group work of John Rowan in this regard.	Myths and legends, comparative and integrative work focused on teachings about soul/spirit or Self; also comparative and integrative focus on body-mind holism, chaos theory and quantum dynamics in human/universal systems.	The void. The antimonian aspects of Jungian psychology, the mysticism of Fox, the superconscious of psychosynthesis, the satori of Zen – in so far as they cannot be explained and cannot be experienced by the single European idea of individual ego. PHYSIS

Training – or rather 'Education', whose root meaning is 'leading forth from within'

A Basket of Fresh Bread
The Prophet Muhammed said,
'There is no better companion
on this Way than what you do. Your actions
will be your best Friend, or if you're cruel and selfish,
your actions will be a poisonous snake that lives
in your grave.'

But tell me, can you do the Good Work
without a teacher? Can you even know what it is
without the Presence of a Master? Notice how
the lowest livelihood requires some instruction.

First comes knowledge, then the doing of the job.
And much later, perhaps after you're dead, something grows from what you've done.

Look for help and guidance in whatever craft
you're learning. Look for a generous teacher,
one who has absorbed the tradition he's in.

Look for pearls in oyster shells
Learn technical skill for a craftsman.

Whenever you meet genuine spiritual teachers,
be gentle and polite and fair with them,.
Ask them questions, and be eager
for the answers. Never condescend.
If a master tanner wears an old, threadbare smock
that doesn't diminish his mastery.

. . . The real truth of existence is sealed,
until after many twists and turns of the road.

As in the algebraical method of 'the two errors',
the correct answer comes only after two substitutions,
after two mistakes. Then the seeker says,

'If I had known the real way it was,
I would have stopped all the looking around.'

But that knowing depends
on the time spent looking!

Just as the Sheikh's debt could not be paid
until the boy's weeping, that story we told in Book II.

You fear losing a certain eminent position.
You hope to gain something from that, but it comes
from elsewhere. Existence does this switching trick,
giving you hope from one source, then satisfaction from another.
It keeps you bewildered and wondering
and lets your trust in the Unseen grow.

(Rumi 1988: 69)

A fuller appreciation of the importance of the realm of meaning for understanding
human beings will require a different kind of training for scholars in the human
sciences . . . **The object of their inquiry, the human being, exists in multiple
strata of reality, which, although interrelated, are organized in different ways**.

(Polkinghorne 1988:183, my emphasis)

My colleagues and I have for some years been experimenting successfully
with a training programme – or rather an educational design for educating
psychologists, psychotherapists, supervisors and organizational consul-
tants (based on the ideas outlined in this paper) called 'Learning by
Enquiry' (*Dieratao*: Clarkson 1998f).

The Dieratao programme at PHYSIS is partly an affirmative response to
the articulation by Samuels (1981) of a psychotherapy training
programme which is better suited to the plurality of the psyche than the
more usual linear, historically based, 'You have to start at the beginning'
brick-by-brick way until the whole edifice of the history of the approach
has been covered in a 'chronological' order.

Furthermore, so many linear-type trainings tend to be developmentally
based in certain 'stages', as if responsible adult learners cannot be trusted
to think for themselves and need to be protected from psychological
fragmentation, independent decision-making about anomalies and
dealing with conflicting ideas.

> . . . these stages usually get referred to as 'years'; 'she's a second year trainee' or
> 'he qualified a year ago' or 'the third year group are monsters'. This calendric
> approach can be seen as a massive defence against fragmentation [or complexity]
> because the implication is of an orderly, logical, in control sort of process, a
> symbol of the dangerous tendency to mass produce our new analysts [and
> counselling psychologists, and counsellors and psychotherapists] . . . It wouldn't
> matter if some aspects of these disputes were over students' heads; they will
> understand more in time and even linear syllabi are not absorbed in a linear
> manner. **Starting at the beginning is no guarantee of comprehension**.

(Samuels 1981: 220–21, 217, original emphasis)

Samuels also quotes Popper, who writes: 'We do not know how or where
to start an analysis of this world. There is no wisdom to tell us. Even the

scientific tradition doesn't tell us. It only tells us where other people started and where they got to' (1972: 129).

Amongst several other recommendations he suggests 'the abandonment of consensus based training and the chronological approach; these would be replaced by a training centred around contemporary arguments or disputes in the field. This may be termed 'conflict-oriented training' (Samuels 1981: 224).

Although I agree that conflict can be valuable, I have, as a practitioner-researcher, even more respect for 'question-oriented' training. An education which, for example, reflects not choosing sides between leading authorities in disputes only, but a learning environment particularly focused on enquiry as the most natural and reliable form of learning in all creatures – particularly healthy children.

There is actually a large body of psychological research supporting this kind of educational approach which privileges current questions, practice-based enquiry and an open mind as well as a responsive body. Research-equipped adult psychotherapists are then not only willing to investigate the assumptions and arguments of their 'elders' (or senior co-learning research partners), but also committed to the exploration of their own assumptions, favoured beliefs, preferred values and methods – as well as of the profession itself. And some of their work even gets published before they 'graduate'!

Unfortunately, like the psychological information that adults can't concentrate for more than 20 minutes at a time – which is usually delivered in 90-minute long lectures – many potentially invaluable scientific facts about learning, cognition and emotion are more likely to be ignored than applied. As Perls says, who was also in favour of a complete reversal of educational method, by dealing directly with a patient, the student would face the human personality, whereas under the present system he studies first the parts of the psyche, then the mechanical functions of the living organism, and at last he sips a drop of knowledge of the 'soul'. Isolated treatment of the different aspects of the human personality only supports thinking in terms of magic [and unquestioning introjection] and bolsters up the belief that body and soul are isolated items, joined together in some mysterious way (Perls 1969a: 31).

(For further information on the educational design and training qualifications I've developed, see Chapter 12 in Clarkson 1998e, and the Physis website).

The two tables reproduced below summarize in brief form a different kind of education by contrasting its key concepts with those of linear, block-by-block incremental Eurocentric educational paradigms of the kind to which psychotherapy or supervision trainees are often subjected. Table 10.4 is from Hilliard (in Hale 1986) emphasizing an African-centred educational perspective.

Table 10.4 Comparison of the different emphases of Euro-centred and African-centred education.

As it is (analytical)	As it could be (relational)
• Rules	• Freedom
• Standardization	• Variation
• Conformity	• Creativity
• Memory for specific facts	• Memory for essence
• Regularity	• Novelty
• Rigid Order	• Flexibility
• 'Normality'	• Uniqueness
• Differences equals deficit	• Sameness equals oppression
• Preconceive	• Improvise
• Precision	• Approximate
• Logical	• Psychological
• Atomistic	• Global
• Egocentric	• Sociocentric
• Convergent	• Divergent
• Controlled	• Expressive
• Meanings are universal	• Meanings are contextual
• Direct	• Indirect
• Cognitive	• Affective
• Linear	• Patterned
• Mechanical	• Humanistic
• Unison	• Individual in group
• Hierarchical	• Democratic
• Isolation	• Integration
• Deductive	• Inductive
• Scheduled	• Targets of opportunity
• Thing-focused	• People-focused
• Constant	• Evolving
• Sign-oriented	• Meaning-oriented
• Duty	• Loyalty

(Hilliard, in Hale 1986: 41)

Table 10.5 is one I developed to supplement and guide the process (method) of training for counselling, counselling psychology, psychotherapy, supervision and consultancy. **Both centralize relationship**. There is no intention on my part that the second column **excludes** the first. Unfortunately, educational or supervisory curricula based on concepts from the first column in both tables tend in practice to exclude, devalue or discriminate against key concepts from the second column.

On the basis of research discussed by Brown et al. (1999), the time of professional organizations would be better spent promoting an approved

Table 10.5 Two kinds of education

Old paradigm of education	New paradigm of education
Expectation of pathology	Expectation of potential
Authority based	Resource based
Motivated by threats/fear	Motivated by curiosity/*élan vital*
Local	Global
Cumulative	Systemic
Content	Context
Rule-bound	Situational
Body of 'knowledge'	Body of 'method'
Consensus driven	Exception-al
Reward for ideological (theoretical) adherence	Reward for rigour and variety of enquiry
Consolidate practice standards when circumstances change	Change practice standards when circumstances change
Sectarian boundaries and disputes	Awe
Scholarship	Authorship
Neutrality and objectivity	Engagement and subjectivity
Absorption of other's knowledge	Learning from other's learning
Compliance	Questioning
Mass-produced	Individual
Incremental progressions	Second-order shifts in knowledge
Imposed teachers, supervisors, therapists	Teachers, supervisors, therapists employed as consultants by autonomously directed individuals to assist their learning process
Introjected collective ethics	Questioned and researched personal ethics
Closed systems	Open systems
Modernist	Postmodernist
Newtonian and Cartesian	Quantum and chaos/complexity inclusive

(From Clarkson 1998f: 245)

method for the routine, systematic, and empirical assessment of outcomes rather than dictating which treatment approaches their members use. Going one step further, actually collecting outcome data from their members would make professional associations active participants in the development of national norms for clinical practice – norms that could, in turn, be used to help third-party payers and other funding agencies determine the appropriateness for psychological treatment based more on ability to benefit rather than psychiatric diagnosis.

> This is not, however, the direction in which the various professional organizations look to be heading. For example, the DSM, in spite of continuing to be plagued by poor reliability and validity and **having absolutely no predictive**

power in terms of treatment outcome . . . is now a fixed part of most graduate training programs and a prominent feature of the whole empirically validated treatment movement.

(Hubble et al. 1999b: 438; my emphasis)

Hogan (1999) points out that psychotherapy regulation as it is currently done 'constitutes control of input since it establishes standards and criteria governing entrance into a profession. Because current require-ments have not been shown to be related to effective performance alter-natives should be considered.' In Hogan's opinion, 'regulation through registration, in which practitioners are required to register with a govern-ment agency or board, but are not required to meet any academic or other prerequisites, is the most desirable form of regulation' (Hogan 1999: 5).

Arguably, anyone who has successfully negotiated the Euro-American educational system to Master's degree or beyond has been schooled in passionless Newtonian, Cartesian analytic thinking and has had to undergo a partial or complete amputation of holistic, organic, full-bodied/spirited relational engagement with other people and the world in which we live. (See e.g. Duffell 1999, for testimonies regarding the effects of British youngsters being sent to boarding schools.)

'How many Zen masters does it take to change a light bulb?' 'I don't know. How many Zen masters does it take to change a light bulb?' 'Three. One to change the lightbulb, one not to change the lightbulb and one neither to change the lightbulb nor not to change the lightbulb.' How then to learn the transpersonal?

. . . in general, the most important concern is for our daily life and our ethical conduct towards family members, friends, and those in our workplace and community. Even our simplest habit or acts are to be approached from an integrated perspective . . . In one Hasidic legend, a renowned eighteenth-century mystical adept is said to have commented how the greatest piece of knowledge he acquired from his own teacher was 'how to sleep properly'. In another parable a disciple is said to have sought out one Hasidic master 'in order to see how he ties his shoelaces' . . . it is in daily life that we must be grounded for all inner growth.

(Boorstein 1996: 172)

Research results show a weak correlation between amount of training and clinical outcome, which strongly suggests that admission to training and eventual credentialing be based on the ability to perform rather than the mastery of various theories or techniques. The survival of the mental health professions, in other words, will be better ensured by identifying empirically validated treat*ers* rather than empirically validated treat*ment*s.

(Hubble et al. 1999b: 439)

From an African-centric perspective, Ani challenges also:

> It is the epistemological tool of 'objectification' that perhaps has the most critical implications for the nature of European culture and behaviour towards others. The mind is trained to objectify. The person believes that by disengaging herself from the phenomenon she wishes to understand, she comes to 'know' it; it becomes an object of her knowledge. She therefore attempts to transform all phenomena in either total 'matter' or pure mathematical symbol. She despiritualizes it. But let us suppose that Plato was essentially mistaken; a good mathematician but a weak humanist (social theorist). If human intelligence is not limited to rationality as defined in terms of order and control (power), but rather is revealed in spirituality that may include but certainly transcend rational order, then the European *utumawazo* does not equip Europeans to deal successfully with the 'human' in themselves or with other human beings.
>
> (Ani 1994: 480)

Continuing education

> Currently, sole emphasis is placed on mastering the skills or techniques associated with a particular version of treatment. By contrast, an accountable system of continuing education would be truly continuous. For example, therapists could routinely receive feedback about their work resulting from the outcome data systematically gathered and analysed . . .
>
> (Hubble et al. 1999b: 440)

I'd like to reiterate the notion that our greatest teachers are not necessarily those of greater seniority, greater political influence, greater degrees than ourselves – or those who promise us referrals. Our greatest learning is just as likely to come from our most disturbed patients, our most junior colleagues, our most disconcerting life experiences.

I vividly remember someone from the British Psychological Society bureaucracy explaining to me with a great display of pained patience that it was impossible to accredit a course as continuing education if beginners and veterans were to be on the same event. That person's opinion was that if you are qualified, you just continue to learn beyond the qualification so to speak, and novices must always start at the beginning – where the others had already proved to have successfully 'ticked off' their list of competencies, psychological knowledge and professionally applied ethics. (See also Samuels above pp. 263–4.)

It was as if nothing new had happened in psychology since the first courses had started decades ago. Learning counselling or clinical psychology was like climbing a ladder, and the people who reached the top first were the best. In contrast, Wittgenstein wrote: 'My propositions are elucidatory in this way: he who understands . . . finally recognizes them as senseless, when he has climbed out through them, on them, over them. He [or she] must so to speak throw away the ladder after he has climbed up on it' (1922: 189).

It was impossible for this person who was clinging to her stated views to conceive that beginners and veterans could both perhaps have something new to learn together which may be infinitely enriching for both sets of professionals and that **unlearning** is as important a part of continuing education as any other.

The learning cycle model reproduced below is an integration of Gestalt with Robinson's (1974) work and my own. Robinson had pointed out in an industrial context that 'conscious competency' usually progresses to 'unconscious mastery' (e.g. car-driving skills becoming habitual). After a while at this point it is likely that, whatever the skill involved, the 'master' may become unconsciously incompetent again. Unless he or she is willing to go through the learning cycle again and experience the void of unlearning, new learning will most likely degenerate into old habits and a commensurate inability to teach or supervise others.

So, in order to keep learning, the teachers themselves need to unlearn everything they had learned so far, fall into the void, risk the awkward clumsiness and the feeling of being de-skilled, tolerate the embarrassment of being seen to 'be at the beginning again' and turn it into shared excitement and a joyful adventure. Then, sometimes, the teachers can fall asleep because the teaching never only depends on them.

A student's dream

'I had a great dream about a state of abundance. I dreamed that there were millions of pounds coming into the household of my teacher. I knew I would benefit from these riches. I then saw myself lying on a couch next to my teacher who was falling asleep on the couch beside me, tired after she had finished her work writing. Suddenly, a big display of ice creams appeared from the ceiling. It was a huge, oblique-shaped display, lit from the inside, with a very rich variety of ice creams in many different shapes and sizes. It was not easy to see from the outside. But, if you were at a certain **level**, it was a delight to look at, the colours were very bright and the ice creams looked very tasty. It almost felt that it was the ice creams themselves that were lighting the display. I immediately took out a cone (there were plenty to choose from, it was a never-ending variety) and started eating it, babbling away with enthusiasm about new research projects while my teacher was happily falling asleep.'

Continuing education in love

Another take on this is that the **coexistent polarity of continuing education may actually be to continue to grow in all the experiential and epistemological levels of love refracted in the interrelationship with our so-called others, whether they be clients, students, colleagues, family, friends or lovers, knowing that we will be waxing and waning in our skill-fullness as the cycle of individual and collective learning and unlearning eternally recurs**.

The five-dimensional process of this love could be translated as follows:

- the working alliance is the love of the **work**;
- the biased relationship is the love of learning by **enquiry**;
- the developmentally needed relationship is the love for **humanity**;
- the dialogic relationship is the love for a **particular person(s)**;
- and the transpersonal relationship is the love of **God/Spirit**.

The seven content **levels** of 'Love' of course, like most other subjective experiences, have their correlate in our epistemological discourses about 'love':

Level 1: there is the love of **SOMA** (the body which loves life even as it risks death);

Level 2: the love of **EROS** (our erotic attachments or revulsions to other creatures);

Level 3: the love of **LOGOS** (the word and images which encode our being, e.g. what 'love' means);

Level 4: the love of **NOMOS** (our allegiances to and betrayals of the collective and cultural laws or norms within which we are embedded – for good or for ill);

Level 5: the love of **TECHNOS** (the love of our capacities to impact on our world with rational thought and action);

Level 6: the love of **MYTHOS** (our love of story-telling, our need for meaning-making, our multivocal disparate narratives about all the rest); and of course

Level 7: the love of **PHYSIS** (our love for the transcendent whole which is both alone in the realm beyond words and bodies as well as a whole encoding all the other **levels**).

PHYSIS AS SOMA, EROS, LOGOS, NOMOS, TECHNOS, MYTHOS AND AS ITSELF. Imagine them all curled up curved into the body of a living ammonite which is both part, and the fractal whole of all time

and of all life. Or yourself in relationship in one single moment. (Refer back to Tables 10.1 and 10.3.)

To become increasingly skill-full at using these different **levels** means that we continue to learn and to strive, differentially and intentionally by discriminating when and how different kinds of love (from confrontational boundary-making to participating in the realm of universal love) are needed by different people in relationship with us at different times. Maturana and Varela conclude:

> To disregard the identity between cognition and action, not to see that knowing is doing, and not to see that every human act takes place in languaging and, as such (as a social act) has ethical implications because it entails humanness, is not to see human beings as living entities . . . **we have only the world that we bring forth with others, and only love helps us bring it forth**.
>
> (Maturana and Varela 1987: 248)

Symbol of **knowledge**, **lifelong education** and **continued education**, and **continued quest for knowledge**. Literal translation: He who does not know can become knowledgeable from learning; he who thinks he knows and ceases to continue to learn will stagnate. The Akan believe that the search for knowledge is a lifelong process. The symbol *nea onnim* incorporates this view of learning and knowledge. (Ani 1994: see also http://www.hunter.cuny.edu/blpr/africana.html – a webpage for African studies at Hunter College, CUNY, New York.)

Summary

If I were to summarize everything written so far at this time, I would say that:

1. All human and non-human existence is based on the between of different modes of relationship.
2. Some form of the transpersonal relationship pervades all forms of healing, including all forms of psychotherapy – whether acknowledged or not. The transpersonal dimension is the hidden curriculum.
3. Human beings exist and experience their lives and their world on a multiplicity of coexistent **levels** (ontology).
4. Human knowledge exists and is encountered in a multiplicity of coexisting domains (epistemology).
5. Most spiritual paths have both normative (cultural/ideological) aspects

as well as transpersonal (mystical/quantum complexity) aspects which also coexist in varying degrees of congruence.

6. The mystical/quantum complexity domain of being and knowing is in the realm beyond words. Yet descriptions and poetry which point to such experiences show a singular convergence and agreement across all cultures and all spiritual traditions.

7. People's choices of which path they follow are determined by many factors, not least their innate temperament or 'first nature'.

8. Transpersonal psychotherapy is any form of psychotherapy which allows for the transpersonal, unexplained or transcendent realm of existence.

9. Human beings have a hunger for meaning and a yearning for spirituality which informs their living and dying. It is as important and basic, and sometimes more important than physical survival.

10. **The psychotherapist is the servant of physis**, the attendant of the cell or the soul's self-healing creative capacity for endurance, transformation or surrender.

As a postscript to everything written so far:

> The language I speak must be ambiguous, must have [at least] two meanings in order to be fair to the dual aspect of the psyche's nature. I strive quite consciously and deliberately for ambiguity of expression, because it is superior to singleness of meaning and reflects the nature of life. My whole temperament inclines me to be very unequivocal indeed. That is not difficult, but it would be at the cost of truth. I purposely allow all the overtones and undertones to chime in, because they are there anyway while at the same time giving a fuller picture of reality. Clarity makes sense only in establishing facts, but not in interpreting them.
>
> (Jung letter, 1952)

C.f also *Mysterium Coniunctionis*, para. 715:

> Unequivocal statements can be made only in regard to immanent objects; transcendental ones can be expressed only by paradox.

Moreover, as Jung (1966) observed: 'Nicholas of Cusa, in his *De docta ignorantia*, regarded antinomial thought as the highest form of reasoning' (1966: 309).

And finally:

One group immediately cut the cords of doubt
and were freed.
Another group let their faith
begin to grow slowly.
And a third segment
of the pilgrims were sour and sceptical
before they came, and sour and sceptical
afterwards.
And that's the end of that story!

(Rumi 1990: 118)

Appendix 1
Psychotherapy of the Dead

Samuel E. Menahem, Ph.D.

> Joking is teaching. Don't be fooled by the lightness,
> or the vulgarity. Jokes are serious.
> (Rumi 1990: 83)

It is time to 'bury the myth' that certain people are untreatable by modern psychotherapy. In recent years people with untreatable 'narcissistic character disorders' have suddenly become treatable. It is the contention of this author that there is one group that has been totally neglected by psychotherapists – the dead. Why have they been so ignored? Probably because fat cat therapists only want to take on articulate, motivated patients. Well, it's time for these lazy doctors to get off their dimpled derrieres and 'break new ground'. People who are dying to get into treatment can no longer be ignored. The author is now treating dead patients and training young therapists to do the same.

Review of the literature

An exhaustive review of the psychological literature turned up only one article related to the subject of therapy of the dead. Dr. I. M. Bananas (1916) reported that death was the crucial turning point in his treatment of Frau Rigormortis, an arrogant, vindictive patient. Dr. Bananas did a five-year follow-up with the patient's family. They reported that there were no incidents of arrogant behaviour since the patient's death. Thus, the case was considered a complete cure.

Dead silence

Many beginning psychotherapists have trouble with long silences during the therapeutic hour. The author has found that one of the best ways to desensitize psychologists in training is to assign them a dead patient. Techniques to deal with the silence include:

Intermittent questioning of the corpse, e.g., 'What brings you here today?', 'What would you really like to get out of therapy?', and 'If you were a tree, what kind of tree would you be?'.

The Gestalt hot seat technique: The cadaver is placed on a chair facing the therapist and encouraged to report 'exactly what he is feeling *right now*'.

Tentative interpretations, e.g. 'You seem to be expressing hostility toward me which you would rather direct at your mother' and 'There seems to be a marked passive-aggressive trend in your silence'.

Rational-emotive therapy: The therapist attempts through logical reasoning to convince the patient that he is nothing more than a whining baby who thinks he can push people around simply because he's dead. An example of a patient's faulty logic and the therapist's analysis follows. (Communication was established through medium Madame Mediocre.)

A. Nobody ever liked me when I was alive.
B. I am now dead.
C. Nobody will ever like me.

The rational-emotive therapist proceeded to argue that 'even if nobody ever liked you, there is no reason to weep and wail and gnash your teeth telepathically. So what if people didn't like you – who gives a shit! Stop that irrational other worldly whining and do something to help yourself. Get a ghost writer, learn the cha cha, do something!'

Transference

Part of the beauty of working with the dead patient is the total lack of transference problems. There is literally nothing to be 'worked through'. It was noted, however, that when a dead patient was placed in water, a 'floating transference' developed immediately. Many of the psychoanalytic therapists were very patient in waiting for either a positive or a negative transference to develop. These therapists believe that cure could be effected only through the development and working through of this 'transference neurosis'. These therapists spent hundreds of hours carefully observing the affect of the patient. All therapists noticed a certain stiffness and 'flattening of affect' as the sessions continued over several months. Many of the therapists also reported a pungent odor, possibly indicative of sweating (anxiety) or passing flatus (passive-aggressive phenomenon).

Many therapists also reported a marked indifference of their dead patients, even when the most provocative statements were made, e.g. 'Your mother wears combat boots', or 'Your father was a leprechaun'. This indifference was hypothesized to be related to erotic longings for passive union with an omnipotent figure.

Countertransference

It has long been accepted that therapeutic impasses can be broken through by the therapist observing his own countertransferential feelings and then using them in the context of psychotherapy. The following exchange was typical of the use of this principle in the psychotherapy of the late I. M. Boring of Beaver Falls, Pennsylvania. The therapist was Marci Cystic, Ph.D.

Dr. C.: How are you feeling today?
Mr. B.: (Silence – 5 minutes pass.)
Dr .C.: You seem very quiet.
Mr. B.: (Silence – 10 minutes pass.)
Dr. C.: Your silence is driving me crackers!
Mr. B.: (Silence – 5 minutes pass.)
Dr. C.: (Angrily) Say something! Anything!
Mr. B.: (Silence – 20 minutes pass.)
Dr. C.: (Shaking the patient) You're not getting any better. I've tried every-thing! What do you want? You want me to beg? All right. (Gets down on all fours and imitates a dog begging.) Arf! Arf!
Mr. B.: (Silence – 5 minutes pass.)
Dr. C.: (Sobbing) Get out of my office you bag of bones you!
Mr. B.: (Doesn't move)
Dr. C.: (Sobbing uncontrollably) If only you knew how much I want you to get better. . . . You'd behave differently . . . I know it.

Dr. Cystic analysed the countertransference with her analyst, Dr. Om Nicient. The following is an excerpt from that session.

Dr. N.: So how is that difficult patient of yours?
Dr. C.: Which one?
Dr. N.: The Dead Head.
Dr. C.: Oy Mein Gott! Do we have to discuss him?
Dr. N.: Is it painful?
Dr. C.: Is duck greasy?
Dr. N.: Not if you cook it right!

Dr. C.: I guess I'm ducking the issue.

Dr. N.: Flight of ideas?

Dr. C.: No, I'm chickening out . . . I got to face the music. I'm not helping Mr. Boring.

Dr. N.: And how do you feel as he sits there in silence?

Dr. C.: Helpless . . . (sobbing) . . . like a lost little girl . . . And when I feel helpless I get angry.

Dr. N.: He won't do what you want and get better?

Dr. C.: That's it! He won't respond. No matter what I do or say. He just sits there!!

Dr. N.: And you want to get a rise out of him?

Dr. C.: Yes! And he won't respond.

Dr. N.: Does this situation remind you in any way of you and your mother?

Dr. C.: Yes! She never came (crying hysterically) when I cried . . . I called and called and I couldn't make her come to me. I couldn't make her do what I wanted.

Thus we see the rich material elicited by analysing the countertransference. The dead patient didn't move but the therapist did. She moved to Purdue, Indiana and opened a Chicken D Light franchise.

Special problems – reluctance to pay bills

One hundred per cent of all dead patients showed a marked reluctance to pay their bills. These dead beats think that just because they're deceased they can get away with murder. Thus, it must be emphasized at the first session (preferably held when the patient is still alive) that payment must be made well in advance. Then, someone in the estate must be appointed to pay the bill monthly. Freud (1937) mentioned this problem briefly in his classical paper 'Analysis terminable or interminable'. He stated 'many analyses are truly interminable due to the depth of unconscious bulemia. . . . Thus, the analyst must make some arrangement to continue the analysis and *payment* (italics ours) interminably.' It is rumoured that Freud's heirs are still collecting fees from the estate of a rich American, D. Warbucks, whose interminable analysis centred on the idea that he was a cartoon character.

Death is not an ending, it's a beginning

This article is not intended to be the last word on psychotherapy of the dead. It was intended to stimulate the stagnant professionals who are reluctant to treat difficult people. The public must become aware of the neglect of the mental health of the dead. Only a public outcry will make services available in the fertile field of the dead. More research is necessary so that better techniques can be added to the therapeutic armamentarium.

> The first time Paul McCartney had a marijuana joint, he recalls being seized by a sense of mystic enlightenment – albeit short-lived. 'I was wandering around looking for a pencil because I felt that I had discovered the meaning of life that evening', he says.
>
> 'I wanted to get it down on a piece of paper. Someone handed me the bit of paper the next morning and on it was written, in very scrawly writing: "There are seven **levels**."'

(Heylin 2000: 50)

Appendix 2
Jesus Christ and the five modes of the therapeutic relationship

Petrūska Clarkson

> And his fame went throughout all Syria; and they brought unto him all sick people that were taken with divers diseases and torments, and those which were possessed with devils, and those which were lunatick, and those that had the palsy; and he healed them.
>
> (Matthew 4: 4)

Modern psychological research into the healing of counselling and psychotherapy has found that the relationship is more important than almost any factor in the helping process. Of course we know from our own experiences how healing a good relationship can be. Human beings are born into relationship, need relationship to thrive and usually find their salvation when they find it through some relationship. Five different kinds of relationship (Clarkson 1995a) have been discovered which are potentially present in every important relationship whether in our communities, in our churches, in our families, between spouses or in other situations such as formation.

This piece is an attempt to look at the life and works of Jesus Christ through the lens of the five kinds of relationship that have been found to characterize the work of counselling and psychotherapy. These five modes of relationship are

the Working Alliance;
the Distorted or Transference relationship;
the Developmentally Needed or Reparative relationship;
the Person-to-Person or I–You relationship; and
the Transpersonal relationship.

Of course they are all interrelated, but it has been found that the work of counselling or formation is improved when we focus on providing

279

different relationships adapted for different people, for different needs and at different phases of growth. Psycho-spiritual counselling and formation can train and develop understanding and capabilities in discerning how, when and with whom (including ourselves) to develop and use the different therapeutic relationships as facets of the whole.

I am not suggesting that Jesus followed the five relationship model – rather that we can find these modern five elements of the therapeutic relationship in the accounts of His life and work. This approach is based on the idea that Jesus Christ was one of the greatest psychotherapist counsellors our world has ever known.

The purpose of this piece is twofold: firstly, to deepen our appreciation of the work of the Christian Lord on earth by studying and exploring it again from another perspective and, secondly, to enrich our counselling, formation and other relationship processes by learning from the examples based on the therapeutic relationships of Christ as told in the Gospel stories.

The therapeutic working relationship

Jesus explains the basis of the working alliance when he says after the parable of the seed which first fell on stony ground: 'Who hath ears to hear, let him hear . . . But he that received seed into the good ground is he that heareth the word, and understandeth it; which also beareth fruit, and bringeth forth, some an hundredfold, some sixty, some thirty . . .' (Matthew 13: 9, 23).

Time after time in the gospel stories, there is a kind of recognition that something significant is required from the person seeking to be healed in addition to that which Jesus will provide. 'Ask, and it shall be given you; seek, and ye shall find; knock and it shall be opened unto you; for every one that asketh, receiveth; and he that seeketh findeth; and to him that knocketh, it shall be opened' (Matthew 7: 7–8).

Usually, there has to be some kind of effort on both sides – or the sides of the interceding families. The nature of this effort (or required commitment) varies. It may be to 'take up your bed and walk', or to 'stretch forth your hand', or to touch the hem of his garment. Sometimes the supplicant has to repeat the request many times to show that they are serious and sincerely want to be healed or she may make a spontaneous gift of oil. Sometimes Jesus requires that the client will take a risk to prove his faith in the healer and is willing to do whatever Jesus bids him or her to do in order to be healed. When the rich young man refuses to give away his wealth, there can be no working alliance and there can be no healing. The young man turns away sadly.

Also in the training of his disciples, a thoroughgoing commitment, some sacrifice and immediate action is required. And he saith unto them, 'Follow me, and I will make you fishers of men and they straightaway left their nets and followed him . . . and they immediately left the ship, and their father, and followed him' (Matthew 4: 20). When the time for the appointment has come, it is important not to delay or be late – for whatever reason. For example, another disciple pleaded that he just wanted some time to bury his dead father before following Jesus, but Christ insisted on a wholehearted and immediate commitment *now*: 'Follow me, Let the dead bury the dead' (Matthew 8: 22).

Finally, it is worth noting that Jesus also prescribes that we keep our working alliances, our contracts with the state: 'Render therefore unto Caesar the things which Caesar's; and unto God, the things that are God's' (Matthew 22: 21).

Distortions (or transference) in the therapeutic relationship

There were several kinds of transference (or distortions of the working relationship) which people experienced towards Jesus as described in the Gospels. He had to bear the unpleasant experience of being 'demonized'. Instead of seeing him for what he was and understanding and using the nature of his work on earth, from early on in his ministry Jesus had to live with the knowledge that some people saw it as the work of the devil: 'But when the Pharisees heard it, they said, this fellow doth not cast out devils, but by Beelzebub the prince of the devils; and Jesus knew their thoughts . . .' (Matthew 12: 24–25).

Of course, although it may sound strange to say, Jesus was also idealized by the people. That means that notwithstanding all his miracles and teaching, he was always expected to do still more – until one day he challenged this too, by refusing to give them 'a sign'. He was expected to cure all ills as well as to bear all pain by himself. His own needs for human person-to-person relationship had sometimes to be met outside of his relationships with his disciples, for example, in some of his spontaneous friendships with women such as Mary who washed his feet with her hair. His disciples often failed to understand his own plight or to take his loneliness seriously enough to stay awake with him when he was troubled. Then the only thing left was his prayerful relationship to his supervisor – God the Father.

On the other hand, when people knew him in his social context with his brothers and sisters as the son of Joseph and Mary, they transferred on to him the prejudice that a man from such a working-class family could not possibly do the wonders he was performing:

> Whence hath this man this wisdom, and these mighty works? Is not this the carpenter's son and is not his mother called Mary? and his brethren James, and Joseph, and Simon, and Judas?
> And his sisters, are they not all with us? Whence hath this man all these things?
> And they were offended in him . . .
>
> (Matthew 13: 545. 56–57)

Every priest and religious leader must have come across similar social prejudice, for example, when people see you as 'too young' to be able to help them through psycho-spiritual counselling. Sometimes people feel that someone who is celibate cannot help someone with sexual problems – as if only people who have problems with alcohol themselves can assist others with similar problems. It is of course possible that some similar experience may help in feeling personally connected to the problem brought for counselling, but it is equally possible that a different perspective may be of more benefit. Ultimately, it depends on the formation and on the ability of the individual counsellor to tolerate and work with and through the transference, giving people the opportunity to discover for themselves how they can use the proffered healing relationship to help them in their quest for understanding, patience or growth.

Jesus did not only deal with the individual and collective transferences towards himself, but also with the ways in which we find transference as prejudice in the community. In his relationships to all people from the Canaanite to the centurion, he gives us models of how to deal with people without prejudice, without bringing to a new relationship with a unique human being the experience of our past, or the judgements of other people based on their past experiences. He himself is free from prejudice, and judges people only by their fruits – their actual behaviour. Christ sits down in public 'by the well' to talk to prostitutes, he has conversations with tax collectors and with others who have lost the respect of their community and perhaps their self-respect – in order for them to find themselves whole again.

> And it came to pass, as Jesus sat at meat in the house, behold, many publicans and sinners came and sat down with him and his disciples;
> And when the Pharisees saw it, they said unto his disciples, Why eateth your Master with publicans and sinners?
> But when Jesus heard that, he said unto them, They that be whole need not a physician, but they that are sick . . .
>
> (Matthew 9: 10–12)

The way in which Christ finally goes to Jerusalem for the last time, and is displayed in death on the cross, indicates the fury and disappointment of people whose transference fantasies were not fulfilled or worked through. From the stories, it seems as if multitudes distorted the meaning of his work according to their political wishes, covering his route in palm leaves, believing him to be the one to deliver them from Roman domination in a triumphal procession fit for a statesman or a world-famous rock star. In studies of famous people we often come across the way in which they are dehumanized, idealized and then pulled viciously off the pedestal as soon as they fail to live up to the fantasies of those who put them there. People of great achievement deserve our admiration and respect. They inspire and set us an example to follow. But when, in excess of the admiration which they may deserve for their achievement, we project our ideals and our aspirations onto those famous people and fail to take responsibility for reaching our own greatness in ourselves, it goes wrong.

We could think that Jesus, by riding on a humble donkey, was trying to confront this collective transference, symbolically demonstrating that the reality of the work he had come to do was different from the fantasies of the adoring crowd who had come to acclaim the 'famous' man. He might have wanted to stress that even the humblest amongst us can achieve greatness in fulfilling the work of God. A similar notion of Jesus as nation-alist saviour of the Jewish nation in exile is also the last taunt above his head as he is crucified: 'THIS IS JESUS, THE KING OF THE JEWS' (Matthew 27: 37).

When we don't clarify expectations in making clear working contracts and frequently reviewing our contracts with our clients, we run the risk of incurring terrible disappointments. Fortunately, most of us will not ever face having to deal with the kind of collective and frenzied transference which was the lot of our Lord. In our much smaller context, however, similar misunderstandings based on falsely idealizing transferential expectations can occur. The counsellor is not the 'saviour' or the 'liberator' of the people who come to him or her for help. The counsellor can only point the way, facilitate the journey, but in the end cannot do it for the client. The client has to do it for himself. But at the end of it all, there is still a lot of work to be done and none of it complete before our death. The effective and realistic counsellor is not there to provide a permanent inoculation against all the difficulties of life, merely to help their clients to resource themselves better in order to deal with it.

Countertransference or counsellor bias in the therapeutic relationship

Countertransference refers to the feelings or attitudes of the counsellor that come into the therapeutic or formation relationship. In many cases, if the counsellor has not done their own personal work, this (proactive transference) can be limiting or distorting to the counselling work, and undermining of the working relationship. In other cases, the feelings and attitudes of the counsellor, if he or she is aware of them, can be used effectively to strengthen and sustain the working relationship. For the sake of illustration, we can look at at least two kinds of such feelings in the Christ story.

There are times when Christ is just so angry at the lack of figs on a tree when he is hungry that he condemns it to wither – or he uncharacteristically curses to hell the cities which had not repented or formed a working alliance with John the Baptist. There may indeed be times when we feel like this about our clients who apparently persist obstinately in self-destructive or abusive behaviour. But it is not going to help if we then become abusive or rejecting of our clients in turn. Declaring such feelings to our clients, however, is unlikely to lead to any progress. It is better to discharge such vehement countertransference feelings in personal therapy, so that when we are in the therapeutic relationship we can find the most useful and effective ways of being with our clients.

Typically for Jesus, the section ends with the gentle promise: 'Come to me all that labour and are heavy laden, and I will give you rest. Take my yoke upon you, and learn from me; for I am meek and lowly in heart: and ye shall find peace unto your souls. For my yoke is easy and my burden light' (Matthew 11: 28–29). This is more in keeping with the kind of merciful countertransference – his personal feelings of loving tenderness – which seems to underlie his whole ministry: 'But when he saw the multitudes, he was moved with compassion on them, because they fainted and were scattered abroad as sheep having no shepherd' (Matthew 9: 6).

The developmentally needed or reparative therapeutic relationship

The developmentally needed or reparative relationship is that mode of the therapeutic relationship that provides what was missing in the person's previous life or repairs the damage or trauma which they had experienced before. There are many models of development of the therapy of trauma that can enlighten this work – in this piece we look at some examples from St Matthew. There are dozens of incidents of the blind made to see, the leprous becoming whole and the seeming dead arising, which illustrate how Jesus came to repair our blindness, our brokenness, our death-like unconsciousness – 'as many as touched were made perfectly whole' (Matthew 14: 6). These stories, as we have said, almost all show how, if there is a sincere mutual commitment and an expectation of being helped, miraculous cures can occur.

The very heart of Christ's ministry is this restoration or repair, not only of the body and the soul, but also of humankind's relationship to God. This is only possible where the human being (a) assumes responsibility for making good use of Christ's gifts (an effective working alliance), *and* (b) where there are no excessive distortions (transferences) or unrealistic anticipations of absolution from the ongoing challenges of life on the one hand or misperceiving God as some kind of magician delivering lottery wins 'on cue' or some kind of devil if we do not get *all* of our wishes *immediately* on the other hand. Or, in other words, as we learn from our personal growth work as well as from supervision: What the client wants is not always what the client needs.

The other major aspect of this kind of corrective therapeutic relationship has to do with providing the education, training and development opportunities which the client needs in a way which the client is most likely to be able to use it. When Jesus is asked by his disciples why he teaches the multitudes in parables, he says, like the good educator he is, that he teaches different people in different ways according to their gifts and their needs: 'lest at any time they should see with their eyes, and hear with their ears, and should understand with their heart, and should be converted, and I should heal them. But blessed are your eyes, for they see; and your ears, for they hear' (Matthew 13: 15).

Jesus is not blinded by his own wishes and fears to the faults of his followers. Indeed, his restorative and formation work is done in the full knowledge of the script patterns and habitual inclinations of his disciples. He uses this knowledge to create growth opportunities for them and to prepare them for their future work and to rehearse skills against temptation when he is not longer there for them.

Perhaps the greatest gift that any teacher can give a student is fully to understand their limitations, and yet to have unswerving faith in their ability to succeed – even when the student panics, despairs and loses their footing:

> And he said, Come. And when Peter was come down out of the ship, he walked on the water, to go to Jesus, But when he saw the wind boisterous, he was afraid, and beginning to sink, he cried, saying, Lord save me. And immediately Jesus stretched forth his hand, and caught him, and said unto him, O thou of little faith, wherefore didst thou doubt? And when they were come into the ship, the wind ceased.
>
> (Matthew 14: 29–32)

Yet Peter's formation in faith was yet to be put to several further tests – just as many as he would need to overcome his impulsiveness and conquer his fears. Only after Peter had denied Christ three times in the night of the sentencing did he remember that Jesus had understood him well enough to predict his actual behaviour – notwithstanding Peter's protestations of loyalty: 'Then he went out and wept bitterly' (Matthew 26: 5). Peter must have been remembering that, in spite of knowing all his faults, Jesus yet had faith in Peter's potential to grow into the rock on which the church would be built.

The person-to-person or I–You therapeutic relationship

The real or I–You relationship is that aspect of the therapeutic relationship that focuses on the counsellor or formator's personal feelings. It usually concerns private or undisclosed feelings and attitudes. This may involve such delight in friends marrying that water is miraculously transformed into wine for the celebration, or it might be a very private grief. Sometimes judicious sharing of such person-to-person feelings can be very beneficial to the counselling work, sometimes it can be very damaging.

We read several moments when Christ expresses not just his message or his mission *on behalf of God the Father*, but when his words sound heart-rendingly human and personal. These are times when his example may be evoking our direct empathy and our profoundest identification with him through having experienced similar feelings of injustice, abandonment and despair in our own lives. Here, he seems to be expressing his raw feelings of betrayal, fear and desolation – when even the son of God feels that his father has forsaken him. What an example he is giving us about the appropriate and whole-hearted voicing of our deepest concerns.

It is sometimes falsely understood that Christians should not get angry. This is in conflict with the example of Christ's life where he shows us several times how to differentiate between times when it is better to turn the other cheek when provoked, times when it is better to talk it over with your opponent and other times when decisive and clear aggressive action should be taken:

> And Jesus went into the temple of God, and cast out all them that sold and bought in the temple, and overthrew the tables of the money-changers, and the seat of them that sold doves;
>
> And said unto them, It is written My house shall be called the house of prayer, but ye have made it a den of thieves.
>
> (Matthew 21:12–13)

Some of the saddest passages in the whole of the Bible concern Christ's longing for his students to accompany him on his most excruciating and fearful journey – but of course they can't:

> Then saith he unto them, My soul is exceedingly sorrowful, even unto death: tarry ye here, and watch with me.
>
> And he went a little farther, and fell on his face and prayed, saying, O my Father, if it be possible, let this cup pass from me; nevertheless, not as I will, but as thou wilt.
>
> And he cometh unto the disciples, and findeth them asleep, and saith to Peter, What, could ye not watch with me one hour?' he asked again and they fell asleep again and for a third time he asked and still they fell asleep.
>
> Then all the disciples forsook him, and fled.
>
> (Matthew 26: 38–40, 56)

Finally, after all the disciples have fled, after he has again pledged submission to do what he would pray he does not have to do, he cries out that even his father who has sent him on this dreadful path has abandoned him in his hour of greatest need: 'And about the ninth hour Jesus cried with a loud voice, saying, Eli, Eli, lama sabachthani? that is to say, My God, my God, why hast thou forsaken me?' (Matthew 27: 45–47).

Sadly, even then the bystanders gossip that he was crying for Elias when they misunderstand his last grief-stricken cry at feeling the final and most desperate loss – his relationship with his beloved Father.

The transpersonal therapeutic relationship

The transpersonal relationship in counselling and formation is concerned with those aspects of the healing relationship that cannot be put into words. It is not to do with ego or self. It is *trans*personal – beyond the personal. It is about awe, mystery and grace. It is about the edges of chaos, the uncertainties of complexity and the unknowable frontiers of quantum physics. The transpersonal never wholly submits to explanation. Often it is wordless silence. It merely requires that we open our hearts and our souls in faith-full expectation – who knows in which hour the bridegroom cometh? 'All things are delivered unto me of my Father and no man knoweth the Son, but the Father; neither knoweth any man the Father, save the Son, and he to whomsoever the Son will reveal him' (Matthew 16: 25–27).

We need to learn as hard as we can as much as we can about being human through our own experiences, through books and through good teachers. There is no denying the importance of such learning. But – such learning, if thoroughly pursued, always leads us ultimately to where we do *not* know. This is neither an insincere humility nor a laziness about putting in the hard work to gain as much personal knowledge about healing relationships as we can. It is that which 'passeth all understanding'.

> . . . we are forced to imagine that we are masters of the It [Physis], of the many It units of the one common It, yes, masters even of the character and the actions of a fellow creature, that we control [or influence] his life, his health, his death. Assuredly this is not so, but it is a necessity of our organism, of our human existence that we should believe it. We live, and because we live we have to believe that we can train our children, that there are causes and effects, that we are able to be useful or harmful in accordance with our thoughts [or deeds]. As a matter of fact we know nothing whatever about the connection of things, we cannot determine for twenty-four hours ahead what we shall do, and we have not the power to do anything of our own design.
> But we are compelled by the It to take its doings, its thoughts, and its feelings for affairs of the conscious mind for our own design, of our 'I'. Only because we are immersed in error, are blind, and ignorant of every little thing, can we be physicians and treat the sick.
>
> (Groddeck 1988: 224)

The notion of the transpersonal merely stresses that in learning or teaching about this mode of relationship we have to cope with ambiguities, contradictions and paradoxes: 'For whomsoever will save his life shall lose it; and whosoever will lose his life for my sake shall find it. For what is profited, if he shall gain the whole world and lose his own soul? Or what shall a man give in exchange for his soul?'; or again, whether mistranslated or not: 'Think not that I am come to send peace on earth; I came not to send peace, but a sword' (Matthew 10: 4).

And finally again, for all counsellors, psychotherapists and their teachers and supervisors, we have assurance that if we create space for the transpersonal therapeutic relationship to manifest itself in our work, healing can happen independently of our gifts of learning, our inevitable limitations or our greatest theoretical understandings. In the preparation of the disciples for their work in healing the people, the greatest trainer taught: 'For it is not you that speaketh, it is the spirit of your Father which speaketh in you . . . With men this is impossible, but with God all things are possible' (Matthew 9: 20, 26).

With grateful thanks to the people of the Institute of St Anselm, Cliftonville, Kent, from whom I have learned so much and without whom this paper would not have been written.

Appendix 3
A gift from someone who has 'come through'

When one is unenlightened, the snows of Mount Fuji are the snows of Mount Fuji and the water of Tassajara is the water of Tassajara.

When one seeks enlightenment, the snows of Mount Fuji are not the snows of Mount Fuji, and the water of Tassajara is not the water of Tassajara.

When one has attained enlightenment, the snows of Mount Fuji are the snows of Mount Fuji and the water of Tassajara is the water of Tassajara.

(Fromm 1986: 75)

My therapist, because I had told her that I would like to write about my therapy, asked me would I like to write something now about my journey from *this point* on the stair-landing looking back: *thank you, yes*.

So today, right now, I feel nervous and I feel grateful. I have moments, hours even, of swimming gratitude and ease, but I can nearly accept that right now isn't one of them. I am of a fine sensitivity today and I am afraid of being interrupted. I'm even interrupting myself as I go with one or two possibilities: suppose my prize-winning carpenter forgets today is a bank holiday and shows up at my freshly painted front door ready to proceed. I remember that I have a physical presence. I have a physical presence that can stop most people, most of the time, from entering my house at any moment or in any way which would feel intrusive to me. No more walking in, without personal regard, leaning into and through my energetic body. This from a woman who started out as a girl with no sense of her own skin. Don't think I exaggerate. There were no walls and everything came in. Now I can see from whence I came, the nearly bottom steps.

What is different?

Nearly everything, except that I am more myself. I began what I think of as my real self, pure and good and incredibly tough, at the age of 19. Now I am 37. Sometimes the toughness was reassuring. But mostly I remember thinking that after everything that had happened to me up to that age, I couldn't believe I had to do another hard thing now as well. Definitely I was convinced the world owed me.

Now I think I have been inordinately blessed. In those days I mostly showed up as mad and bad and unpredictable and difficult. I was misshapen certainly. Inside I had something I'd protected but I didn't know anything about how to live well or please my real self. I was lucky beyond my wildest and most desperate dreams – which were usually about finding someone to love/save me – to come together with my particular therapist.

First of all she spoke to me in a language that made resounding emotional sense. I remember she told me once, in the early days, that my heart was tight like a drum. I'd never even thought of *my* heart in terms of my relationship to the world before, not much and certainly not in what condition.

We also drew up a contract, jointly worded but drafted by me alone. In it I agreed to pay for my therapy, to keep my appointments, not to hurt myself or anyone else. There was something about psychiatric hospitals. I forget the wording but I know the idea was to approach my therapy with reasonable good will. I had no concept like it. I don't think I do myself a disservice in saying I had never consciously applied reasonable good will to anything before in my life. I'd tried to be perfect (childhood) and I knew mad/bad and in despair well enough, but reasonable good will was novel, and quite frankly, engaging.

At the same time I begun emotionally thawing and that hurt like hell. I saw how frozen I'd been and I didn't know if I would successfully thaw or if I'd be fingerless for ever or if I would regrow my fingers or what – but I did begin to experience myself within a new perspective. From where I'm standing now on this particular step, high up and breathing well, I feel awed by the importance of my back-then decision. I began to support myself with glimpses, albeit painful, of the person I could be. Instead of how sick I was, I became interested in my health.

What is the same?

Nothing, except that I am still myself. I have also been unable to change my biological family. I have no idea how invested my mother, father and sister and brother really were in my being mad and visible with it for the rest of their lives. Thankfully now, having expressed and expanded enough, I can love and forgive my father. A beautiful, sensitive man who supported my creativity to the best of his ability – at considerable personal cost – while my mother campaigned against my very being with an increasing fury. By the time I was an older child I was in trouble every-where. As a young teenager I was taken into care (a decision which prevented my mother killing me or me killing myself); my father stood by helplessly and let me go because he couldn't do any different.

He and I only speak of it now if he brings the subject up (almost never) or if I lose my temper when I'm speaking to him (almost never as well). To be honest, these days the history of my family according to me is not often in the foreground. I can even experiment with being lovingly casual and humorous about my childhood. I have asked my therapist – if I pay her, and it's appropriate and she's free, of course – would she accompany me to my mother's funeral. (Death by natural causes, and not yet.) Maybe, and it's fine and good that I ask. That's her answer for now and I can live with it.

Then from my position of radical sameness and difference, I start up, like an echo of my 18-year-old self, Why Does Everything To Do With My Family Always Have To Be So Difficult? What I realize with a sudden bolt of joy is how that's no longer true – I don't believe that any more. Why does everything to do with my family always have to be so difficult? It doesn't have to be and it isn't. It isn't.

Finally intense gratitude for my therapist and to Life for the dramatic and the subtle changes that keep on happening. Every single thing in my life is better now – including my past.

Love,

Anon.

Postscript from her therapist

Analysis of this letter is left to the reader. Suffice it to say that in this fractal all the major themes and processes about which I have been writing in this book are present as a whole. Thank you all. Yes.

Appendix 4
Summary of Systemic Integrative Relational Psychotherapy

The praxis of Systemic Integrative Relational Psychotherapy (or of any 'pure' form of effective psychotherapy from any 'school' – Kleinian analysis to Bio-energetics) is probably:

- based on **intentional** *being* – physis – which is understood as a relational co-creation of healing, growth and emergent creativity – auto-poiesis (e.g. Clarkson 1996a);
- based on **a consciously or unconsciously philosophically informed choice of known or invented interventions between seven epistemological and ontological levels of complexity** – physiological, emotional, nominative, normative, rational, theoretical and transpersonal (e.g. Clarkson 1975; Clarkson 1992a);
- **manifested through the five relationship modalities**: the working alliance, the transference/countertransference relationship, the developmentally needed or reparative relationship, the dialogic relationship and the transpersonal relationship. These five relational modes are present in any relationship from supervision to parent–child relationships to casual sexual encounters (Clarkson 1990, 1995b, 1996b);
- **guided by the decision-making priority sequence of action** – danger, confusion, conflict, deficit, development (see e.g. Clarkson 1998c);
- expressed in terms of the understanding and appropriate **use of systems principles** as articulated by Von Bertalanffy, Maturana and Varela, and current quantum physics and complexity understandings of the world (Clarkson and Lapworth 1992; Clarkson 1998d).

Characteristics of training at PHYSIS

Transdisciplinarity *and* **valuing singular theories** (e.g. Clarkson 1992b)
Culturally pluralistic (e.g. Clarkson and Nippoda 1997)
Beyond schoolism (e.g. Clarkson 1998b)
Integrating practice and research (e.g. Clarkson 1998e) with **ethics** (e.g. Clarkson 1995a, 1996c and 2000a), **culture** (e.g. Clarkson 1997b), and **organizational context** (e.g. Clarkson 1995b)
Attentive to **contemporary debates** as well as to **history** and **future aspirations** (e.g. Clarkson 1993a).
Consultation, training, supervision and **practice-based PhD research** can be formal and structured or based on psychologically based principles of '**Learning by Enquiry**' (*Dieratao*) as Heraclitus advised (in Clarkson 1998e: 242–72)

Outcomes

Turner (1998) commented (without information or evidence) on the attempts by Clarkson 'to straddle the lines of both respect for purism and a concurrent facilitation of inter-school communication by favouring the development of a common language (like the transtheorists). One could question the feasibility of such a monumental project for individual practitioners and especially trainees' (1998: 451).

I hope I have clarified the language question. Our common language is everyday English. Furthermore, contrary to Turner's unchecked expectations, veterans **and** trainees find it very valuable, as evidenced by their success, for example, with BAC and UKCP registration, BPS Counselling Psychology examinations as well as practice-based Master's and Doctoral degrees at different universities.

Appendix 5
Scientist-practitioner supervision in action

Here follows a verbatim transcript from a section showing a supervisor doing live coaching with two or three students in using the scientist-practitioner paradigm which I earlier described in action. You can use this as an exercise in identifying and/or imagining the five relational dimensions and the seven experiential and discursive levels.

Background

The client has already said that the issue of taking responsibility for everything and everybody is one of the ways that she is in the world. The therapist has just made a self-disclosure to the person bringing a problem that has resulted in movement in the session coming to a halt. The client's eye-blink rate is down and she breaks eye-contact. The therapist feels uncomfortable and requests live coaching.

Supervisor: Use your eyes after an intervention, along with the whole of the rest of your body, to see how she responds to it. She's not responding well to that last intervention you made. There's no sign of increased liveliness, contact. She's probably had people who were supposed to help her self-disclose and trying to help her too much anyway. It may be well for you to avoid that intervention for a very long time.

Therapist: That is the same thing – somebody told me about that immediate thing that I do. I rush in and start talking. I feel I am needing to listen to that, I have to start helping them and listening to them.

Supervisor to therapist: So you want to avoid that. Not that you did it wrong in that case, it's an experiment. So, if I give her this information and she goes, 'Oh . . . what about you?', it stops. You could say to yourself, 'Oh, we'll get ourselves out of that. If I do that, that's what happens with this person and I can see it's not working.' So we'll get ourselves out of that dead spot and we won't try that intervention again for a long time. She's already told us that she takes too much responsibility for other people.

Therapist: You told us you are worried about attacking responses when you do that – standing up for others.

Client: (*Animatedly*) I think it is me, it's the most central thing of my life!

Supervisor to
therapist: But you don't know that until you made the experiment right? You've seen that, that's what we're saying. Every inter-action is an experiment – you watch what happens. Then, if it doesn't work, you don't do that one again. Now this exper-iment worked. You reminded her of what she's worried about. You've shown her you're interested in her – and just see how she comes to life.

Therapist: Yeah. It's very obvious.

Therapist to
client: And people will tell you how they want to be helped or if they want to be helped, and what I am really impressed by is the fact that in that situation nobody wanted to be helped.

(*Laughter*)

Therapist: You don't want to be helped.

Client: No, not at all.

Therapist: You want to be understood. You don't want to be helped. You want, I think, recognition for the existential position you've taken in the world, you don't want to be sent on holiday to recover from stress. You want to be recognized for the position that you've taken up, and what that costs.

Client: Oh don't please, (*Laughter*) you see?

Therapist: It's not help you want, it's understanding.

Client: Oh, I don't want to cry. (*Laughter*) No I don't want to cry. No, no.

Supervisor: Now you see, you don't listen to the words, because we can see that her body wants to cry. Look, she is crying.

Therapist to
supervisor: That, that's the skill because it's not always, it's not always . . . just hearing the words?

Supervisor: No, not, not only the words.

Therapist to
supervisor: For her, particularly not hearing the words.

Supervisor: Particularly not hearing the words.

Therapist to
supervisor: Very helpful. And you were showing me and she proved it by crying – that you don't just listen to the words, most of the words you can ignore.

Supervisor: You're only listening for some words. You listen for 'I need', I want', 'I feel'. And how you know that, that whether she means what she says or whether an intervention of yours is working is by looking at and feeling into the body of the other person.

Client: But when I talk about it, which is what I like to do because it's so important to me . . . if I can keep up the lightness I can try and avoid the pool of emotion – brush past my feelings very quickly, Oh . . .

Therapist: Yes, yes.

Supervisor: So what do we learn about her? – If it's OK to talk about you some more?

Client: (*Nods*)

Therapist to
supervisor: So I might really work on its OK for her to get into her pool.

Supervisor: Yes. The last thing we'll do of course, knowing what we know now, and we didn't know it before, is to use a self-disclosing intervention because her ears are full of parental figures who have leaned on her self-disclosing to her and they have not helped her at all.

Client: Very true, very true.

Supervisor: Who wants to learn more about working like this? Munir, do you want to have another shot?

Munir: Yes? (*Throat-clearing sound*)

Supervisor: Do you think we believe him?
(*Laughter*)

Supervisor: Let's do some fine-tuning here – Does he mean that, does he really want that?

Munir: I think I should do that.

Supervisor: Sounds like Stella has to take medicine that doesn't taste very nice. So, if I were going to check out with you now, Stella, I would say that something like that I hear the yes and I am just checking if you really mean the yes, I do that with people a lot.

Munir:	It's not a yes, but its more a yes than a no.
Supervisor:	Is it enough of a yes?
Munir:	Yeah.
Supervisor:	But we can see and hear and sense the hesitancy. Is there maybe something we can do to help that?
Munir:	Hmm.
Supervisor:	Maybe we can do a little bit?
Munir:	Hmm.
Supervisor to others:	It's a bit like, stop listening to people in order to really listen to them. It's just going a little bit further in. Just gathering the string in a little bit further. Listen with all of you at all levels, not just with your ears.
Aminda:	It isn't deeper, it's more obvious.
Supervisor:	Yes, its right here in our faces, obvious.
Aminda:	Looking at how she moves, I understand. Yes, I understand. I don't have to worry does she or does she not understand. She's moved right back and settled down. (*Mirroring*)
	(*To Munir*) When you first said 'Yes', your body said, 'A little bit yes', like so.
Client:	(*Tells her issue at high speed and without any apparent feeling.*)
Supervisor:	One thing we know, she has talked about this a lot.
(*Laughter*)	
Munir:	How do you know?
Supervisor:	I'll tell you why it's obvious – because of the smoothness and the fastness with which it comes out. There's nothing new or felt or fresh about it. The story hardly matters, it's dead material.
Munir:	Oh yes, yes.
Supervisor:	It lacks her organism involvement. So the question is, How can you listen to her in a way in which she's not been listened to before?
(*Puzzled look*)	
Supervisor:	By your face you look as if you don't know the answer? I don't know either. But we can try many psychological experiments.
Munir:	OK . . .
Supervisor:	And we'll stop every now and then and we'll do one or two and then we'll stop again for some reflection.
Munir:	Yeah, that's good. OK.

Supervisor to
group: You see she likes that – did you see? That worked.
(*Laughter*)
Munir as
therapist: It seems as if you had already talked about it a lot or
                        rehearsed in your mind. Is that right? About your existential
                        position.
Stella as
client: There is something, going on from what the supervisor was
                        saying, which is very accurate, and I think it was about the
                        recognition that I want for the position that I've taken by
                        people who I think would appreciate it, and when I meet
                        that envy and fear I feel pain. When that doesn't occur the
                        position I've taken doesn't appear to be a threat, it's like
                        being understood at that very deep level.
Munir as
therapist: What do you mean by people understand your position?
                        People understand that in a hierarchical position?
Stella as
client: No, the opposite. The same attitude and existential position,
                        the sense that in them and I have one friend whom I value, I
                        value lots of friends, but I have this one friend and I think we
                        do understand each other's position and the pain of it too,
                        of that sense of conscience.
Munir: Do you get enough recognition? Do you each recognize each
                        other, what you do?
Stella: Yes, Yes. Essential for my mental health. (*Affirmative nod*)
Supervisor: That intervention worked. What was the last thing she said?
Munir to
Supervisor: That . . . did that feel really good?
Supervisor: She said 'yes, essential for my mental health'. Did you see
                        that one go down?
Munir: Yes.
Supervisor: Good, there's a loose emotional word lying around, the
                        loose word is PAIN.
Munir to
Stella: You have somebody to share this with, your existential
                        position in your work, and sharing maybe the pride in your
                        conscience, and your actions, and you also share the pain?
Stella: The pain of sharing from the outside, of writing the postcard
                        from the edge.
Munir: Uh uh.

Stella: Taking on the risk to be different, taking the risk that when I
             hear spitefulness . . . not anger, I think for many years I
             confused angry feelings with just negativity, I don't hold that
             position any more, but I don't like experiencing or seeing
             people intent on humiliating others, I don't let that happen
             to me any more, I have in the past let that happen to me, that
             pain was as bad as it could be, quite unbearable,

Munir: Quite

Stella: It touches me deeply, so much about human prejudice and
             alienation and it touched so much in me around quality. It
             exacted from me . . . when I hear about . . .

Munir: Maybe you're doing a bit too much. You're getting too much
             pain from this position that you're taking. Maybe you could
             think of doing it less.

Stella: (*With a look of total incomprehension on her face*) . . . Yeah.
(*Laughter*)

Supervisor: OK? You got it? So, that's not a mistake you made. That was
             an experiment. That's simply not the way she wants to go.
             Then you could say something like, 'Oh, it looks to me that
             this is not an option you want to take'. So do something like
             that in your own way and let's see what happens.

Munir: OK. This is not an option you want to take. You're quite
             happy with how you...

Stella: I am not entirely . . . But I don't want to cop out (?)

Munir: But you think there are ways to make your position more
             bearable? One of which you told me is take into your confi-
             dence friends who have similar values. That's always for you
             to, to support you in this.

Stella: Yes. Yes.

Munir: Give you strength.

Stella: Gives me strength.

Supervisor: Good work.

Munir: Because maybe that's what tied in with the aloneness bit.
             When you were talking about aloneness.

Stella: Ahmm. And I felt that aloneness in groups. When I've
             spoken out. I've seen similar words in people's mouths,
             because everything we say is trapped in our mouth. It's all
             going on like a silent movie. And I make it manifest what is
             hidden . . . unspoken.
             I think my husband put it very well, and I think it is probably
             something that has taken him a long time to say. He has been
             able to say it, and it is a very healing thing. I, I understand

	that I must be very difficult to be around sometimes. What he says is, the thing that he loved and wants about me is my integrity – he says it shines from me . . .
Munir:	Hmm.
Stella:	But the glare is very dazzling sometimes. And I can really understand what he's saying. And it's not about making mistakes. There are cues I get wrong. You know, I'm not always as sensitive as I would like to be. I get angry. I have a full range of emotions, and I own those and I work with them. But I really understood how hard it is for him sometimes, and I think he would just . . . Can that – can't she just let that go? Can't you just be a witness without intervening? . . .
Munir:	Hmm. Do they want to, maybe... Do they want to be more with you and not have you go and . . .
Aminda:	Yes, yes. That's in my marriage. I need a place sometimes where my husband can't go, where I don't want him to be. And I respect that in him. And he feels very terrified of that in me.
Munir:	There's a fear in him?
Stella:	Yes, because he says I'm his only friend.
Munir:	And you are friends with the whole world? He has to share.
Stella:	It must be hard for him.
Supervisor to Stella as client:	Do you feel that Munir understands you now?
Aminda:	Yeah, absolutely.
Supervisor to Munir:	Do you feel you're getting to her?
Munir:	Yes.
Supervisor:	Do you feel the difference inside you? Do you feel the difference in the atmosphere? It becomes richer, juicier, more moist.
Stella:	I mean, I still feel that I'm concentrating quite hard but – I can feel it.
Supervisor:	You can feel it?
Munir:	I can feel it.
Supervisor:	You can feel it. That when it feels right. It's when it becomes rich and moving and full of life.
Stella:	This wasn't rehearsed.
Munir:	You were thinking – slowly... you don't know, you're feeling your way through it.

Stella:	This has been, this stuff was my life for the past three years. Trying to turn about a 20-year relationship. Many threads.
Supervisor:	This session has to end in a minute. So, reflect on what's happened without tidying it up. You may even experiment with self-disclosure again. See if it works now. She has now told you that she wanted that recognition from other people who have stood up for their values. She's now asked for it – told you that she wants it. This is different from you giving it to her at the beginning of the session without first having established understanding.
Munir:	But . . . (?) (*Laughter*)
Supervisor:	Go on! Try it.
Munir:	I . . . um . . . feel moved by what you have shared with me. Having taken that position myself sometimes in life, I really feel it and respect you for it . . .
Supervisor:	Beautiful. How beautiful! What does that feel like Aminda?
Stella:	Thank you. I feel understood. Thank you.
Munir:	I feel that it may be something maybe not proper to say in psychotherapy.
Supervisor:	It's fine. It's much more proper in terms of what she was now asking for in terms of your contract. It's not proper by the book. It's proper by this person at this moment.
Munir:	You think there are these things that you must and mustn't do. And then experience shows you, and in workshops you say, 'Oh well, I do this' – and I think, ' You're not supposed to do that according to the book'.
Supervisor:	People aren't books. Question is: Does it work?
Munir:	Yeah, that must be right.
Supervisor:	You have to listen to their story and in their story how they want you to be with them.
Munir:	I have just experienced that.
Supervisor:	So it's much more sophisticated than 'playing by ear'. Clients will tell you what they want from you. You told us exactly what worked for you. You said what you want. Any one of us at this moment could be therapists for people because we have all the treatment planning information. I am exaggerating somewhat, but in principle, in truth, in the fractal has told us . . . Stella doesn't want to be alone, she wants accompaniment, she wants things to be broken down into little pieces, she wants to be respected. She says she places too high expectations on herself . . . She wants to be accompanied alongside and that this must be in little pieces

	– she told you she didn't want one big chunk. To check out a lot, not to take things for granted . . . To give her lots of space. What a lot of information we got. Stella wants to be respected and valued by being listened to, not given advice.
Munir:	It's a recognition – it's a recognition from not just anybody – it's a recognition other people who can identify with her after having shown that they understand her.
Supervisor:	Yes. But it's what she's looking for, person-to-person, around the issue of values.
Stella:	I just wanted to be listened to.
Supervisor to Stella:	You wanted to be listened to, and that's what worked . . . (*To Munir*) What Stella was saying at that earlier moment felt incongruent, because she was saying, 'I'm fine' and yet she was crying.
Stella:	What is that painting? – 'The Scream' by Edvard Munch. A silent movie.
Supervisor:	And then you described it as a silent movie – I loved that! You're like the pianist, aren't you, accompanying the film?
Munir:	Yeah. It all comes out.
Stella:	. . . And I do it myself!
Munir:	Of course.
Supervisor:	So it's both more complicated and simpler than it appears. You, the therapist, don't actually have to do very much. You have to be there, pay attention, try things – if they don't work, people will tell you. People are very much more clever than you read in the books. And there are so many clues. About the way you said your joints are aching . . . You were talking about sitting down. That was telling us about your physical comfort. You know, like it's – right there. This is not mysterious. You know, this person's body is important for them. It's almost like that. And yours is not mysterious. You say, 'I am frightened of going to do the psychotherapy on my own.' There it is! It's like that! It's all there, right in the little fractal. Almost in the first transaction.
Munir:	I give off fear. I was frightened about going in first. I thought, I've got to keep a bit centred here, because otherwise I won't be able to do this, be there to listen to you. So there was all that going on, too. All my self-consciousness, not available for being conscious of you.

Supervisor: If we track it back to my first interaction: I remember coming into the room with you guys sitting here looking all very formal, and I went, sort of 'Aaagh!' (*Laughter*) Aaagh! – I was thinking that I don't want to be part of all of this frightened-ness. But I find a cathartic way of releasing it a little bit for us all. So that I didn't get caught into doing what you were doing. Being frightened of you getting frightened.

Munir: Well I kind of thought, 'Well, the bullshitting is over.' (*Laughter*) Here it is. This is it!

Supervisor: This is the REAL THING. It's only a summary of the things you've learned. You can see all of them, the relationship. You see the developmental relationship fail when the person is not ready for it. You see the working alliance work when it's there. They're just the things I taught you about Scientist-Practitioner. Does it work? Oh, it works! – I'll do that again. No, that doesn't work – let me try something else. Working from inside yourself. And attending to the flow of the client's physis. And not working from – 'because this works for me, I'll apply it to everybody'. Working from inside myself, with this person and their difference. Sometimes other people are just totally incomprehensible.

Stella: What do you do then?

Supervisor: You just work with them in making them more comprehensible to themselves. And then they'll tell you again. They'll help. They'll help you. In a way, we've done that with everybody here – making them slightly more comprehensible to themselves. So, next time you go to a therapist, you are then a better client because you are in a better position to say to them, 'Look, I don't like so much of that – I need more warmth, or . . .'.

Stella: I've never said anything like that, ever.

Supervisor: Or 'I feel you leave me alone too much – I need more feedback from you'.

Stella: What if the therapist can't take that?

Supervisor: You have said you weren't so sure about continuing with your current therapist.

Stella: Yeah. Yeah. It doesn't feel like much is happening. Something has happened which has been good, and I'm enjoying it. But I'm not sure if I shouldn't stop it for a while because there doesn't seem to be anything of urgency in my life, and a lot of the time I don't feel as though something is really happening. I am not sure. With the space thing that I have, I think groups would be quite helpful.

Supervisor: And you can see this in the calibration – that's the word. It's how to calibrate to this person, and to this person. That's too much, That's too little, faster, slower, different, the same and come back again. And that is good to learn.

Stella: It's also good to learn in this form of coaching.

References

Abrams D (1997) The Spell of the Sensuous. New York: Random House.

Adams MV (1997) The Multicultural Imagination: 'Race', Color, and the Unconscious. London and New York: Routledge.

Adler G (1979) Dynamics of the Self. London: Coventure. (First published 1951)

Alther L (1985) Other Women. Harmondsworth: Penguin.

Anderson WT (1990) Reality Is Not What It Used To Be. San Francisco: Harper and Row.

Anderson CM, Stewart S (1983) Mastering Resistance – A Practical Guide to Family Therapy. New York: Guilford Press.

Andre G (2000) Chereau Interview b. Time Out, 16–23 August: 75.

Angelo M (1992) Image intelligence – a psychological study of active imagination as education. Unpublished PhD thesis, Sussex University.

Angelo M (1997) Placing the sublime – cosmology in the consulting room. In Clarkson P (Ed.) On the Sublime. London: Whurr. pp 15–45.

Ani M (1994) Yurugu – An African-centred Critique of European Cultural Thought and Behaviour. Trenton, NJ: African World Press.

Archambeau E (1979) Beyond countertransference: the psychotherapist's experience of healing in the therapeutic relationship. Doctoral dissertation, San Diego: California School of Professional Psychology.

Arden M (1993) Thoughts on the healing process. International Forum on Psychoanalysis 2, Stockholm.

Arendt H (1964) Eichmann in Jerusalem: A Report on the Banality of Evil. New York: Viking Press.

Aspy D (1974) Towards a Technology for Humanizing Education. Champaign: Research Press.

Assagioli R (1971) Psychosynthesis. New York: Viking Press..

Atlas J (1992) Review of Nicholson Baker's 'Vox'. Vogue, March.

Austin JH (1999) Zen and the Brain: Toward an Understanding of Meditation and Consciousness. Cambridge, MA: MIT Press.

Avens R (1984) The New Gnosis: Heidegger, Hillman and Angels. Dallas, TX: Spring Publications.

BAC (1999) Counselling On Line . . . opportunities and risks in counselling clients via the Internet. Available from the British Association for Counselling and Psychotherapy, Rugby, UK.

305

Bachelor A, Horvath A (1999) The therapeutic relationship. In Hubble MA, Duncan BL, Miller SD (Eds) The Heart and Soul of Change: What Works in Therapy. Washington DC: American Psychological Association. pp 133–78.

Barkham M (1995) Editorial: Why psychotherapy outcomes are important now. Changes 13(3): 161–63.

Barry WA, Connolly WJ (1986) The Practice of Spiritual Direction. San Francisco: HarperCollins.

Bauman Z (1993) Postmodern Ethics. Oxford: Blackwell.

Beck AT (1976) Cognitive Therapy and Emotional Disorders. New York: International Universities Press.

Beitman BD (1994) Stop exploring! Start defining the principles of a psychotherapy integration: Call for a consensus conference. Journal of Psychotherapy Integration 4(3): 203–28.

Bergson H (1965) Creative Evolution. London: Macmillan.

Berne E (1961) Transactional Analysis in Psychotherapy: A Systematic Individual and Social Psychiatry. New York: Grove Press.

Berne E (1966) Principles of Group Treatment. New York: Grove Press.

Berne E (1971) Away from a theory of the impact of interpersonal interaction on non-verbal participation. Transactional Analysis Journal 1(1): 6–13.

Berne E (1972) What You Say after You Say Hello. New York: Grove Press.

Bernstein L (1964) Kaddish. Recording: Manhattan Center, New York, 15 and 17 April.

Bion WR (1970) Attention and Interpretation. London: Karnac.

Bird L (1999) The Fundamental Fact. London: The Mental Health Foundation.

Black DM (2000) The functioning of religions from a modern psychoanalytic perspective. Mental Health, Religion and Culture 3(1): 13–26.

Bloom W (1996) Psychic Protection. London: Piatkus Books.

Bly R (1990) Iron John: A Book About Men. Shaftesbury: Element.

Blyth RH (1960) Zen in English Literature and Oriental Classics. New York: Dutton.

Boadella D (1987) Lifestreams – An Introduction to Biosynthesis. London: Routledge and Kegan Paul.

Bohm D (1980) Wholeness and the Implicate Order. London: Ark Paperbacks.

Bolen JS (1984) Goddesses in Everywoman: A New Psychology of Women. New York: Harper and Row.

Bonaparte M, Freud A, Kris, E (Eds) (1954) Sigmund Freud – The Origins of Psychoanalysis. Letters to Wilhelm Fliess, Drafts and Notes 1887–1902. (Trans. E Mosbacher, J Strachey) London: Imago.

Boorstein S (Ed.) (1996) Transpersonal Psychotherapy. (2nd edn) Albany, NY: State University of New York Press.

Boradori G (1986) 'Weak thought' and the 'Aesthetics of quotationism': the Italian shift from deconstruction. Working Paper No. 6: Center for Twentieth Century Studies.

Brandon D (1976) Zen in the Art of Helping. London and Henley: Routledge and Kegan Paul.

Braud W, Anderson R (Eds) (1998) Transpersonal Research Methods for the Social Sciences. Thousand Oaks, CA: Sage.

Breakwell AM (due 2001) Identity. London: Sage.

Bridges W (1980) Transitions: Making Sense of Life's Changes. Reading, MA: Addison-Wesley.

Briggs J, Peat FD (1990) Turbulent Mirror. New York: Harper and Row. (First published 1989)

Brock W (1949) Notes. In Heidegger M, Existence and Being. Chicago, IL: Gateway. pp 363–69.

Brodribb S (1992) Nothing Mat(t)ers: A Feminist Critique of Postmodernism. North Melbourne: Spinifex Press.

Brown J, Dreis S, Nace DK (1999) What really makes a difference in psychotherapy outcome? Why does managed care want to know? In Hubble MA, Duncan BL, Miller SD (Eds) The Heart and Soul of Change: What Works in Therapy. Washington DC: American Psychological Association. pp 389–406.

Buber M (1962) Ten Rungs: Hasidic Sayings. New York: Schoken.

Buber M (1987) I and Thou. (Trans. R Gregor Smith) Edinburgh: T and T Clark. (First published 1937).

Burman E (1994) Deconstructing Developmental Psychology. London: Routledge.

Camus A (1948) The Plague. (Gilbert S Trans.) New York: Knopf.

Caplan G (1951) A public health approach to child psychiatry. Mental Health 35: 18.

Capra F (1976) The Tao of Physics. London: Fontana.

Capra F (1983) The Turning Point: Science, Society and the Rising Culture. London: Fontana.

Carroll L (1986) Through the Looking-glass. London: Victor Gollancz.

Casement P (1985) On Learning from the Patient. London: Tavistock.

Chambers I (1990) Border Dialogues: Journeys in Postmodernity. London: Routledge.

Chanter T (1995) Ethics of Eros: Irigaray's Rewriting of the Philosophers. New York: Routledge.

Charles R (1996) Mind, Body and Immunity – Enhancing Your Body's Natural Defences for Good Health and Long Life. London: Cedar.

Clarkson P (1975) The seven-level model. Paper delivered at University of Pretoria, November.

Clarkson P (1988) Crisis and aspiration. ITA News 21: 12.

Clarkson P (1989a) Gestalt Counselling in Action. London: Sage.

Clarkson P (1989b) Metanoia: a process of transformation. Transactional Analysis Journal 19(4): 224–34.

Clarkson P (1990) A multiplicity of psychotherapeutic relationships. British Journal of Psychotherapy 7(2): 148–63.

Clarkson P (1991a) Through the looking glass: explorations in transference and countertransference. Transactional Analysis Journal 21(2): 99–107.

Clarkson P (1991b) Further through the looking glass: transference, countertransference, and parallel process in transactional analysis psychotherapy and supervision. Transactional Analysis Journal 21(3): 174–83.

Clarkson P (1992a) Systemic integrative psychotherapy training. In Dryden W (Ed.) Integrative and Eclectic Therapy: A Handbook. Buckingham: Open University Press. pp 269–95.

Clarkson P (1992b) Transactional Analysis Psychotherapy – An Integrated Approach. London: Routledge.

Clarkson P (1993a) New perspectives in counselling and psychotherapy, or adrift in a sea of change. In Clarkson P (Ed.) On Psychotherapy. London: Whurr. pp 209–32.

Clarkson P (1993b) Metanoia: a process of transformation. In Clarkson P (Ed.) On Psychotherapy. London: Whurr. pp 55–71.

Clarkson P (1994) The Achilles Syndrome: The Secret Fear of Failure. Shaftesbury: Element.

Clarkson P (1995a) The Therapeutic Relationship in Psychoanalysis, Counselling Psychology and Psychotherapy. London: Whurr.

Clarkson P (1995b) Change in Organisations. London: Whurr.

Clarkson P (1996a) The archetype of physis: the soul of nature – our nature. Harvest: Journal for Jungian Studies 42(1): 70–93.

Clarkson P (1996b) Researching the 'therapeutic relationship' in psychoanalysis, counselling psychology and psychotherapy – a qualitative inquiry. Counselling Psychology Quarterly 9(2): 143–62.

Clarkson P (1996c) Values in counselling and psychotherapy. Changes 13(4): 299–306.

Clarkson P (1996d) The Bystander (An End to Innocence in Human Relationships?). London: Whurr.

Clarkson P (1996e) Counselling psychology in Britain – the next decade. Counselling Psychology Quarterly 8(3): 197–204.

Clarkson P (1996f) The eclectic and integrative paradigm: between the Scylla of confluence and the Charybdis of confusion. In Woolfe R, Dryden W (Eds) Handbook of Counselling Psychology. London: Sage. pp 258–83.

Clarkson P (1996g) Accreditation procedures in psychotherapy. Self and Society 23(6): 14–15.

Clarkson P (Ed.) (1997a) On the Sublime in Psychoanalysis, Archetypal Psychology and Psychotherapy. London: Whurr.

Clarkson P (1997b) The sublime in psychoanalysis and archetypal psychotherapy. In Clarkson P (Ed.) On the Sublime in Psychoanalysis, Archetypal Psychology and Psychotherapy. London: Whurr. (Revised version of 'The sublime in psychoanalysis and psychotherapy.' Paper delivered at the Tenth Jung Studies Day held at University of Kent, Canterbury, 25 November 1995.)

Clarkson P (1998a) Supervised supervision: including the archetopoi of supervision. In Clarkson P (Ed.) Supervision: Psychoanalytic and Jungian Perspectives. London: Whurr. pp 136–46.

Clarkson P (1998b) Beyond schoolism. Changes 16(1): 1–11.

Clarkson P (1998c) Supervision in counselling, psychotherapy and health: an intervention priority sequencing model. European Journal of Psychotherapy, Counselling and Health 1(2): 195.

Clarkson P (1998d) The Organisational Psychology of Complexity. OACES: Organisations as Complex Evolving Systems Conference, Warwick University.

Clarkson P (1998e) Counselling Psychology: Integrating Theory, Research, and Supervised Practice. London: Routledge

Clarkson P (1998f) Learning through inquiry (the Dierotao programme at PHYSIS). In Clarkson P (Ed.) Counselling Psychology: Integrating Theory, Research and Supervised Practice. London: Routledge. pp 242–72.

Clarkson P (1999) Racial and cultural issues for counselling psychologists. Symposium at BPS Division of Counselling Psychology Annual Conference, 21–23 May, Brighton.

Clarkson P (2000a) Ethics: Working with Ethical and Moral Dilemmas in Psychotherapy. London: Whurr.

Clarkson P (2000b) Similar processes operate in the internal world. Psychotherapy Review 2(7): 319–21.

Clarkson P (2000c) On Psychotherapy, Vol. 2. London: Whurr.

Clarkson P (Ed.) (in press, a) Cross-cultural Issues in Psychotherapy. London: Whurr.

Clarkson P (in press, b) The Therapeutic Relationship: A Practitioner's Guide. London: Whurr.

Clarkson P (in press, c) The Therapeutic Relationship. (2nd edn) London: Whurr.

Clarkson P (in press, d) Working with countertransference. Accepted by Psychodynamic Counselling.

Clarkson P, Angelo M (2000) In search of supervision's soul: a research report on competencies for integrative supervision in action. Transpersonal Psychology Review 4(2): 29–34.

Clarkson P, Clayton (1995) New paradigms of group dynamics. In Clarkson P (Ed.) Change in Organisations. London: Whurr.

Clarkson P, Lapworth P (1992) Systemic integrative psychotherapy. In Dryden W (Ed.) Integrative and Eclectic Therapy: A Handbook. Buckingham: Open University Press. pp 41–83.

Clarkson P, Nicolopoulou K (in press) Organisational relational psychology in five dimensions: research and practice. Report presented to Andersen Consulting, 1999. (Submitted for publication.)

Clarkson P, Nippoda Y (1997) The experienced influence or effect of cultural/racism issues on the practice of counselling psychology – a qualitative study of one multi-cultural training organisation. Counselling Psychology Quarterly 10(4): 415–37.

Clarkson P, Nuttall J (2000) Working with countertransference. Psychodynamic Counselling 6(3): 359–79.

Cleminson D (in press) Historical perspective. In Clarkson P (Ed.) Cross-cultural Issues in Psychotherapy. London: Whurr.

Coe S, Metz H (1983) How to Commit Suicide in South Africa. London: Knockabout Comics.

Copi IM (1961) Introduction to Logic. (2nd edn) New York: Macmillan.

Corney R (1997) A Counsellor in Every General Practice? London: Greenwich University Press.

Cortright B (1997) Psychotherapy and Spirit. Albany, NY: State University of New York Press.

Costall A, Reddy V, Williams E, Draghi-Lorenz R (1997) Unexplaining social development. Poster presented at the 27th Annual Symposium of the Jean Piaget Society, 19–21 June, Santa Monica, California.

Cottone RR (1988) Epistemological and ontological issues in counselling: implications of social systems theory. Counselling Psychology Quarterly 1(4): 357–65.

Cowie H, Clarkson P (2000) Narratives of psychotherapy in modern English literature. Accepted for publication in the European Journal of Psychotherapy, Counselling and Health.

Cox M, Thielgaard A (1987) Mutative Metaphors in Psychotherapy. London and New York: Tavistock Publications.

Crown M (2000) Random reality. New Scientist 165 (2227: 26 February).

Csikszentmihalyi M (1992) Flow – The Psychology of Happiness. London: Rider.

Cutler BL, Penrod SD (1995) Assessing the accuracy of eye-witness identifications. In

Bull R, Carson D (Eds) Handbook of Psychology in Legal Contexts. Chichester: John Wiley. pp 193–213.

Dale B (in press) Five relational dimensions in person-centred psychotherapy. In Clarkson P (Ed.) Cross-cultural Issues in Psychotherapy. London: Whurr. (In preparation: available from PHYSIS, London)

Davies P (1992) Does this give God His P45? (Interview by A MacPherson). The Mail on Sunday, 26 April: 17.

de Chardin T (1966) Man's Place in Nature. London: Collins.

de Shazer S (1985) Keys to Solution in Brief Therapy. New York: Norton.

Derrida J (1992) Acts of Literature. (Ed. D Attridge) New York and London: Routledge.

Descartes R (1969) A Discourse on Method – Meditations and Principles. (Trans. J. Veitch) London: Dent: Everyman's Library.

Descartes R (1973) Le Monde. In Alqui F (Ed.) Oeuvres Philosophiques de Descartes, Vol. 1. Paris, Garnier Freres. pp 227–441.

Diamond N (1996) Can we speak of internal and external reality? Group Analysis 29: 303–17.

Dixon VJ (1976) World views and research methodology. In King LM, Dixon VJ, Nobles WW (Eds) African Philosophy: Assumptions and Paradigms for Research on Black Persons. Los Angeles: Fanon Center Publications. pp 51–102.

Don NS (1996) The story of Wendy – a case study in multi-modal therapy. In Boorstein S (Ed.) Transpersonal Psychotherapy. (2nd edn) New York: State University Press. pp 343–76.

Draghi-Lorenz R, Reddy V, Costall A (in press) Re-thinking the development of 'non-basic' emotions: a critical review of existing theories. Accepted for publication in Developmental Review.

Duffell N (1999) The Making of Them – The British Attitude to Children and the Boarding School System. London: Lone Arrow Press.

Dunn J (1995) Intersubjectivity in psychoanalysis: a critical review. International Journal of Psycho-Analysis 76: 723–38.

Edwards D, Ashmore M, Potter J (1995) Death and furniture: the rhetoric, politics, and theology of bottom line arguments against relativism. History of Human Sciences 8: 25–49.

Elkin I (1995) The NIMH treatment of depression collaborative research program: major results and clinical implications. Changes 13(3): 178–85.

Elliott S, Williams KL (1991) Modelling people using cellular slime moulds. Australian Natural History 23(8): 609–16.

Ellis A (1962) Reason and Emotion in Psychotherapy. Secaucus, NJ: Citadel Press.

Erickson M (1967a) Indirect hypnotic therapy of an enuretic couple. In Haley J (Ed.) Advanced Techniques of Hypnosis and Therapy. Selected Papers of Milton H. Erickson. New York and London: Grune and Stratton. pp 410–12.

Erickson M (1967b) Naturalistic techniques of hypnosis. In Haley J, (Ed.) Advanced Techniques of Hypnosis and Therapy. Selected Papers of Milton H. Erickson. New York and London: Grune and Stratton. pp 424–30.

Fabricius J (1994) Alchemy – Medieval Alchemists and their Royal Art. London: Diamond Books.

Farrell BA (1979) Work in small groups: some philosophical considerations. In Babington Smith B, Farrell BA (Eds) Training In Small Groups: A Study of Five Groups. Oxford: Pergamon. pp 103–15.

Feather NT (Ed.) (1982) Expectations and Actions: Expectancy-value Models in Psychology. Hillsdale, NJ: Lawrence Erlbaum.

Feltham C, Dryden W (1993) Dictionary of Counselling. London: Whurr.

Fiedler FE (1950) A comparison of therapeutic relationships in psychoanalytic nondirective and Adlerian therapy. Journal of Consulting Psychology 14: 436–45.

Field N (1991) Projective identification: mechanism or mystery? Journal of Analytical Psychology 36(1): 93–110.

Field N (1996) Breakdown and Breakthrough. London: Routledge.

Fiumara GC (1995) The Metaphoric Process. London: Routledge.

Flew A (1971) An Introduction to Western Philosophy. London: Thames and Hudson.

Foucault M (1967) Madness and Civilization – A History of Insanity in the Age of Reason. (Trans. R Howard) London: Tavistock.

Foucault M (1974) The Archaeology of Knowledge. (Trans. AM Sheridan Smith) London: Tavistock Publications.

Foucault M (1979) Discipline and Punish – The Birth of the Prison. Harmondsworth: Penguin.

Foulkes SH (1983) Introduction to Group-Analytic Psychotherapy – Studies in the Social Integration of Individuals and Groups. London: Maresfield. (First published 1948)

Fox M (1994) The Re-invention of Work – A New Vision of Livelihood for our Time. San Francisco: Harper Collins.

Frank JD (1973) Persuasion and Healing. (2nd edn) Baltimore, MD: Johns Hopkins University Press.

Frank JD, Frank JB (1993) Persuasion and Healing: A Comparative Study of Psychotherapy. Baltimore, MD: Johns Hopkins University Press.

Frankl VE (1973) Man's Search for Meaning: An Introduction to Logotherapy. London: Hodder and Stoughton. (First published 1959)

Freud S (1900) The Interpretation of Dreams. Standard Edition, 4. London: Hogarth Press (1953). pp 1–630.

Freud S (1907) Obsessive Acts and Religious Practices. Standard Edition, 9. London: Hogarth Press (1959). Harmondsworth: Penguin edition. pp 115–27.

Freud S (1937) Analysis Terminable and Interminable. Standard Edition, 23. London: Hogarth Press (1957). pp 209–54.

Freud S (1938) Three contributions to the theory of sex. In The Basic Writings (Trans. and Ed. AA Brill) New York: Modern Library. pp 553–629.

Friedman M (Ed.) (1964) The Worlds of Existentialism. New Jersey: Humanities Press.

Fromm E (1986) Psychoanalysis and Zen Buddhism. London: Unwin Paperbacks.

Fromm-Reichman F (1974) Principles of Intensive Psychotherapy. Chicago: Chicago University Press.

Geertz C (1973) The Interpretation of Cultures. New York: Basic Books.

Gendlin E (1967) Subverbal communication and therapist expressivity: trends in client-centred therapy with schizophrenics. In Rogers CR, Stevens B (Eds) Person to Person – The Problem of Being a Human: A New Trend in Psychology. Lafayette, CA: Real People Press. pp 119–49.

Genet J (1963) Our Lady of the Flowers. New York: Grove Press.

Gergen KJ (1990) Toward a postmodern psychology. The Humanistic Psychologist 18: 23–34.

Gergen KJ (1992) Toward a postmodern psychology. In Kvale S (Ed.) Psychology and Postmodernism. London: Sage. pp 17–30.

Gergen KJ, Kaye J (1992) Beyond narrative in the negotiation of therapeutic meaning. In McNamee S, Gergen KJ (Eds) Therapy as Social Construction. London: Sage. pp 166–85.
Gergen KJ, Gloger-Tippelt G, Berkowitz P (1990) The cultural construction of the developing child. In Semin GS, Gergen KJ (Eds) Everyday Understanding: Social and Scientific Implications. London Sage. pp 108–29.
Gergen M (1994) Free will and psychotherapy: complaints of the draughtsmen's daughters. Journal of Theoretical and Philosophical Psychology 14(1): 13–24.
Glass JM (1993) Shattered Selves: Multiple Personality in a Postmodern World. Ithaca and London: Cornell University Press.
Gleick J (1989) Chaos: Making a New Science. London: Heinemann.
Goertzel Z (1965) Cradles of Eminence. New York. Constable.
Goleman D (1999) Working with Emotional Intelligence. London: Bloomsbury.
Gooch S (1995) Cities of Dreams, London: Aulis.
Goodman P (1962) Seating arrangements. In Utopian Essays and Practical Proposals. New York: Vintage Books.
Gorrell-Barnes G (1979) Infant needs and angry responses – a look at violence in the family. In Walrond-Skinner S (Ed.) Family and Marital Psychotherapy. Routledge and Kegan Paul: London. pp 68–90.
Greenberg IA (Ed.) (1975) Psychodrama: Theory and Therapy. London: Souvenir Press. (First published 1974)
Greene M (2000) It's a sister act. Daily Mail Weekend Magazine, 22 July: 14–15.
Greenfield S (2000) The Private Life of the Brain. London: Allen Lane, The Penguin Press.
Grinberg L, Sor D, Tabak de Bianchedi E (1975) Introduction to the Work of Bion. Strath Tay: Clunie Press.
Groddeck G (1988) The Meaning of Illness – Selected Psychoanalytic Writings. (Trans. G Mander) London: Maresfield Library. (First published 1923)
Grof S (1985) Beyond the Brain: Birth, Death and Transcendence in Psychotherapy. New York: State University of New York.
Grosskurth P (1986) Melanie Klein: Her World and her Work. New York: Alfred A Knopf.
Gudjonsson GH (1997) Accusations by adults of childhood sexual abuse. Applied Cognitive Psychology 11: 3–18.
Guerrière D (1980) Physis, Sophia, Psyche. In Sallis J, Maly K (Eds) Heraclitean Fragments: A Companion Volume to the Heidegger/Fink Seminar on Heraclitus. Alabama: University of Alabama Press. pp 86–134.
Guggenbühl-Craig A (1971) Power in the Helping Professions. Dallas, TX: Spring Publications.
Hale K (1986) Black Children – Their Roots, Culture and Educational Needs. London, Baltimore: Brigham Young University Press, John Hopkins University Press.
Haley J (Ed.) (1967) Advanced Techniques of Hypnosis and Therapy. Selected Papers of Milton H. Erickson. New York and London: Grune and Stratton.
Haley J (1984) Ordeal Therapy. San Francisco: Jossey-Bass Inc. Publishers.
Haney C, Banks C, Zimbardo P (1973) Interpersonal dynamics in a simulated prison. International Journal of Criminology and Penology 1: 69–97.
Haritos-Faroutos M (1983) Antecedent conditions leading to the behaviour of a torturer: fallacy or reality. Unpublished manuscript, University of Thessaloniki,

Greece.

Hart TN (1980) The Art of Christian Listening. New York/Ramsey: Paulist Press.

Haslam D (2000) Understanding our dreams – idle visions or pearls of great price? Self and Society 28(2): 5.

Hauke C (2000) Jung and the Postmodern: The Interpretation of Realities. London: Routledge.

Hawkins JM, Allen R (Eds) (1991) The Oxford Encyclopaedic English Dictionary. Oxford: Oxford University Press.

Heaton J (1999) Scepticism and psychotherapy: a Wittgensteinian approach. In Mace C (Ed.) Heart and Soul – The Therapeutic Face of Philosophy. London: Routledge. pp 47–64.

Hedges LE, Hilton R, Hilton VW, Caudill B (1997) Therapists at Risk. New Jersey: Jason Aronson.

Heidegger M (1987) An Introduction to Metaphysics. (Trans. R Mannheim) New Haven: Yale University Press. (First published 1959)

Heidegger M (1998) Pathmarks. (Ed. W McNeill) Cambridge: Cambridge University Press.

Heimann P (1950) On counter-transference. International Journal of Psycho-Analysis 31: 81–84.

Hekman SJ (1995) Moral Voices, Moral Selves: Carol Gilligan and Feminist Moral Theory. Cambridge: Polity Press.

Helman CG (1994) Culture, Health and Illness: An Introduction for Health Professionals. (3rd edn) Oxford: Butterworth-Heinemann.

Heylin C (2000) Sex, drugs, Armageddon and the Messiah of rock and roll. Daily Mail, 26 August: 50.

Hillman J (1985) Archetypal Psychology: A Brief Account. Dallas: Spring Publications.

Hillman J (1990) The Essential James Hillman: A Blue Fire (Ed. T Moore) London: Routledge.

Hillman J (1996) The Soul's Code – In Search of Character and Calling. New York: Random House.

Hillman J, Ventura M (1992) We've Had a Hundred Years of Psychotherapy and the World's Getting Worse. San Francisco, CA: Harper.

Hogan DB (1999) Professional Regulation as Facilitation, not Control: Implications for an Open System of Registration versus Restrictive Licensure. London: Midfields.

Holdstock L (1990) Can client-centred therapy transcend its monocultural roots? In Lietaer G, Rombauts J, van Balen R (Eds) Client-Centred and Experiential Psychotherapy in the Nineties. Leuven, Belgium: University Press. pp 109–21.

Houston J (1982) The Possible Human. Los Angeles: Tarcher.

Howard K, Kopta S, Krause M, Orlinsky D. (1986) The dose – effect relationship in psychotherapy. American Psychologist 41: 159–64.

Hubble MA, O'Hanlon (1992) Theory countertransference. Dulwich Centre Newsletter 1: 25–30.

Hubble MA, Duncan BL, Miller SD (Eds) (1999a) The Heart and Soul of Change: What Works in Therapy. Washington DC: American Psychological Association.

Hubble MA, Duncan BL, Miller SD (1999b) Directing attention to what works. In Hubble MA, Duncan BL, Miller SD (Eds) The Heart and Soul of Change: What Works in Therapy. Washington DC: American Psychological Association. pp 407–47.

Huxley A (1970) Perennial Wisdom. London: Harper and Row.

Ireland J (1987) Life Wish. London: Century Hutchinson.

Irigaray L (1985) Speculum of the Other Woman. (Trans. GC Gill) Ithaca, NY: Cornell University Press. (Originally published 1974).

Irigaray L (1991) The Irigaray Reader. (Ed. M Whitford) Oxford: Blackwell.

Isham CJ (1995) Lectures on Quantum Theory – Mathematical and Structural Foundations. London: Imperial College Press.

Jacobs P, Landau S, Pell E (1971) To Serve the Devil, Vols I and II. New York: Vintage.

James J (2000) The Shadow – a critical enquiry into the significance of the concept of the shadow in analytical psychology. Unpublished Master's Thesis, University of Essex.

James M, Savary L (1977) A New Self: Self-therapy with Transactional Analysis. Reading, MA: Addison-Wesley.

James W (1985) The Varieties of Religious Experience. Gifford Lectures delivered 1901–1902. Glasgow: Fount Paperbacks.

Jaques E (1988) Death and the midlife crisis. In Spillius EB (Ed.) Melanie Klein Today, Vol. 2. London: Routledge. pp 226–48.

Jeffers S (1987) Feel the Fear and Do it Anyway. New York: Arrow

Jung CG (1928) Analytical psychology and education. In Contributions to Analytical Psychology (Trans. HG Baynes, FC Baynes). London: Trench Trubner. pp 313–82.

Jung CG (1944) Psychological Types or the Psychology of Individuation. (Trans. HG Baynes) London: Kegan Paul.

Jung CG (1951) Aion: Researches into the Phenomenology of the Self. Collected Works, Vol. 9(ii). (2nd edn) London: Routledge and Kegan Paul.

Jung CG (1952) Memories, Dreams, Reflections. Original Swiss edition.

Jung CG (1956) Symbols of transformation: an analysis of the prelude to a case of schizophrenia. Collected Works, Vol. 5. (Trans. RFC Hull) London: Routledge and Kegan Paul.

Jung CG (1963) Memories, Dreams, Reflections. (Ed. A Jaffe) London: Routledge and Kegan Paul.

Jung CG (1964) Man and his Symbols. London: Aldus Books.

Jung CG (1966) The Practice of Psychotherapy. Collected Works, Vol.16. (2nd edn) London: Routledge and Kegan Paul.

Jung CG (1967) Alchemical Studies. Collected Works, Vol. 13. London: Routledge and Kegan Paul.

Jung CG (1968) Psychology and Alchemy. Collected Works, Vol. 12. (2nd edn) London: Routledge and Kegan Paul.

Jung CG (1969a) Synchronicity: an acausal connecting principle. Collected Works, Vol. 8. (Trans. RFC Hull) (2nd edition) London: Routledge and Kegan Paul. pp 416–531.

Jung CG (1969b) On the nature of the psyche. Collected Works, Vol. 8. (Trans. RFC Hull) (2nd edition) London: Routledge and Kegan Paul. pp 159–234.

Jung CG (1969c) Constitution and heredity in psychology. Collected Works, Vol. 8. (Trans. RFC Hull) (2nd edition) London: Routledge and Kegan Paul. pp 417–519.

Jung CG (1969d) Psychology and Religion: West and East. Collected Works, Vol. 11. (Trans. RFC Hull) (2nd edition) London: Routledge and Kegan Paul.

Jung CG (1970) The Conjunction. Collected Works, Vol. 14 (Trans. RFC Hull) (2nd edn) London: Routledge and Kegan Paul. pp 457–553.

Jung CG, Pauli W (1955) The Interpretation of Nature and the Psyche. London: Routledge and Kegan Paul.

Kahn C (1981) The Art and Thought of Heraclitus. Cambridge: Cambridge University Press.

Kazantzakis N (1960) The Saviors of God – Spiritual Exercises. (Trans. K Friar) New York: Simon and Schuster.

Khenpo N, Surya Das L (1995) Natural Great Perfection – Dzogchen Teachings and Vajra Songs. New York: Snow Lion Publications.

Kierkegaard S (1954) Fear and Trembling and the Sickness unto Death. (Trans. W Lowrie) Garden City, NY: Doubleday.

Kiersey D, Bates M (1984) Please Understand Me – Character and Temperament Types. Del Mar, CA: Gnosology Books.

Kingston K (1996) Creating Sacred Space with Feng Shui. London: Piatkus

Kirk SA, Hutchins H (1992) The Selling of DSM: The Rhetoric of Science in Psychiatry. New York: Aldine.

Klein M (1984) Envy, Gratitude and Other Works. London: Hogarth Press and Institute for Psychoanalysis. (First published 1957)

Kleinman A (1988) The Illness Narratives. New York: Basic Books.

Klossowski de Rola S (1973) Alchemy: The Secret Art. London: Thames and Hudson.

Koestler A (1972) The Roots of Co-incidence. London: Hutchinson.

Koestler A (1989) The Act of Creation. London: Arkana. (First published 1964)

Kohut H (1977) The Restoration of the Self. New York: International Universities Press.

Kramer H, Sprenger J (1971) The Malleus Maleficarum. (Trans. M Summers) New York: Dover.

Kuhn TS (1970) The Structure of Scientific Revolutions. Chicago: University of Chicago Press. (First published 1962.)

Kutchins H, Kirk SA (1997) Making Us Crazy. New York: Free Press.

Lacan J (1968) The Language of the Self: The Function of Language in Psychoanalysis. New York: Johns Hopkins University Press.

Lago C, Thompson J (1996) Race, Culture and Counselling. Buckingham and Philadelphia: Open University Press.

Langs R (1976) The Bipersonal Field. New York: Jason Aronson.

Lao Tsu (1973) Tao Te Ching. (Trans. G-F Feng, J English) New York: Vintage.

Lawrence DH (1992) Selected Poems. (Ed. M Kalnins) London; Dent and Sons.

Lax WD (1992) Postmodern thinking in a clinical practice. In McNamee S, Gergen K (Eds) Therapy as Social Construction. London: Sage. pp 69–85.

Lee D (Ed.) (1980) Wittgenstein's Lectures, Cambridge 1930–1932. Oxford: Basil Blackwell.

Levenson EA (1976) A holographic model of psychoanalytic change. Contemporary Psychoanalysis 12: 338–42.

Levenson EA (1991) The Purloined Self – Interpersonal Perspectives in Psychoanalysis. (Ed. AH Feiner) New York: William Allison White Institute.

Levin DM (1985) The Body's Recollection of Being: Phenomenological Psychology and the Deconstruction of Nihilism. London: Routledge and Kegan Paul.

Levy S (1992) Artificial Life – The Quest for a New Creation. London: Jonathan Cape.

Lewin R (1992) Complexity – Life at the Edge of Chaos – The Major New Theory that Unifies All Sciences. London: Macmillan.

Leytham G (1995) Review of 'The Transpersonal: Psychotherapy and Counselling' by John Rowan. Network (Scientific and Medical Network) 56: 80–81.

Liotti G (1989) Resistance to change in cognitive psychotherapy: theoretical remarks from a constructivistic point of view. In Dryden W, Trower P (Eds) Cognitive Psychotherapy: Stasis and Change. London: Cassell. pp 28–56.

Lorimer D (1987) The near-death experience and spiritual health. Holistic Medicine 2: 79–184.

Lovelock J (1989) Gaia: A New Look at Life on Earth. Oxford: Oxford University Press. (First published 1979)

Lowen A (1976) Bioenergetics. Harmondsworth: Penguin.

Lynch G (2000) Pastoral counselling in the new millennium. Counselling 11(6): 340–42.

Lyotard J-F (1989) The Postmodern Condition: A Report on Knowledge. Manchester: Manchester University Press.

Lyotard J-F (1997) Domus and the megapolis. In Leich N (Ed.) Rethinking Architecture: A Reader in Critical Theory. Routledge, London. pp 297–385.

MacDonald AM (1972) Chambers Twentieth Century Dictionary. London: Chambers.

McLeod J (1997) Narrative and Psychotherapy. London: Sage.

McNamee S (1992) Reconstructing identity: the communal construction of crisis. In McNamee S, Gergen KJ (Eds) Therapy as Social Construction. London: Sage. pp 186–99.

McNamee S, Gergen KJ (Eds) (1992) Therapy as Social Construction. London: Sage.

MacPherson A (1992) Does this give God his P45? (Interview with P Davies) The Mail on Sunday, 26 April: 17.

Macy J (1991) World as Lover, World as Self. Berkeley: Parallax Press.

Mahrer AR (1985) Psychotherapeutic Change: An Alternative Approach to Meaning and Measurement. New York: Norton.

Mandelbrot BB (1974) The Fractal Geometry of Nature. New York: Freeman.

Marcel G (1950) The Mystery of Being. (Trans. GS Fraser, R Hague) Chicago: Regnery.

Marshall I, Zohar D (1997) Who's Afraid of Schrodinger's Cat? – All the New Science Ideas You Need to Keep up with the New Thinking. New York: William Morrow and Company.

Marton F (1992) Phenomenography and 'the art of teaching all things to all men'. Qualitative Studies in Education 5: 253–67.

Maslow A (1968) Toward a Psychology of Being. (2nd edn) New York: Von Nostrand.

Massimini F, Csikszentmihalyi M, Carli M (1987) The monitoring of optimal experience: a tool for psychiatric rehabilitation. Journal of Nervous and Mental Disease 175(9): 545–49.

Masson JM (Ed. and Trans.) (1985) The Complete Letters of Sigmund Freud to Wilhelm Fliess, 1881–1904. Cambridge, MA: Harvard University Press.

Masson JM (1989) Against Therapy. London: Collins.

Masterson JF (1985) The Real Self: A Developmental, Self, and Object Relations Approach. New York: Brunner/Mazel.

Maturana HR, Varela FJ (1987) The Tree of Knowledge: The Biological Roots of Human Understanding. Boston, MA: Shambala.

May R (1991) The Cry for Myth. New York: WW Norton.

Maybury-Lewis D (1992) Millennium: Tribal Wisdom and the Modern World. Harmondsworth: Viking Penguin.

Megill A (1987) Prophets of Extremity – Nietzsche, Heidegger, Foucault, Derrida. Berkeley, CA: University of California Press.

Merleau-Ponty M (1983) La Nature. Unpublished manuscript. (Trans. X Tilliere 1998)

Midgley M (1992) Science as Salvation – a Modern Myth and its Meaning. London: Routledge.

MIND Report (2000) Strategies for Living. London: MIND.

Mingers J (1995) Self-Producing Systems: Implications and Applications of Autopoiesis. New York: Plenum Press.

Minkowski E (1970) Lived Time. (Trans. N. Metzel) Evanston, IL: Northwestern University Press. (First published 1933)

Molino A (Ed.) (1997) Freely Associated – Encounters in Psychoanalysis. London: Free Association Books.

Mollon P (1996) The memory debate: a consideration of clinical complexities and some suggested guidelines for psychoanalytic therapists. British Journal of Psychotherapy 13(2).

Moodley R (1998) Cultural return to the subject: traditional healing in counselling and therapy. Changes 16(1): 45–56.

Moore T (1992) Care of the Soul: How to Add Depth and Meaning to Your Everyday Life. London: Piatkus.

Moore T (1996) The Re-Enchantment of Everyday Life. New York: Harper Collins.

Morgan N (2000) The bizarre healing that gave me back my life. Daily Mail, 30 May: 49.

Mountjoy L (in press) Relationship with self. In Clarkson P (Ed.) Practitioner's Guide to the Five Relationships. London: Whurr.

Muhlhausler P, Harré R (1991) Pronouns and the People. Oxford: Blackwell.

Murray D (1986) One writer's secrets. College Composition and Communication 37: 146–53.

Murray G (1955) Five Stages of Greek Religion. Garden City, NY: Doubleday Anchor Books.

Naddaf G (1993) Origine et l'Evolution due Concept Grec de Phusis. Canada: E. Mellen.

Nobuyuki Y (Trans.) (1966) The Narrow Road to the Deep North and Other Travel Sketches. London: Penguin Books.

Norcross JC (1999) Foreword. In Hubble MA, Duncan BL, Miller SD (Eds) The Heart and Soul of Change: What Works in Therapy. Washington DC: American Psychological Association. pp xvii–xix.

Nuttall J (2000) The Rosarium Philosophorum as a universal relational psychology: Jung and object relations. Psychodynamic Counselling 6(1): 79–99.

Ogden T (1994) The analytic third: working with intersubjective clinical facts. International Journal of Psycho-Analysis 75: 3–19.

O'Hara M (1991) Horizons of reality: demystifying postmodernism (book review). Networker, Jul/Aug: 71–74.

O'Hara M (1995) Why is this man laughing? AHP Perspective 19: 3–31.

Onions CT (Ed.) (1973) The Shorter Oxford English Dictionary. Oxford: Oxford University Press.

Ormay T (2000) Counselling and psychotherapy online. Paper delivered at the BAC and UKCP Conferences, Warwick.

Padesky CA, Greenberger D (1995) Clinician's Guide to Mind over Mood. New York: Guilford Press.

Panikkar R (1989) The Silence of God. Maryknoll, NY: Orbis Books.

Parad HJ (1969) Crisis Interventions: Selected Readings. New York: Family Services Association of America.

Parikh J (1991) Managing Your Self. Bombay: India Books.
Parry G, Richardson A (1996) NHS Psychotherapeutic Services in England. London: Department of Health.
Peat D (1996) Blackfoot Physics. London: Fourth Estate.
Peck S (1978) The Road Less Traveled: A New Psychology of Love, Traditional Values and Spiritual Growth. New York: Simon and Schuster.
Pepinster C (1992) Lost generation. Time Out 1135: 13.
Pepperell R (1995) The Post-Human Condition. Exeter: Intellect.
Perera SB (1992) Descent to the Goddess – A Way of Initiation for Women. Toronto: Inner City.
Perls FS (1969a) Gestalt Therapy Verbatim. Moab, Utah: Real People Press.
Perls FS (1969b) Ego, Hunger and Aggression. New York: Vintage Books. (First published 1947)
Perls FS, Hefferline R, Goodman P (1951) Gestalt Therapy: Excitement and Growth in the Human Personality. New York: Julian Press.
Phillips A (1998) A Defence of Masochism. London: Faber and Faber.
Pierrakos JC (1974) The Core of Man. New York: Institute for the New Age.
Pierrakos JC (1987) Core Energetics – Developing the Capacity to Love and Heal. San Francisco, CA: Life Rhythm Publication.
Plato (1987) The Republic. London: Penguin.
Polanyi M (1958) Personal Knowledge. London: Routledge and Kegan Paul.
Polkinghorne DE (1988) Narrative Knowing and the Human Sciences. Albany, NY: State University of New York Press.
Ponterotto JG, Casas JM, Suzuki LA, Alexander CM (1995) Handbook of Multicultural Counselling. California: Sage.
Pope-Davis D, Coleman HLK (1997) Multicultural Counselling Competencies – Assessment, Education and Training, and Supervision. California: Sage.
Popper KR (1972) Conjectures and Refutations: The Growth of Scientific Knowledge. London: Routledge and Kegan Paul.
Prigogine I (1995) A (very) brief history of certainty. Network – The Scientific and Medical Network Review, Winter, 56: 6–7.
Progroff I (1975) At a Journal Workshop. New York, NY: Dialogue House Library.
Rank O (1989) Art and Artist – Creative Urge and Personality Development. New York: Norton. (First published 1932)
Rank O (1998) Psychology and the Soul – A study of the Origin, Conceptual Evolution and Nature of the Soul. (Trans. GC Richter, EJ Lieberman) Baltimore: Johns Hopkins University Press.
Rawlinson A (1997) The Book of Enlightened Masters: Western Teachers in Eastern Traditions. Chicago: Open Court.
Redfeld J (1994) The Celestine Prophesies. New York: Bantam.
Reed G (1988) The Psychology of Anomalous Experience. (Rev. edn) New York: Prometheus Books.
Reich W (1972) Character Analysis. (3rd edn) New York: Touchstone.
Rilke RM (1964) Selected Poems. (Trans. JB Leishman) London: Penguin.
Rinzler D (1984) Human disconnection and the murder of the earth. Transactional Analysis Journal 14(4): 231–36.
Roberts D, Clarkson P (1996) Empowerment-based education vs. shame-based education. ITA News.

Robinson WL (1974) Conscious competency – the mark of a competent instructor. Personnel Journal 53: 538–39.

Rogers CR (1961) On Becoming a Person: a Therapist's View of Psychotherapy. London: Constable.

Rogers CR (1986) Client-centred Therapy: Its Current Practice, Implications and Theory. London: Constable. (First published 1951)

Ronan S (Ed.) (1992) The Goddess Hekate – Studies in Ancient Pagan and Christian Religion and Philosophy, Vol. 1. Hastings: Chthonios Books.

Roob A (1997) Alchemy and Mysticism. Cologne: Taschen.

Rorty R (1979) Philosophy and the Mirror of Nature. Princeton, NJ: Princeton University Press.

Roustang F (1982) Dire Mastery. (Trans. N. Luckacher) London: Johns Hopkins University Press.

Rowan J (1990) Sub-Personalities – The People Inside Us. London: Routledge.

Rowan J (1993) The Transpersonal: Psychotherapy and Counselling. London: Routledge.

Rowan J (1996) The psychology of furniture. In Palmer S, Dainow S, Milner P (Eds) Counselling: The BAC Counselling Reader. London: Sage and BAC. pp 350–56.

Rowe D (1983) Depression: The Way Out of Your Prison. London: Routledge.

Rumi J (1952) Divan Shams-i-Tabriz. (Trans. and Ed. RA Nicholson) Cambridge: Cambridge University Press.

Rumi J (1988) This Longing. (Versions by Barks C, Moyne J) Putney, VT: Threshold.

Rumi J (1990) Delicious Laughter: Rambunctious Teaching Stories from the Mathnawi. (Barks C, Ed.) Athens, GA: Maypop.

Rumi J (1991) One-handed Basketweaving. Athens, GA: Maypop. (Versions by Barks C)

Rumi J (1994) True Religion. (Version by Noel Cobb) Sphinx 6: 217–18.

Runes DD (1966) Dictionary of Philosophy. Totawa, NJ: Littlefield, Adams and Co.

Rycroft C (1968) A Critical Dictionary of Psychoanalysis. Harmondsworth: Penguin.

Ryle G (1966) Dilemmas: The Tarner Lectures. Cambridge: Cambridge University Press.

St John of the Cross (1973) The Dark Night of the Soul. Cambridge: James Clarke.

Sampson EE (1988) The debate on individualism: indigenous psychologies of the individual and their role in personal and social functioning. American Psychologist 43: 15–22.

Samuels A (1981) Fragmentary vision: a central training aim. Spring: 215–25.

Samuels A (1993) The Political Psyche. London: Routledge.

Samuels A, Shorter B, Plaut F (1986) A Critical Dictionary of Jungian Analysis. London: Routledge and Kegan Paul.

Sartre JP (1938) Nausea. Harmondsworth: Penguin.

Schimmel A (1993) The Triumphal Sun: A Study of the Works of Jalaloddin Rumi. Albany, NY: State University of New York Press.

Schlamm L (2000) Wilber's 'Spectrum model' and Jung's 'Elevationism': identifying alternative soteriological perspectives. Unpublished article.

Searles HF (1955) The informational value of the supervisor's emotional experiences. Psychiatry 18: 135–46.

Seligman MEP (1995) The effectiveness of psychotherapy. American Psychologist 50(12): 965–74.

Shah I (1985) The Exploits of the Incomparable Mulla Nasrudin. London: Octagon Press.

Shapiro DA (1996) Foreword. In Roth A, Fonagy P (Eds) What Works for Whom? A Critical Review of Psychotherapy Research. New York: Guilford Press. pp viii–x.

Sheenan (1993) Reading a life: Heidegger and hard times. In Guignon CB (Ed.) The Cambridge Companion to Heidegger. Cambridge: Cambridge University Press. pp 70–91.

Sheldrake R (1988) The Presence of the Pat: Morphic Resonance and the Habits of Nature. New York: Random House.

Shorter B (1996) Susceptible to the Sacred. London: Routledge.

Shotter J (1992) Getting in touch: the meta-methodology of a postmodern science of mental life. In Kvale S (Ed.) Psychology and Postmodernism. London: Sage. pp 58–73.

Silverman D (1997) Discourses of Counselling – HIV Counselling and Social Interaction. London: Sage.

Simon FB, Stierlin H, Wynne LC (1985) The Language of Family Therapy – A Systemic Vocabulary and Sourcebook. New York: Family Process Press.

Simons HW (1989) Distinguishing the rhetorical from the real: the case of psychotherapeutic placebos. In Simons HW (Ed.) Rhetoric in the Human Sciences. London: Sage. pp 109–18.

Smith D (1991) Hidden Conversations: An Introduction to Communicative Psychoanalysis. London: Routledge.

Smith ML, Glass GV, Miller TI (1980) The Benefits of Psychotherapy. Baltimore: Johns Hopkins University Press.

Smuts JC (1987) Holism and Evolution. Cape Town, SA: N and S Press. (First published 1926)

Snyder CR, Michael ST, Cheavens JS (1999) Hope as a psychotherapeutic foundation of common factors, placebos, and expectancies. In Hubble MA, Duncan BL, Miller SD, (Eds) The Heart and Soul of Change: What Works in Therapy. Washington DC: American Psychological Association.

Solzhenitsyn A (1973) Lecture. (Trans. N Bethell) London: Stenvalley Press.

Some M (1996) Ritual Power, Healing and Community. San Francisco: Gateway.

Spinelli E (1989). The Interpreted World: An Introduction to Phenomenological Psychology. London: Sage.

Stallybrass P, White A (1993) Bourgeois hysteria and the carnivalesque. In During S (Ed.) The Cultural Studies Reader. London: Routledge. pp 284–92.

Stein M (1983) In Midlife – A Jungian Perspective. Dallas, Spring Publications.

Steiner C, Wyckoff H, Marcus J, Lariviere P, Goldstine D, Schwebel R, and members of the Radical Psychiatry Center (1975) Readings in Radical Psychiatry. New York: Grove Press.

Stern D (1985) The Interpersonal World of the Infant. New York: Basic Books.

Steuer JS (1993) Defining virtual reality: dimensions determining telepresence. Journal of Telecommunication 42(4): 17–24.

Stoppard T (1993) Arcadia. London: Faber and Faber.

Sutich AJ (1969) Some basic considerations regarding transpersonal psychology. Journal of Transpersonal Psychology 1(1): 11–20.

Suzuki DT (1964) An Introduction to Zen Buddhism. New York: Panther.

Suzuki DT (1972) Living by Zen. London: Rider. (First published 1950)

Symington N (1986) The Analytic Experience: Lectures from the Tavistock. London: Free Association Books.

Symington N (1990) Religion and psychoanalysis. In Groups, Crowds and Culture. London: Free Association Books.

Symington N (1994) Emotion and Spirit. London: Cassell.

Tacey DJ (1993) Jung's ambivalence toward the world soul. Sphinx 5: 278–87. London: Convivium for Archetypal Studies.

Tausch R, Tausch A (1998) Erziehungpsychologie. (10th edn) Gottingen: Hofrefe.

Thomas D (1980) The force that through the green fuse drives the flower. In Collected Poems 1934–1952. London: Dent. p 8.

Thorne B (1998) Person-centred Counselling and Christian Spirituality – The Secular and the Holy. London: Whurr.

Tilley J (1999) Life and soul. Editorial. Mental Health Nursing 19(2): 3.

Tillich P (1952) The Courage to Be. New Haven: Yale University Press.

Trevarthen C (1979) Communication and cooperation in early infancy: a description of primary intersubjectivity. In Bullowa M, (Ed.) Before Speech: The Beginnings of Early Communication. Cambridge: Cambridge University Press. pp 321–48.

Turner M (1998) Moving beyond modernist discourses of psychological therapy. European Journal of Psychotherapy, Counselling and Health 1(3): 435–57.

Uexküll J (1926) Theoretical Biology. (Trans. DL MacKinnon) London: Kegan Paul, Trench, Trubner & Co.

UNESCO (1998) International Symposium of Transdisciplinarity – Towards Integrative Process and Integrated Knowledge. New York: United Nations. pp 1–12.

Valle R (Ed.) (1998) Phenomenological Inquiry in Psychology: Existential and Transpersonal Dimensions. New York: Plenum Press.

van Deurzen-Smith E (1988) Existential Counselling in Practice. London: Sage.

van Deurzen-Smith E (1997) Existential Psychotherapy. London: Sage.

von Franz M-L (1978) Time: Rhythm and Repose. London: Thames and Hudson.

von Franz M-L (1980) Alchemy: An Introduction to the Symbolism and the Psychology. Toronto: Inner City Books.

von Franz M-L (1995) Shadow and Evil in Fairytales. Boston: Shambala.

Vyasa K-D (1990) The Mahabharata, Vol. XII, Mahaprathanika Parva, section III. (Trans. Kisari Mohan Ganguli) New Delhi: Munishiram Manoharlal.

Walker M, Antony-Black J (Eds) (1999) Hidden Selves – An Exploration of Multiple Personality. Buckingham: Open University Press.

Washburn M (1988) The pre/trans fallacy reconsidered. In Rothberg D, Kelly S (Eds) Ken Wilber in Dialogue: Conversations with Leading Transpersonal Thinkers. Wheaton: Quest Books. pp 62–83.

Watson L (1974) Supernature. London: Coronet.

Watts AW (1968) The Meaning of Happiness – The Quest for Freedom of the Spirit in Modern Psychology and the Wisdom of the East. New York: Perennial Library.

Webster N (Ed.) (1944) Webster's Collegiate Dictionary. (2nd edn) Springfield, MA: Miriam Webster.

Weedon C (1987) Feminist Practice and Poststructuralist Theory. Oxford: Basil Blackwell.

Weinberg S (1993) The First Three Minutes. London: Flamingo.

White TH (1987) The Once and Future King. London: Fontana.

Whitman W (1955) Leaves of Grass. New York: The New American Library.

Wilber K (1980) The Atman Project: A Transpersonal View of Human Development. Wheaton, IL: Theosophical Publishing House.

Wilhelm R (Trans.) (1951) The I Ching or Book of Changes. London: Routledge and Kegan Paul.

Wilhelm R (1962) The Secret of the Golden Flower. London: Arkana.

Williams L (1992) Torture and the torturer. The Psychologist 5(7): 305–8.

Williams T (1959) Cat on a Hot Tin Roof. London: Penguin.

Winnicott DW (1958) Collected Papers: Through Paediatrics to Psycho-analysis. London: Tavistock Publications.

Winnicott DW (1986) Home is Where We Start From. Harmondsworth: Penguin.

Winter DA (1997) Everybody has still won but what about the booby prizes? Inaugural address as Chair of the Psychotherapy Section, British Psychological Society, University of Westminster, London.

Wittgenstein L (1922) Tractatus Logico-Philosophicus. (Trans. DF Pears, BF McGuinness) Reprinted London: Routledge, 1961.

Wittgenstein L (1980) Remarks on the Philosophy of Psychology, Vol. 1. (Trans. GEM Anscombe) Oxford: Blackwell.

Wolfe LM (1951) John Muir: Son of the Wilderness. New York: Houghton Mifflin.

Wolman BB (Ed.) (1965) Handbook of Clinical Psychology. New York: McGraw-Hill.

Yalom I (1975) The Theory and Practice of Group Psychotherapy. New York: Basic Books. (First published 1931)

Young-Eisendrath P (1997) Jungian constructivism and the value of uncertainty. Journal of Analytical Psychology 42(4): 637–52.

Youngson HA, Alderman N (1994) Fear of incontinence and its effects on a community-based rehabilitation programme after severe brain injury – successful remediation of escape behaviour using behaviour modification. Brain Injury 8(1): 23–36.

Zohar D (1990) The Quantum Self. London: Bloomsbury.

Index